ACCESSING THE WEB STUDY GUIDE IS EASY!

1. Visit www.HumanKinetics.com/MotorLearningAndPerformance.
2. Click on the "View resources for the sixth edition" link next to the book cover.
3. Click on the "Sign In" link on the top left of the page. If you do not have a Human Kinetics account, click on the "New to Human Kinetics? Create an account now!" link to create an account.
4. **If you purchased a new book**, in the **Ancillary Items** box on the left side of the page, click on the "Enter Key Code" link.
   - Enter the key code exactly as printed below, including hyphens.
   - Click on the Submit button to unlock your online product. Once submitted, the key code cannot be used again. On subsequent visits, you will only need to sign in to your account; you will not need to enter the key code again.

   If you purchased a used book, you may purchase access to the web study guide by visiting https://US.HumanKinetics.com and searching for "Motor Learning and Performance web study guide."
5. To access your materials for the first time, please sign out of your account, refresh your browser, and click the "Sign In" link and sign in again.
6. For future visits, Sign In to your account and under MY ACCOUNT, click the "My eProducts" link to follow the step-by-step instructions.

Product: Motor Learning and Performance, Sixth Edition web study guide

Key code: LEE-JYKMQT-OSG

For technical support, send an email to:

U.S. and international customers........................ info@hkusa.com
Canadian customers .... info@hkcanada.com

5-2021

Motor Learning and Performance

From Principles to Application

SIXTH EDITION

Richard A. Schmidt
Timothy D. Lee

HUMAN KINETICS

Library of Congress Cataloging-in-Publication Data

Names: Schmidt, Richard A., 1941- author. | Lee, Timothy Donald, 1955- author.
Title: Motor learning and performance : from principles to application / Richard A. Schmidt Timothy D. Lee.
Description: Sixth edition. | Champaign, IL : Human Kinetics, [2020] | Includes bibliographical references and index.
Identifiers: LCCN 2019012425 (print) | LCCN 2019012997 (ebook) | ISBN 9781492592860 (epub) | ISBN 9781492571193 (PDF) | ISBN 9781492571186 (print)
Subjects: | MESH: Motor Activity | Learning | Psychomotor Performance | Kinesthesis
Classification: LCC BF295 (ebook) | LCC BF295 (print) | NLM BF 295 | DDC 152.3/34--dc23
LC record available at https://lccn.loc.gov/2019012425

ISBN: 978-1-4925-7118-6 (paperback)
ISBN: 978-1-4925-7468-2 (loose-leaf)

Copyright © 2020 by Timothy D. Lee
Copyright © 2014 by Richard A. Schmidt and Timothy D. Lee
Copyright © 2008, 2004, 2000 by Richard A. Schmidt and Craig A. Wrisberg
Copyright © 1991 by Richard A. Schmidt

Human Kinetics supports copyright. Copyright fuels scientific and artistic endeavor, encourages authors to create new works, and promotes free speech. Thank you for buying an authorized edition of this work and for complying with copyright laws by not reproducing, scanning, or distributing any part of it in any form without written permission from the publisher. You are supporting authors and allowing Human Kinetics to continue to publish works that increase the knowledge, enhance the performance, and improve the lives of people all over the world.

The web addresses cited in this text were current as of April 2019, unless otherwise noted.

Acquisitions Editors: Andrew L. Tyler and Diana Vincer; **Developmental Editor:** Melissa J. Zavala; **Indexer:** Beth Nauman-Montana; **Permissions Manager:** Dalene Reeder; **Graphic Designer:** Dawn Sills; **Cover Designer:** Keri Evans; **Cover Design Associate:** Susan Rothermel Allen; **Photograph (cover):** © Thomas_EyeDesign / Getty Images; **Photographs (interior):** © Human Kinetics, unless otherwise noted; **Photo Asset Manager:** Laura Fitch; **Photo Production Manager:** Jason Allen; **Senior Art Manager:** Kelly Hendren; **Illustrations:** © Human Kinetics; **Production:** Westchester Publishing Services; **Printer:** Walsworth

Printed in the United States of America 10 9 8 7 6 5 4

The paper in this book was manufactured using responsible forestry methods.

Human Kinetics
1607 N. Market Street
Champaign, IL 61820
USA

United States and International
Website: **US.HumanKinetics.com**
Email: info@hkusa.com
Phone: 1-800-747-4457

Canada
Website: **Canada.HumanKinetics.com**
Email: info@hkcanada.com

E7393 (paperback)/E7444 (loose-leaf)

Tell us what you think!
Human Kinetics would love to hear what we can do to improve the customer experience. Use this QR code to take our brief survey.

In Memoriam

Richard Allen (Dick) Schmidt (1941–2015) was one of the most influential scientists in the history of motor control and learning research. Dick's work influenced how research was conducted in the laboratory, how theories were developed, how the field of motor control and learning was taught to undergraduate and graduate students, and how practical issues and problems encountered in everyday life could be better understood by applying this scientific knowledge. Thank you, Dick.

Contents

Preface

Most of us feel tremendous excitement, pleasure, and perhaps envy when we watch a close race, match, or performance, focusing on the complex, well-controlled skills displayed by the players or musicians. We marvel at those who succeed in executing their skill on the spot, at how the person with high-level skills is able to excel, sometimes under extreme pressure to do so.

This book was written for people who appreciate high-level skilled activity and for those who would like to learn more about how such incredible performances occur. Thus, readers in fields related directly to kinesiology (such as teaching and coaching) will benefit from the knowledge provided here. But the material extends far beyond these fields and should be relevant for those who study rehabilitation in physical and occupational therapy, as well as for instructors and facilitators of many other areas in which motor skills play an important role, such as music, ergonomics, and the military. The text is intended for beginners in the study of skill and requires little knowledge of physiology, psychology, or statistical methodologies.

The level of analysis of the text focuses on motor *behavior*—the overt, observable production of skilled movements. Of course, there are many scientific areas or fields of study involved in the understanding of skilled behavior. Motor skill is the outcome of processes studied in many different fields, such as neurology, anatomy, biomechanics, biochemistry, and social and experimental psychology, and this text could have focused on any number of these fundamental fields. But the focus of the text is broader than the fundamental fields that support it. The focus is *behavioral*, with the major emphasis on humans performing skills of various kinds. To be sure, we will talk about these other levels of analysis from time to time throughout the book in an attempt to explain what processes or events occur to support these high-level skills. Therefore this text should be appropriate for courses in elementary motor learning and motor performance in a relatively wide group of scientific areas.

Throughout the text, we construct a conceptual model of human performance. The term *model* is used in a variety of ways in many branches of science, and models are found frequently. A model typically consists of a system of parts that are familiar to us; when assembled in a certain way, these parts mimic aspects of the system we are trying to understand. One example is the pump-and-pipe model of our circulatory system, in which the heart is represented by a pump and the arteries and veins are pipes of various diameters and lengths. One could actually construct the model (although some models are purely conceptual); such a model could be used in classroom demonstrations or experiments on the effects of blood pressure on capillaries of the hand.

Our first goal in writing this text was to build a strong, general, conceptual understanding (or overview) of skills. We believe that instructors, coaches, therapists, and trainers, as well as others dealing with the learning or teaching of skills, will profit greatly from such a conceptual understanding of skilled behavior. In striving toward this goal, we have adopted the idea that skills can be understood, for the most part, through the use of concepts concerning information and its processing. We set about to build a conceptual model that would explain many of the intricacies of skilled motor performance. We begin this process by considering the human as a very simple input–output system; then gradually, as we introduce new topics in the text, we expand the model by adding these new concepts. Gradually, by building on knowledge and concepts presented in earlier parts of the text, we add increasing complexity to the conceptual model. Simply presenting the finished conceptual model would make it very difficult for students to understand, and we hope that the systematic process of constructing the model, assembled with parts as they are presented in the text, forms a logical basis for increasing the model's complexity. This construction process should make the final version of the model understandable.

Our second goal was to organize the book in the best way to aid student understanding based on many years of teaching experience. The text is divided into two parts. After the introduction to the study of motor skills in chapter 1, part I examines how the motor system works by investigating the major principles of human performance and progressively developing a conceptual model of human actions. The focus is mainly on human performance as based on an information-processing perspective, although alternative theoretical approaches are provided as well. Chapter 2 discusses the nature of information processing, decision making, and movement planning. Chapter 3 considers the concepts of attention and memory. Chapter 4 concerns the information received from various sensory sources that is relevant to movement. Chapter 5 examines the processes underlying the production of movement, with particular emphasis to the role of motor programs. Chapter 6 considers the basic principles of performance that form the building blocks of skilled performance—analogous to the fundamental laws of physics. This analysis is extended in chapter 7, by examining different approaches taken to the performance of more complex skills—from the traditional approach of examining differences in movement abilities among people to the more contemporary examination of how movements are coordinated, both within and between individuals. On completion of part I, the student should have a reasonably coherent view of the conceptual and functional properties of the motor system. These principles seem appropriate for maximizing the performance of already learned skills.

Part II of the text uses the conceptual model to impart an understanding of the processes involved in human motor *learning*. Much of this discussion uses the terms and concepts introduced in part I. This method works well in our own teaching, probably because motor learning is usually inferred from changes in motor behavior; therefore, it is logical to discuss these changes in terms of the behavioral principles presented in part I. In this second part, chapter 8 treats some methodological problems unique to the study of learning, such as how and when to measure performance, which also have application to measuring performance in analogous teaching situations. Chapter 9 considers broad issues of learning, retention, and transfer, such as the important role of practice. Chapter 10 concerns the issue of how and when to practice, dealing with the many factors that instructors can control directly to make practice more effective. Finally, chapter 11 deals with the critical topic of feedback, examining what kinds of movement information students need for effective learning, when it should be given, and so on. By the end of the text, readers will have a progressive accumulation of knowledge that, in our experience, provides a consistent view of how skills are performed and learned.

Many real-world examples of motor performance and learning principles are discussed in the main body of the text. In addition, we've included Focus on Application sections set off from the main textual materials. Strategically located directly after pertinent discussions of principles, these sections indicate applications to real-world teaching, coaching, or therapy. We wanted to write a text that could be used by performers, teachers, coaches, physical therapists, and other instructors in various fields to enhance human performance in real-world settings. To meet this goal, we have worked to focus the text on the topics most relevant to practical application.

As a third goal, we wanted a presentation style that would be simple, straightforward, and highly readable for those without extensive backgrounds in the motor performance area. As a result, the main content does not stress the research and data that contribute to our knowledge of motor skill acquisition and performance. Important points are occasionally illustrated by data from a critical experiment, but the emphasis is on an integrated conceptual knowledge of how the motor system works and how it learns. However, for those who desire a tighter link to the basic data, we have included sections called Focus on Research, which are set off from the main text and describe the important experiments and concepts in detail.

Finally, we demanded that the principles discussed should be faithful to the empirical data and thought in the study area. From decades in doing basic research in motor learning and motor performance, we have developed what we believe to be defensible, coherent, personal viewpoints (conceptual models, if you will) about how skills are performed and learned, and our aim was to present this model to the reader to facilitate understanding. Our viewpoints are based on a large literature of theoretical ideas and empirical data, together with much thought about competing ideas and apparently contradictory research findings. We have tried to write from this perspective as we would tell a story. Every part of the story can be defended empirically, or it would not have been included. Our goal has been to write the truth, at least as we understand it and as it can be understood with the current level of knowledge. We have included a brief section at the end of each chapter describing additional readings that provide competing viewpoints and additional scientific justifications.

Students will find a range of learning aids within each chapter, including chapter-opening outlines, objectives, and lists of key terms, as well as an end-chapter summary of the activities in the accompanying web study guide and "Check Your Understanding" and "Apply Your Knowledge" questions. Instructors using this text in their courses will find a wealth of updated ancillary materials at www.humankinetics.com/MotorLearningAndPerformance, including a presentation package and image bank, instructor guide, and test package.

New to this edition is a web study guide that contains narratives from Tim Lee's book, *Motor Control in Everyday Actions*. The narratives relate to real-life encounters with objects and tasks in day-to-day routines. The purpose of the narratives is not only to motivate interest in concepts important to this field of study but also to stimulate thinking regarding how to conduct new research on these topics, and serves as a relevant and relatable companion to the present book. The narratives that correspond to each chapter are indicated throughout the book.

This sixth edition of *Motor Learning and Performance* extends the approach used in the previous five editions. As with the previous editions, we have tried to integrate the latest findings together with the research evidence that has remained relevant for longer periods of time. Since motor learning and performance are probably the most widespread activities that humans from all walks of life experience on a daily basis, our goal was to touch on as many of these applications as possible. The generality and limitations of these principles represent a core of human existence, and we hope that our treatment of them in this book resonates well with each person who reads it.

Richard A. Schmidt
(deceased)

Timothy D. Lee
Professor Emeritus
Department of Kinesiology
McMaster University, Hamilton, Ontario

Student and Instructor Resources

Student Resources

Students, visit the free web study guide, available at www.humankinetics.com/MotorLearningAndPerformance. The web study guide has been fully revised for the sixth edition to offer a more focused and interactive set of activities to aid learning. The activities in this study guide will help you to assess and build your understanding of concepts from each chapter of the text as you study.

In each chapter of the web study guide, you will be presented with a series of two to four interactive activities that test your understanding of important concepts. These include matching, multiple-choice, and diagram-based activities. For each chapter, you will be also be presented with a principles-to-application exercise that prompts you to take your knowledge beyond the classroom by using principles of motor control and learning to analyze an activity. There is no single right answer for the principles-to-application problems, but it is important to provide evidence and reasoning to support your ideas. Each principles-to-application exercise includes sample student answers and critiques of those answers to guide you as you develop your analysis. By completing the exercises included in this study guide, you will build your knowledge of important concepts from the textbook and learn to apply that knowledge to real-world situations.

The web study guide also contains narratives from Tim Lee's 2010 book, *Motor Control in Everyday Actions*. The narratives are referenced throughout this text and organized by chapter on the web study guide.

Instructor Resources

The instructor guide, test package, chapter quizzes, presentation package, and image bank are free to course adopters and are accessed at www.humankinetics.com/MotorLearningAndPerformance.

Instructor Guide

The instructor guide includes chapter summary notes for preparing lectures and ideas for presenting topics and engaging students in class discussions, as well as practical laboratory activities. The instructor guide also features answers to the questions posed in the captions of some of the photos in the book.

Test Package

The test package includes about 250 true-or-false, multiple-choice, fill-in-the-blank, and short-answer questions that can be used to create exams. The test package is available for download in Respondus and LMS formats as well as in Rich Text Format (.rtf) for use with word processing software.

Chapter Quizzes

New for the sixth edition, these ready-to-use quizzes help assess students' comprehension of the most important concepts in each chapter. Chapter quizzes can be imported into learning management systems or be used in RTF format by instructors who prefer to offer a written quiz.

Presentation Package

The presentation package includes more than 270 PowerPoint text slides that highlight material from the text for use in lectures and class discussions. The slides can be used directly in PowerPoint or can be printed to make transparencies or handouts for distribution to students. Instructors can easily add, modify, and rearrange the order of the slides as well as search for images based on key words.

Image Bank

The image bank, included with the presentation package, includes most of the figures, content photos, and tables from the text, sorted by chapter, which can be used to develop a customized presentation.

Acknowledgments

This edition of *Motor Learning and Performance* owes a debt of gratitude to many people. It was Rainer Martens who first conceptualized the idea of the book, and his encouragement led to the publication of the first edition (Schmidt, 1991). Dick and Craig Wrisberg coauthored the next three editions (Schmidt & Wrisberg, 2000, 2004, 2008). I coauthored the fifth edition with Dick and took on the responsibility of preparing the revision for the current edition. Over the past 20 years I have worked with many wonderful people at Human Kinetics, who made the sometimes tedious process much more enjoyable, for which I am very grateful. For this edition I would especially like to thank Drew Tyler, Melissa Zavala, and Diana Vincer for their efforts and support in seeing this project through to completion. I think of these people and their colleagues at HK as much more than just employees of a company. Rather, they are dedicated to producing the best possible learning experience for their readers, and I sincerely thank them for all of their hard work. I also thank Liz Sanli (again) for preparing the book's ancillaries. Lastly, I thank my wife, Laurie, our kids, and our grandchildren for helping me understand the bigger picture.

Credits

Figures

Figure 2.2 Adapted from Attneave (1959).

Figure 2.7 Reprinted by permission from R.A. Schmidt and T.D. Lee, et al., *Motor Control and Learning: A Behavioral Emphasis,* 6th ed. (Champaign, IL: Human Kinetics, 2019), 65; Data from Merkel 1885.

Figure 2.8 Reprinted by permission from R.A. Schmidt and T.D. Lee, et al., *Motor Control and Learning: A Behavioral Emphasis,* 6th ed. (Champaign, IL: Human Kinetics, 2019), 65; Data from Merkel 1885.

Figure 2.9 Reprinted by permission from R.A. Schmidt and T.D. Lee, et al., *Motor Control and Learning: A Behavioral Emphasis,* 6th ed. (Champaign, IL: Human Kinetics, 2019), 70.

Figure 2.11 Data from Brosnan et al. (2017).

Figure 2.12 Adapted from Adams and Dijkstra (1966).

Figure 3.1 Based on Posner and Keele (1969).

Figure 3.3 Reprinted by permission from D.J. Simons and D.T. Levin, "Failure to Detect Changes to People in a Real-World Interaction," *Psychonomic Bulletin & Review* 5 (1999): 644–649.

Figure 3.4 Metamorworks/iStock/Getty Images

Figure 3.5a: Data from Davis (1959).

Figure 3.5b: Reprinted by permission from R.A. Schmidt and T.D. Lee, et al., *Motor Control and Learning: A Behavioral Emphasis,* 6th ed. (Champaign, IL: Human Kinetics, 2019), 108; Data from Davis 1959.

Figure 3.7 Reprinted from M.I. Posner and S.W. Keele, Attentional Demands of Movement, in *Proceedings of the 16th Congress of Applied Physiology* (Amsterdam, Amsterdam: Swets and Zeitlinger, 1969). By permission of M.I. Posner.

Figure 3.8 Reprinted by permission from R.A. Schmidt and T.D. Lee, *Motor Control and Learning: A Behavioral Emphasis,* 5th ed. (Champaign, IL: Human Kinetics, 2011), 129. Data from Weinberg and Ragan (1978).

Figure 4.8 Reprinted from D.N. Lee and E. Aronson, "Visual Proprioceptive Control of Standing in Human Infants," *Perception & Psychophysics* 15 (1974): 529–532. By permission of D.N. Lee.

Figure 4.9 Data from Keele and Posner (1968).

Figure 5.3a: Reprinted by permission from R.A. Schmidt, T.D. Lee, et al., *Motor Control and Learning: A Behavioral Emphasis,* 6th ed. (Champaign, IL: Human Kinetics, 2019), 185.

Figure 5.3b: Reprinted by permission from R.A. Schmidt, T.D. Lee, et al., *Motor Control and Learning: A Behavioral Emphasis,* 6th ed. (Champaign, IL: Human Kinetics, 2019), 186.

Figure 5.4 Reprinted from W.J. Wadman et al., "Control of Fast Goal-Directed Arm Movements," *Journal of Human Movement Studies* 5 (1979): 10. By permission of W.J. Wadman.

Figure 5.5 Adapted from T.R. Armstrong, *Training for the Production of Memorized Movement Patterns: Technical Report No. 26* (Ann Arbor, MI: University of Michigan, Human Performance Center), 35. By permission of the Department of Psychology, University of Michigan (1970).

Figure 5.6 Reprinted by permission from R.A. Schmidt, T.D. Lee, et al., *Motor Control and Learning: A Behavioral Emphasis,* 6th ed. (Champaign, IL: Human Kinetics, 2019), 203.

Figure 5.7 Adapted by permission from J.M. Hollerback, *A Study of Human Motor Control Through Analysis and Synthesis of Handwriting.* Doctoral Dissertation (Cambridge, MA: Massachusetts Institute of Technology, 1978).

Figure 5.8 Reprinted from M.H. Raibert, *Motor Control and Learning by The State-Space Model: Technical Report No. A1-TR-439* (Cambridge, MA: Artificial Intelligence Laboratory, Massachusetts Institute of Technology, 1977), 50. By permission of M.H. Raibert.

Figure 6.1 Adapted from P.M. Fitts, "The Information Capacity of the Human Motor System in Controlling the Amplitude of Movement," *Journal of Experimental Psychology* 47 (1954): 381–391.

Figure 6.2 Reprinted by permission from R.A. Schmidt, T.D. Lee, et al. *Motor Control and Learning,* 6th ed. (Champaign, IL: Human Kinetics, 2019), 217; Data from Fitts 1954.

Figure 6.3 Adapted from P.M. Fitts, "The Information Capacity of the Human Motor System in Controlling the Amplitude of Movement," *Journal of Experimental Psychology* 47 (1954): 381–391.

Figure 6.4 Reprinted by permission from R.A. Schmidt et al., "Motor-Output Variability: A Theory for the Accuracy of Rapid Motor Acts," *Psychological Review* 86 (1979): 425. Copyright © 1979 by the American Psychological Association.

Figure 6.5 Reprinted by permission from R.A. Schmidt et al., "Motor-Output Variability: A Theory for the Accuracy of Rapid Motor Acts," *Psychological Review* 86 (1979): 425. Copyright © 1979 by the American Psychological Association.

Figure 6.8 Adapted by permission from R.A. Schmidt and D.E. Sherwood, "An Inverted-U Relation Between Spatial Error and Force Requirements in Rapid Limb Movements: Further Evidence for The Impulse-Variability Model," *Journal of Experimental Psychology: Human Perception and Performance* 8 (1982): 165. Copyright © 1982 by the American Psychological Association.

Figure 6.10 Reprinted by permission from R.A. Schmidt and T.D. Lee, et al., *Motor Control and Learning: A Behavioral Emphasis,* 6th ed. (Champaign, IL: Human Kinetics, 2019), 227.

Figure 7.2 Reprinted by permission from P.A. Bender, *Extended Practice and Patterns of Bimanual Interference.* Unpublished Doctoral Dissertation (Los Angeles, CA: University of Southern California, 1987).

Figure 7.3 Reprinted by permission from T.D. Lee et al., "Do Expert Golfers Really Keep Their Heads Still While Putting?" *Annual Review of Golf Coaching* 2 (2008): 135–143.

Figure 7.6 Based on Kelso, Scholz, and Schöner (1986).

Figure 7.7 Reprinted by permission from R.C. Schmidt, C. Carello, and M.T. Turvey, "Phase Transitions and Critical Fluctuations in the Visual Coordination of Rhythmic Movements Between People," *Journal of Experimental Psychology: Human Perception and Performance* 16 (1990): 229. Copyright © 1990 by the American Psychological Association.

Figure 8.2 Adapted by permission from R.B. Ammons and L. Willig, "Acquisition of Motor Skill: IV. Effects of Repeated Periods of Massed Practice," *Journal of Experimental Psychology* 51 (1956): 118–126. Copyright © 1956 by the American Psychological Association.

Figure 8.3 Adapted by permission from R.B. Ammons and L. Willig, "Acquisition of Motor Skill: IV. Effects of Repeated Periods of Massed Practice," *Journal of Experimental Psychology* 51 (1956): 118–126. Copyright © 1956 by the American Psychological Association.

Figure 8.4 Adapted by permission from H.P. Bahrick, P.M. Fitts, and G.E. Briggs, "Learning Curves—Facts or Artifacts?" *Psychological Bulletin* 54: 256–268. Copyright © 1957 by the American Psychological Association (1957).

Figure 9.1 Data from Leavitt (1979).

Figure 9.3 Adapted by permission from R.A. Schmidt and T.D. Lee, *Motor Control and Learning: A Behavioral Emphasis,* 6th ed. (Champaign, IL: Human Kinetics, 2019), 386; Adapted from MacKay (1976), personal communication.

Figure 9.4 Reprinted by permission from K. Davids, C. Button, and S. Bennett, *Dynamics of Skill Acquisition: A Constraints-Led Approach* (Champaign, IL: Human Kinetics, 2008), 40.

Figure 9.5 Adapted by permission from R. Gray, "Comparing Cueing and Constraints Interventions for Increasing Launch Angle in Baseball Batting," *Sport, Exercise and Performance Psychology* 7 (2018): 318–332. Copyright © 2018 by the American Psychological Association.

Figure 9.6 Reprinted by permission from E. Neumann and R.B. Ammons, "Acquisition and Long Term Retention of a Simple Serial Perception Motor Skill," *Journal of Experimental Psychology* 53 (1959): 160. Copyright © 2011 by the American Psychological Association.

Figure 9.7 Reprinted from E.A. Fleishman and J.F. Parker, "Factors in the Retention and Relearning of Perceptual Motor Skill," *Journal of Experimental Psychology* 64 (1962): 218. Copyright © 1962 by the American Psychological Association.

Figure 9.8 Alvis Upitis/The Image Bank/Getty Images

Figure 10.1 Adapted by permission from B.A. Boyce, 1"Effects of Assigned Versus Participant-Set Goals on Skill Acquisition and Retention of a Selected Shooting Task," *Journal of Teaching in Physical Education* 11, no. 2 (1992): 227.

Figure 10.2 Based on Lewthwaite and Wulf (2010).

Figure 10.3 Based on Lewthwaite and Wulf (2010).

Figure 10.4 Data from Hird et al. (1991).

Figure 10.5 Reprinted by permission from R.A. Schmidt and T.D. Lee, et al., *Motor Control and Learning: A Behavioral Emphasis,* 6th ed. (Champaign, IL: Human Kinetics, 2019), 323; Data from Baddeley and Longman (1978).

Figure 10.6 Reprinted by permission from L.E. Bourne and E.J. Archer, "Time Continuously on Target as a Function of Distribution of Practice," *Journal of Experimental Psychology* 51 (1956): 27. Copyright © 1956 by the American Psychological Association.

Figure 10.8 Data from Catalano and Kleiner (1984).

Figure 10.9 Reprinted by permission from K.M. Keetch, R.A. Schmidt, T.D. Lee, and D.E. Young, "Especial Skills: Their Emergence With Massive Amounts of Practice," *Journal of Experimental Psychology: Human Perception and Performance* 31 (2005): 970–978. Copyright © 2005 by the American Psychological Association.

Figure 10.10 Adapted by permission from J.B. Shea and R.L. Morgan, "Contextual Interference Effects on the Acquisition, Retention, and Transfer of a Motor Skill," *Journal of Experimental Psychology: Human Learning and Memory* 5 (1979): 179–187. Copyright © 1979 by the American Psychological Association.

Figure 10.11 Reprinted by permission from T.D. Lee et al., "Modeled Timing Information During Random Practice Eliminates the Contextual Interference Effect," *Research Quarterly for Exercise and Sport* 68 (1997): 100–105. Reprinted by permission of the publisher Taylor & Francis Ltd, http://www.tandf.co.uk/journals.

Figure 10.12 Data from Simon and Bjork (2001).

Figure 11.3 Adapted by permission. ©Bob Scavetta. Any adaptation or reproduction of "1.5 Seconds of Thought" is forbidden without the written permission of the copyright holder.

Figure 11.4 Reprinted by permission from R.A. Schmidt and T.D. Lee, et al., *Motor Control and Learning: A Behavioral Emphasis,* 6th ed. (Champaign, IL: Human Kinetics, 2019), 349; Data from Kernodle and Carlton (1992).

Figure 11.5 Reprinted by permission from C.J. Winstein and R.A. Schmidt, "Reduced Frequency of Knowledge of Results Enhances Motor Skill Learning," *Journal of Experimental Psychology: Learning, Memory, and Cognition* 16 (1990): 910. Copyright © 1990 by the American Psychological Association.

Figure 11.7 Data from Guadagnoli et al. (1996).

Figure 11.8 Based on Yao, Fischman, and Wang (1994).

Figure 11.10 Adapted by permission from R.A. Schmidt and T.L. Lee, et al., *Motor Control and Learning: A Behavioral Emphasis,* 6th ed. (Champaign, IL: Human Kinetics, 2019), 338. Adapted from Armstrong 1970.

Figure 11.11 Reprinted by permission from S.P. Swinnen et al., "Information Feedback for Skill Acquisition: Instantaneous Knowledge of Results Degrades Learning," *Journal of Experimental Psychology: Learning, Memory, and Cognition* 16 (1990): 712. Copyright © 2011 by the American Psychological Association.

Figure 11.12 Based on Guadagnoli and Kohl (2001).

Photos

Page iii: ©Timothy D. Lee

Page 1: Lars Baron/Bongarts/Getty Images

Page 7: LuisPortugal/E+/Getty Images

Page 11: Tim Mosenfelder/Getty Images

Page 21: Dylan Buell/Getty Images

Page 24: David Madison/Getty Images

Page 24: Kyodo News via Getty Images

Page 26: Christian Petersen/Getty Images

Page 32: Takashi Aoyama/Getty Images

Page 32: LOIC VENANCE/AFP/Getty Images

Page 37: Clive Mason/Getty Images

Page 51: Michael H/DigitalVision/Getty Images

Page 53: Matthew Maxey/Icon Sportswire via Getty Images

Page 60: Devin Manky/Getty Images

Page 65: Larry Marano/Getty Images

Page 78: Matjaz Tancic/The Image Bank/Getty Images

Page 78: ©DR P. MARAZZI/Science Source

Page 78: Roberto Machado Noa/LightRocket via Getty Images

Page 91: Photo courtesy of Philip de Vries.

Page 101: Ross Kinnaird/Getty Images

Page 118: Michele Eve Sandberg/Corbis via Getty Images

Page 123: ©Liv Friis-larsen - Fotolia.com

Page 123: Richard Heathcote/Getty Images

Page 131: Jose Luis Pelaez Inc/DigitalVision/Getty Images

Page 138: ET-ARTWORKS/DigitalVision/Getty Images

Page 151: Stan Grossfeld/The Boston Globe via Getty Images

Page 154: Alex Menendez/Getty Images

Page 168: Fatemah Bahrami/Anadolu Agency/Getty Images

Page 175: ©Photodisc/Getty Images

Page 185: ©Timothy D. Lee

Page 195: ©Timothy D. Lee

Page 200: imacoconut/iStock/Getty Images

Page 207: Photo courtesy of Sinah Lee

Page 223: JMichl/E+/Getty Images

Page 245: ©imageBROKER RM/Denis Meyer

Page 259: CasarsaGuru/E+/Getty Images

About the Authors photos page 307: Courtesy of Laurie Wishart.

1

Introduction to Motor Learning and Performance

How Skills Are Studied

KEY TERMS

absolute constant error (|CE|)
absolute error (AE)
closed skill
constant error (CE)
continuous skill
correlation coefficient
discrete skill
open skill
root-mean-square error (RMSE)
serial skill
skill
tracking
variable error (VE)

CHAPTER OUTLINE

CHAPTER OBJECTIVES

Chapter 1 provides an overview of research in human motor skills with particular reference to their study in motor learning and performance. This chapter will help you to understand

- the scientific method in skills research,
- different taxonomies used to classify skills,
- common variables used to measure motor performance, and
- the rationale for developing a conceptual model of motor performance.

Parkour videos can be scary to watch, let alone being a performer in one. The traceur or traceuse performs acts of balance, agility, and dexterity, usually across great expanses of space and often at dizzying heights above ground. And yet they perform these skills with grace and confidence. How people perform these skills at such high levels, how such skills are developed, and how you can develop some approximation of these skills in yourself, your children, or your students—all of these questions generate fascination, encouraging further understanding about human movement.

A description of the study of motor performance and learning starts here. The overview presented in this chapter introduces the concept of skill and discusses various features of its definition. The chapter then gives examples of skill classification schemes important for later applications. Finally, the logic behind the book's organization is described to help you understand skills effectively: first, the principles and processes underlying skilled performance, followed by how such capabilities can be developed with practice.

The remarkable human capability to perform skills is a critical feature of our very existence. It is almost uniquely human, although various animals relatively high on the evolutionary scale can be trained to produce what you might call skilled behaviors (e.g., circus dogs doing somersaults, bears riding bicycles). Without the capacity for skilled performance, we could not type the page we are preparing now and you could not read it. And for students involved in physical education and kinesiology, coaching, physical (or speech or occupational) therapy, chiropractic, medicine, or human factors and ergonomics, here is the opportunity to learn about the fundamentals of a wide variety of sports and athletic endeavors, music, and simply ordinary everyday actions that are so strongly fascinating and exciting.

Human skills take many forms, of course—from those that emphasize the control and coordination of our largest muscle groups in relatively forceful activities such as soccer or tumbling, to those in which the smallest muscle groups must be tuned precisely, as in typing or repairing a watch. This text generally focuses on the full range of skilled behavior because it is useful to understand that many common features underlie the performance of skills associated with industrial and military settings, sport, the reacquisition of movement capabilities lost through injuries or stroke, or simply the everyday activities of most people.

Most humans are born with the capability to produce many skills, and only some maturation and experience are necessary in order to produce them in nearly complete form. Walking and running, chewing, balancing, and avoiding painful stimuli are some examples of these relatively innate behaviors. But imagine what simple and uninteresting creatures we would be if these inherited actions were all that we could ever do. All biological organisms have the remarkable facility to profit from their experiences, to learn to detect important environmental features (and to ignore others), and to produce behaviors that were not a part of their original capabilities. Humans seem to have the most flexibility of all, which allows gains in proficiency for occupations as chemists or computer programmers, for competition in music or athletics, or simply for conducting daily lives more efficiently. Thus, producing skilled behaviors and the learning that leads to their development are tightly intertwined in human experience. This book is about both of these aspects of skills—skilled human performance and human learning.

This book is *not* about skills in which the degree of success is determined by deciding which of many already learned actions the performer is to do. When the laboratory rat learns to press a bar at the presentation of a sound, the rat is not learning how to press the bar; rather, the animal is learning when to make this already learned bar-pressing action. As another example, in the card game of bridge, it does not matter *in what fashion* the various cards are played (i.e., moved). What matters is cognitive decision making about which card to play and when to do it. The study of these kinds of decision-making processes falls mainly into fields such as experimental psychology and cognitive neuroscience, and these processes are deliberately not included here.

Why Study Motor Skills?

Because skills make up such a large part of human life, scientists and educators have been trying for centuries to understand the determinants of skills and the factors that affect their performance. The knowledge gained is applicable to numerous aspects of life. Important points apply to the instruction of skills, where methods for efficient teaching and effective carryover to life situations are primary concerns. There is also considerable applicability for improving high-level performances, such as sport, music, and surgical skills. Of course, much of what coaches and music and physical education teachers do during their professional activities involves, in one way or another, skills instruction. The practitioners who understand these skill-related processes most effectively undoubtedly have an advantage when their trainees perform their activities.

Other application areas can be emphasized as well. There are many applications in training skills for industry, where effective job skills can mean success in the workplace and can be major determinants of satisfaction both with the job and with life in general. Teaching job skills most effectively, and determining which of a large number of individuals are best suited to particular occupations, are common situations in which knowledge about skills can be useful in industry. Usually these applications are considered within human factors (ergonomics). The principles also apply to physical therapy and occupational therapy settings, where the concern is for the (re)learning and production of movements that have been lost through head or spinal cord injury, stroke, birth defects, and the like. Although all these areas may be different and the physical capabilities of the learners may vary widely, the principles that lead to successful application are generally the same.

The Science of Motor Learning and Performance

It is not uncommon that as an area of interest grows, the systematic study of the principles involved also develops. Motor learning and performance are no different, in that a science has emerged that allows the formalization of terms and concepts for others to use. When we use the word *science*, what do we mean?

The concept of a science implies several things: (1) the active use of theory and hypothesis testing to further our knowledge, (2) a certain infrastructure that involves books and journals, scientific organizations that deal with both the fundamental aspects of the science and ways to apply the knowledge to real-world situations, and granting agencies to provide funds for research, and, of course, (3) the existence of courses of study of the area in universities and colleges.

Theories and Hypotheses

Certainly at the heart of every science are theories that purport to explain how things work. A theory's purpose is to explain how phenomena occur. The theorist devises *hypothetical constructs*—elements or pieces that interact in various ways in the theory. The theorist then describes the ways in which the hypothetical constructs interact with each other so as to explain some empirical phenomenon. Then, using logical deduction, scientists determine certain predictions that the theory makes in its current form. These predictions form the basis of hypotheses that can be tested, typically in the laboratory. These hypotheses take the form of statements such as "If I ask learners to practice under condition *x*, then learning should be better than for others who practice under condition *y*."

Theories are typically tested by doing experiments, which determine whether or not the hypothesis correctly predicted what happened. In the field of motor learning and performance, these experiments typically take the form of having at least two groups of research participants randomly assigned to experimental treatments, with one group performing a task under condition *x* (as in the example just mentioned) and the other group performing under some other conditions that are reasonably well understood (sometimes called a control condition). If, in this example, the group practicing under condition *x* outperforms the group in the control condition, then we say that the hypothesis is supported. However, a given theory might predict an outcome that would make sense for several different theories, so an experiment that supports the hypothesis cannot be said to *prove* that is theory is correct. What is usually far stronger is if the results come out *contrary* to the prediction; this leads to the logical inference that the theory must be incorrect, allowing us to reject one of the possible theories. This is so because a theory cannot survive for long if something predicted from it turns out not to be the case. Because of this difference in the power of the ways in which hypotheses are tested, scientists tend to search out predictions from a theory that might not hold if tested in the laboratory.

What Skills Have Been Studied and Who Studies Them?

The science of motor learning and performance has been used to study many varieties of skills. Initially, skills research was primarily the domain of psychologists and physiologists who used movement tasks as tools to examine theories of learning and coordination. For example, in the 1890s, Bryan and Harter studied the complex processes involved in sending and receiving Morse code. In the 1920s, the psychologist E.L. Thorndike used blindfolded line drawing to examine the role of augmented feedback to test his Law of Effect. Rotary pursuit tracking was a common tool used to examine Hull's theory of learning in the 1940s. And simple line-drawing tasks came back into popularity again in the 1960s to study the forgetting of information over short retention periods.

Focus on
RESEARCH 1.1

Paul M. Fitts

Have you ever wondered why some keys on a calculator or your computer keyboard are larger than others, or why they are arranged to occur in specific locations? If so, then you can probably credit Paul Fitts with the underlying rationale. His research was designed to answer fundamental questions about human performance in situations that required speed and accuracy, often under stressful situations. Some of his many contributions included research on stimulus–response compatibility effects (see chapter 2), the effects of target size and distance on movement time, now known as Fitts' Law (chapter 6), and the stages of learning (chapter 9). His work was largely responsible for the growth of the research area now called ergonomics or human factors.

In the late 19th century, physiologists such as Sir Charles Sherrington were interested in the role of various biological systems concerning the fundamental mechanisms of neural control of muscle and the study of the nervous system. Nikolai Bernstein and Erich von Holst contributed essential research to our understanding of movement coordination during the first half of the 20th century. And Edward Taub performed controversial experiments on monkeys that revealed evidence about lost and retained movement capabilities in the absence of sensory feedback.

Perhaps motivated by discoveries in these more traditional fields, researchers in other disciplines began to study motor skills as a means to answer domain-specific issues. Paul Fitts (see Focus on Research 1.1) contributed to the war effort in the 1940s by studying piloting errors—why errors occurred and how movements are limited in speed and accuracy by task demands. Fitts' work represented an emerging field called ergonomics (also called human factors), which broadly studied the limits of human performance in the execution of industrial tasks.

Physical education and kinesiology departments, led by researchers such as Franklin M. Henry (see Focus on Research 1.2), studied motor skills as a research topic of direct interest in and of itself. Later, researchers added to this effort by establishing testable theories regarding the learning and control of motor skills.

It is common now to find research being conducted in various fields of application in which skills are used as components of daily living, such as medicine, dentistry, physical rehabilitation, fire prevention, law enforcement, and the interface of humans with various forms of computing devices. And, of course, the study of how highly skilled performance is acquired and executed remains an ongoing field of study in sport and music. All of these influences, in the pursuit of both practical and theoretical advances to our knowledge, have served to drive the study of motor learning and performance.

Defining Skills

As widely represented and diverse as skills are, it is difficult to define them in a way that applies to all cases. Guthrie (1952) provided a definition that captures most of the critical features of skills that we emphasize here. He defined **skill** as "the ability to bring about some end result with maximum certainty and minimum outlay of energy, or of time and energy" (p. 136). Next, we consider some of the important components (or features) of this definition.

First, performing skills implies some desired goal, such as holding a handstand in gymnastics, expressing thoughts using a keyboard, or being able to walk again after

Focus on
RESEARCH 1.2

Franklin M. Henry, Father of Motor Behavior Research

Before World War II and during the 1950s and 1960s when much effort was directed at military skills such as pilotry, most of the research in movement behavior and learning was done by experimental psychologists, studying relatively fine motor skills. Little effort was devoted to the gross motor skills that would be applicable to many sports. Franklin M. Henry, trained in experimental psychology but working in the Department of Physical Education at the University of California, Berkeley, was filling this gap with a new tradition of laboratory experimentation that started an important new direction in research on movement skills. He studied gross motor skills, with performances intentionally representative of those seen on the playing fields and in gymnasiums. But he used laboratory tasks, which enabled the rigorous study of these skills employing methods analogous to those used in experimental psychology. Two of his major contributions to research were (1) evidence that initiation times increase as movements-to-be-made increase in complexity, providing evidence in support of the motor program concept (see chapter 5), and (2) evidence that skills are highly uncorrelated within individuals (see the section "Correlation: The Association Strength Between Scores" later in this chapter), which dispelled the general motor ability concept (see chapter 7).

a stroke. Skills are usually thought of as different from *movements*, which do not necessarily have any particular goal, such as idly wiggling one's little finger. Of course, skills consist of movements because the performer could not achieve the goal without making at least one movement.

Second, to be skilled implies meeting this performance goal, this end result, with maximum *certainty*. For example, suppose that a darts player makes a bull's-eye. This by itself does not ensure that he is a skilled darts player, because there is no evidence that this result was achieved with much certainty. Such an outcome could have been the result of one lucky throw in the midst of hundreds of others that were not so lucky. To be considered skilled requires that a person produce the skill reliably, on demand, without luck playing a very large role. This is one reason why people value so greatly the champion athlete who, with but one chance and only seconds remaining at the end of a game, makes the play that allows the team to win.

Third, a major feature in many skills is the minimization, and thus conservation, of the energy required for performance. For some skills this is clearly not the goal, as in the shot put, where the only goal is to achieve the maximum distance. But for many other skills the minimization of energy expenditure is critical, allowing the marathon runner to hold an efficient pace or allowing the wrestler to save strength for the last few minutes of the match. We evolved to walk as we do, in part, because our walking style minimizes energy expenditure for walking a given distance. This minimum-energy notion applies not only to the physiological energy costs but also to the psychological or mental energy required for performance. Many skills have been learned so well that the performers hardly have to pay attention to them, freeing their cognitive processes for other features of the activity, such as strategic planning in team sports or artistic expressiveness in dance and music. A major contributor to the efficiency of skilled performance is, of course, practice,

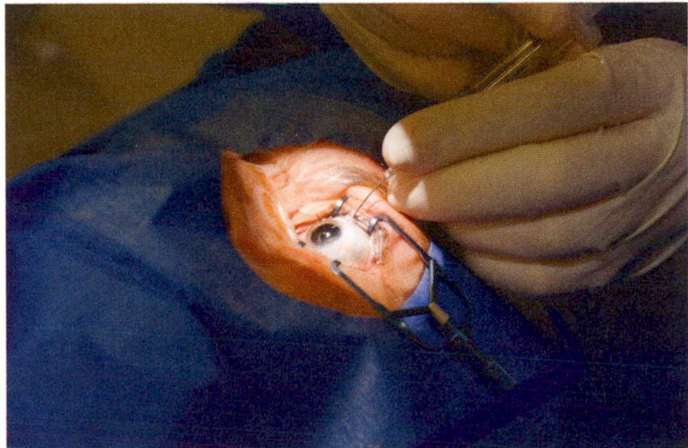

Identify the main emphases in each of these photos with respect to the definition of skill.

with learning and experience leading to the relatively effortless performances so admired in highly skilled people.

Finally, another feature of many skills is for highly proficient performers to achieve their goals in minimum time. Many skills have this as the only goal, such as a swimming race. Minimizing time can interact with the other skill features mentioned, however. Surgeons who conduct invasive surgery need to work quickly to minimize the opportunity for infections to enter the body. Yet surgeons obviously need to work carefully too. Speeding up performance often results in imprecise movements that have less certainty in terms of achieving their goals. Also, increased speed generates movements for which the energy costs are sometimes higher. Thus, understanding skills involves optimizing and balancing several skill aspects that are important to different extents in different settings. In sum, skills generally involve achieving some well-defined goal by

- maximizing the certainty of goal achievement,
- minimizing the physical- and mental-energy costs of performance, and
- minimizing the time used.

Components of Skills

The elegant performance of the skilled dancer and the artistic talents of an expert sculptor may appear simple, but the performance goals actually were realized through a complex combination of interacting mental and motor processes. For example, many skills involve considerable emphasis on sensory–perceptual factors, such as detecting that a tennis opponent is going to hit a shot to your left or that you are rapidly approaching a car that has suddenly stopped on the road ahead of you. Often, sensory factors require the split-second analysis of *patterns* of sensory input, such as discerning that the combined movements of an entire football team indicate that the play will be a running play to the left side. These perceptual events lead to decisions about what to do, how to do it, and when to do it. These decisions are often a major determinant of success. Finally, of course, skills typically depend on the quality of movement generated as a result of these decisions. Even if the situation is correctly perceived and the response decisions are appropriate, the performer will not be effective in meeting the environmental goal if she executes the actions poorly.

These three elements are critical to almost any skill:

- Perceiving the relevant environmental features
- Deciding what to do and where and when to do it to achieve the goal
- Producing organized muscular activity to generate movements that achieve the goal

The movements have several recognizable parts. Postural components support the actions; for instance, the arms and hands of a surgeon need to be supported by a stable platform in order to perform accurately. Body transport components move the body toward the point where the skill will take place, as in carrying a package of shingles up a ladder to place on the roof of a house.

It is interesting, but perhaps unfortunate, that each of these skill components seems to be recognized and studied in isolation from the others. For example, sensory factors in perception are studied by cognitive psychologists, scientists interested in (among other things) the complex information-processing activities involved in seeing, hearing, and feeling. Sometimes these factors are in the realm of psychophysics, the branch of psychology that examines the relationship between objective physical stimuli (e.g., vibration intensity) and the subjective sensations these stimuli create when perceived (e.g., loudness). Factors in the control of the movement itself are typically studied by scientists in the neurosciences, cognitive psychology, biomechanics, and physiology. Skill learning is studied by yet another group of scientists in kinesiology, in experimental or educational psychology, or in the field of human factors and ergonomics. A major problem for the study of skills, therefore, is the fact that the several components of skill are studied by widely different groups of scientists, often with little overlap and communication among them.

All of these various processes are present in almost all motor skills. Even so, we should not get the idea that all skills are fundamentally the same. In fact, the principles of human performance and learning depend to some extent on the *kind* of movement skill to be performed. So the ways in which skills have been classified are discussed next.

Classifying Skills

There are several skill classification systems that help organize the research findings and make application somewhat more straightforward. These are presented in the following sections.

Open and Closed Skills

One way to classify movement skills concerns the extent to which the environment is stable and predictable throughout performance. An **open skill** is one for which the environment is variable and unpredictable during the action. Examples include most team sports and driving a car in traffic where it is difficult to predict the future actions of other people. A **closed skill**, on the other hand, is one for which the environment is stable and predictable. Examples include swimming in an empty lane in a pool and drilling a hole in a block of wood. These open and closed designations actually mark only the end points of a continuum, with the skills lying in between having varying degrees of environmental predictability or variability (see Gentile, 2000, for more discussion).

This classification points out a critical feature for skills, defining the performer's need to respond to moment-to-moment variations in the environment. It thus brings in the subprocesses associated with perception, pattern recognition, and decision making (usually with the need to perform these processes quickly) so the action can be tailored

TABLE 1.1 Open and Closed Skills Continuum

Closed skills ◄		► Open skills
Predictable environment	**Semipredictable environment**	**Unpredictable environment**
Gymnastics Archery Typing	Walking a tightrope Steering a car Playing chess	Playing soccer Wrestling Chasing a rabbit

to the environment. These processes are minimized in closed skills, where the performer can evaluate the environmental demands in advance without time pressure, organize the movement in advance, and carry it out without needing to make rapid modifications as the movement unfolds. These features are summarized in table 1.1.

Discrete, Serial, and Continuous Skills

A second scheme for classifying skills concerns the extent to which the movement is an ongoing stream of behavior, as opposed to a brief, well-defined action. At one end of this dimension is a **discrete skill**, which usually has an easily defined beginning and end, often with a very brief duration of movement, such as throwing a ball, firing a rifle, or turning on a light switch. Discrete skills are particularly important in both sport and daily actions, especially considering the large number of discrete hitting, kicking, and throwing skills that make up many sport activities, as well as everyday skills of fastening buttons, writing your signature, and pointing a computer mouse. Discrete skills often result in a measured outcome score, which can be combined with other scores to result in several types of error scores, discussed later in this chapter.

At the other end of this dimension is a **continuous skill**, which has no particular beginning or end, the behavior flowing on for many minutes, such as swimming or knitting. As discussed later, discrete and continuous skills can be quite different, requiring different processes for performance and demanding that they be taught somewhat differently as a result.

One particularly important continuous skill is **tracking**, in which the performer's limb movements control a lever, a wheel, a handle, or some other device to follow the movements of a target. Steering a car involves tracking, with steering wheel movements made so the car follows the track, defined by the roadway. Tracking movements are very common in real-world skills situations, and much research has been directed to their performance and learning. Tracking tasks are sometimes scored using a particular error score, called root-mean-square error (RMSE) presented in detail later in this chapter.

Between the polar ends of the discrete–continuous skill continuum is the **serial skill**, which is often thought of as a group of discrete skills strung together to make up a new, more complicated skilled action. See table 1.2 for a comparison summary. Here the word *serial* implies that the order of the elements is usually critical for successful performance. Cars that have a manual transmission involve a serial skill that combines discrete arm movements along with movements of both feet performed in a precisely timed sequence to create a larger action. Other examples include performing a gymnastics routine and most types of cooking. Serial skills differ from discrete skills in that the movement durations tend to be somewhat longer, yet each component retains a discrete beginning and end. One view of learning serial skills suggests that the individual skill elements present in early learning are somehow combined to form one larger, single element that the performer controls almost as if it were truly discrete in nature (e.g., the smooth, rapid way a gymnast shifts from one maneuver to another on the rings).

TABLE 1.2 Discrete–Serial–Continuous Skills Continuum

Discrete skills	Serial skills	Continuous skills
Distinct beginning and end	**Discrete actions linked together**	**No discrete beginning or end**
Throwing a dart Flipping a light switch Shooting a rifle	Hammering a nail Assembly-line work Gymnastics routine	Steering a cart Swimming Tracking task

Object Manipulation and Body Transport

Gentile (2000) identified two other factors that help to more precisely define the nature of skills. One concerns whether the body is stationary or in motion during the performance of the skill. For example, a dentist usually performs her work while standing still, in contrast to a table busser in a restaurant, who is constantly on the move. The other factor is whether or not the performer is manipulating an object during performance. Figure skaters express artistry in motion on ice skates, in contrast to puck control, which is the primary goal in ice hockey.

The four factors described above define skills as a complex classification system. Ultimately, almost every skill that you can think of can be described as an interacting product of these four dimensions.

Measuring Skilled Performance

Quite frequently, researchers are called on to generate methods for computing scores for a participant who was attempting to perform a series of trials on a test. As we shall see, there are various ways to calculate these measures, depending on whether the task is discrete or continuous.

Error Scores in Discrete Tasks

Suppose that you are testing individuals on a throwing task, in which they are trying to throw a ball exactly 50 ft away from where they are currently standing. Two hypothetical participants perform this task for five trials, and the results are illustrated in figure 1.1 and presented in table 1.3.

Which of these two individuals was more skillful in this task? It appears from the figure that there is a difference in skill, but looking at a figure and making decisions based on one's impression is less scientific and precise than developing measures that are based on the actual numbers and inferential statistics. Therefore, researchers have come up with ways of combining the scores on the five throwing trials into a single number that reflects their skill in the task. Several candidate measures are possible, and each represents a unique assessment of skill.

The worksheet presented in table 1.3 presents a detailed description of how to calculate various methods that represent the skills illustrated by the two throwers in figure 1.1.

Visit the web study guide to read "Public Opinion Polls" and complete the self-directed learning activities.

Constant Error (CE)

The simplest way to determine which person was more accurate is to compute the error deviation of each throw, relative to the target, and then calculate the average of these error deviations (column 4 in table 1.3). For example, on trial 1, Chester's error score was –4 (his throw was 46 ft, and thus, 4 ft short of the target of 50 ft). The error score on the second trial was +2 (his 52 ft throw was 2 ft too far), and so on. After the error scores for each trial are computed, the mean can then be calculated to determine the average error

Classify the actions depicted here along the four skill classification dimensions: discrete/continuous/serial; open/closed; body in motion or stationary; object or no object.

deviation from the target. This is termed the participant's average **constant error (CE)**. The interpretation is that Chester tended to overthrow the 50 ft target by only 0.4 ft; John-Lee tended to underthrow the target by 2.6 ft, therefore Chester tended to be closer to the goal than John-Lee, based on average CE.

The formula for constant error is

$$CE = [\Sigma (X_i - T) / N]$$

where: Σ = the "sum of," i = trial number, X_i = score for the ith trial, T = the target distance, and N = the number of trials.

Absolute Error (AE)

Another simple way to combine the scores into a single number is to consider the *absolute value* (i.e., with the sign ignored or removed) of the error on each trial, and take the average

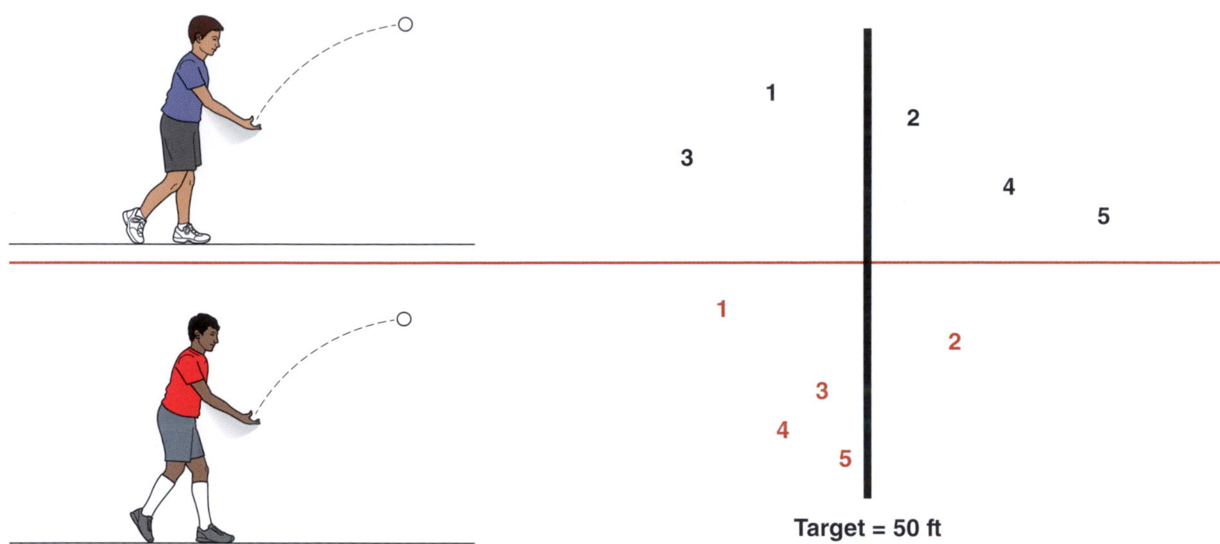

FIGURE 1.1 Two performers are attempting to throw a ball exactly 50 feet. The numbers (1–5) represent the individual results of each of five trials. The numerical results are presented in table 1.3.

TABLE 1.3 Error Scores in Discrete Tasks

Chester					
Trial	X_i	T	CE $X_i - T$	AE $\|X_i - T\|$	VE $[(X_i - T) - CE]^2$
1	46	50	−4	4	19.36
2	52	50	+2	2	2.56
3	39	50	−11	11	129.96
4	55	50	+5	5	21.16
5	60	50	+10	10	92.16
			$\Sigma(X_i - T) = 2.0$	$\Sigma(\|X_i - T\|) = 32.0$	$\Sigma[(X_i - T) - CE]^2 = 265.2$
			$\Sigma(X_i - T)/N = +0.4$	$\Sigma(\|X_i - T\|)/N = 6.4$	$\Sigma[(X_i - T) - CE]^2 / N = 53.04$
					$\sqrt{[\Sigma[(X_i - T) - CE]^2 / N]} = 7.3$
John-Lee					
Trial	X_i	T	CE $X_i - T$	AE $\|X_i - T\|$	VE $(X_i - CE)^2$
1	40	50	−10	10	54.76
2	54	50	+4	4	43.56
3	48	50	−2	2	0.36
4	46	50	−4	4	1.96
5	49	50	−1	1	2.56
			$\Sigma(X_i - T) = -13$	$\Sigma(\|X_i - T\|) = 21$	$\Sigma[(X_i - T) - CE]^2 = 103.2$
			$\Sigma(X_i - T)/N = -2.6$	$\Sigma(\|X_i - T\|)/N = 4.2$	$\Sigma[(X_i - T) - CE]^2 / N = 20.64$
					$\sqrt{[\Sigma[(X_i - T) - CE]^2 / N]} = 4.5$

of those unsigned error scores for the various trials (column 5 in table 1.3). For example, Chester has an error of –4 ft on the first trial; when we take the absolute value, the first trial has an absolute error of 4 ft; the second trial has an error of +2 ft, whose absolute value is 2. If we do this procedure for the remainder of the trials for Chester, and all the trials for John-Lee, the computed average absolute error for Chester is 6.4; for John-Lee it is 4.2. Here, with the direction of the errors being disregarded, the interpretation is that Chester was off-target more than was John-Lee.

The formula for average **absolute error (AE)** is

$$AE = [\Sigma\,(|X_i - T|) \,/\, N]$$

where: Σ, *i*, *X*, *T*, and *N* are defined as before for constant error, and the vertical bars (|) mean "absolute value of."

Variable Error (VE)

The third measure of skill is not actually a measure of accuracy but rather an assessment of the participant's inconsistency—that is, how different each individual score was in comparison to his average (CE) score. To compute **variable error (VE)**, we square the difference between each trial's error score and the individual's own constant error $[(X_i - \mathrm{T}) - CE]^2$, sum those squared values over all of the trials, and divide by *N*. Now, since these are squared values, we return them to their original state by computing the square root of this value (see column 6 in table 1.3).

In this example, for Chester's first trial, the difference between X_1 and Chester's average CE (which was +0.4) is [(–4 – (+0.4)] = –4.4 ft, which, when squared, is 19.36 ft. For the second trial, the difference between X_2 and Chester's average CE is [(+2) – (+0.4)] = 1.6 ft, which, when squared, is 2.56 ft. Now do the same thing for trials 3, 4, and 5; add up all five squared differences; divide this number by *N* = 5; then take the square root of that number; and you finally have VE. The score is interpreted as the inconsistency in responding—that is, how variable the performance is about the person's own average CE. Of course when computing the value for John-Lee, we would use his CE (which was –2.6) in the computations. The computed VE score for Chester was 7.3 ft, and for John-Lee the VE was 4.5 ft. The interpretation is that even though Chester's average throw was closer to the goal than was John-Lee's average throw, Chester was more inconsistent in those throws than was John-Lee.

The formula for variable error is

$$VE = \sqrt{\Sigma\,\left[\left(X_i - \mathrm{T}\right) - CE\right]^2 / N}$$

where Σ, *X*, *i*, *CE*, and *N* are defined as before, and √ is the square root.

AE was employed as a measure of error very frequently until investigators Schutz and Roy (1973) pointed out some statistical difficulties with it. Today, investigators tend to use CE (as a measure of average bias or directional error) and VE (as a measure of inconsistency). Sometimes investigators use a statistic called **absolute constant error** (abbreviated **|CE|**) instead of CE for an individual's measure of bias. The |CE| is simply the average absolute value of the computed CE score as defined previously. The advantage is that |CE| retains the magnitude of average deviation from the target but prevents two scores from canceling out when data from more than one person are averaged together to present a group score. Much more on these error scores is presented in chapter 2 of Schmidt et al. (2019).

Visit the web study guide to read "Cutting Wood and Missing Putts" and complete the self-directed learning activities.

Error Scores in Continuous Tasks

Continuous tasks, such as tracking, are capable of producing many error scores on a single trial. Consider figure 1.2 as an example of a portion of a single trial of a tracking task for one individual. The wide blue path represents the goal, such as a highway lane along which a driver might navigate a car. The red line represents the exact (but usually unmarked) center of the track from edge to edge. The black dotted line represents a person's tracking behavior—in this case, how close to the center of the road the car is maintained. How

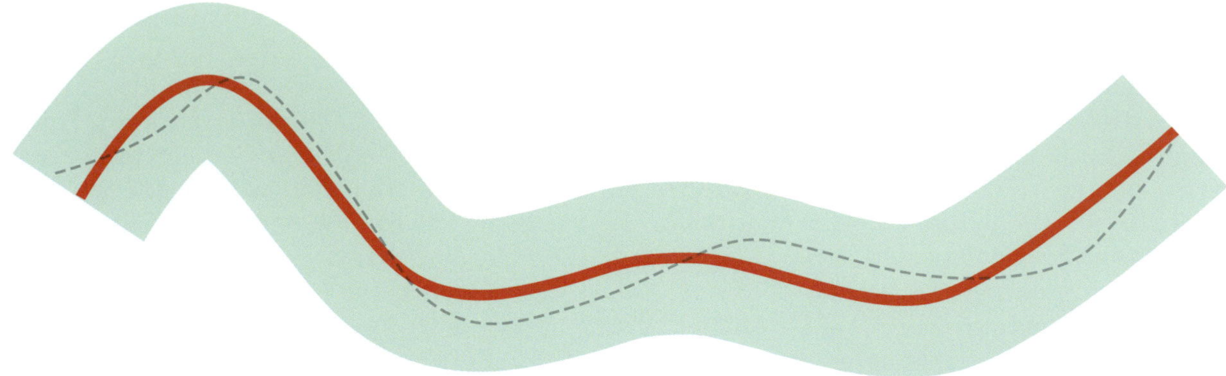

FIGURE 1.2 Measuring RMSE in a tracking task. The blue area represents the track (such as a highway lane); the red (solid) line represents the unmarked center of the lane, and can be considered the participant's goal track. The black dotted line represents the participant's performance in attempting to follow the red line.

can skill be measured in this single trial of a continuous performance?

A common method used by researchers who study tracking tasks is to compute a measure called **root-mean-square error (RMSE)**. One does this by computing the distance of the person's tracking behavior from the target line at preset *distance points* along the track (e.g., every 10 ft of highway traveled) or, more commonly, at a constant interval of time along the track (e.g., every 100 ms). This method effectively slices the continuous movement into equal, discrete intervals of tracking behavior, from start to finish.

With each slice of the track, the researcher then computes how far the participant's tracking position is from the target. Since the red line in figure 1.2 represents the center of the track, it is convenient to define the red line as the zero position. Therefore, if the participant is to the right of the target, the measure is given a positive error value; if the tracking position is to the left of the target, the measure gets a negative value. The root-mean-square error score is computed by first calculating the squared deviations for each measured position along the track, then taking the square root of the sum of those scores.

The RMSE is a more complex measure of performance than any of the error scores for discrete tasks, because it represents two components of behavior. The RMSE reflects both the bias tendency (e.g., on average, to drive closer to the right edge of the lane than the left edge) as well as inconsistency in the tracking behavior (how variable the performance tends to be). The RMSE is well recognized as a very good measure of how effectively the person tracked.

Correlation: The Association Strength Between Scores

Sometimes researchers are interested in discovering how sets of scores are related to each other. Franklin M. Henry (see Focus on Research 1.2) was an early pioneer of using correlations as a measure of determining one such relationship. His reasoning was this: Assume that a relatively large number of people are tested on each of two skills, A and B. Henry reasoned that if one person was an outstanding performer on skill A, then this person would be assumed to have a strong general motor ability. If so, this person should also score well on skill B, which also depended on the general motor ability. Conversely, if another person did not score well on skill A, at least part of the reason would be that this person had a weak general motor ability, and this person would be expected to score relatively poorly on skill B also. In this way, skill A and skill B are *related* to each other, in that good scores on A go with good scores on B, and poor scores on A go with poor scores on B.

With this kind of relationship, if we were to plot performances of skill A against performances of skill B, as we have done in figure 1.3, where each dot represents a single individual measured on both tests A and B, these two tests should plot linearly with each other, which they tend to do in figure 1.3*a*. However, if skill A and skill B are not related to each other, then they should plot more or less as seen in figure 1.3*b*. One interpretation of these scatter plots is that in figure 1.3*a*, skill A and skill B tend to be measures of the same thing, and the usual interpretation is that they are both measures of the same ability. In figure 1.3*b*, on the other hand, we would be forced to say that skill A and skill B are not measures of the same ability. This leads to the straightforward prediction that if general motor ability exists, with all skills being dependent on a single general motor ability, then all skills should show strong relationships among them, as in figure 1.3*a*.

As we mentioned previously, however, determining conclusions based on the visual inspection of trends in data is imprecise. Fortunately, a statistic called the **correlation coefficient** provides a way to determine the exact strength of a relationship, for example, between the data that are illustrated in figure 1.3.

The correlation can range in size from −1.0 to +1.0. The size of the correlation indicates the strength of the relationship, or how close the individual dots are to the best-fitting line passing through them. If the line is sloped negatively—downward to the right—then the sign of the correlation will be negative. If the dots are close to the line, as they are in figure 1.3*a*, the correlation is close to +1.0, indicating a very strong tendency for skill in A to be associated with skill in B ($r = +.90$). If the dots lie relatively far from the line, as they do in figure 1.3*b*, the correlation is closer to zero, indicating a relatively weak tendency for scores in A to be associated with scores in B ($r = +.15$). The strength of a relationship is estimated by the squared correlation coefficient multiplied by 100. Thus, the correlation of +.15 means that the two tests have $.15^2 = (.15 \times .15) \times 100$, or about 2% in common with each other. Note that the size of the correlation has nothing to do with its sign, because a strong correlation can be either positive or negative. Finally, a correlation of .00 indicates that the line of best fit is a horizontal line (a slope of 0), with the dots scattered about it in a random way. In such a case, tests A and B would not be related at all. We will have much more to say about the findings uncovered by this research in chapter 7.

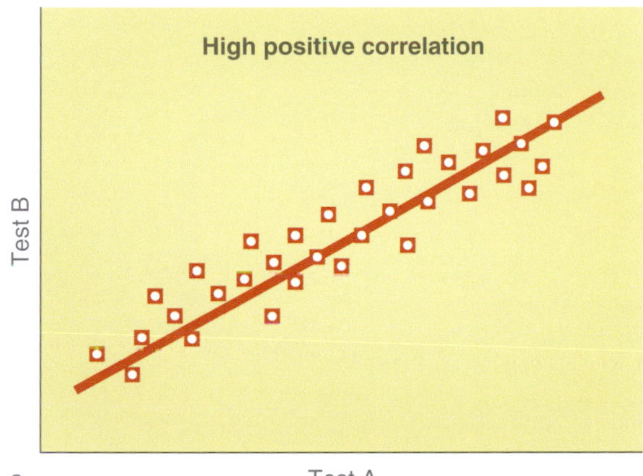

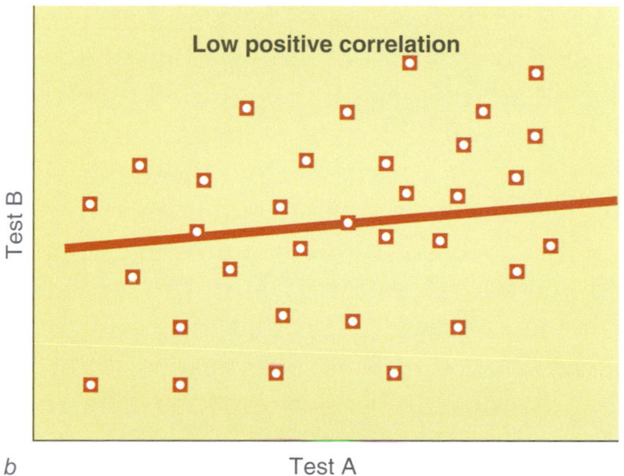

FIGURE 1.3 Scatter plot of two tests revealing a high positive correlation (*a*) and a very low positive correlation (*b*). Each dot in the figure represents the performance of one individual, plotting performance on one test against performance on the other test.

Visit the web study guide to read "The Hot Hand" and complete the self-directed learning activities.

Understanding Performance and Learning

In some ways, skilled performance and motor learning are interrelated concepts that cannot be easily separated for analysis. Even so, a separation of these areas is necessary for presentation and making eventual understanding much easier. Many of the terms, principles, and processes that scientists use to describe the improvements with practice and learning (the subfield of motor learning) actually come from the literature on the underlying processes in the production of skilled motor performance (the subfield of human performance; the field of motor behavior often includes both motor learning and human performance). Therefore, whereas at first glance it might seem most logical to treat motor learning before motor performance (a person has to learn before performing), it turns out to be awkward to present information on learning without first having provided this background performance information.

For this reason this book is organized into two parts, the first of which introduces the terminology, concepts, and principles related to skilled human performance without very much reference to processes associated with learning. The principles here probably apply most strongly to the performance of already skilled actions. Having examined the principles of how the motor system produces skills, the discussion turns to how these processes can be altered, facilitated, and trained through practice, which involves motor learning.

Figure 1.4 illustrates a simplified relationship between motor learning and performance in the context of the issues discussed in this chapter. Measurable performance is the result of processes that culminate in movement. Just as the skill has different identifiable dimensions, so too does the individual, and the first part of this book is devoted to describing the processes that influence motor performance. Learning, which represents a relatively permanent improvement in the performance of a skill, occurs when those processes are repeated and refined, which is the topic of the second part of this book.

When studying motor performance and learning, it is helpful to understand where each concept fits into the complex process of performing a skill. For this reason, and to help apply skills information to a variety of settings, this book develops a conceptual model. This model represents the big picture of motor performance. As new topics are introduced, they are added to the model, tying together most of the major processes and events that occur as performers produce skills. Models of this type are critical in teaching and in science because they embrace many seemingly unrelated facts and concepts, linking real-world knowledge with the concepts being discussed.

Models can be of many types, of course, such as the plumbing-and-pump model of the human circulatory system and the variety of balls that model the structure of atoms, the

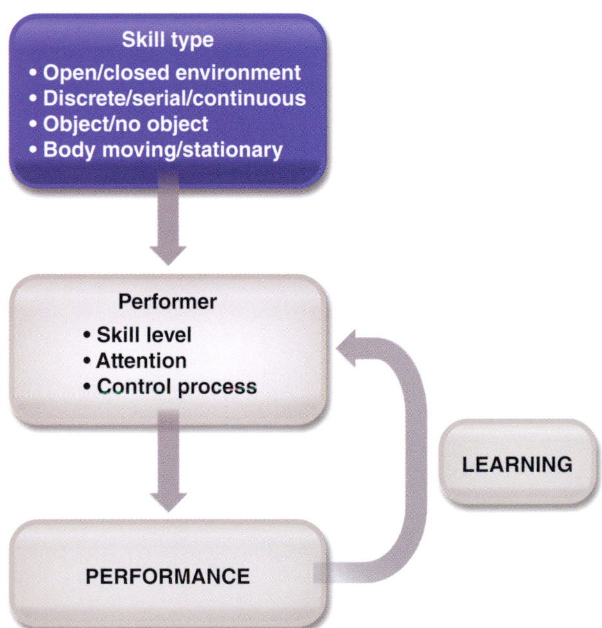

FIGURE 1.4 An overview of the processes involved in motor learning and performance. The next part of the book is devoted to the processes that influence performance. The latter part concerns issues that influence learning.

solar system, and molecules in chemistry. For skills, a useful conceptualization is an information-flow model, which considers how information of various kinds is used in producing and learning a skilled action. The first portions of the text build this model, first considering how the sensory information that enters the system through the receptors is processed, transformed, and stored. To this is added how this sensory information leads to other processes associated with decision making and planning action. To the emerging conceptual model are then added features of the initiation of action as well as the activities involved while the action is unfolding, such as controlling muscular contractions and detecting and correcting errors; this is highly related to the performer's analysis of the sensations produced as a result of performing the action—processes related to feedback. In the second portion of the text, which deals with learning, the model provides an effective understanding of the processes that are, and are not, influenced by practice.

Summary

People regard skills as an important, fascinating aspect of life. Knowledge about skills has come from a variety of scientific disciplines and can be applied to many settings, such as sport, teaching, coaching, industry, and physical therapy.

Skill is usually defined as the capability to bring about some desired end result with maximum certainty and minimum time and energy. Many different components are involved; major categories are perceptual or sensory processes, decision making, and movement output. Skills may be classified along numerous dimensions, such as open versus closed skills, and discrete, serial, and continuous skills. These classifications are important because the principles of skills and their learning often differ for different skill categories.

The text's particular organization of materials should facilitate an understanding of skills. After this introduction, the remainder of part I addresses the principles of human skilled performance and the underlying processes, focusing on how the various parts of the motor system act to produce skilled actions. Part II examines how to modify these various processes by practice and motor learning. Understanding how all of these components can operate together is facilitated by a conceptual model of human performance that is developed throughout the text.

WEB STUDY GUIDE ACTIVITIES

The student web study guide offers these activities to help you build and apply your knowledge of the concepts in this chapter.

Interactive Learning

Activity 1.1: Classify skills as discrete, serial, or continuous in nature by selecting the appropriate category for each of five examples.

Activity 1.2: Review the types of error measured in motor learning research by matching various error measures with their definitions.

Principles-to-Application Exercise

Activity 1.3: The principles-to-application exercise for this chapter applies the concepts in this chapter to your own experience by asking you to analyze a motor skill that you have learned in the past or are currently learning. You'll describe the skill as open or closed and as discrete, serial, or continuous and identify the goals of the skill and the factors that contribute to your success when performing it.

Motor Control in Everyday Actions Narratives

Public Opinion Polls
Cutting Wood and Missing Putts
The Hot Hand

Check Your Understanding

1. Define a skill and indicate why each of the following terms is important to that definition.
   - Environmental goal
   - Maximum certainty
   - Minimum energy costs
   - Minimum time
2. Distinguish between open and closed skills and between discrete, serial, and continuous skills. Give one example of each.
3. List and describe three elements critical to almost any skill.
4. Define a theory and describe how scientists use theories to design experiments.

Apply Your Knowledge

1. List three motor skills that you have learned, either recently or when you were younger (e.g., swinging a baseball bat, tying your shoelaces, or playing a chord on the piano). Classify each of the skills you have listed, distinguishing between open and closed and between discrete, serial, and continuous skills. Are maximum certainty, minimum energy costs, and minimum time equally important for each of the tasks you have listed? Why or why not?

Suggestions for Further Reading

Historical reviews of motor skills research were conducted by Irion (1966), Adams (1987), and chapter 1 in Schmidt et al. (2019). The first edition of *Motor Control and Learning* (Schmidt, 1982) contains a chapter devoted to the scientific study of motor skills. A biography of Paul Fitts was written by Pew (1994). The book by Snyder and Abernethy (1992) contains an autobiographical chapter on the early stages of the career of Franklin M. Henry. Chapter 2 of Schmidt et al. (2019) goes into much greater detail about error measures and experimental methods. Skills classification systems are reviewed in Poulton (1957), Gentile (1972, 2000), and Farrell (1975). See the references list for these additional resources.

PART I

Principles of Skilled Performance

Chapter 1 introduced a few of the types of motor performance that fascinate us—from the powerful movements of elite athletes to virtuoso musical performances. We now begin a two-part exploration of such skills. In part I, we emphasize the research-based principles of how such motor performances occur. As we introduce the various concepts concerning motor performance, we build a conceptual model of human skilled performance. This model contains and summarizes many of the major factors that underlie such performances and is useful as a guide for understanding how motor skills are performed. In part I, the focus is mainly on the factors that allow skilled motor performances to occur, without much reference to practice and learning of skills. After we explain the terminology and fundamental concepts of human performance in part I, we turn in part II to some of the principles governing how motor skills are acquired with practice and augmented feedback.

2

Processing Information and Making Decisions

The Mental Side of Human Performance

KEY TERMS

choice reaction time
foreperiod
Hick's Law
information-processing approach
long-term memory (LTM)
memory
movement time (MT)
population stereotypes
reaction time (RT)
response time
short-term memory (STM)
short-term sensory store (STSS)
simple RT
spatial anticipation
temporal anticipation

CHAPTER OUTLINE

CHAPTER OBJECTIVES

Chapter 2 describes a conceptualization of how decisions are made in the performance of motor skills. This chapter will help you to understand

- the information-processing approach to understanding motor performance,
- the stages that occur during information processing,
- various factors that influence the speed of information processing,
- the role of anticipation in hastening the speed of responding, and
- memory systems and their roles in motor performance.

The batter felt ready this time. The pitcher had just thrown three curveballs in a row. Although the batter had two strikes against him, he was confident because he felt certain that the next pitch would be a fastball, and he was prepared for it. As the pitch was coming toward him, he strode forward and began to swing the bat to meet the ball, but he soon realized it was another curve. He could not modify his swing in time, and the bat crossed the plate long before the ball arrived. The pitcher had beaten him again.

How did the batter's faulty anticipation interfere with his performance? What processes were required to amend the action? To what extent did the stress of the game interfere with his batting? Certainly a major concern for the skilled performer is the evaluation of information, leading to decision making about future action. But what information was the batter reflecting on while the pitch was coming toward the plate—the spin of the ball? its velocity? its location? the type, speed, and location of previous pitches? how fast to swing the bat? where to try to hit the ball? Processing all, or even some, of this information would surely have affected the batter's success in hitting the ball.

Visit the web study guide to read "Preventing Penalties and Batting Baseballs" and complete the self-directed learning activities.

One of the most important features of skilled performance is deciding what to do (and what not to do) when these decisions are needed quickly and accurately. After all, the most beautifully executed baseball throw to first base is completely ineffective if the ball should have been thrown to a different base instead. This chapter considers factors contributing to these decision-making capabilities, including processing environmental information, and some of the factors that contribute to the actual decision. We begin with a general approach for understanding how the motor system uses information, which will form the basis of the conceptual model of human performance.

The Information-Processing Approach

Researchers have found it useful to think of the human being as a processor of informa-

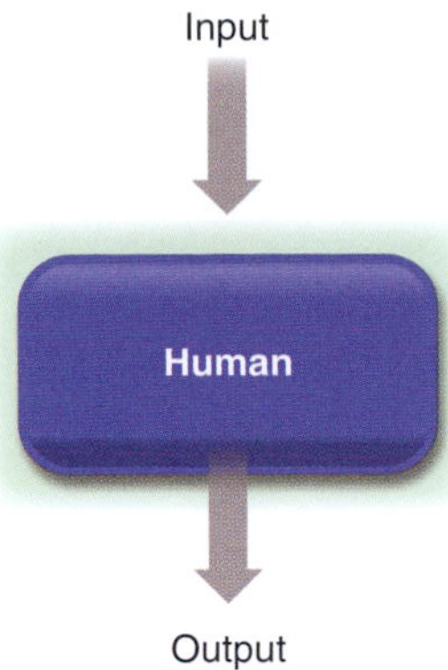

FIGURE 2.1 A simplified information-processing approach to thinking about human performance.

tion very much like a computer. Information is presented to the human as input, various stages within the human central nervous system generate a series of operations that process this information, and the eventual output is skilled movement. The most basic representation to illustrate this **information-processing approach** is shown in figure 2.1.

What Is Input?

Appearing at the top of diagram in figure 2.1 is the term *input*, which refers to the information to be processed by the human. Information comes in all sensory forms, with visual input being the most common in motor skills, as well as the most complex. One important issue to be discussed about the processing of information concerns the amount of the input. Similar to a computer, the human information-processing system will require more time to process a larger amount of data than it will to process a smaller amount.

Let's consider amount of information as the equivalent to the amount of uncertainty in a situation. A good analogy is presented in figure 2.2 (after Attneave, 1959). Suppose someone secretly placed an X in one of the 64 squares in figure 2.2 (top), and your task was to guess the correct square by asking questions about its location. You could discover the answer by asking only six questions, with each question eliminating one-half of the incorrect locations. For example, if your first question was "Is the X located in the top half of the squares?" the answer would be no because it is located in the bottom half. But even if your question was answered with a yes, it still would eliminate the top half of the figure, effectively reducing the uncertainty by one-half, from 64 to 32 squares. By asking questions in this manner, reducing uncertainty

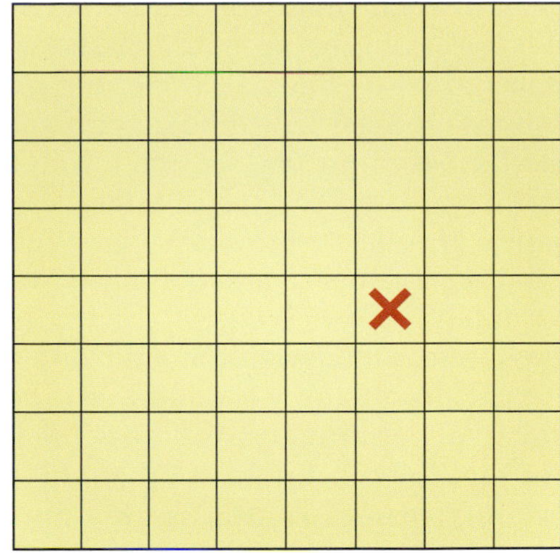

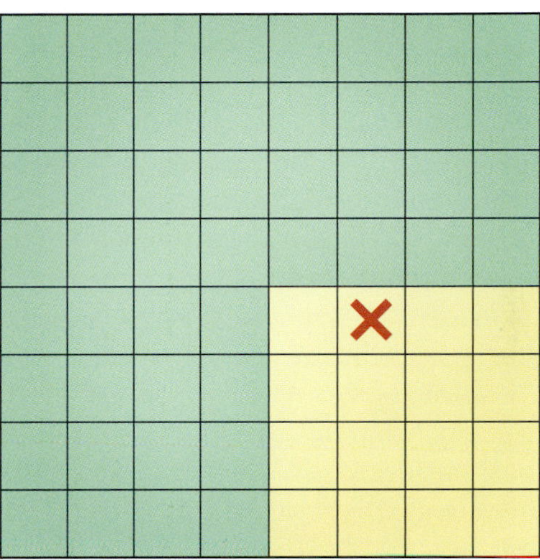

FIGURE 2.2 In the top figure, there are 64 possible locations of the X, requiring 6 bits of information to process. By eliminating 75% of the possible locations (bottom figure) the task has been reduced to only 16 possible locations, or 4 bits of information.

by one-half each time, you would solve the question by asking just six questions. Reducing the uncertainty by one-half each time allows the information gained to be quantifiable in terms of a base unit of 2. In the example in figure 2.2 (top), the amount of information to be gained is equal to 6 binary digits (bits) of information because 2 must be raised to the power of 6 (2^6) to reach 64.

Now suppose there was a situation in which three-quarters of the 64-square grid could be effectively eliminated as a possible location of the X, as in figure 2.2 (bottom). The uncertainty of its location is substantially reduced. In quantifiable terms, the amount of information to process has been reduced from 64 squares to 16 squares, or from 6 bits to 4 bits of information (because $2^4 = 16$).

How the amount of information to be processed is reduced represents an important component of our discussion in various parts of this book. Using anticipation is one method to reduce the amount of information to process. Performers who know what to expect in a certain situation, or who can eliminate certain alternatives, will reduce the amount of information to process. For example, most baseball batters know that a pitcher is likely to throw a fastball on a 3-0 count, because the pitcher needs a strike and usually the pitcher's most accurate pitch is the fastball. Also, because the pitcher needs a strike, he is likely to throw the ball near the center of the strike zone. In this case, the batter has been able to reduce the uncertainty about the upcoming pitch in terms of both its type (fastball) and its location (center of strike zone). Of course, there is no guarantee that the anticipation will be correct, but the reduction in the amount of information to process will make for an easier and faster decision to swing at the pitch or not.

In many sports, becoming skilled allows the performer to effectively reduce the amount of information to process. Skilled athletes have the advantage of knowing what components of the environment are likely to reveal critical information and what components are unlikely to. Therefore, they are able to eliminate some of the uncertainty *prior* to the presentation of the input.

In these photos, identify situations in the game in which the defense (a) or batter (b) are likely to have less uncertainty (information) to process.

The Human

A major goal of researchers interested in the performance of motor skills is to understand the specific nature of the processes in the box labeled "Human" in figure 2.1. There are many ways to approach this problem; a particularly useful one assumes that there are separable information-processing stages through which the information must pass on the way from input to output. For our purposes, here are three of these stages:

- Stimulus identification
- Response selection
- Movement programming

The stage analysis approach generally assumes that peripheral information enters the system and is processed in the first stage. When and only when this stage has completed its operations, the result is passed on to the second stage, which carries on the information processing, and then the stage 2 result is passed to the third stage, and so on. A critical assumption is that the stages do not overlap. All of the processing in a given stage is completed before the product is passed to the next stage; processing in two different stages cannot occur at the same time (referred to as parallel processing). This process finally results in an output—the action. Let's consider some of what goes on in these stages of processing.

Stimulus Identification Stage

During this first stage, the system's problem is to decide whether information has been presented and, if so, what it is. Thus, stimulus identification is primarily a sensory stage, analyzing environmental information from a variety of sources, such as vision, audition, touch, proprioception, and smell. The components, or separate dimensions of these stimuli, are thought to be assembled in this stage, such as the combination of edges and colors that form a representation of a car in traffic. Patterns of movement are also detected, such as whether other objects are moving, in what direction and how quickly they are moving, and so on, as would be necessary for driving a car in heavy traffic. The result of this stage is thought to be some representation of the stimulus, with this information being passed on to the next stage—response selection.

Visit the web study guide to read "Friendly Fire" and complete the self-directed learning activities.

Response Selection Stage

The activities of the response selection stage begin after the stimulus identification stage provides information about the nature of the input. This stage has the task of deciding what response to make, given the nature of the situation and environment. In the driving example, the choice from available responses might be to go around another vehicle, to slow the car, or to make an avoidance maneuver. Thus, this stage requires the key process of determining what to do and how it should be done.

Movement Programming Stage

This final stage begins its processing upon receiving the decision about what movement to make as determined by the response selection stage. The movement programming stage has the task of preparing the motor system to make the desired movement. Before producing a movement, the system must ready the lower-level mechanisms in the brainstem and spinal cord for action, and it must retrieve and organize a motor program that will eventually control the movement. In the driving example, if the response selection stage determined that a braking response was required, then the organization of the motor program responsible for executing a braking action would occur in the movement programming stage.

Output

Once the movement programming stage has completed its processing of information, the task is passed along to further stages that are responsible for producing a motor output. The stages involved in producing movement will occupy the middle chapters of this book and represent a major focus of researchers whose interests lie in motor control.

Focus on
APPLICATION 2.1

Intent to Blow Whistle Rule in NHL

There are not many sports in which the stages of information processing are built into the official rule book. The National Hockey League (NHL) is a rare exception. A game in early 2017 provided an example of when the rule was applied. A play in the first period of a game between the Nashville Predators and Vancouver Canucks saw a scramble for the puck in front of the Canucks' goalie, Ryan Miller. The referee, Ghislain Hebert, no longer being able to see the puck loose in the goal crease, justifiably determined that the goalie had covered the puck with his body and blew his whistle to stop play, just milliseconds *after the puck crossed the goal line into the net.* After a meeting with the other officials, Hebert confirmed that the apparent goal would not count.

The Predators' players and coaches were enraged—it was clear that the sound of the whistle occurred after the puck was in the net, so why would the goal not count? In response, the officials cited Rule 78.5, Section xii, which states that "Apparent goals shall be disallowed . . . when the Referee deems the play has been stopped, even if he had not physically had the opportunity to stop play by blowing his whistle." *(National Hockey League Official Rules [2018–2019],* p. 117*).* This ruling is further clarified by rule 31.2, which states that "As there is a human factor involved in blowing the whistle to stop play, the Referee may deem the play to be stopped slightly prior to the whistle actually being blown. The fact that the puck may come loose or cross the goal line prior to the sound of the whistle has no bearing if the Referee has ruled that the play had been stopped prior to this happening" (p. 51).

For our purposes, the key phrase in the rule above is "human factor involved in blowing the whistle." The human factor that the rule refers to involves the stages of processing described in this chapter, all of which add up to a time lag that applies in the "intent to blow" rule: the time lag starts when the referee detects the stimulus (in this case, the puck no longer being visible), decides on the appropriate response (to stop play), begins the movement programming process (to blow the whistle), and executes the action (resulting in the sound of the whistle). As we shall see in this chapter and those to follow, these stages of processing can take up to several hundred milliseconds, leaving plenty of time for a puck to cross the goal line after the decision has been made.

The rationale underlying these rules may not be well understood and represents a source of frustration for fans and players. The rule is designed to let the referee's decision, *at the time the decision was made*, be the key determining factor. In our view, by acknowledging this human factor the NHL has achieved a remarkably insightful way to protect the integrity of their referees.

The "intent to blow whistle" rule allows referees to make a final decision based on the timing of the intent to blow the whistle, not when the whistle was actually blown. Identify another situation in a different sport where an official's decision or a player's intent did not match what was actually seen or heard.

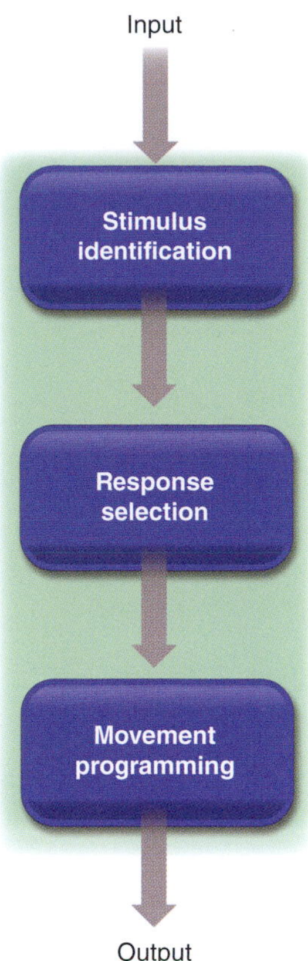

FIGURE 2.3 An expanded information-processing model, highlighting three critical processing stages in thinking about human performance.

Expanding the Conceptual Model

Figure 2.3 adds some detail to the simple notion of information processing described in figure 2.1 by including the stages of processing just described. This elaboration is the first revision of our conceptual model, which will be expanded throughout the text as we introduce more fundamental ideas of human performance.

Clearly, these stages are all included within the human information system and are not directly observable under usual circumstances. However, several laboratory methods allow scientists to learn many details about these stages. **Reaction time** (abbreviated **RT**) is one of the most important tools that researchers have used for many decades to learn about these stages. We will examine RT in much more detail to understand how information processing operates.

Reaction Time and Decision Making

An important performance measure indicating the speed and effectiveness of decision making is the RT interval—the interval of time that elapses following a suddenly presented, often unanticipated stimulus until the *beginning* of the response. The concept and assessment of RT are important because it represents a part of some everyday events, such as braking rapidly in response to an unanticipated traffic event, responding to catch a glass that has been accidentally tipped over, and, in sport, in such events as sprint races, where an auditory tone serves as a stimulus to begin a race.

There is an old saying that a picture is worth a thousand words. This is certainly borne out by the redrawn photo of a long-ago sprint race (figure 2.4) reprinted from Scripture (1905). The starter on the left side of the photo has already fired his gun, perhaps a couple of hundred milliseconds earlier, as you can see by the position of the pistol smoke rising above the starter. And yet the runners are all still in their ready positions and are only now just beginning to move. The photo illustrates nicely the substantial delay involved in RT. Being able to minimize RT in such a situation is critical to getting the movement under way as rapidly as possible. Because RT is a fundamental component of many skills, it is not surprising that much research attention has been directed toward it.

Visit the web study guide to read "Jumping the Gun" and complete the self-directed learning activities.

But RT has important theoretical meaning as well, which is the major reason it has attracted so much research attention. Sometimes there is confusion about what RT is and how it is measured. To review, researchers define the RT interval very precisely; it is the period of time beginning when the stimulus is first presented and ending when the movement response *starts*. Note that the RT interval

FIGURE 2.4 Illustration of the RT delay in a sprint start; the starting gun has been fired, yet the athletes are still on their marks because of the delay in processing the signal from the starting gun (the delay is contained in the reaction-time interval).

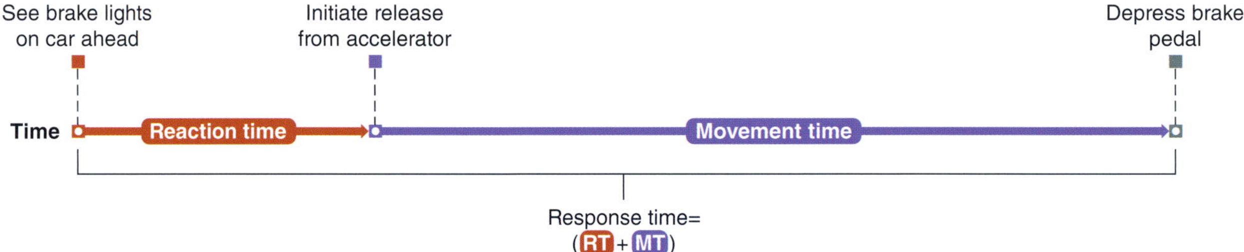

FIGURE 2.5 Illustration of the relationship between reaction time, movement time, and response time when pressing the brake pedal in a car.

does not include the time that is taken to complete the movement, as illustrated in figure 2.5. That period of time, from the end of RT until the completion of the movement, is typically called the **movement time** (or simply **MT**). For example, the term *brake RT*, used to describe the time it takes a person to press the brake pedal in a car, is technically incorrect, as the time taken to press the brake includes the time for the foot's movement from the accelerator to depress the brake, which occurs *after* the reaction interval is completed. What many refer to as brake RT is actually the total of RT plus MT—what is called **response time**.

Visit the web study guide to read "Red Light, Green Light" and complete the self-directed learning activities.

Factors That Influence Decision Making

The RT interval is a measure of the accumulated durations of the three stages of processing seen in figure 2.5. Any factor that increases the duration of one or more of these stages will thus lengthen RT. For this reason, scientists interested in information processing have used RT to measure the duration of these stages. Some of the more important factors related to human performance are considered in the next sections.

Number of Stimulus–Response Alternatives

Consider the following example that involves driving a car. In light traffic, the number of possible emergency situations that require an evasive response is usually less than in heavy traffic. One of the most important factors influencing the time to start an action is the number of stimuli (each having its own response) that can possibly occur at any given time. For example, the response to someone who swerves into your lane might be a rapid evasive turn into an empty lane, whereas the appearance of brake lights on the car you are following might require you to apply your brakes. In such situations, unexpected events from multiple vehicles around you serve to amplify the possible trouble situations that could occur, compared to extremely light or no traffic. Controlled laboratory experiments that have been conducted to examine the effects of the number of choices generally involve several possible stimuli, such as lights, and several different responses from which the research participant is to choose, such as pressing different keys depending on which stimulus light has been illuminated.

Figure 2.6 illustrates a typical experimental setup in which the stimulus array contains eight possible lights that could turn on and a response panel with eight corresponding response keys. In each of the four panels in this figure (2.6a, b, c, d), focus only on the yellow (stimulus) circles and the brown (response) squares. Although all eight stimulus lights and response keys are seen in each version of the experiment, the researcher gives the participant prior instructions about the number of stimulus–response (S-R) alternatives from which to expect a stimulus (a light suddenly illuminated) on any given block of trials. For example, in figure 2.6*c*, the participant would know that only one of the middle four lights could be lit, which would require the response of pressing the assigned corresponding key. It is important to note, however, that on any given trial, only one

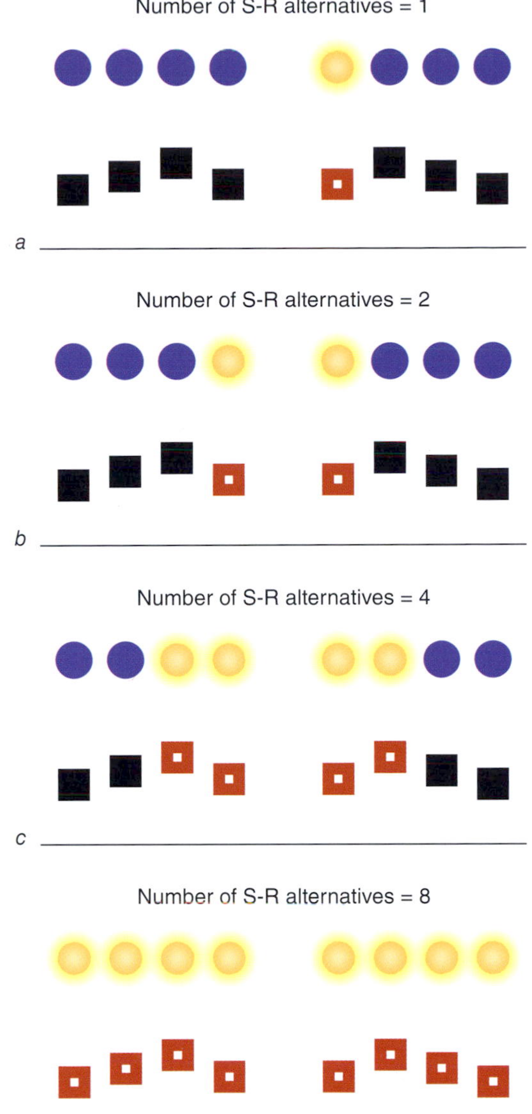

FIGURE 2.6 Different combinations of number of stimulus–response alternatives. The circles represent potential visual stimuli; the squares represent the keys to press in response to these stimuli. Yellow circles and brown squares represent the possible S-R events that are possible; blue circles and black squares represent stimuli and response keys that would not be used on that block of trials. In figure 2.6a, only one stimulus and response alternative are used for a block of trials; in figure 2.6b, the stimulus could be one of the two yellow circles, responding with the associated brown square, and so on.

stimulus light will be illuminated so only one key needs to be pressed.

This is termed a **choice reaction time** task, in which the performer must choose one response from a subset of possible predetermined responses. Typically the performer receives a warning signal, followed by a **foreperiod** of unpredictable length (e.g., 2, 3, or 4 s, the order being randomly determined). When the reaction stimulus is suddenly presented, it is only then that the performer is informed about which button to press. As always, RT is the measured duration that starts at the presentation of the stimulus and ends when the response is initiated. In this particular example, RT is the time required to detect and recognize the stimulus and select and initiate the proper response.

Generally, as the number of possible S-R alternatives increases, there is an increase in the time required to respond to any one of them. The fastest situation involves only one stimulus and one response, termed **simple RT**. Increased RT due to a greater number of S-R alternatives is of critical importance in understanding skilled performance, forming the basis of **Hick's Law** (see Focus on Research 2.1). The increase in RT is very large when the number of alternatives is increased from one to two. As seen in figure 2.7, RT might increase from about 190 ms with simple RT (figure 2.6*a*) to more than 300 ms for a two-choice case (figure 2.6*b*)—a 58% increase in the time required to process the stimulus information into the response! Adding extra choices still increases RT, but the increases become smaller and smaller (e.g., the increase from 9 to 10 choices might be only 20 ms, or about 2% or 3%). But even this small amount of delay can be critical in determining success in many situations.

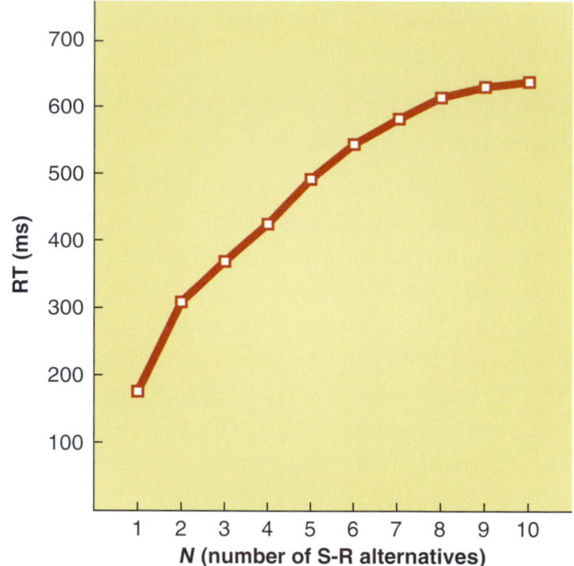

FIGURE 2.7 The relationship between the number of possible stimulus–response (S-R) alternatives and reaction time.

Stimulus–Response Compatibility

An important determinant of RT is S-R compatibility, usually defined as the extent to which the stimulus and the response are connected in a natural way. Turning the handlebars of a bicycle to the right to move in that direction is an example of S-R compatibility because the movement of the handlebars and the change in the intended direction are the same—that is, they are said to be directionally compatible. Imagine how difficult it would be to require a movement of the handlebars to the left in order to turn right (in fact, someone has done just that—search "backwards bicycle" for a video). Perhaps that explains some of the reason that steering a sailboat is trickier than steering a bicycle—the sailor needs to move the tiller to the left in order to change the heading of the boat to the right.

Figure 2.9 illustrates two examples of S-R spatial compatibility mappings used in research. The ensemble of stimuli and responses in illustration 2.9*a* is the more compatible of the two because either of the stimulus lights calls for the participant to respond in the same direction and on the same side of the body as the light. In the example in 2.9*b*, however, the right light calls for the left hand to be used and the left light calls for the right hand to be moved. The spatial mapping of the stimuli and required response is not nearly so spatially direct and unambiguous; this situation is said to be S-R incompatible (or more accurately, less spatially compatible than in figure 2.9*a*).

Focus on
RESEARCH 2.1

Hick's Law

In another very early RT experiment, Merkel (1885, cited by Woodworth, 1938) asked participants in a choice-RT experiment to press a reaction key when one of up to 10 possible stimuli was presented. The stimuli were the Arabic numerals 1 through 5 and the Roman numerals I through V. Each stimulus was paired with one finger or thumb and response key. For example, the possible stimuli on a set of trials might be 2, 3, and V (a three-choice case), and the participants were to respond with either the right index, right middle, or left thumb if and when the associated stimulus was presented. Merkel varied the number of possible stimulus–response alternatives in different sets of trials. (It is important to remember that only one of the *N* possible stimuli is ever presented on a given trial.)

Merkel's results are shown in figure 2.7, where RT is plotted as a function of the number of S-R alternatives. You can see that as the number of alternatives was increased there was a sharp rise in RT (roughly 120 ms; see figure 2.7) from $N=1$ to $N=2$; this rise becomes smaller as the number of alternatives is increased toward 10 (from $N=9$ to $N=10$, where RT increases roughly 3 ms; see figure 2.7).

Much later Hick (1952) and, independently, Hyman (1953) discovered that the relationship between RT and the logarithm to the base 2 of the number (*N*) of S-R alternatives, abbreviated $\text{Log}_2(N)$, was *linear* (see figure 2.8). This relationship has become known as Hick's Law, and it holds for a wide variety of situations using different movements and stimulus materials. It is one of the most important laws of human performance. [See the earlier discussion of information and figure 2.2. $\text{Log}_2(N)$ is the power to which the base 2 must be raised to equal *N*. For example, the logarithm to the base 2 of 8 is 3, abbreviated $\text{Log}_2(8)=3$, because the base 2 raised to the third power, $(2^3)=8$.]

Hick's Law in equation form is $\text{RT}=a+b\log_2(N)$, where a is the RT-intercept and b is the slope. The relationship implies that RT increases a constant amount every time the number of stimulus–response alternatives (*N*) is *doubled* (e.g., from $N=2$ to $N=4$, where the $\text{Log}_2(N)$ is 1 or 2, respectively; or from $N=8$ to $N=16$, where the $\text{Log}_2(N)=3$ and 4, respectively). This led to an important interpretation of Hick's Law: Because the amount of information needed to resolve the uncertainty among *N* possible choices is $\text{Log}_2(N)$, Hick's Law says that RT is linearly related to the *amount of information* that must be processed to resolve the uncertainty about the various possible

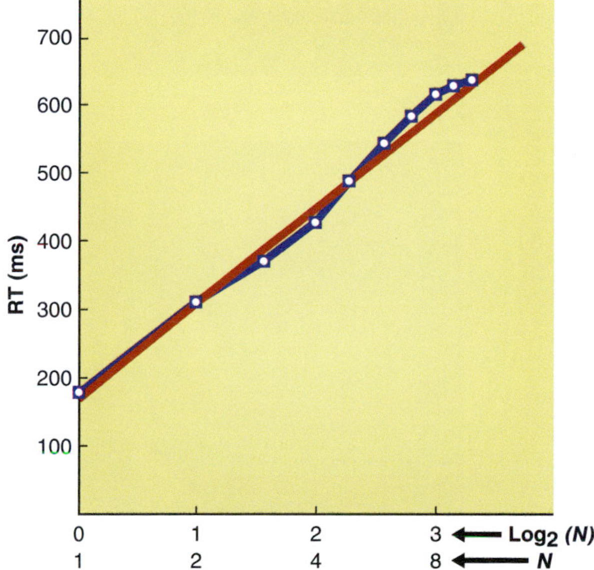

FIGURE 2.8 Hick's Law: The relation between RT and number of S-R alternatives (*N*) is replotted using Merkel's data from figure 2.7, with RT as a function of $\text{Log}_2(N)$.

> *continued*

> Hick's Law *continued*

stimulus–response alternatives. Doubling the amount of information to be processed by doubling *N* therefore increases RT by a constant amount. This constant amount is equal to the slope (*b*) in the equation of Hick's Law.

Exploring Further

1. How does the concept of uncertainty relate to the amount of information in Hick's law?
2. Name two factors that would be expected to influence the magnitude of the slope (*b*) of Hick's Law, and describe how variations in these factors would be predicted to increase or decrease the slope.

In each of these photos, how can the team (top) or player (bottom) who controls the ball create more uncertainty for the opposition, thereby increasing the amount of information that they must process?

Focus on RESEARCH 2.2

Donders' Stages of Processing

Determining the durations of mental activities goes back many years, and one of the first experiments involving humans was undertaken by Dutch physician F.C. Donders in 1868. Donders followed the logic of physiology experiments by von Helmholtz, who studied the nerve conduction velocity in frogs. In von Helmholtz' research, he would stimulate and measure the conduction durations for one dissected nerve that was *x* cm long and one that was perhaps *x*+2 cm long. By subtracting the known times of the shorter nerve from the longer nerve, and given the known difference in distance, von Helmholtz could then compute the conduction velocities that would be expected to produce the duration differences.

Donders basically used a similar logic—that insight into the durations of the various stages could be understood by subtracting the time taken for specific task requirements. Have a look at the illustrations in figure 2.6. The illustration in figure 2.6*a* represents the simplest situation—the participant's task is to press the response key as rapidly as possible when the stimulus above it appears. No other stimulus will appear and no other response will be required—the task is merely to respond as quickly as possible in this situation. According to Donders, such a task (which he called an A-type, or what is now called a simple RT task) requires only the process of stimulus detection, as the performer knows the response to make before the stimulus comes on.

Contrast this task with another in which the participant is required to respond to the signal, as in figure 2.6*a*, with a rapid key press. However, in this task (a C-type, now called a "go/no-go" RT task), one of the other stimuli will appear at times. The participant's task is to *not respond* with a button press in these trials, but to respond only when the specified stimulus appears. Donders reasoned that this task also required stimulus detection, as in the A-type task. But, in addition, this task requires that the participant perform a stimulus identification process—identifying that the stimulus was the specified one before responding. Hence the difference in RTs between the two tasks supposedly required the additional stage of stimulus identification.

Lastly, Donders considered a third type of task—a B-type task (a choice-RT task)—that required participants to respond to one of the alternative stimuli with an appropriate key press as shown in figure 2.6, *b* through *d*. This task is similar to the C-type task in that the stimulus must be detected and identified. But, in addition, the B-task requires that the participant respond by selecting the appropriate key to press. Thus, compared to the C-task, the additional RT required to complete a B-response is caused by the insertion of a response selection stage of processing.

Requirements of Donders' Three Task Types

Type	Stimulus detection	Stimulus identification	Response selection
A-type reaction	Yes	No	No
C-type reaction	Yes	Yes	No
B-type reaction	Yes	Yes	Yes

Years later, Sternberg (1969) critically analyzed Donders' methods, noting among other things that the logic depended on the processing stages operating in serial—

> *continued*

> Donders' Stages of Processing *continued*

that is, no parallel or partially overlapping operations. Sternberg's research found evidence that some operations did indeed overlap, thus casting doubt on Donders' simple-subtraction technique to estimate the duration of processing activities. More details about Sternberg's alternative methods are presented in Schmidt et al. (2019).

Exploring Further

1. According to Donders' logic, if the A-type RT was 150 ms, the B-type RT was 240 ms, and the C-type RT was 180 ms, what would be the durations of the stimulus identification and response selection stages?
2. Donders was one of the first to explore the contents and workings of the stages of information processing by rearranging task conditions to be able to add or subtract specific processing requirements systematically. The approach is not without problems, however. Critically examine the following assumptions of this method:
    a. That processing stages are serially arranged, with no overlaps in time
    b. That, as compared to the A-reaction, the C-type reaction task requires only the additional stage of stimulus recognition, and no others; an analogous assumption involves the B- and C-tasks and the response selection stage

    How might you conduct research to test if these assumptions are correct?

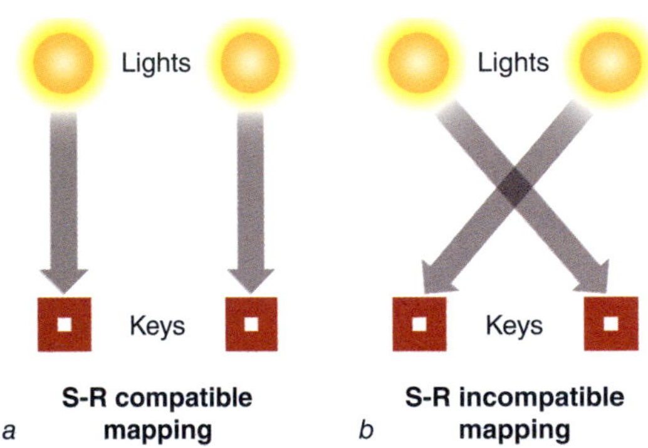

FIGURE 2.9 The relationship between the two stimuli and the two responses is more spatially S-R compatible in the array on the left (*a*) than in the array on the right (*b*).

It is well established that for a given number of S-R alternatives, increasing S-R compatibility decreases RT. This is thought to be the effect of the relative difficulty of information processing in the response selection stage, where the more natural linkages between compatible stimuli and responses lead to faster resolution of uncertainty and thus to shorter RTs. Note, however, that the general rules regarding the number of possible stimuli and RT still apply to incompatible S-R arrangements (i.e., Hick's Law).

So, what exactly makes a natural linkage and how does it improve S-R compatibility (or conversely, what makes an unnatural linkage)? As we have discussed above, the *spatial relationship* between a moveable object and what it controls is an obvious one. A rightward movement of the mouse on my desktop sends the cursor on the computer screen to the right. Any other result would be less natural from a spatial compatibility view. The scene in Figure 2.10 is probably one that most readers have experienced. Most stovetop burners are manufactured with a set of spatially incompatible controls, even though better, more compatible spatial arrangements could easily be used. But what are some other compatibility relationships that researchers have studied?

Visit the web study guide to read "Push or Pull?" and complete the self-directed learning activities. 

FIGURE 2.10 A watched pot never boils, and neither will this one. Turning on the wrong stovetop element because of spatially incompatible controls is an all-too-frequent problem when cooking. Identify two other spatially incompatible situations that cause problems where you live.

Another S-R compatibility relationship that has been extensively studied can be attributed to the response to spoken stimuli. For example, suppose you were wearing stereo headphones and were told to respond appropriately to a message presented to one ear (such as "press the right reaction key"). Such a task is performed faster and more accurately if that message is presented to the right ear than to the left ear. Thus, responding to a verbal command is not immune from anatomical relationships.

Compatibility has also been studied with respect to end-consequences. Suppose a friend asked you to move an upside-down glass from one spot on the table to another. Your response would likely be to simply pick up the glass and move it using a normal upright hand posture. However, if she asked you to place the glass upside down after you had moved it, then your hand posture would likely have been inverted to start, such that it was in the normal upright position as you placed it on the table. Note that in both cases the stimulus (the glass) was the same—the nature of the response selected to perform the task differed as a function of what David Rosenbaum termed "end-state comfort." The initially selected hand posture was determined based on what would be most compatible with the comfort of the final hand posture (see Rosenbaum, 2010, for more).

Some S-R compatibility effects have emerged due to societal norms. For example, we tend to turn dials clockwise in order to increase the loudness of an auditory source or the speed of a fan. In North America, we move a light switch upward to turn the light on; in Europe, this relationship is reversed. However, in these cases it is more difficult to argue that the mapping of the stimulus and response represents a naturally existing relationship and not a purely arbitrary one. Instead, the likely association is a learned societal one—we sometimes act habitually due to specific cultural learning, referred to as **population stereotypes**.

Focus on
APPLICATION 2.2

Light Switches

Stimulus–response (S-R) compatibility and population stereotypes are a large part of our daily existence. We usually take notice of them only in situations in which unexpected issues arise. One common example occurs when you walk into a room and flip a switch to turn on a light or a bank of lights. In North American culture (but not in some other parts of the world), we turn lights on by flipping the light switch *up*; moving it *down* turns the lights off. We act accordingly when we enter a room and tend not to give the action a moment's thought. However, a light switch that has been installed upside down will bring the issue to our conscious attention.

A similar issue occurs with respect to the spatial organization of switches in relation to the spatial locations of the lights in the room that they control. Suppose you enter a room that has three lights under control of three separate switches. One light is near you, one is in the middle of the room, and one is in the far corner of the room; and they are controlled by the switches located on the wall near the room entrance. Which switch would you flip to turn the middle light on? A panel that has been compatibly mapped will have the nearest switch control the nearest light, the middle switch control the light in the middle of the room, and so on. But how often have you been tricked into turning on the wrong light because of an incompatible light-to-switch mapping? Once again, the issue mainly comes to our attention when the unexpected occurs.

The examples could go on and on. Why is the brake pedal always to the left of the accelerator pedal in cars? Why does the CD system in your car have larger numbers assigned to later tracks on a CD? Why does your car always increase its speed when the accelerator is pushed down? In all of these examples, the designer who came up with the very first automobile accelerator pedal, CD numbering system, or steering wheel logic could have done it either way. Now, however, we all have had sufficient benefit of experience with a particular organization that has become a population stereotype. Imagine the bother and wasted movements—or indeed the dangerousness—of the system designed with some other stimulus–response relationship.

Visit the web study guide to read "The Grocery Store" and complete the self-directed learning activities.

Some colors represent common population stereotypes. Red is often associated with stop or danger, green with go or safety. Traffic lights exploit this relationship, as do many other lights in our environment. The small LEDs (light-emitting diodes) on my coffee machine are red while the coffee is being brewed, and they turn to green when the coffee is ready to drink. Importantly, we only pay attention to these stereotypes in our day-to-day activities when the expected relationship is violated.

Amount of Practice

Highly practiced performers can overcome the disadvantages of low S-R compatibility, such as the highly experienced racing sailor who doesn't even have to think to move the tiller to the right when the boat needs to turn left. For a given number of stimulus–response alternatives, the higher the level of practice, generally the shorter the RT will be. Overall, practice reduces the steepness of the increase in RT as the number of stimulus–response alternatives increases. This means that there is only a small effect of practice on reducing simple RT, but there are large effects of practice on choice RT. With extremely large amounts of practice, high-level performers can produce reactions that approach automatic processing; these reactions are very fast and are slowed little, if at all, as the number of S-R alternatives is increased further.

This fits well with practical experience. To a beginning driver, the connection between the presentation of a red light to stop and the response of pressing the brake pedal is very clumsy. However, after thousands of hours of driving practice, the link between the red light and the brake pedal becomes extremely natural, leading almost automatically to the movement.

Anticipation: Minimizing Processing Delays

As mentioned earlier in this chapter, one fundamental way to reduce RT is to anticipate. Typically, a highly skilled performer predicts what is going to happen in the environment

Practice can overcome the processing delays caused by low stimulus–response compatibility. For example, a skilled sailor knows to move the tiller the opposite direction the boat needs to turn.

and when it will occur, and will then perform various information-processing activities in advance of the stimulus. A soccer goalkeeper anticipates that a player taking a penalty will aim her kick at the upper-left corner of the goal and starts moving in that direction before the kick is made. An experienced long-haul truck driver knows that many car drivers do not understand the stopping distance of an 18-wheeled vehicle and takes evasive actions to avoid a potential accident.

Highly skilled people know what stimuli are likely to be presented, where they likely will appear, and when they will occur, so these people can predict the required actions to take with a high level of probability. Armed with this information, a performer can organize movements in advance, completing some or all of the information-processing activities usually conducted during the response selection or movement programming stage. This allows the performer to initiate the movement much earlier or in coordination with the timing of movements in the environment, as in predicting where and when a pitched ball will arrive at the plate so that it can be struck with a well-timed bat swing. Because of these capabilities to anticipate, skilled performers seem to behave almost as if they had all the time they need, without being rushed to respond to stimuli using the reaction-time processes previously discussed.

Types of Anticipation

Anticipation can occur in different ways. One type is called **spatial anticipation** (sometimes called event anticipation). For example, two important shots in badminton are the clear and drop shots. The clear shot is high and long and sends the opponent to the back of the court. The drop shot is intended to land just on the other side of the net, which brings the opponent to the front of the court. Spatial anticipation in badminton involves predicting the type of shot your opponent will hit and being in the correct position to return the shot when it is hit. In other situations, it might be obvious what is going to occur and where, but there might be uncertainty about when it will occur, as in anticipating the snap of the ball in American football. This is usually called **temporal anticipation**. Although there is a strong advantage in knowing when some event will occur, not being able to predict *what* will occur prevents the performer from organizing the movement completely in advance.

Benefits of Anticipation

Several factors affect the capability to predict effectively. One is the regularity of the events. For example, if our racquetball opponent always serves the ball to our (weak) backhand side, we can predict this event and counter it in various ways. Clearly, the capability to anticipate would be minimized if three or four different serves were randomly used instead. Similarly, if the football quarterback always has the ball snapped on the second of two rhythmical verbal signals, the defensive team can anticipate the critical event and be highly prepared for it. Varying the timing of the snap signals keeps the defensive team from anticipating temporally, yet still allows the quarterback's offensive teammates to anticipate both temporally and spatially (as they have learned what is to be done, and when, in the huddle). The goals here are for the offensive team to respond as a single unit to the snap count and to allow the defensive team no capability to anticipate. This provides the offense the greatest relative advantage.

Costs of Anticipation

There are several strong advantages to anticipation, but, as with most strategies for trying to gain an advantage, it comes with risks. The primary disadvantage occurs when the anticipated action is not what actually happens. In American football again, if the defensive lineman anticipates that the snap will occur on the second sound but the quarterback takes the snap on the third sound, the lineman could move too early, incurring a penalty for his team. In a similar way, when anticipating that an opponent will hit the ball to the left side of the court, a tennis player will move in

Focus on **RESEARCH 2.3**

Assessing Anticipation Skills

What skills separate an expert from a novice? Most would agree that an expert batter in baseball or cricket possesses motor skills that are more accurate, less variable, and generally more efficient than those of a less-skilled batter. The expert's motor skills are simply better and more finely tuned. For some skills, however—and most importantly, for open skills—researchers have shown that experts also have a large advantage in perceptual anticipation (anticipating the movements of objects in the outside world). How do the researchers know this?

One of the frequently used experimental techniques is to show edited videos of athletes in action and to ask the viewer to make certain predictions. For example, a video of a baseball pitcher might be edited such that a certain body part (e.g., the pitching arm) has been blocked from the viewer's vision. Presumably, editing out a body part (e.g., the grip on a fastball or a curveball) would interfere with an anticipation *only if* the batter was using that perceptual information to determine what type of pitch was being thrown. In contrast, editing out a nonessential body part should not interfere with anticipation. Another method involving video editing is to freeze the display at certain time points in the action. Presumably, a skilled viewer would be able to pick up more information in an earlier frozen video frame than a less-skilled viewer. The purpose that underlies both of these occlusion edit methods is to discover how and when information is being used by more highly skilled performers. Understanding this information should then be useful in training less-skilled performers.

Exploring Further

1. What is an eye tracker? How is this equipment used to assess the "quiet-eye" effect?
2. What are point-light displays? How are they used in research to assess biological motion?

that direction before the shot is hit but is at risk of losing the point if the shot is actually hit to the right. Clearly, anticipating correctly can result in many benefits, but the costs of anticipating incorrectly can be disastrous.

Earlier, we discussed the idea that anticipating allows various information-processing activities to take place in advance so they do not have to occur after the reaction stimulus is presented. Suppose that a performer has gone through these preparatory processes but now the events in the environment change. The information-processing costs in this case are actually magnified. First the performer must stop, or unprepare, the already prepared (falsely anticipated) action, and this process will require time to complete. Then the correct action must be prepared and initiated, which extends the processing delay even further. Thus, while a correct anticipation might reduce the lag period to essentially 0 ms, an incorrect anticipation will require more processing activities, and longer delay, compared to a response to a neutral or unanticipated event.

An additional problem occurs if the incorrect anticipation has resulted in a movement, as you have seen many times in sport events.

As before, the performer still has the problem of inhibiting the incorrect action and preparing the correct one. But there can be an additional problem: The inappropriate action might be in the incorrect direction, taking the person farther from the best location and producing a biomechanical disadvantage because of her wrong direction. This makes the corrective action even more costly, difficult, and time consuming to overcome.

Visit the web study guide to read "Method to His Bratness" and complete the self-directed learning activities.

Memory Systems

We change tack here slightly to discuss an important concept in thinking about skills, namely, memory, which is usually seen simply as the storage of the results of the various information-processing activities discussed so far. The various types of memory and their characteristics will be useful later during the discussion of several aspects of human performance. First we consider three distinct memory systems involved in movement control: short-term sensory store, short-term memory, and long-term memory.

Short-Term Sensory Store

The briefest of all memories, the **short-term sensory store (STSS)**, is thought to retain sensory information for a very short period of time. We rely on this memory store during almost all of our daily activities whenever we see, hear, or feel things. For example, after spotting the milk container in the refrigerator, we use that brief visual memory to reach for it as we then shift the eyes to a search for something else. Visual information is taken in by the eyes and acoustic information by the ears; and the aftereffects of movements are remembered as well. How long does the sensory information last? Early research by Sperling (1960) suggested that visual information may last no more than about 1 s in STSS. The basic idea is that STSS is responsible for storing vast amounts of sensory information only long enough for some of it to be abstracted and further processed (in short-term memory, STM). The STSS is not considered to be sustained by attention—it is simply a brief holding cell for sensory information.

Short-Term Memory

Short-term memory (STM), which researchers sometimes call working memory, is a temporary holding place for information, such as a phone number given to you verbally. We all know that unless we repeat it this phone number will be lost from memory in a short period of time (probably within a few minutes

A skilled defensive lineman may be able to anticipate the timing of the snap and the play about to be run, reducing his effective reaction time to near zero.

Focus on
APPLICATION 2.3

Cost/Benefit of Anticipating in Sprint Starting

The story "Jumping the Gun" on the web study guide describes how and why a false start is determined in a sprint race. Since the goal of the race official is to have all sprinters react to the sound of the "gun" (which now is often a speaker behind each runner controlled by an electronic "pistol"), temporal anticipation is discouraged by a preset, 100-ms cutoff—any racer having an RT less than 100 ms is penalized with a false start and the race must start again. Can you guess why, then, RTs became longer for both males and females in the time period 2004 to 2009, and then again in the period 2010 to 2014 (see figure 2.11)? The answer lies in a cost–benefit analysis of anticipating.

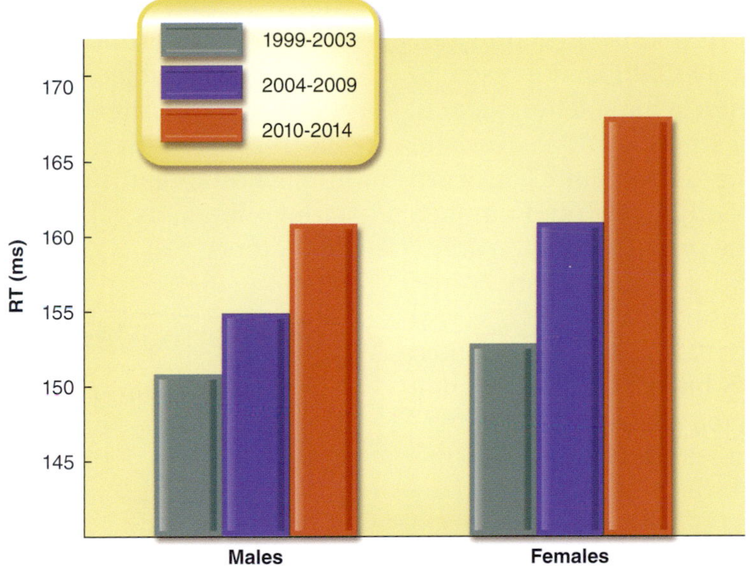

FIGURE 2.11 International sprint race RTs during three separate eras under which different rules for false starting had been implemented.

Prior to 2004, the rules of sprint racing permitted each runner in a race to make one false start. The runner was disqualified if he or she made a second false start in that race. Thus, there was a slight strategic benefit to anticipating the sound of the gun. If the sprinter started his response just before hearing the sound of the gun, but not too much before, then a legal RT (of just over 100 ms) would be a huge advantage over the other racers. The cost of such a strategy was that if RT was less than 100 ms, then the sprinter would need to be more cautious not to jump the gun in the do-over.

A rule change in 2004 changed that cost–benefit analysis. No longer was *each* runner allowed to make a false start. Instead, only one of the runners in the field was allowed to make a false start. After that the entire field of runners for that race was essentially put on notice—any further false starts would result in an immediate disqualification, regardless of who it was. Such a rule change made the false start much

> *continued*

> Cost/Benefit of Anticipating in Sprint Starting *continued*

more penalizing, and as a result, sprinters tended to be more cautious about jumping the gun, especially so after the field was put on notice. Hence, average RTs increased.

The cost of anticipating became even more devastating following a further rule change in 2010. This rule change effectively removed the "on notice" clause—any sprinter who false started was disqualified immediately. The rule change made the cost of jumping the gun catastrophic, and sprinters responded by lengthening their RTs even more (see figure 2.11).

at most). Information requires *rehearsal* as the process by which we keep from losing it from STM. Repeating the phone number over and over to yourself, either silently or out loud, is a process of rehearsing the information and thereby keeping it available in STM.

For example, participants in a study by Peterson and Peterson (1959) were presented with verbal information (a three-letter trigram), and were prevented from saying it over and over again by having them count backward by threes from a two-digit specified number. Within about 10 s, the probability of recalling the trigram successfully was less than .20 and it was below .10 after about 20 s. Thus, verbal information (eight items) in STM is retained longer than in STSS but was still lost quite rapidly when not given sustained attention.

A study similar to Peterson and Peterson's but using motor skills was conducted by Adams and Dijkstra (1966) to study the STM of movement information. In one condition (labeled 1 in figure 2.12), blindfolded participants moved a slide on a track from a start position to a mechanical stop and tried to repeat this movement (with the stop removed) after various periods of time (retention intervals). In two other conditions, the movement of the slide to the mechanical stop was repeated either 6 or 15 times, amounting to additional rehearsals of the movement-to-recalled. In this experiment, memory loss is represented by increase in absolute error over time. There are two important results from the Adams and Dijkstra study to note in figure 2.12. First, as in the Peterson and Peterson study, rapid forgetting occurred during the first 20 s of the retention period, with further decreases occurring over the next 60 s, especially if there were no additional rehearsals provided (i.e., the 1 condition). Second, the addition of rehearsals (6 or 15) reduced the amount of error due to forgetting over the retention intervals. This evidence suggests that information can be retained for a period of time that is much longer than STSS but is subject to forgetting if not given sustained attention. As well, the strength of the representation in memory also has an impact on forgetting, as information that was strengthened by rehearsals slowed the speed of memory loss.

Long-Term Memory

Long-term memory (LTM) contains well-learned information that has been collected over a lifetime. Experiments show that LTM

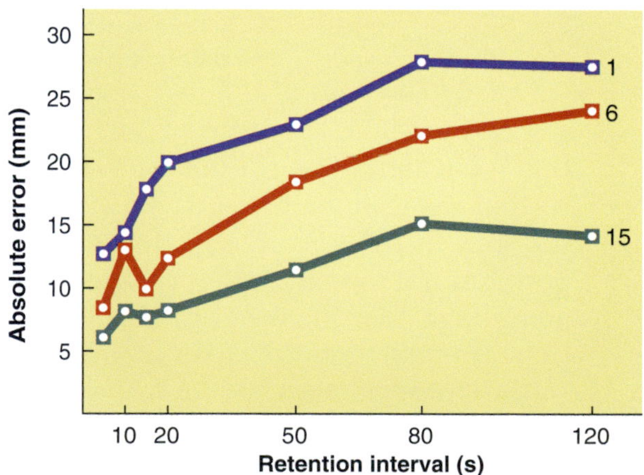

FIGURE 2.12 Absolute error in blind positioning recall increases rapidly over different retention intervals (5 to 120 s) depending on the number of rehearsals (1, 6, or 15 rehearsals).

must be essentially limitless in capacity, as indicated by the vast amount of information that can be stored for very long periods of time. Such information might never be completely forgotten: You never seem to forget how to ride a bicycle or throw a ball, even after many decades of no practice. Even an apparent loss of information from memory, such as someone's name or your old phone number, may just be due to a temporary inaccessibility of the stored information. For example, you might recognize a person's name if someone else mentions it—suggesting that the memory was there but that retrieval of it posed a problem. The items stored in LTM are thought to be very abstract, with information coded by elaborate connections to other stored information and by imagery, sounds, smells, and the like, which neuroscientists are beginning to understand more completely.

Essentially, a vast amount of information can be stored in LTM by processing in STM (rehearsal, connecting the information to other information, and so on), so getting information into LTM storage generally requires effort. To say that someone has learned something means that information was transferred in some way from STM to LTM. This also applies to movement skills, with motor programs for action (discussed in chapter 5) stored in LTM for later execution. For many motor skills, particularly continuous ones such as riding a bicycle or swimming, evidence and common experience suggest almost perfect retention after years, even decades, without intervening practice; this is quite contrary to the forgetting seen with well-learned verbal and cognitive skills (e.g., foreign language vocabulary). However, discrete skills, such as throwing or gymnastics stunts, are more easily forgotten. More on retention is presented in chapter 9.

Summary

The human motor system can be thought of as a processor of information—for motor skills, information is received from the various sense organs, processed through various stages, and output as movements. The system has three main stages: a stimulus identification stage, which detects the nature of environmental information; a response selection stage, which resolves uncertainty about what action should be made; and a movement programming stage, which organizes the motor system for action. Reaction time is an important measure of information-processing speed. Its duration is strongly affected by stimulus–response alternatives (described by Hick's Law), by the naturalness of the relationship between stimuli and their associated movements (stimulus–response compatibility), and by anticipation of the upcoming events. Three memory systems are described: Short-term sensory store (STSS) holds sensory information for a few seconds at most. Short-term memory (STM) is capable of holding about eight items of information for longer periods of time, but these items last only as long as can be maintained by attention. Long-term memory (LTM) is capable of holding information permanently.

WEB STUDY GUIDE ACTIVITIES

The student web study guide offers these activities to help you build and apply your knowledge of the concepts in this chapter.

Interactive Learning

Activity 2.1: Identify the stage of information processing in which each of a list of actions occurs.

Activity 2.2: Arrange the stages of information processing in the correct order.

Activity 2.3: Review the memory systems by matching each with its definition.

Principles-to-Application Exercise

Activity 2.4: The principles-to-application exercise for this chapter prompts you to choose a skill you can perform or are learning how to perform. You will describe the skill, including the goal of the movement and the basic actions involved. You will also select someone else to perform this skill and describe one processing activity for each stage of information processing and one factor that might influence making decisions about the skill.

Motor Control in Everyday Actions Narratives

Preventing Penalties and Batting Baseballs

Friendly Fire

Jumping the Gun

Red Light, Green Light

Push or Pull?

The Grocery Store

Method to His Bratness

Check Your Understanding

1. Describe the information-processing activities that might occur in the stimulus identification, response selection, and movement programming stages for a hockey goalie in a game and for a kayaker navigating a set of rapids.
2. Describe and provide an example where spatial anticipation is important to a sport outcome, and describe and provide an example where temporal anticipation is important to a sport outcome.
3. Provide an example of stimulus–response compatibility and an example of stimulus–response incompatibility that you have encountered today.

Apply Your Knowledge

1. Three memory systems are involved in the learning process. The short-term sensory store (STSS) stores large amounts of sensory information before processing by short-term memory (STM), which is a temporary holding place for information, which can remain in STM through rehearsal. Information in STM can be processed in order for it to be stored in long-term memory (LTM). This processing from STM to LTM can be described as learning. Explain how each of the three memory systems (STSS, STM, and LTM) is involved in learning a new dance routine. Provide examples of specific information that would be processed.
2. Anticipation can play a role in many contexts. One activity where the success or failure of anticipation can be particularly clear is racket sports, where players must anticipate the next shot of the opponent. Discuss how anticipation in a game of squash can be both beneficial and harmful, depending on the situation. What factors can affect the outcome of anticipation?

Suggestions for Further Reading

Many good references can be found on the information-processing approach in psychology, including work by Chubb et al. (2013) and Sternberg (1969). Marteniuk (1976) applied this approach to thinking about motor-skills research (see also Magill & Anderson, 2017). Welford's (1980) book on reaction times provides a good overview of the various applications of this method. Rasmussen (1986) discusses many applications of information processing. Proctor and Vu (2006) provided a comprehensive review on stimulus–response compatibility. Roediger (2008) is an excellent, rich source for discussions of memory. Adams (1976) discusses memory with particular relevance to motor skills. See the references list for these additional resources.

3

Attention and Performance

Limitations on Information Processing

KEY TERMS

arousal
attention
automatic processing
choking
cocktail-party effect
constrained action hypothesis
double-stimulation paradigm
external focus of attention
hypervigilance
inattentional blindness
internal focus of attention
inverted-U principle
ironic effects
"looked-but-failed-to-see" accidents
movement programming
perceptual narrowing
probe-task technique
psychological refractory period (PRP)
response selection
stimulus identification
stimulus-onset asynchrony (SOA)
sustained attention
unintended acceleration

CHAPTER OUTLINE

CHAPTER OBJECTIVES

Chapter 3 describes the role of attention as a limiting factor in human performance. This chapter will help you to understand

- attention and its various properties and definitions,
- attention as a limitation in the capacity to process information,
- attention as a limitation in the capability to perform actions, and
- performance under conditions of increased stress.

The task of driving to the store illustrates why the topic of attention is so complex. Consider the following:

- On the drive to the supermarket you suddenly remember that you left the shopping list on the refrigerator door, and try to reconstruct what might have been on it—eggs, milk, peanut butter, hmm, no, not milk, I bought some yesterday . . . You receive a phone call. It's your roommate, and she asks you to pick up some pasta for dinner, as well as some green peppers.
- There's an intersection ahead; the light has been green for quite a while and may turn to yellow at any moment, so better be ready . . .
- The temperature is pretty warm today; maybe some air conditioning is needed. Which of these control buttons should I push?
- What was it that my roommate asked me to get? Think hard, I'll remember—pasta and . . . green onions, yeah, that's it.
- Oops, the lane departure feature on my car just made my steering wheel vibrate and pushed the car back toward the center of the lane.
- There's the yellow light; do I have time to make a safe stop, or should I accelerate through the intersection?

And on it goes. In a very short time this scenario has illustrated the nature of attention and factors that influence it. Attention appears to be limited in that only a certain amount of information-processing capacity seems to exist. If attention is overloaded, much information can be missed. Also, attention appears to be serial in that it can be focused on one thing, then on another, and only with great difficulty (if at all) can we focus attention on two things at the same time. Sometimes attention is directed to external sensory events (where other cars are going). Sometimes it is focused on internal mental operations (trying to remember the items on the shopping list). And sometimes it is focused on internal sensory information (sensations from the muscles and the joints,

Focus on
APPLICATION 3.1

William James on Attention

Consider the following statement, made over a century ago by the famous psychologist William James (1890):

> Everyone knows what **attention** is. It is the taking possession by the mind, in clear and vivid form, of one out of what seem several simultaneously possible objects or trains of thought. Focalization, concentration of consciousness, is of its essence. It implies withdrawal from some things in order to deal effectively with others.

In only a few words, William James identified the complexity of the topic. In this statement, James suggests that attention takes on at least three different roles. First, he says that attention involves "taking possession by the mind . . . of one out of . . . several . . . trains of thought." By this statement, James suggests that attention involves a process of *selection* in which the individual is juggling several ongoing lines of thinking, each competing for current resources (or consciousness). Second, he states that attention involves "focalization . . . of consciousness." This is a subtle, but important, difference from the first idea because it implies an active, *directive* process of current thinking, presumably one that is dynamic—that changes with the changing needs of the performer. And last, James suggests that attention requires "withdrawal from some things in order to deal effectively with others." Here, James is again implying something subtly different—that there is a limit to the *amount* of attention that can be allocated, and that we don't have enough capacity to allocate to two or more tasks at the same time. Therefore, the performer must be able to shift the amount of attention allocation as changes occur in the demands of the task.

As we will discuss in this chapter, James' intuitions and descriptions about attention back in 1890 remain quite accurate today.

---

such as feeling the steering wheel vibrate). In addition, there are the difficulties in doing two tasks at the same time, such as talking or texting on a cell phone while driving. Attention involves many different things, as is clearly evident in the historical quote from William James in Focus on Application 3.1.

What Is Attention?

All of the preceding examples represent different uses of attention. But what *is* attention? In our view, attention is a resource (or pool of resources) that is available and that can be used for various purposes. In many respects, attention is like a bank account, which contains financial resources that fund our daily living. The ways in which these attentional resources are allocated define how we *use* attention.

A way to think of attention is related to the limitations in doing two things at the same time. Psychologists have approached the limitations in information processing by first trying to understand the separate requirements of tasks that interfere with each other. The idea has been that if two tasks interfere with each other, they both demand some access to the limited capacity to process information—that is, they both require attention. Figure 3.1 illustrates this idea. Both circles represent the total capacity of resources available to be allocated. In the bank account example,

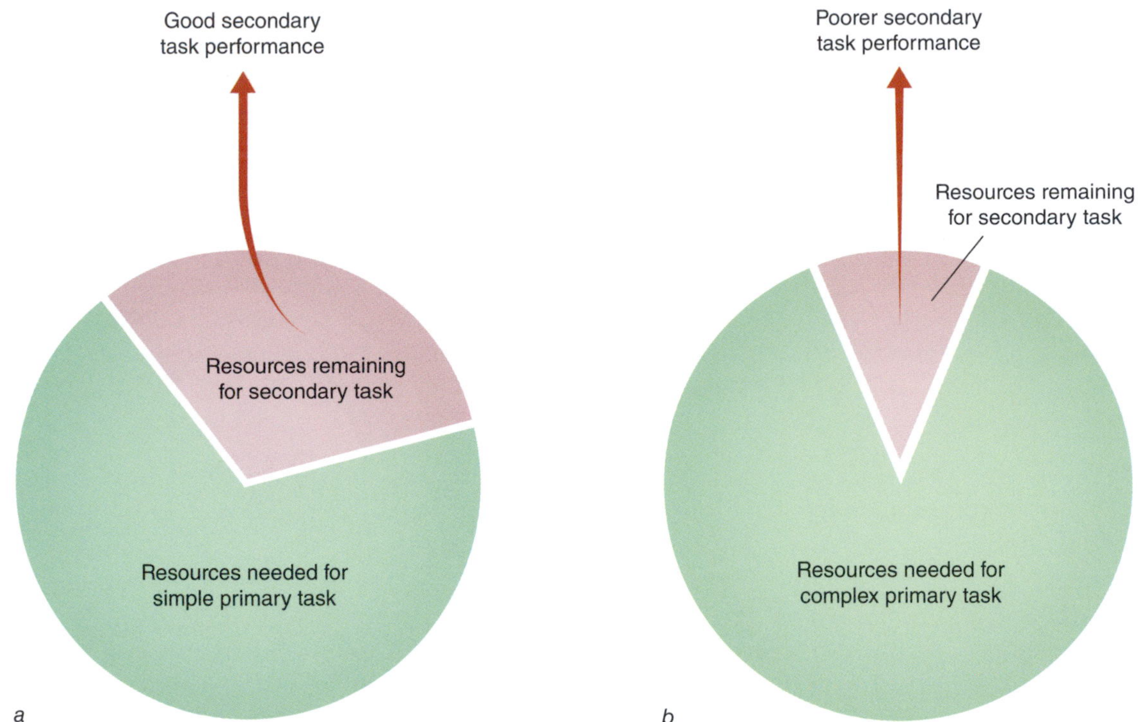

FIGURE 3.1 Attention remaining for a secondary task is reduced when the primary task is more complex (*b*) compared to when the primary task is simple (*a*).

this would represent all the money that we have available. Figure 3.1 illustrates how the fixed amount of attention (capacity resource) must be divided between a main task and a secondary task. When the main task is relatively simple and does not require very much attention, as depicted in figure 3.1*a*, then more attentional capacity remains for other tasks. In the bank account example, consider the money allocated to paying your rent as the main task. When that amount is a relatively small proportion of your paycheck, as in 3.1*a*, then more resources are available to be spent elsewhere. However, when the rent takes up a larger proportion of your monthly income, as in figure 3.1*b*, then less is available to be spent elsewhere.

Visit the web study guide to read "Gumbo" and complete the self-directed learning activities.

This notion has strong implications for understanding skilled performance. In many skills, there is an overwhelming amount of information that could be processed, some of it relevant to performance (e.g., what other drivers are doing, as in the driving example) and some of it irrelevant to performance (e.g., the color of the other cars on the road). The performer's problem is how to cope with this potential overload of information. The performer must learn what to attend to and when, and must shift attention skillfully between events in the environment, monitoring and correcting her own actions, planning future actions, and doing many other processes that compete for the limited resources of attentional capacity.

The following sections turn to the question of when and under what conditions tasks interfere with each other. One way to understand the kinds of multiple-task interference involves the stages of information processing described in chapter 2—**stimulus identification**, **response selection**, and **movement programming** (see figure 2.3). It is useful to ask whether, within each stage, there is interfer-

Multitasking is an example of an attentional capacity problem in which the demands of the individual tasks exceed the capability to devote full attention to each of them. In this case, explain how the performer might try to achieve multitasking.

ence between two processes competing for the available capacity. There is evidence that some processing can occur in parallel (that is, without attention) in the stimulus identification stage, but that much less parallel processing occurs in the response selection stage. Finally, considerable interference often exists among tasks in the movement programming stage.

Limitations in Stimulus Identification

Some evidence suggests that information processing in the peripheral, sensory stages of the information-processing model can be done in parallel. With parallel processing, two or more streams of information can enter the system and be processed together without interfering with each other. For other tasks, however, the amount of information exceeds the capacity limits of attention, requiring that we *switch* attention between competing sources. Still other research reveals that **sustained attention** tends to wane after extended periods of information processing. These influences on sensory information processing are discussed in the next sections.

Parallel Processing

Information from different aspects of the visual display, such as the color and the shape of objects, can apparently be processed together without interference. Evidence for parallel processing in stimulus identification comes from an analysis of the Stroop effect (Stroop, 1935; MacLeod, 1991, 2015). Imagine that you are a research participant being asked to respond as quickly as possible by naming the font color in which words are

a	b
HOUSE	BLUE
PENCIL	BLACK
HORSE	ORANGE
WATCH	GREEN
RIVER	YELLOW
LETTER	RED

FIGURE 3.2 The Stroop effect. Time yourself while naming the font colors of the words printed in each list. (Note that the font colors in each list are the same, yet the color names in list *b* are more difficult to produce quickly and accurately.)

printed, as in figure 3.2. In some cases, the words printed have no semantic relationship to the colors in which they are printed, as in list *a*. In other cases, as in list *b*, the font colors compete with the names of the words themselves. The Stroop effect is the finding that it requires more time to name the colors for the set of stimuli in list *b* than in list *a*. Evidence suggests that the reason for the delay is due to the competition between name of the font color and the name of the word in list *b*. Even though you try to ignore the name of the word on the page and focus solely on the font color, that name gets at least some automatic processing along with the parallel processing of the font color. Performance is slowed because interference arises later on when the two stimuli compete for different responses.

In important early research on this topic, Cherry (1953) developed the "dichotic listening" task to investigate how auditory sensory information could be processed in parallel. Participants wore headphones with separate streams of information directed to each ear and were instructed to pay attention to the information presented in one channel and to disregard the other. After a short period of time the participants removed the headphones and were asked to repeat the information that had been presented to the "attended" ear. Unexpectedly, they were also asked to repeat what had been presented to the "unattended" ear. Participants were largely unable to remember the information from the unattended ear, although they could identify some surface features of the message, such as the speaker's gender and loudness of the voice.

Cherry called this the **cocktail-party effect**, and it represents another example of parallel processing. The effect is this: Imagine yourself in a large room at a party, in which many groups of people are engaged in conversations. There is considerable noise surrounding the conversation in which you are engaged—loud music, other conversations, and so on—yet you can still engage in a conversation successfully, effectively shutting out the background noise. But not all information is blocked. You can be engaged in an ongoing conversation and suddenly hear your name being spoken in a conversation in which you are not involved at all. Even though you have effectively shut out that background noise, some of it must have been processed in parallel in the stimulus identification stage in order that you could hear your own name. Like the Stroop effect, the cocktail-party effect illustrates that even some unattended features of sensory processing are processed in parallel with other attended information in the very early stages of sensory processing.

Inattentional Blindness

The previous section illustrates how stimulus information can be processed in parallel, even despite efforts to block it out. And yet, sometimes a very simple, goal-directed visual search, such as looking for a specific entrance or building number, seems to absorb our attention, making us "blind" to other things. Some remarkable findings by several research groups have shown that we can miss seemingly obvious features in our environment when we are engaged in attentive visual

Focus on
RESEARCH 3.1

Automatic Stimulus Processing in Basketball

Recall from the Stroop effect that response times are slow and errors increase when naming the font color of a printed word that is not the same as the word itself (e.g., responding with "red" when the word *green* is printed in red font). The slowing occurs because when we look at the word we automatically read its name (e.g., green), and must inhibit responding with that word in order to come up with name of the font color. Research suggests that a process similar to the Stroop effect occurs in responding to head fakes in sport—such as a basketball player who passes the ball in the direction opposite to where he is looking, or a soccer player who kicks the penalty to the left of the goalkeeper while looking to her right.

Kunde, Skirde, and Weigelt (2011) conducted a set of elegantly simple studies in which participants responded to static pictures of a basketball player who was passing a ball to his left or to his right. The player was either looking in the same direction of the pass or looking in the opposite direction. The findings were clear: responses to incongruent pictures (looking and passing in opposite directions) were 7.4% slower and 3 times more errorful than to congruent pictures. However, in a follow-up study, the same pictures resulted in no differences between the congruent and incongruent pictures when the face of the player was obscured. These findings indicate very clearly that humans automatically process the direction that is implied when responding to where people are looking and have difficulty in blocking that process when incongruent (i.e., defending the direction of the pass itself).

In this photo the offensive player is trying to create a Stroop-like delay in the defense by using a no-look pass. Describe another sport situation in which the direction of gaze by an offensive player is intended to fool the behavior of the defender.

These results are not surprising. As Kunde et al. point out, humans are very attuned to the faces of other people. Even very young infants try to imitate the actions of others, such as attempting to stick out their tongues in response to what they observe. But, like the Stroop effect (and its many variations), this is a learned behavior that can largely be eliminated with practice. Expert basketball players are less prone to no-look passes because they have learned to focus less on where the opponents' heads are turned and concentrate more on where the hands and the ball are going when playing defense.

search. For example, research participants in Simons and Chabris' (1999) study watched a video of six people who passed basketballs among themselves while all players were in motion. Three players on one team wore black shirts, and three players on the other team wore white shirts. Each team passed their ball among players on their own team. The research participants who watched a video of this activity were told to count the number of passes made by the team dressed in white shirts. (The Simon and Chabris video and others like it are readily available on YouTube.)

After the 30 s video ended, the experimenter asked the participants how many passes were made, and followed this by asking if they had seen anything unusual in the video. About half of all participants responded "no" to the second question. The other half responded by saying that they had seen someone dressed in a gorilla suit walk through the group of players, pound his chest (gorilla style), and walk away (see figure 3.3). When the video was replayed to the participants who had not seen the gorilla, they were shocked at having missed it, some even claiming that the researcher must have shown them a different video (Chabris & Simons, 2010).

FIGURE 3.3 The inattentional-blindness effect. Participants (observers of the video) counted the number of basketball passes made among the participants in white shirts. Later, about half of these participants did not recall seeing the gorilla walk through the middle of the group.

Visit the web study guide to read "Turn Right at the Next Gorilla" and complete the self-directed activities.

This phenomenon, which has been given the label **inattentional blindness**, was originally discovered by Neisser and Becklen (1975). These findings reveal that missing the rather obvious gorilla is likely to occur only when the viewer is engaged in a specific search task. Watching the video under no specific search instructions, or being asked to count the passes made by the team in black shirts, produced very few cases of this inattentional blindness (Simons & Chabris, 1999). Watching the video a second time, or thinking that something unexpected might occur, also eliminated the effect. Furley and colleagues (2010) found that highly skilled basketball players were also less likely to miss the gorilla than were low-skilled players.

Still, other findings reveal that the inattentional blindness effect is not restricted to watching videos but can be demonstrated in live action events. For example, people who are engaged in attention-demanding tasks are likely to miss quite obvious things such as a change in a person to whom they are giving directions (Simons & Levin, 1998) or a person dressed in a clown suit riding a unicycle (Hyman et al., 2010). In fact, a number of automobile accidents seem linked to this phenomenon. These have been given the label **"looked-but-failed-to-see" accidents**. In these accidents, even though there is evidence that the driver looked in the correct direction, he still drove into the path of a pedestrian, bicycle, or another vehicle (Brown, 2005; Langham et al., 2002). The driver simply did not see the other object coming, even though he looked at it, perhaps because he was searching for something else in the environment, such as a specific sign or building.

Inattentional blindness also explains why we momentarily fail to recognize a friend that we happen to encounter while looking for someone else in a crowd. Our search has been directed toward a person with specific visual characteristics, and we become temporally oblivious to people who don't match those search criteria, even though we would have instantly recognized them otherwise. Magicians and pickpockets exploit essentially the same concept. When the victim is directed by the magician or thief to focus attention on one thing, the victim becomes essentially blind to the other person's actions (Stephen et al., 2008).

Sustained Attention

World War II generated research on sustained attention in order to better understand the limits of radar operators who were on the lookout for enemy aircraft. One task, devised by Mackworth (1948), who was a leader in this research, required participants to watch the pointer of a clocklike apparatus jumping second by second. Occasionally, after long, irregular (unpredictable) intervals, the pointer would jump by 2 s. Detection of these 2 s jumps was found to be reliable for the first 30 min of work but declined dramatically thereafter. These were termed "vigilance decrements" (see Hancock, 2017, for historical overview).

A number of factors are known to affect vigilance or sustained attention; these include the operator's motivation, arousal, secondary tasks, and, of course, fatigue (clearly related to the accumulated amount of time in performing the task). Environmental factors, such as temperature and noise, are also known to affect sustained attention (see Davies & Parasuraman, 1982, for more). After a period of time, concentrating on a single target of our attention becomes a progressively more difficult task.

These effects are quite obvious on a daily basis, as they influence many occupations in which vigilance is a necessity. For example, consider the task of working as a security agent at a busy airport. Before people can board their aircraft, they must go through a series of security checks, which includes an X-ray scan of their carry-on luggage. Each X-rayed piece of luggage must undergo a visual search by a human operator, who looks for the presence of objects that are not permitted on the aircraft. The obvious ones (guns, knives) should be relatively easy to spot. But the problems faced by the security agent include trying to decide whether something that looks like a banned object is actually one or not, which slows the checkpoint process. Experiments on visual search tasks reveal that the number and similarity of distracting objects play an important role in the success of the search. The agent's task is made even more difficult by the fact that finding banned objects is (thankfully) a rare occurrence—so sustained attention to the task is of primary concern (Wolfe et al., 2005).

The role of vigilance is an obvious factor in driving. Long periods of driving without rest are hazardous to sustained attention. However, the act of driving itself provides some benefits to maintaining vigilance. We worry, however, how vigilance will be affected as automated driving vehicles take over the roads (figure 3.4; see also Greenlee et al., 2018). Will drivers be prepared to assume control of the vehicle in an emergency?

Limitations in Response Selection

Interference between tasks is never more obvious than when the performer must perform two actions simultaneously, with each task requiring mental operations, such as answering a telephone call while pouring water into a coffee maker. Both activities are thought to be done during response selection because they require that choices be made among several possible alternatives—which hand to use to pour the water and pick up the telephone, which ear to listen with, monitoring the water so as to not spill any and not pour too much, and so on. These activities are governed by *controlled processing*, which is thought to be (1) slow, (2) attention demanding, with interference caused by competing processing, (3) serially organized, with a given processing

FIGURE 3.4 The driver of an automated vehicle is susceptible to vigilance decrements over long periods of time.

task coming before or after other processing tasks, and (4) volitional, easily halted or avoided altogether. Relatively effortful, controlled processing is a very large part of conscious information-processing activities, involving mental operations among relatively poorly learned, or even completely novel, activities. Having to perform two information-processing tasks together can disrupt one or both tasks.

A separate, very different kind of information processing seems to occur in highly practiced people. Some years ago, Peter Vidmar, an Olympic silver medalist in gymnastics, claimed that before mounting the apparatus, he paid attention just to the first move in his routine—the mount; the remainder of the elements occurred more or less automatically, that is, without requiring attention (Vidmar, 1984). These later elements required only minor adjustments while being run off, allowing Vidmar to focus on such higher-order aspects of his routine as style and form. It is as if much of the information processing necessary in this complex gymnastics routine was fundamentally different from controlled processing, not requiring very much attention. This way of dealing with information, **automatic processing**, is (1) fast, (2) not attention demanding, in that such processes do not generate (very much) interference with other tasks, (3) organized in parallel, occurring together with other processing tasks, and (4) involuntary, often unavoidable.

Automatic information processing is thought to be the result of an enormous amount of practice. Your capability to quickly recognize collections of letters as the words you are reading now has come from years of practice. Many years ago, Bryan and Harter (1897, 1899) conducted studies of telegraph operators, whose job it was to identify (receive) and send Morse code, which is composed of varying bursts of brief noise (called dots and dashes) that combine to define letters and numbers. Bryan and Harter found that telegraph operators focused on individual letters at the earliest stage of learning but that as they gained proficiency, they processed Morse code as combinations of letters, then later as whole words, and even as phrases.

The effectiveness of automatic processing has strong implications not only for many everyday tasks (like reading) but also for high-level performance skills. If a task is performed automatically, many important information-processing activities can be produced not only quickly but in parallel with other, simultaneous tasks and without disrupting performance. It is as if certain stages (e.g., response selection) are bypassed altogether.

Costs and Benefits of Automaticity

Automatic performances are related to processing information in parallel, quickly, and without interference from other processing tasks. For example, after much practice, high-level volleyball players can interpret their opponents' movement patterns automatically to mean that the ball will be spiked from, say, their left side (e.g., see Allard & Burnett, 1985). But what if, after consistently producing a pattern leading to a play to the left, the opposing team uses the same pattern leading to a play to the right? The defenders' automatic processing of the pattern would lead to a quick decision and a movement to counter the *expected* play, a response that would be hopeless as far as combating the actual play is concerned.

Clearly, then, automaticity can have drawbacks, as well as benefits. Although very fast processing is effective when the environment is stable and predictable, it can lead to terrible errors when the environment (or an opponent) changes suddenly. Thus, automaticity seems most effective in closed skills, where the environment is relatively predictable. With open skills, so many more patterns are possible that the performer must develop an automatic response to each of them; this is generally possible only after many years of experience.

Automaticity allows highly skilled athletes to process information about their opponents' movements quickly and respond.

Developing Automaticity

How do people develop the capability to process information automatically? One approach to this question was addressed in experiments by Schneider and Shiffrin (1977). They found that practice, and lots of it, was a very important ingredient. Automaticity developed gradually and most effectively under a "consistent-mapping" condition, where the response generated was related *consistently* to a particular stimulus pattern. For example, the response to a red light during driving is always to bring the vehicle to a stop. This is in contrast to a "varied-mapping" condition, where a given stimulus sometimes leads to one response and sometimes to a different response. An example is the variety of button layouts on different brands of remote-control units, where a given function (changing the volume) requires pressing different buttons depending on the brand and the type of device being controlled. The diversity of such varied-mapping conditions makes automatic processing almost impossible to achieve, and such tasks require considerable controlled processing to avoid making errors.

Response Selection and Distracted Driving

The NHTSA (National Highway Traffic and Safety Administration) defines distracted driving as "any activity that diverts attention from driving, including talking or texting on your phone, eating and drinking, talking to people in your vehicle, fiddling with the stereo, entertainment or navigation system—anything that takes your attention away from the task of safe driving" (Currin, 2018, para. 1). Distracted driving is an excellent example of attention's limited capacity, and more specifically, the limitations due to response selection and movement programming.

Texting is an obvious distraction problem, as it places limitations on stimulus identification, due to sensory disengagement with the activities of driving (e.g., looking away from the road), response selection (e.g., deciding where to touch the phone), and movement programming (e.g., sequencing a series of presses). Manipulating the entertainment or navigational system would likely suffer similar decrements to all processes. But an interesting dilemma has surfaced when comparing hands-free and handheld cell phones—do they represent equal or unequal demands on attentional capacity?

Laws passed in many U.S. states and in other countries have banned the use of handheld cell phones during driving but allow the use of hands-free units. The underlying assumption of these laws is that the *manual* handling of a cell phone interferes with the operation of a motor vehicle. Thus, this argument lays the blame for the cell phone–driving dual-task deficit as a movement programming limitation. But the research suggests otherwise and is quite conclusive that hands-free and handheld phones are about equally problematic in exceeding the attentional capacity limits of the driver. The source of the problem lies in the capacity demanded by the phone *conversation*, and not whether the driver is holding on to, looking at, or manipulating the phone (e.g., Strayer & Johnston, 2001). The physical actions involved in manipulating the cell phone do not add significantly to the attention demands required in carrying on a conversation while driving (see Ishigami & Klein, 2009, and Caird et al., 2018, for important reviews of this research). The discussion in Focus on Research 3.2 provides more information about the methods used to understand the attention demands of distracted driving.

Remember, though, that using a cell phone can also be dangerous when done at the same time as performing other types of activities. For example, in an observational study, Thompson and colleagues (2013) found that people who texted or talked on a cell phone while they crossed a busy intersection walked about 20% slower than nondistracted pedestrians. The texting pedestrians were also less likely to look both ways for oncoming traffic before entering the intersection.

Limitations in Movement Programming

As you will recall from chapter 2, the movement programming stage is the third in the sequence of information-processing stages. Here, after the performer has perceived information from the environment, and after having chosen an appropriate action, the performer must still organize the motor system in order to actually execute the movement. In this stage, the performer must make critical adjustments that occur at various levels (e.g., in the limbs, muscles, and spinal cord). These adjustments take time, of course. A good example is the action of a fencer, who must preprogram a movement despite having to execute the movement in the face of a potentially changing environment. In the following example, the programmed action is somewhat complicated, involving a move toward the center shoulder and then followed by a sudden change in the action.

A fencer moves the foil toward the opponent's shoulder but then quickly alters the direction and contacts the waist instead. The opponent, in responding to the first move (the fake), will often be delayed in the speed of responding to the second move. The delay in responding occurs because of interference to the movement programming stage, which has the task of organizing the motor system to make the desired movement. Specifically, the programming of one response (the fake to the shoulder) interferes with the programming of a second response (to the waist).

Focus on
RESEARCH 3.2

Distracted-Driving Research

Researchers have used varying approaches to understand the effects of distractions on the control of a vehicle. The obvious problem with doing the most logical type of research—using drivers in real traffic situations—is that it brings other drivers, the research participants, and sometimes the experimenters themselves into potentially dangerous situations, which is an unethical research practice. So researchers have devised different methods to assess the attentional cost of performing various tasks while driving.

A statistical approach to the specific problem of cell phone use during driving uses call records of individuals who were involved in an accident. The findings of one study using this method revealed that the likelihood of being involved in a car accident increased by 400% when a driver was talking on a cell phone (Redelmeier & Tibshirani, 1997). These authors also found that the increase in accident rate while talking on a cell phone during driving is about the same as when driving with a .08% blood alcohol concentration (BAC)—the legal definition of driving under the influence (DUI) of alcohol concentration in some states and countries.

The most common type of experimental procedure involves humans performing in driving simulators in laboratory environments. Some simulators provide extremely realistic driving environments, enabling researchers to have control over the traffic conditions and varying distractions without endangering anyone.

A few experimenters have gone further to create outdoor environments, using an actual car and a simulated driving environment in an otherwise safe area such as a large empty parking lot. In fact, one of the very first studies of its kind was performed over a half-century ago, and the authors suggested back then that mobile phones and automobile drivers were a dangerous mix (Brown, Tickner, & Simmons, 1969).

Of course, each method has advantages and disadvantages. Phone records involve actual data about calls that have occurred. But the co-occurrence of an accident and records of a call says very little about the state of the individual during the call. Simulators provide the researcher with excellent control of mental workloads, ongoing distractions, the timing of critical events, the measurement of behaviors, and so on. But these are all simulations of a driving environment, not the real thing. Outdoor environments, in actual cars but with simulated driving conditions, also have the advantage of good experimenter control of events, but, again, without the reality of an actual driving experience in real traffic. In the end, the information provided by all types of research activities together provides researchers with the best answers to these critical questions about distracted driving (see Simmons, Hicks, & Caird, 2016, for more).

Exploring Further

1. How might the nature of a particular cell phone conversation affect a person's capacity to attend to the task of driving?
2. Do you think that a driver having a discussion with an in-car passenger would have the same effects on driving as the driver talking on the cell phone? Why or why not?

Visit the web study guide to read "Fakes" and complete the self-directed learning activities.

Support for this reasoning comes from considerable research evidence using the so-called **double-stimulation paradigm**, where the participant is required to respond, with separate responses, to each of two stimuli presented very closely together in time (see Focus on Research 3.3). In many ways, this paradigm is in many ways analogous to the problem facing the fencer who must first respond to one move and then to another in rapid succession. The delay in responding to the second move occurs because of the interference that arises in programming the first and second movements as rapidly as possible.

Psychological Refractory Period

The delay in responding to the second of two closely spaced stimuli is termed the psychological refractory period (PRP). An important question concerns how soon a person can switch from (1) making a goal-directed response to one stimulus to (2) making a different goal-directed response to a different stimulus. The system processes the first stimulus and generates the first response. If the experimenter presents a second stimulus during the time the system is processing the first stimulus and its response, the onset of the second response will be delayed considerably (the PRP effect).

A leading explanation for the PRP effect is that there is a kind of bottleneck in the movement programming stage, and that this stage can organize and initiate only one movement at a time, as illustrated in figure 3.6. Any other action must wait until the movement programming stage has finished initiating the first movement. This delay is largest when the time between stimuli (SOA) is short, because at this time the movement programming stage has just begun to generate the first response. The first movement must be initiated before the stage can begin to generate a second response. As the SOA increases, more of the first response will have been prepared by the time the second stimulus is presented, so there is less delay before the movement programming stage is cleared.

One more finding is of interest here. When the SOA is very short—say, less than 40 ms—

The fencer on the left has faked one move and is now in the process of making a second move, allowing her to score a point and revealing limitations in the movement programming stage.

Focus on RESEARCH 3.3

The Double-Stimulation Paradigm

Research on the **psychological refractory period (PRP)** uses what is called the double-stimulation paradigm. Here, the participant typically is asked, for example, to respond to a tone (S_1, the first stimulus) by lifting the right hand from a reaction key as quickly as possible. Following a very short time delay (called the **stimulus-onset asynchrony** or **SOA**) a light (S_2, the second stimulus) might then appear. The participant's task is to respond to the light by lifting the left hand from another key as quickly as possible. The SOA might range from zero to a few hundred milliseconds. Of critical interest to researchers is the reaction time (RT) to the second stimulus (RT_2) depending on the length of the SOA. (The timeline shown in figure 3.5*a* might help to make this paradigm easier to understand.)

The findings from one study using this paradigm are graphed in figure 3.5*b*, where RT_2 is plotted as a function of the SOA. The horizontal line (labeled Control RT_2) is the value of RT_2 when the first stimulus is *not presented at all*; it represents the normal RT to this stimulus using this response when there is no interference. Responding to S_2 following a presentation of S_1 usually results in an RT_2 that is much

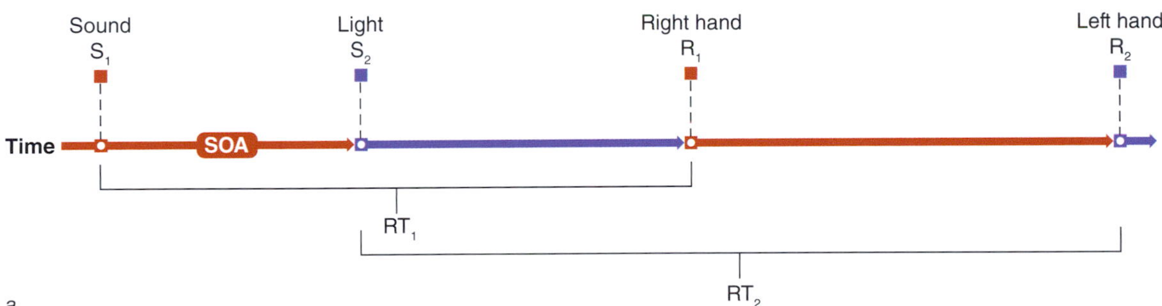

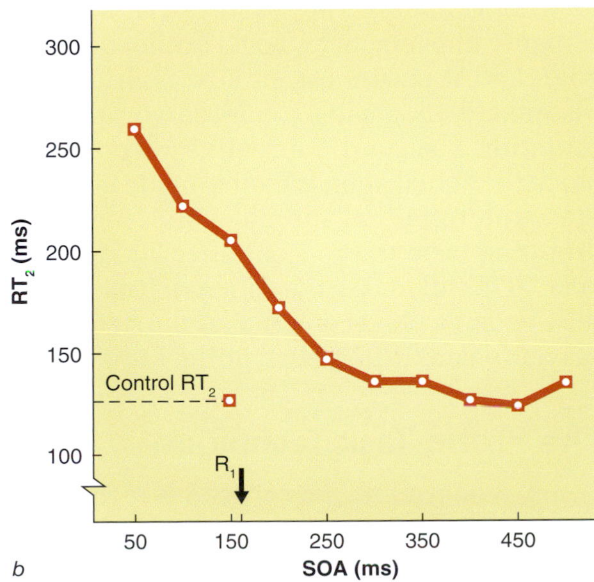

FIGURE 3.5 Illustration of critical events in the double-stimulation paradigm *(a)* and results from experiment by Davis (1959, cited in Schmidt et al., 2019) *(b)*, showing that RT_2 is lengthened greatly at the shortest SOAs.

> *continued*

> The Double-Stimulation Paradigm *continued*

longer than the Control RT_2. But that all depends on the length of the SOA. When the SOA is about 50 ms, the delay in responding is very large, and it can more than double the value of RT_2 as compared to its control value. As the SOA lengthens, the delay in RT_2 decreases, but there is still some delay in producing RT_2 even with SOAs of 200 ms or more (see Figure 3.5*b*). This delay is called the psychological refractory period.

The original single-channel hypothesis (Welford, 1952), which was proposed to account for effects like these, argues that the processing of the first stimulus and response completely blocks the processing of the second stimulus and response until the processing of the first stimulus and response has been completed. More recent thinking about data such as these holds that the major delay in RT_2 arises from interference between the movement programming stages of these actions (Klapp, Maslovat, & Jagacinski, 2019).

Exploring Further

1. Why is the most important comparison in this paradigm the RT to the second of two closely spaced stimuli rather than to the response to the first stimulus?
2. How would the magnitude of the PRP effect be expected to change depending on the number of choices involved in responding to the first stimulus?

the motor system responds to the second stimulus in a very different way. The system responds to the first and second stimulus as if they were one, which produces both responses simultaneously. In this phenomenon, termed *grouping*, the early processing stages presumably detect both stimuli as a single event and organize a single, more complicated, temporally coordinated action in which both limbs respond simultaneously (Miller & Ulrich, 2008). We will have much more to say about coordinated actions in chapter 7.

The PRP effect just discussed accounts for many of the underlying delays that occur in response to fakes. In basketball, for example, the player taking the shot preprograms a single, relatively complex action that involves a move to begin a shot, a delay to withhold it, and then the actual shot—all done in rapid succession. The shooter's movement is organized as a single unit and is prepared as any other movement would be in the movement programming stage. However, the defensive player sees only the first part of this action; this can be thought of as the first stimulus (S_1) in the double-stimulation paradigm, and it triggers the response to block the shot (recall from Focus on Research 3.1 that avoiding the automatic processing of the fake stimulus would only likely occur in the most skilled players). The processing of the first stimulus leads to large delays in responding to the new information that the shot has been withheld, that it is a fake (as indicated by the fact that the second stimulus, S_2, the actual shot, is now being made). The result is that the first response (movement to block) cannot be withheld, and it occurs essentially as originally planned. This creates a very large delay in initiating a second, corrective response to block the actual shot, which is made at about the same time that the defensive player is dropping back to the floor after "taking the fake." This all makes the shot much easier for the offensive player and makes the defensive player look a little foolish at the same time.

The Probe-Task Technique

Some researchers have used a different approach to studying the attention demanded

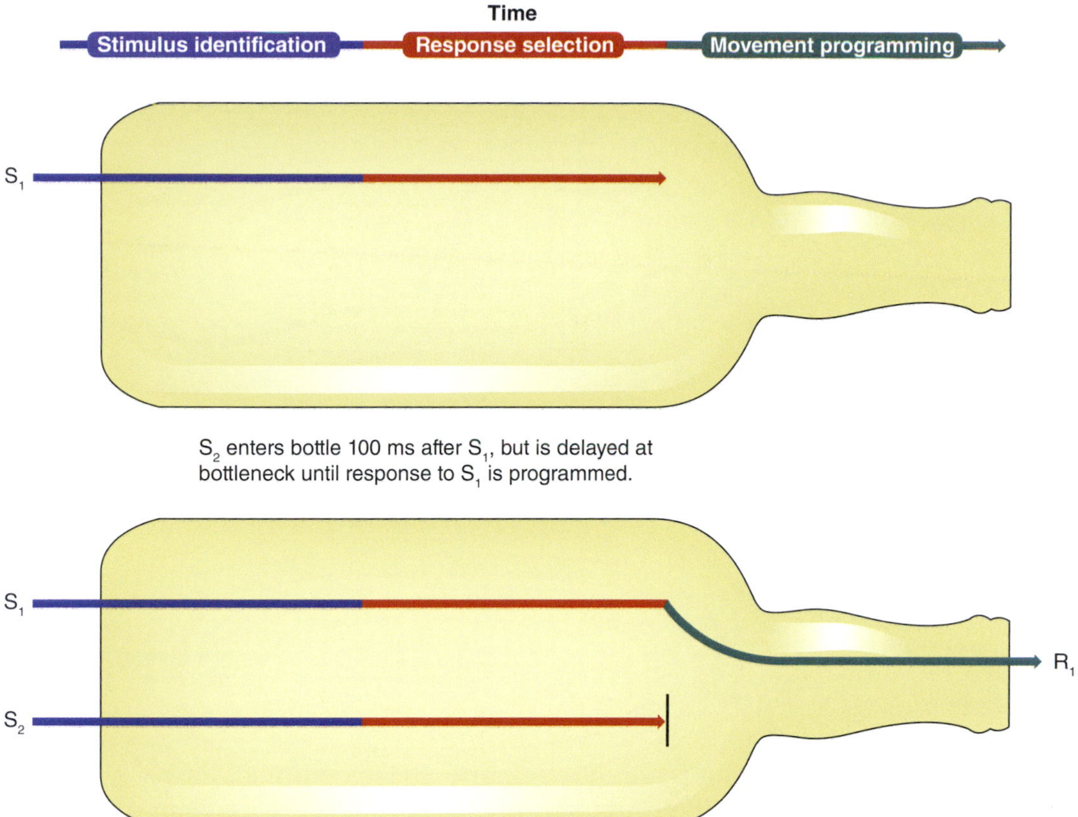

FIGURE 3.6 An information-processing bottleneck in the movement programming stage occurs when two stimuli (S_1 and S_2) are presented 100 ms apart. In *(a)*, the first stimulus enters the information-processing system. In *(b)*, the second stimulus is introduced, but it is delayed at the bottleneck while the first response is programmed. This is similar to what happens in response to a fake in rapid sports. The bottleneck analogy is used to convey the idea that the rate of flow from the bottle is restricted—in this case, specifically at the movement programming stage.

during the movement programming stage, called the **probe-task technique**. Here, the researcher would have the participant perform one task (called the primary task; it could be either discrete or continuous movement). At some unexpected point in the performance of the primary task, the researcher would probe (or test) the attention it demanded by presenting a secondary task, usually a discrete stimulus, such as tone or light (the probe stimulus). Now the participant's additional task would be to respond to the probe stimulus as rapidly as possible with either a manual response (e.g., a key press) or a vocal response (e.g., saying "stop") and RT would measure the delay in responding to the probe. With this strategy, the researcher would use the RT to the probe as a measure of the attention demanded by the primary task; a more attention-demanding primary task would result in slower RTs to the probe stimulus than would a primary task that demanded less attention.

An example of how this technique is used in research is the work of Posner and Keele (1969). In their study, participants were asked to make a rapid, visually guided aiming movement using a lever to a target. Participants made these movements to either large or small targets—the idea being that smaller targets require more of the attentional capacity due to the increased precision

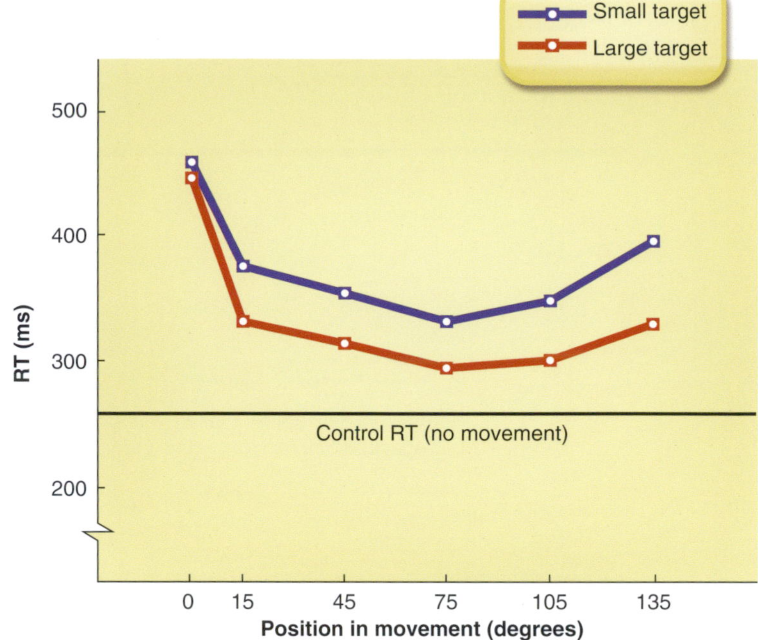

FIGURE 3.7 The attention demands as measured by probe RT at various points during the visually guided pointing movement to either a small or large target. The straight line denotes average RT to the probe stimulus when no pointing movement is being made.

requirements of aiming. The probe technique was used to assess attention demands at various points during the movement, including the start and end positions. Trials that assessed RT were also conducted in a control condition, in which no aiming movement was made.

The results of the Posner and Keele study are presented in figure 3.7. There are several things of interest here. First, the control-RT value (represented as the solid line across the figure near 260 ms) was considerably less than the probe RTs for any of the other data points in the graph. This was interpreted as indicating that all parts of both types of aiming movements required some attention, since RT was elevated relative to the no-movement (control) condition. Second, the bowed nature of both the small-target and large-target curves in the graph suggests that attention demands were not evenly distributed throughout the movement. The elevated probe RTs at positions representing the beginning (0° position) and end (135° position) of the movement suggested that these were more attention-demanding parts of the movement than were the middle positions (i.e., the 15°, 45°, 75°, and 105° positions). Lastly, the probe RT for the small target was generally larger than for the large target, indicating that movements with greater precision requirements are more attention demanding than movements with less precise requirements.

These secondary-task probe techniques are not without their limitations and problems, however. As we will see in chapter 7, producing two movements at the same time introduces special coordination challenges to the processing system. If the movements are compatible (e.g., keeping a rhythm beat with two hands, as in drumming), then two limbs can be coordinated in such a way that there is no detriment to performance (e.g., Helmuth & Ivry, 1996). A problem arises when two or more separate actions have distinct and incompatible *spatial* or *temporal* requirements. The problem for the probe technique is that responding manually to a probe can produce specific interference effects (over and above those associated with attention) with a manual primary task (McLeod, 1980). In McLeod's study, this occurred because the nature of the manual response to the probe was incompatible with the movement

Producing two or more movements at the same time introduces a greater challenge if the movements are incompatible, as when a drummer plays a faster beat with one hand than with the other hand or a foot. Experienced drummers, such as Neil Peart of Rush, are able to do this skillfully.

required for the primary task. Thus, attention demands assessed by the delay in probe RT were contaminated by the competition between movement requirements. McLeod (1980) found that much less competition occurred between a primary limb task and a vocal probe response, for example, and provided a less contaminated assessment of attention demand. This sort of idea prompted the notion of pools of attention, where a given pool would be related to vocal responses, and another pool would be related to motor responses. We will have much more to say about moving two limbs at the same time in chapter 7.

Visit the web study guide to read "The Preshot Routine" and complete the self-directed learning activities.

Focus of Attention During Action

A somewhat different approach to the role of attention in movement concerns the object, or *focus*, to which attention is directed. Although empirical research on the topic has been relatively recent, theorists speculated about it many years ago. Cattell (1893) wrote, "In piano playing, the beginner may attend to his fingers but the practiced player attends only to the notes or to the melody. In speaking, writing and reading aloud, and in games and manual work, attention is always directed to the goal, never to the movement. In fact, as soon as attention is directed to the movement, this becomes less automatic and less dependable." And later, Bernstein (writing in Russian in the 1940s but translated in 1996) offered this advice: "The attention of a person who has learned to ride a bicycle should be fixed not on his legs or arms but on the road in front of the bicycle; the attention of a tennis player should be directed at the ball, the top edge of the net, the movements of the opponent, but certainly not at his own legs or on the racket."

The empirical research addressing the effects of attentional focus has mostly agreed with Cattell and Bernstein. Studies by Wulf and her colleagues, as well as others, suggest that, in almost all situations, an **external focus of attention** results in better performance than an **internal focus of attention**. These studies have revealed very impressive benefits to performance, seen in a wide variety of laboratory and sport tasks and for people of all ages (see Wulf, 2007, 2013, for a review).

External Versus Internal Focus of Attention

Investigations typically address the issue of focus of attention by giving participants explicit instructions about what to think when performing an action. For example, instructions to focus internally could involve cues to think about how the fingers are shaped when releasing a football, the tension in the arms when putting in golf, or the force exerted in the legs when trying to jump as high as possible. These instructions are considered internal because the participant is encouraged to think about how the body is producing movement or perhaps about sensing how the body is moving while the action is ongoing. In contrast, instructions to focus externally might direct the participant to think about the intended target of the football, where the golf ball is being struck with the putter, or a spot on the wall above which the jumper is trying to touch. In this case the instructions serve to direct attention to some end-product of the action or the influence of the action on the environment.

A running sprint-start experiment by Ille et al. (2013) is a good example of the effects of internal versus external attention focus instructions. On separate days of study, the participants were instructed to think about the motions of the arms and legs during the sprint start (internal instructions) or were told simply to get across the finish line as quickly as possible (external instructions). Even just this seemingly minor difference in instructions had a large impact on performance. The external condition resulted in RTs that were about 9% faster and MTs that were close to 3% faster than under internal focus instructions—which represents a relatively large amount of time in a sprint race.

Another approach to inducing different focus of attention conditions was used by Sherwood, Lohse, and Healy (2014) in a dart-throwing task. Rather than varying instructions, Sherwood et al. asked their participants to make a performance assessment after each throw, with the specific nature of the assessment designed to induce either an internal or external focus of attention on subsequent throws. Post-throw judgments about elbow position were considered to induce an internal focus, and judgments about the final position of the dart relative to the target created an external focus. The results for radial error (a two-dimensional equivalent to absolute error, see chapter 1) were comparable to the Ille et al. study described before—external-focus throws were more accurate than internal-focus throws.

The Sherwood et al. study also contained an important third (control) condition, in which no post-movement assessments were made. Dart throws in this condition were as accurate as in the external condition. This finding is important because it suggests that it was not necessarily the positive benefit to performance induced by the external focus, but rather the negative impact of an internal focus that had the critical influence on performance.

A leading explanation of attentional focus effects on performance was offered by Wulf, McNevin, and Shea (2001), termed the **constrained action hypothesis**. The underlying idea was that a conscious, moment-to-moment type of movement control is typical of less-skilled performance, and that a more free-flowing, automated type of movement control is typical of skilled performance. They theorized that consciously controlled movements were typical of an internal focus of attention and that automated movement control was used in externally focused performances. The hypothesis has been supported with kinematic evidence, as reviewed in Schmidt et al. (2019, ch. 4). This view may also help us to understand why a good performance can sometimes turn disastrous, as presented in the next section.

Visit the web study guide to read "The Toad and the Centipede" and complete the self-directed learning activities.

Choking

One of the most dramatic occasions in high-profile sporting events occurs when an individual seemingly on the way to certain victory does the unimaginable—plays sloppily and loses. Famous examples of **choking** under pressure in sports include Boston Red Sox first-baseman Bill Buckner's error on a routine ground ball at a critical point in the World Series, and collapses by Rory McIlroy (2011) and Jordan Spieth (2016) on the final nine holes of the Masters golf tournament. Everyone can probably recall events like this, and there is no shortage of examples in every sport, it seems.

What is a choke, why does it occur, and how can it be avoided? By most accounts, choking is more than simply a failed performance in an important situation. Researchers such as Beilock (2010) suggest that choking often occurs when there is a change in one's attentional focus. Consistent with the Wulf et al. constrained action view, presented earlier, as the pressure builds to perform well in a critical situation, athletes who choke often shift from performing in an overlearned, automatic type of external attentional focus to thinking about how to perform the movement, or how the movement will feel when it is performed. This shift to an internal focus changes how movements are controlled, reducing performance quality. The heightened anxiety that accompanies poor performance can lead to further internalized focus and a dismal, downward spiral toward failure. Other explanations of choking exist, but Beilock's view fits well with the attentional focus literature and theory.

Visit the web study guide to read "Choking Under Pressure" and complete the self-directed learning activities.

Ironic Effects

An anecdotal belief among many athletes is that trying hard *not* to do something will often result in doing that very thing, revealing a specific form of choking. For example, golfers who see a large lake to the right of the fairway might intuitively think "don't hit it to the right," and more often than not, do just that. Pitchers who try to not walk a batter seem more likely to do so, compared to when they try to throw a strike. And football linemen who tell themselves "just don't jump offside" seem to be prone to doing just that (Janelle, 1999).

This tendency to do something you are trying not to do was termed the "ironic effect" by Wegner (1994), who reviewed a number of experimental studies about "counter-intentional" errors. Holding a pendulum in an outstretched arm and trying not to let it sway in the y-dimension, for example, will result in more y-dimensional sway than under various control instructions. Although other, nonmotor **ironic effects** are known to exist (e.g., try not thinking about a fuzzy, white puppy), the influence of negative thoughts on motor control are largely considered to be the end-result of a specific internal focus of attention. Switching to a conscious mode of processing, with a directive to not move or act in a specific manner, seems to be associated with reduced performance that mimics the intended "do not do" instruction.

Decision Making Under Stress

Arousal, the level of excitement produced under stress, is a common aspect of skill performance situations. This is certainly true of many athletic events, where the pressure to win and the threat of losing, as well as crowd influences, are important sources of emotional arousal for players. The level of arousal imposed by a situation is an important determinant of performance, particularly if the performance is dependent on the speed and accuracy of decision making.

Inverted-U Principle

One can think of arousal as the level of excitement or activation generated in the central nervous system. For example, low levels of arousal are associated with sleeplike states, and high levels are associated with the agitated and extremely alert states found in life-threatening situations. The influences of arousal level on performance have been studied for many years. The **inverted-U principle** (or the Yerkes-Dodson law [1908]) represents an early view of the relationship between arousal and performance. The idea is that increasing the arousal level generally enhances performance but only to a point. Performance quality peaks at some intermediate value of arousal, and performance actually deteriorates as the arousal level rises further—hence the inverted-U function.

Support for the application of the inverted-U principle to human motor performance was provided in a study by Weinberg and Ragan (1978). The task involved throwing balls at a target, and levels of stress were induced by (falsely) comparing participants' performances to those of other participants like them (junior high school boys). In the high-stress condition, 90% of this comparison group supposedly performed more accurately than the test participants did. The authors assumed—with good justification, we think—that junior high school boys would find this sort of information feedback to be arousing or stressful. The moderate- and low-stress groups were told that 60% and 30%, respectively, of the comparison group had scored more accurately than they had. When the participants performed the task again, following these stress-inducing false statements, their performances conformed well to the predictions of the inverted-U principle, as shown in figure 3.8.

The inverted-U principle might be surprising to many who deal with sport and coaching, because it is generally believed that the higher the level of motivation or arousal, the more effective the performance will be. Coaches often spend a great deal of time before games attempting to raise the team's arousal level, and we hear sportscasters argue that a team's performance was poor because the players were not "psyched up" enough for the contest. Yet this general view is contradicted by experimental evidence: A high level of arousal is effective only to a point, whereas further raising the arousal level actually damages performance.

Variations of the Inverted-U Principle

Over the years, the general shape of the inverted U has been a good guideline for thinking about the relationship between arousal and performance. However, it is probably best not to put too much faith in the symmetrical shape of this U-function. As shown in figure 3.9, task differences, as well as indi-

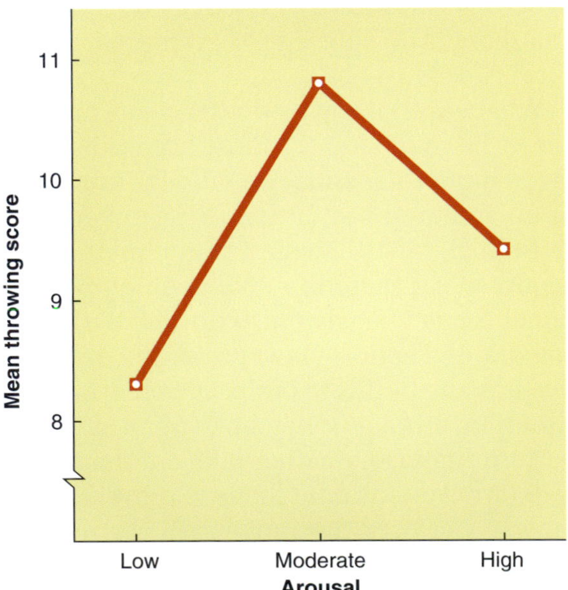

FIGURE 3.8 Stress-inducing instructions have effects on performance that are consistent with the predictions of the inverted-U principle.

vidual differences in the participant's excitability, can result in changes to the shapes of the curve, with optimal performance occurring at either the lower or higher ends of the arousal continuum.

Consider the three hypothetical curves illustrated in figure 3.9. The red curve labeled A shows a steep rise in performance at relatively low levels of arousal, with performance peaking and then beginning to decline even before a moderate level in arousal. Such a curve might represent the shape of the arousal–performance function for a particularly complex task, perhaps requiring fine motor control (threading a needle) or cognition (playing chess), or for an individual who functions best under calm conditions. In contrast, the green curve labeled C could represent the arousal–performance function for a very simple task, perhaps requiring great amounts of force with very little cognition (e.g., powerlifting) or for a person who thrives under pressure. The point here is that the simple inverted U (the blue curve labeled B in figure 3.9) might best represent many other tasks that have medium levels of complexity, cognitive involvement, and so on. These principles have been recognized and studied in the fields of sport and exercise psychology, where the general problem has been to understand the effects of stress and arousal on performance, and to examine how arousal-regulation procedures can be used to manage arousal levels before performance (e.g., Weinberg & Gould, 2019).

Visit the web study guide to read "The Farmer's Market" and complete the self-directed learning activities.

Perceptual Narrowing

One important change in information processing that occurs with high arousal is **perceptual narrowing**—the tendency for the perceptual field to shrink under stress. (This phenomenon is sometimes known as "tunnel vision," in which the world seems to be viewed as through a pipe such that the entire focus is on central vision. It has also been referred to as "weapon focus," in which the panicked victim of an armed robbery cannot identify the robber because her attention had been riveted on the gun.) For example, consider how vision changes for the novice in the relatively stressful sport of deep sea diving. Weltman and Egstrom (1966) presented reaction stimuli in various peripheral locations to diving students who had been asked to perform a simple motor task. On land, where the diver can operate under a low level of arousal, the range of possible stimulus sources to which the participant can

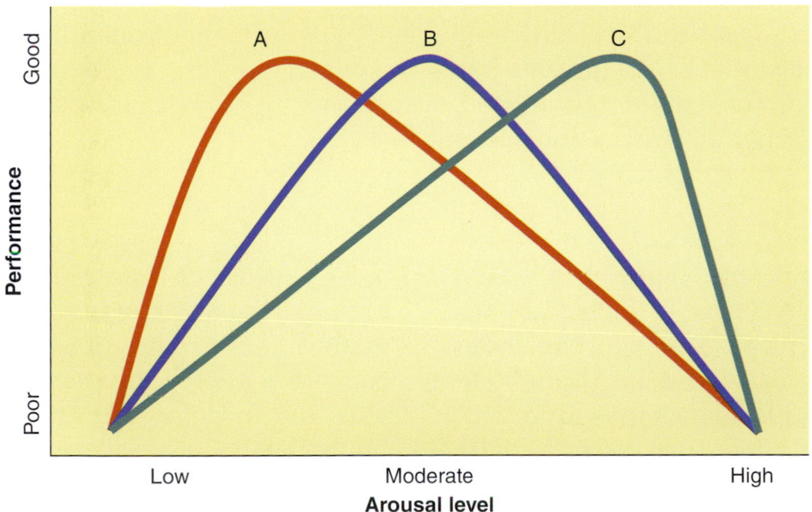

FIGURE 3.9 Variations to the inverted-U principle.

Focus on
APPLICATION 3.2

Driver Panic and Unintended Acceleration

It was a fairly normal morning—the 35-year-old teacher reported that she had just dropped her son at day care before heading to school. She stopped for coffee at the local drive-through and moved the transmission lever from Drive to Neutral in order to reach for her purse. After putting her coffee in the cup holder, she intended to put her foot on the brake while she changed the transmission from Neutral back to Drive. Suddenly, the car lurched forward and gathered speed. Pressing harder on the brake pedal seemed only to make the car go faster. Thinking that the brakes had failed, the teacher pressed harder still, and this time the pedal went all the way to the floor. The car sailed across the parking lot, wildly out of control, with the driver in a complete panic state, before crashing into a parked vehicle on the other side of the street. The air bags engaged, and fortunately nobody was seriously hurt. It was only then, as the motor continued to race with the wheels still squealing, that the woman realized her mistake—she had pressed the accelerator instead of the brake.

This story illustrates a number of important issues about motor control that we will return to later in the book: how we guide movements in the absence of visual feedback; how movement selection errors can occur without our detection; how and when we make error corrections; and lastly, and most important for our present discussion, the fact that normal modes of information processing can cease to operate when we are in a heightened state of panic, sometimes called **hypervigilance**.

As you reflect on this story, there are a number of easy solutions to the situation that come to mind. Turning off the ignition, moving the transmission into Neutral, and removing the foot from the pedal would have all solved the problem. But in these cases of **unintended acceleration**, a phenomenon that occurs far too commonly, none of these corrective actions are typically made (Schmidt, 1989). Instead, it is usually some external agent, such as a tree, wall, or another vehicle, that brings the car to a halt.

Hypervigilance occurs at the very highest levels of arousal. In cases of unintended acceleration, the driver seems to freeze at the wheel, in terms of both normal movement control and information-processing activities. In a hypervigilant state, decision making is severely limited, resulting in an inability to produce creative actions (e.g., switching off the ignition key) and an ineffective performance generally. Fortunately, hypervigilant states are relatively rare. But when they do occur, the fate of the individual is almost completely turned over to the "fight-or-flight" functioning of a panicked information-processing system.

---

respond is relatively wide, representing most of the visual field. However, at the bottom of a swimming pool, and especially on the ocean floor, where arousal would be thought to increase, the visual field becomes more narrowly and intensely focused; systematically fewer peripheral stimuli are detected, with increased focus on the expected or important aspects of the task and increased focus on those sources of information most pertinent to or expected in the task (located in central vision). This is an important mechanism because it allows the person to devote more attention to those stimulus sources that are immediately most likely and relevant. Perceptual narrowing is not limited to vision but apparently occurs with each of the senses in an analogous way.

Easterbrook's (1959) cue-utilization hypothesis also helps to explain the inverted-U principle. When the arousal level is low and the perceptual field is relatively wide, the performer has access to, and uses, a wide range of cues, only a few of which are relevant to effective performance, so performance is suboptimal. As the arousal level rises and the attentional focus narrows onto the most relevant cues, more and more of the irrelevant cues are excluded, so proficiency increases because the performer is responding to mostly relevant cues. When further arousal increases, though, the increased perceptual narrowing means missing even some of the relevant cues, so performance begins to suffer, particularly where the cues are not highly expected. The optimal level of arousal is presumably one in which the narrowed attentional focus excludes many irrelevant cues yet allows most of the relevant cues to be detected.

Summary

A good way to think about attention is to imagine a pool of resources such that, if the information-processing activities from a given task exceed the resources available, performance of this task and perhaps a second task attempted at that the same time will suffer. Under a limited set of circumstances, processing can be done in parallel; that is, performance on two tasks can be done together, without interference. In common cocktail-party circumstances, we can ignore the conversations around us, focusing on a conversation with a given person until, for example, your name is spoken in a nearby conversation. Other findings tend to agree; information about the font color of a word and the meaning of the word appear to be processed in parallel, but there is considerable interference involving selection of the action (the Stroop test). People can become "blind" to certain stimuli if attention is directed strongly elsewhere, for example failing to perceive the gorilla in plain sight when participants' attention was directed strongly to another target. This appears to be related to a class of motor vehicle crashes in which one driver looked but failed to see (that is, to perceive) an oncoming vehicle. On the other hand, many highly practiced tasks tend to be performed without very much attention; this is difficult to achieve without extensive practice under the proper conditions. While we might appear to be able to drive a car without any attention, studies of drivers attempting to drive and converse on a cell phone at the same time show that this is a dangerous combination. The biggest attentional limitation of all appears to be in the movement programming stage. The so-called psychological refractory period (PRP) provides the evidence. The overall viewpoint appears to be that, while we may be able under certain circumstances to respond without attention in the stimulus identification and response selection stages, only one action can be programmed at a time during the movement programming stage.

Focus of attention on an external event results in generally better performance than an internally focused attention. And changing from an external to an internal focus has been associated with dramatic performance changes, such as choking. Shifts in attention are also associated with changes in levels of an individual's anxiety, resulting in dramatic effects on performance.

WEB STUDY GUIDE ACTIVITIES

The student web study guide offers these activities to help you build and apply your knowledge of the concepts in this chapter.

Interactive Learning

Activity 3.1: Review the concepts associated with limitations in attention by matching related terms to their definitions.

Activity 3.2: Indicate whether each in a list of characteristics applies to controlled processing or automatic processing.

Activity 3.3: Using a figure from the text, explore how the inverted-U relationship between arousal and performance varies by situation and person.

Principles-to-Application Exercise

Activity 3.4: The principles-to-application exercise for this chapter prompts you to choose an activity and analyze the attentional demands of three performance situations within that activity. You will also indicate whether the demand for attention relates primarily to stimulus identification, response programming, or movement programming, and examine how stress might affect decision making during this activity.

Motor Control in Everyday Actions Narratives

Gumbo

Turn Right at the Next Gorilla

Fakes

The Preshot Routine

The Toad and the Centipede

Choking Under Pressure

The Farmer's Market

Check Your Understanding

1. Both parallel and serial processing can occur during the stimulus identification stage of information processing. Provide examples of the types of information that might be processed in parallel and in serial as a rock climber decides which move to make next.
2. Explain how a fake in wheelchair basketball illustrates a strong interference between activities in the movement programming stage of information processing.
3. Regarding attention, explain why a lifeguard at a crowded pool may find it more difficult to perform his job as he nears the end of his shift. What factors influence his ability to sustain attention? Suggest two policies that a pool could put in place to make sustained attention easier for lifeguards.

Apply Your Knowledge

1. The way information is processed during the response selection stage of information processing can be very different between a novice and an expert performing the same task. Describe the differing types of processing, highlighting the key features of each. How is task interference related to each type of processing? How might a person performing a waltz perform differently as a novice and as an expert?
2. When mountain biking, some cyclists who have no trouble riding along a straight trail have difficulty performing the identical task (riding in a straight line) on a bridge that is the same width (or wider) than the trail, resulting in a less smooth performance or even a fall. What role might focus of attention play in this phenomenon? How could the inverted-U principle be used to help explain why a bridge over a ravine may make the task of riding in a straight line more difficult?

Suggestions for Further Reading

Many books and review articles about attention and human performance have been written. The works by Wickens and McCarley (2008), Chun, Golomb, and Turk-Browne (2011), and Kahneman (2011) are excellent recent resources. Wulf's (2007) book on attentional focus is of special relevance to motor performance and learning. Chabris and Simons (2010) discuss inattentional blindness and other fascinating attention-related issues. Davies and Parasuraman (1982) discuss sustained attention in detail. Weinberg and Gould (2019) discuss arousal, stress, and other topics of particular importance in sport and exercise psychology. Beilock's (2010) book on choking is also a fascinating read. See the references list for these additional resources.

4

Sensory Contributions to Skilled Performance

Feedback Processing in Motor Control

KEY TERMS

blindsight
closed-loop control system
comparator
cutaneous receptor
dorsal stream
exteroception
feedforward
Golgi tendon organs
joint receptors
M1
M2
M3
muscle spindle
optical array
optical flow
proprioception
quiet-eye effect
tau
ventral stream
vestibular apparatus

CHAPTER OUTLINE

CHAPTER OBJECTIVES

Chapter 4 describes the roles of sensory feedback in human motor control. This chapter will help you to understand

- the types of sensory information available for motor control,
- motor control as a closed-loop processing system,
- how feedback and feedforward information work in the conceptual model, and
- the roles of vision in motor control.

Success in skilled performance often depends on how effectively the performer detects, perceives, and uses relevant sensory information. Frequently, the winner of a competition is the one who has more quickly detected a pattern of action in their opponent. Success can also be measured by the correct detection of errors in one's own body movements and positions, which provides a basis for subsequent movement (or positional) modifications, as in dance or gymnastics. A surgeon requires skilled touch (haptic) perception to detect an abnormal growth during a physical exam of a patient. Consequently, considerable emphasis is directed toward improving the skill with which performers detect and process *sensory information* because these improvements can lead to large gains in performance.

Sources of Sensory Information

Information for skilled performance arises from a number of sources and can be categorized into two major types. One type comes from the environment and is termed *exteroceptive* (the prefix "extero-" means "outside" and here refers to information provided from outside the body). The other type of sensory information is termed *proprioceptive* (the prefix "proprio-" means "one's own" and here refers to information arising from within the body). **Exteroception** provides information to the processing system about the state of the environment in which one's body exists, and **proprioception** provides information about the state of the body itself. These sources of information are types of inherent (sometimes called intrinsic) feedback. The term *feedback* is used for situations in which, during a movement, sensations arise because the body is moving through the environment, resulting in information that is "fed back" to the performer. For example, when we move from one place to another, information is available from the contracting muscles, and there are also changes in what we see while moving.

For feedback to be inherent means that the information is directly available to the performer and is available naturally through the senses. A major distinction is made later in the book when we discuss the provision of *augmented* feedback—information about which the performer is not normally aware; this is extra information provided by an external source. An example is a teacher or instructor who provides a critical assessment to a learner after performing a skill.

Exteroception

The most prominent of the exteroceptive information sources, of course, is vision. Seeing serves the important function of providing information about the physical structure of the environment, such as the edge of a stairway or the presence of an object blocking one's path. Vision also provides information about the movement of objects in the environment in relation to your own movements—such as the flight path of a ball while you are running to catch it—which can be used to make certain predictive judgments about the movement direction to take. Another function of vision is to detect your own movement within the (stable) environment, such as your path toward an external object and how much time will elapse before you arrive.

The second major kind of exteroceptive information comes from hearing, or *audition*. Although audition is not as obviously involved in motor skills as vision, there are many activities that depend heavily on well-developed auditory skills; obvious examples are the sounds of a musical instrument as it is played and the role of hearing in speech production. However, audition is important for many other skills too, such as using the sounds of the sailboat's hull moving through the water as cues to boat speed, the sound of a power tool as a skilled carpenter cuts through different materials, or the sounds of an engine as an auto mechanic adjusts a carburetor.

Proprioception

The second major type of information is from the body's movement, usually termed proprioception. This term refers to sensing the movements of joints, tensions in muscles, and so on, giving information about the state of the body parts in relation to each other and relative to the environment. Several important receptors provide this information.

The **vestibular apparatus** in the inner ear provides information related to head movements and body orientation (e.g., upside down) in the environment. The vestibular apparatus consists of three structures (the saccule, utricle, and semi-circular canals), which are positioned to detect the head's orientation with respect to gravity. Not surprisingly, these structures are strongly implicated in posture and balance control.

Several other structures provide information about what the limbs are doing. Receptors in the capsule surrounding each of the joints, called the **joint receptors**, give information about extreme positions of the joints. Embedded within the belly of the skeletal muscle are **muscle spindles**, oriented in parallel with the muscle fibers. Because muscles change lengths when the joints they span are moved, the muscle spindle lengths are changed as well. These changes provide information about joint position and the state of the muscle (e.g., stretch information). Near the junction between the skeletal muscle and its tendon lie the **Golgi tendon organs**, which are very sensitive to muscle tension and serve to regulate the levels of force produced in the attached muscle. Finally, in most skin areas are **cutaneous receptors**, including several kinds of specialized detectors of pressure, temperature, touch, and so on. The cutaneous receptors are critical for the haptic sense, the sense of touch.

None of these proprioceptors respond to just one physical characteristic, however. The signal from a particular source, such as the muscle spindles, provides ambiguous information about joint position because the receptor can be affected by several other physical stimuli (movement velocity, muscle tension, and the orientation with respect to gravity) at the same time. For this and other reasons, the central nervous system is thought to use a complex combination of the inputs from these various receptors as a basis for body awareness.

Alterations in proprioception can be used in a positive way too, as when they are exploited by human factors engineers in the design of equipment. Experienced typists prefer keyboards that provide some haptic

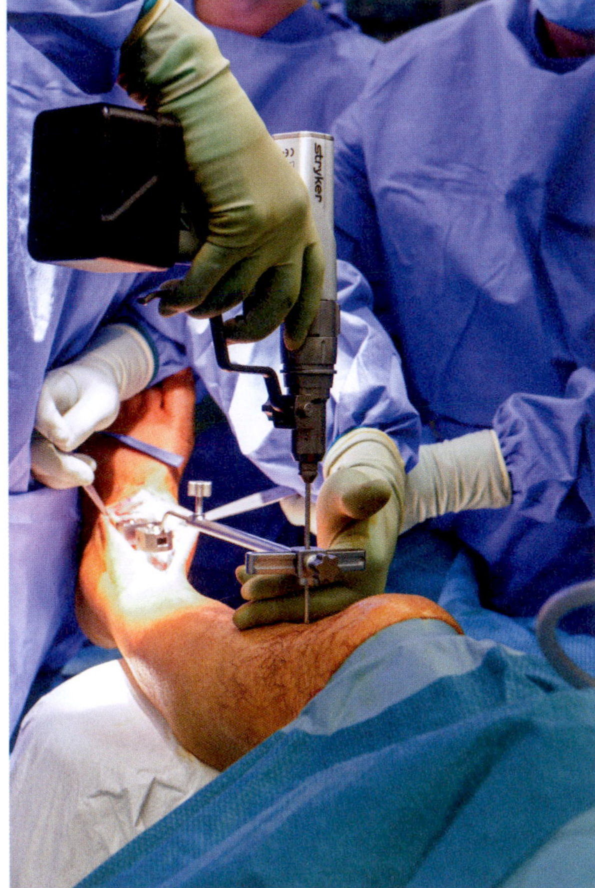

Identify the types of sensory information likely used by the performers in these photos.

feedback which provides the satisfying auditory click, indicating to the operator that the key has been fully pressed (Asundi & Odell, 2011). Supplying aircraft instrument knobs of different shapes and locations for different functions makes confusion among them less likely by associating distinct proprioceptive

A brew pub uses draft tap handles that differ in shape, size, color, and proprietary design. These different designs encourage rapid decision making while reducing errors.

sensations with each knob. A similar strategy can be seen in the brew pub photo in this section.

Multisensory information produces redundancies that provide assistance during performance. For example, automobiles are equipped with sensors that provide visual and auditory feedback about the location of objects in a driver's blind spot, and auditory plus haptic (vibration) information regarding lane departures. Having multisensory redundancies increases the likelihood of responding to one of these inputs with a rapid and accurate response.

However, more information is not always better information, as multiple inputs can also lead to performance failures. Gray (2008) describes situations in which visual, proprioceptive, and vestibular information conflict to confuse airplane pilots about the spatial orientation of the plane's heading. Such conflicts can create perceptual illusions that could lead to failure.

Visit the web study guide to read "The Magnetic Hill" and complete the self-directed learning activities.

There are many different sources of sensory information for motor control, varying not only in terms of where the information is detected but also in terms of how it is processed and used. We reduce the complexity of this discussion in the next sections by considering this variety of sensations as a single group, focusing on the common ways the central nervous system processes this information for skilled performance.

Processing Sensory Information

One important way to think about how sensory information is processed during movement is by analogy to closed-loop control systems, a class of mechanisms used in many applications in everyday life. Figure 4.1 provides an example of a simple closed-loop system.

Closed-Loop Control Systems

The simple **closed-loop control system** illustrated in figure 4.1 can be started in a number of ways, but one common way occurs when you input a desired state or system goal, such as the desired temperature in your house in the winter. Sensory information about the system's output (the room's actual temperature) is measured by a thermometer and is compared to the expected temperature. Any difference between the expected and actual temperature represents an error (e.g., the temperature is too low); this error signal is transmitted to an executive to decide what action to take to eliminate or reduce the error. The executive sends a command to an effector, in this case turning on the furnace, which carries out the action. This action raises the room temperature until the actual state equals the expected state (where the error in temperature is now zero); this new information is sent to the executive, and the executive sends a new instruction to switch off the heat production. This process continues indefinitely, maintaining the temperature near the desired value throughout the day. This kind of system is termed *closed-loop* because the loop from the executive to the effector and back to the executive again is completely closed by sensory information, or feedback.

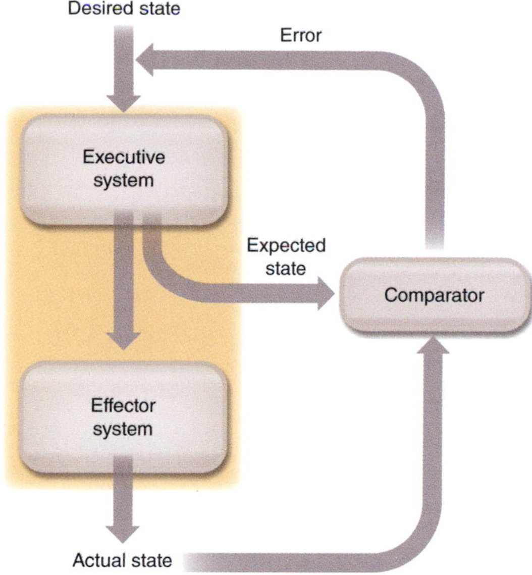

FIGURE 4.1 A basic closed-loop control system.

The same general processes operate in human performance, as in reaching to pick up a cup. Visual information about the hand's position relative to the cup represents the feedback. Differences between the hand's location and the desired location are sensed as errors. An executive determines a correction, modifying the effector system to bring the hand into the proper location. Of course, in more complicated skills, feedback consists of a collection of different kinds of sensory information arising from a variety of receptors both within and outside the body (exteroceptors and proprioceptors).

All closed-loop control systems have four distinct parts:

1. An executive for decision making about errors
2. An effector system for carrying out the decisions
3. A reference of correctness against which the feedback is compared to define an error
4. An error signal, which is the information acted on by the executive

Closed-Loop Control in the Conceptual Model

These closed-loop processes fit within the expanded conceptual model for movement control as shown in figure 4.2. This is simply an expansion of the conceptual model of human performance presented in chapter 2, which introduces the stages of information processing (see figure 2.3). However, now are added the notions of closed-loop control seen in figure 4.1 to achieve a more complete system that complements our discussion of human motor performance.

This conceptual model is useful for understanding the processes involved not only in relatively slow movements (e.g., slow positioning of a limb in physical therapy) where compensations can be made during the action but also in relatively fast movements (e.g., swinging an ax) where the correction of the error must wait until the movements have been completed.

The executive system consists of the decision-making processes discussed in chapter 2—the stimulus identification, response selection, and movement programming stages. The executive then sends commands to an effector system consisting of several parts. One is the motor program, which produces commands for lower centers in the spinal cord, which finally result in the contraction of muscles and the movement of joints. At the same time, information is specified to define the sensory qualities of the correct movement, such as the feel of an effective ax swing. This information represents the performer's anticipated sensory feedback—that is, the sensations that would be generated if the movement was performed correctly. An example is the state of the thermostat when it is set to, say, 70°; incoming feedback from the room's air temperature (the actual feedback) is then compared to the anticipated feedback (70°, indicated by the thermostat's state) and an error is computed, which is then delivered to the executive. As such, the information that specifies that the thermostat should be anticipating a temperature of 70° is often termed *feedforward* information. The term **feedforward** is used to distinguish it from feedback, or the sensory qualities of the action itself. Feedforward information represents anticipated sensory consequences of the movement that should be received if the movement is correct, so that the error signal would be zero.

The output of the system (the movement) results in proprioceptive and exteroceptive feedback information, collectively termed movement-produced feedback. When muscles contract, the system receives feedback about forces as well as about the pressures exerted on objects in contact with the skin. Contracting muscles cause movement, and, as a result, feedback from moving joints and the changes in body position with respect to gravity. Finally, movements usually produce alterations in the environment, which are sensed by the receptors for vision and audition, generating yet more feedback. These movement-produced stimuli, whose nature is critically dependent on the production of a particular action by the performer, are compared against their anticipated states in the **comparator**. The computed difference represents error, which is the information returned to the executive. This process refines and maintains the performer's behavior, holding errors at acceptably low levels.

Notice that the stages of processing are critically important in the closed-loop model in figure 4.2. Every time an action's feedback goes to the executive for correction, it must go through the stages of processing. The various stages of processing are all subject to the mechanisms of attention, as discussed in chapter 3. However, this is not the only way in which feedback can be used, and we discuss various lower-level, reflex-like loops later in the chapter.

The closed-loop model in figure 4.2 is useful for understanding the maintenance of a particular state, as is necessary to perform many long-duration activities. For example, simply maintaining posture, where the goal is a natural, upright position, requires feedback. Various learned postures might be controlled in the same way, such as positioning the body

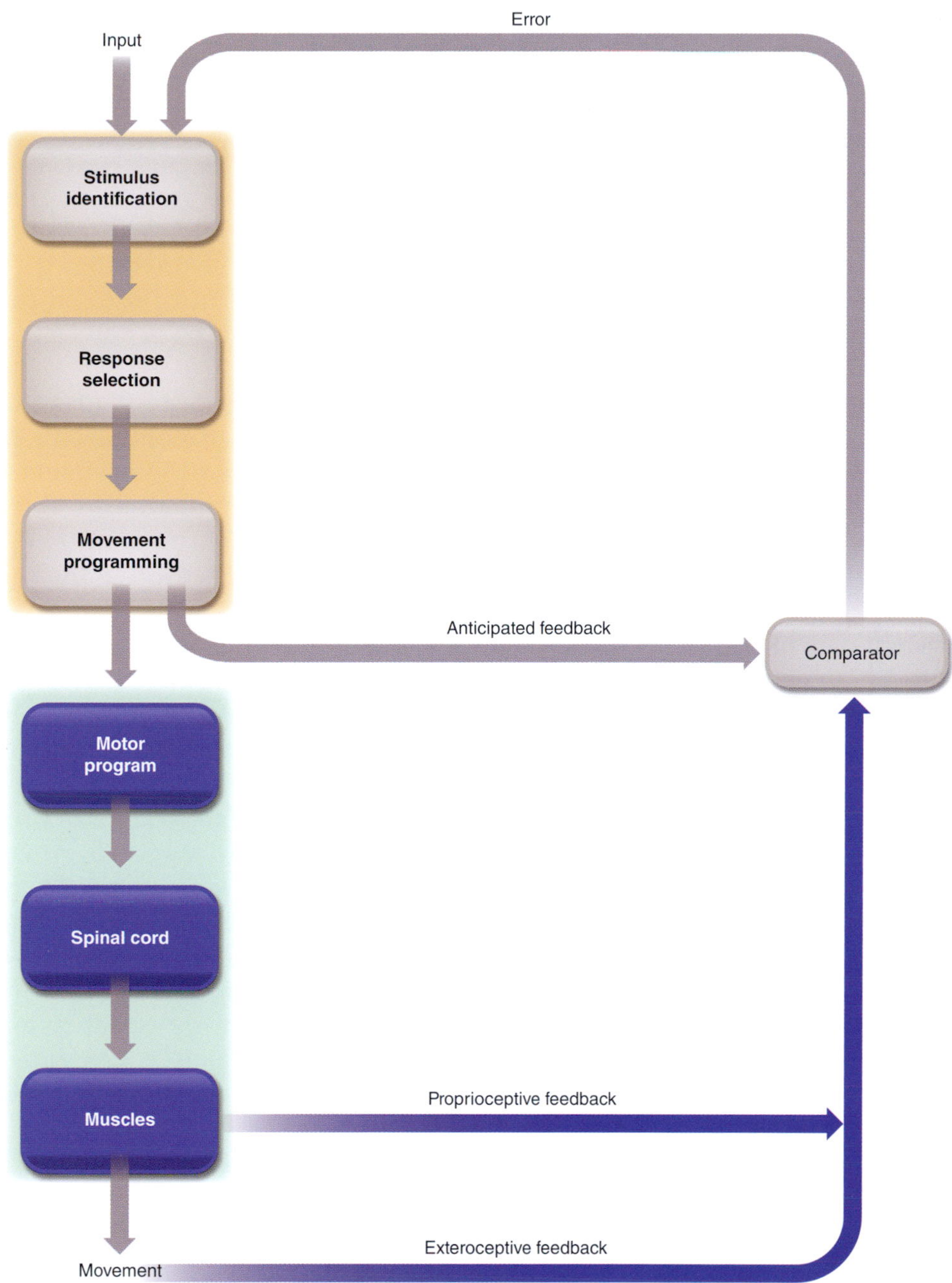

FIGURE 4.2 Expanded conceptual model with the addition of closed-loop components.

in a handstand on the still rings in gymnastics. Also, most movement skills involving the various limbs require an accurate, stable posture as a platform. Without this stable base, the movement, such as throwing darts or shooting a pistol, would be inconsistent. The comparator is thought to define and maintain the desired relative positions of the various limbs as well as the general orientation in space.

Other tasks are far more dynamic. For instance, in a continuous tracking skill, a performer must follow some constantly varying track by moving a control. Steering a car is a classic example, where movements of the steering wheel result from visually detected

Focus on
APPLICATION 4.1

Force Escalation Between Siblings

How often have you seen (or done) this? One sibling pokes the other. The other pokes back. The first pokes again and then the other pokes back. Soon the light poke becomes a jab, then a punch, and often a parent steps in before things get worse. The usual first words are "she started it." But for the motor control student the more interesting issue is why the escalation occurred, perhaps even though neither sibling really intended it to escalate.

The most reasonable explanation appears to be related to the part in the conceptual model (figure 4.2) that goes from movement programming to the comparator, labeled as the anticipated feedback. The anticipated feedback refers to the sensory consequences that are expected to arise from movement, called feedforward information. One important consequence is that feedforward information has a dampening effect on the actual feedback signals that are received, causing a reduction in the intensity of the actual feedback that is experienced. In fact, sometimes the anticipated feedback can actually cancel out the impact of the sensory signals altogether, such as when you try to tickle yourself.

A clever study by Shergill et al. (2003) showed this force-escalation effect quite clearly. They created a mock force-reproduction task between pairs of participants in which each member of the pair simply tried to match the force that they had received from the other participant. The results were dramatic—the force produced by each participant escalated about 38% on each turn. The explanation for the escalation was that since the actual feedback from each self-generated push was dampened (or attenuated) by the anticipated signal, a higher force would need to be generated in order for it to feel like the one just received from the other person. The back and forth increase in force production was not an attempt to injure or one up the other, it was simply a means to overcome the attenuation of the actual proprioceptive feedback by the anticipated feedback signal.

errors in the car's position on the road. There are countless other examples, as this class of activity is one of the most frequently represented in real-world functioning.

Without a doubt, closed-loop control models such as that shown in figure 4.2 are the most effective for understanding these kinds of behavior. Thus, understanding how such a model operates provides considerable insight into human performance and allows many important applications. Understanding the model's limitations for movement control is also important, as discussed next.

Visit the web study guide to read "The Curling Draw" and complete the self-directed learning activities.

Visit the web study guide to read "The Tickle" and complete the self-directed learning activities.

Limitations of Closed-Loop Control

The inclusion of the stages of information processing in the system, as depicted in figure 4.2, illustrates the flexibility in movement control, allowing various strategies and options and altering the nature of the movement produced, depending on the particular circumstances. However, these stages of processing can also represent a big disadvantage—they are slow, especially when there is high demand for processing time, resources, or both, as in many complex actions (discussed in chapter 3). The following sections describe cases in which the closed-loop model is less effective for guiding movement.

Tracking Tasks

One important generalization arising from chapters 2 and 3 was that the stages of information processing require considerable time. Hence the closed-loop system with these processes embedded in it should be slow as well. The stages of processing are critical components in reaction time (RT) situations, where presenting a stimulus requires various processes leading to a movement. The closed-loop model can be regarded in the same way, but the stimulus in this instance is the error that is sent to the executive, and the movement is the correction selected by the executive. Numerous studies of tracking suggest that the system can produce separate corrections at a maximum rate of about three per second. This is about the rate that would be expected if the system were using RT processes as a critical component, reacting to errors by making corrections.

In the conceptual model presented in figure 4.2, each correction is based on a collection of information about the errors that have occurred over the past few hundred milliseconds. This error is processed in the stimulus identification stage; a movement correction is chosen in the response selection stage; and the correction is organized and initiated in the movement programming stage. Therefore, tracking tasks that involve more than three changes in direction per second are often performed very poorly. What makes a fumbled football difficult to retrieve is the frequently unpredictable nature of the bounces it takes. For this reason, closed-loop control processes are most relevant to tasks that are relatively slow or have a long duration in time.

Rapid, Discrete Tasks

A feedback-based view of movement control fails to account adequately for movement production in skills that are very quick, such as the ballistic actions in sport skills (e.g., throwing and kicking) and keypressing while texting. As a general rule with the most rapid human actions, the performer initiates a fully planned movement to achieve the goal. If later sensory information indicates that this movement will be incorrect and thus should be stopped or radically altered, this information is processed relatively slowly and sluggishly, so the first few hundred milliseconds of the original movement occur more or less without modification. As you will see later in this chapter, though, sensory information plays an increasingly important and effective role if the movement is made more slowly.

This sluggishness of feedback processing has implications for controlling the moment-to-moment adjustments in very rapid movements (say, movements less than 250 ms or so), such as typing a text message or plucking the strings of a banjo in a bluegrass song. According to the conceptual model, feedback arising from the rapid movement would not have enough time to be processed before the movement was completed. Thus, the feedback could not influence the fine, moment-to-moment control. More than any other observation, this sluggishness of feedback control has led scientists to believe that most rapid movements must be organized (programmed) in advance. In this view, the moment-to-moment control of rapid movement is included as part of the preorganized program and is not dependent on the relatively slow processes associated with feedback (this idea is discussed more fully in chapter 5).

However, feedback can also act reflexively (bypassing the information-processing stages) to modify movements far more quickly than indicated by the basic closed-loop model presented in figure 4.2. This aspect of feedback control is discussed next.

Proprioceptive Closed-Loop Control

To this point, only one kind of closed-loop processes has been considered: conscious, voluntary control of actions by sensory information. But there are other ways in which sensory information is involved in movement control, especially considering the many kinds of corrections, modifications, and subtle changes in skills that occur automatically (without conscious awareness).

There are a number of reflexive mechanisms that operate below our level of consciousness. One of the most well-known of these is the so-called knee-jerk (or patellar) reflex. If one sits on a table with knee bent and lower leg freely hanging and then a small tap is applied to the patellar tendon (usually with a small rubber hammer, as done by a neurologist), the response to the tap is a brief contraction of the quadriceps muscle (on the thigh) resulting in a small extension (straightening) of the knee. The time from the tap until the quadriceps is activated is only 30 to 50 ms. This reflexive response occurs without any active, voluntary control and occurs far too quickly to have come via the stages of information processing.

Here is what happens. In this seated position, a tap to the patellar tendon, which attaches the kneecap (patella) to the tibia of the lower leg, applies a brief downward movement of the kneecap. Then, because the kneecap is attached to the quadriceps muscle, which (together with the muscle spindles in the quadriceps) is stretched a small amount too, the muscle spindles respond by sending a signal to the spinal cord via afferent (sensory) neurons. These neurons synapse (connect) with efferent (motor) neurons that lead back to the same muscle that was stretched (here, the quadriceps), causing a brief contraction. This occurs very quickly and involuntarily, in part because the afferent and efferent neurons travel a relatively short distance and are connected by a single synapse. Hence, this reflex has been termed the *monosynaptic* stretch reflex. Nearly every skeletal muscle in the body can display this reflex, operating in the same general way.

Take a look at figure 4.3, which is another expansion of our conceptual model. Within the effector box (motor program–spinal cord–muscles), we have added a feedback loop (the so-called M1 loop) from the muscle to the spinal cord and back to the same muscle. This loop is an important component of the monosynaptic stretch reflex. This feedback loop is at a relatively low level in the spinal cord, so the responses do not involve conscious, voluntary control and reflect stereotyped, involuntary, usually very rapid responses to stimuli.

Now suppose that you are a participant in a simple experiment. You are standing, and your task is to hold one of your elbows at a right angle to support a moderate load (such as a book) on your outstretched, palm-up hand. You are instructed to hold the book at the same height and to maintain that position. Suddenly, without you being able to anticipate it, the experimenter adds another book to the load. Your hand begins to drop, but after a delay you compensate for the added load and bring your hand up to the target position again. In all likelihood, your response was nearly immediate and involuntary, but this time more than one reflex was involved. The monosynaptic reflex just described was responsible for an initial, very brief, response to the added load. However, bringing the hand back to the target position likely involved one or more additional reflexes.

The slightly slower (50–80 ms latency) response occurs because the stretched biceps muscle delivered a signal (via afferent neurons from the muscle spindles) to the spinal cord. Here, though, this signal is also sent up the spinal cord, and these neurons synapse with several higher-level neurons. Then the signal is sent back down the pathway in the spinal cord where it synapses with the motor neurons leading to the biceps muscle, causing a second burst of biceps activity. This second burst of activity (labeled M2 in figure 4.3) is stronger and more sustained than the first one (the monosynaptic, **M1**, response), but it arrives with a slightly greater delay (50–80 ms) because the signal had to travel farther and because several synapses were involved. The M2 loop in figure 4.3 goes from the muscle to higher levels in the CNS. Together, these monosynaptic (M1) and multisynaptic (**M2**) reflexes are just two of the many types of reflexive mechanisms by which actions can be modified quickly (and automatically), leading toward goal achievement in a closed-loop manner.

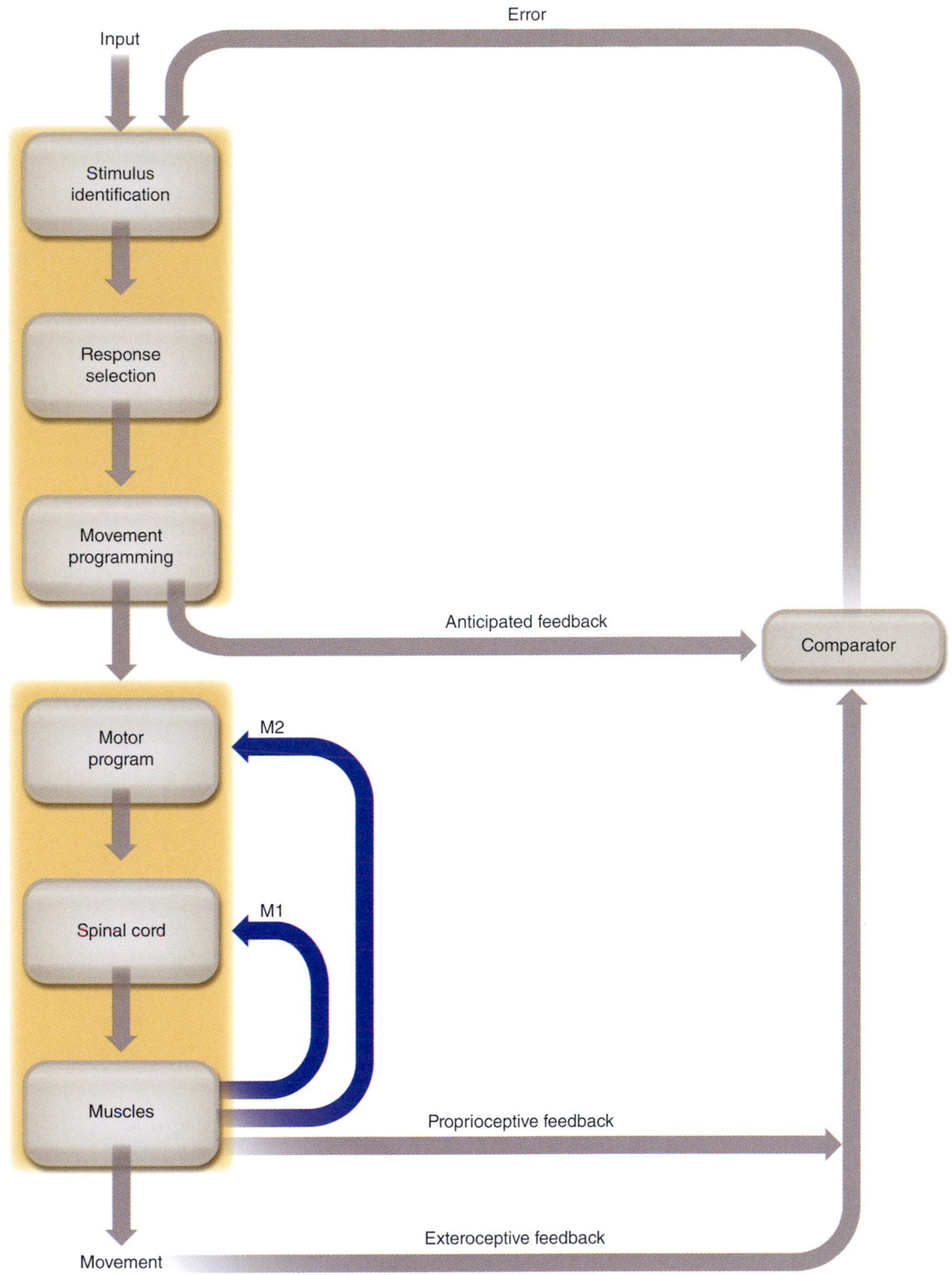

FIGURE 4.3 Conceptual model with the addition of M1 and M2 loops.

Principles of Visual Control

Vision seems to operate somewhat differently than the proprioceptive reflexes we have just seen. Vision, of course, has a very important role in everyday activities, and people deprived of vision have a relatively difficult time functioning in our visually dominated world. But vision also appears to operate somewhat differently from the other senses in the support of skills. For these reasons, vision deserves a place of its own in this chapter.

Two Visual Systems

Over the past 40 years or so, it has become increasingly clear that two essentially separate visual systems underlie human functioning, rather than just one. Visual information is delivered from the retina of the eye along two separate processing streams to different places in the brain, and there is good evidence that these two pathways of information are used differently in the control of behavior.

These two systems, illustrated in figure 4.4, are called the **dorsal stream** and the **ventral stream** because of their anatomical distinctions (Ungerleider & Mishkin, 1982). Visual information in both streams travels first from the retina of the eye to the primary visual cortex. However, at that point it is thought that visual information processing becomes specialized. Information useful for the identification of an object is sent to the inferotemporal cortex via the ventral stream. Information that is used specifically for the control of movement within the visual environment is sent to the posterior parietal cortex via the dorsal stream.

The ventral stream is specialized for conscious identification of objects that lie primarily in the center of the visual field. Its major function seems to be providing answers to the general question, "What is it?" Hence we use this system to look at and identify something, such as the words on this page you are reading now. This system contributes to conscious perception of objects and is severely degraded by dim lighting conditions, as you know from your attempts to read a book without adequate light.

The dorsal stream is believed to be specialized for movement control. Distinct from the ventral stream, which is sensitive only to events in central vision, dorsal vision involves the entire visual field, central and peripheral. Dorsal vision operates nonconsciously, contributing to the fine control of movements without our awareness (see Focus on Research 4.1). Clearly, one reason it is difficult to recognize the existence of dorsal vision is that it is nonconscious. Its function is to provide answers to the questions "Where is it?" or perhaps "Where am I relative to it?"

Visual Control of Movement

How is visual information used for movement control, and what factors determine its effectiveness? It is useful to divide this discussion

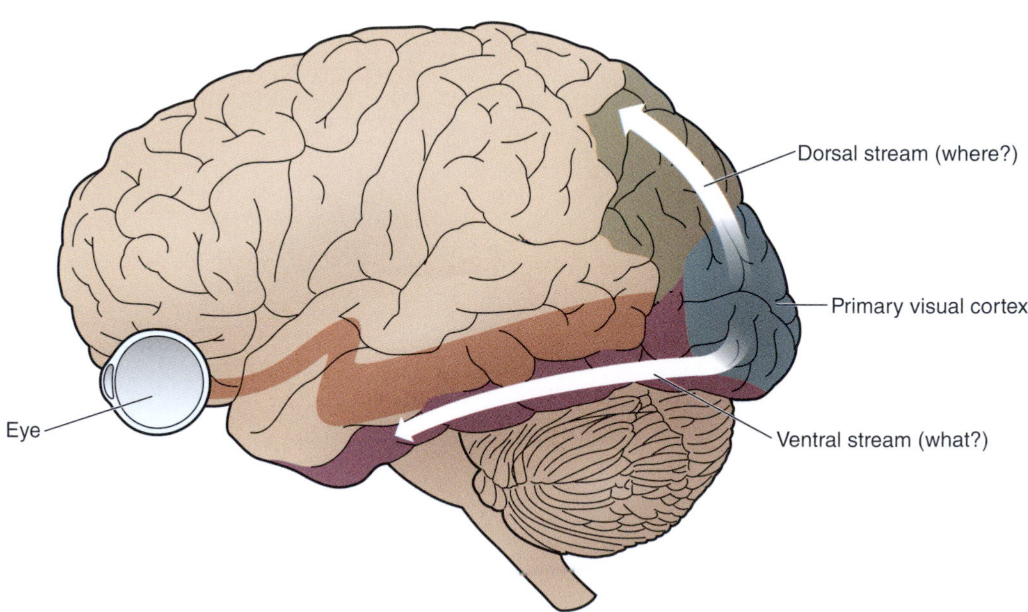

FIGURE 4.4 Illustration of dorsal and ventral stream pathways in the brain.

Focus on RESEARCH 4.1

Blindsight Reveals Dorsal and Ventral Stream Processing

The term **blindsight** might seem to be an oxymoron, but this curious phenomenon led many to the discovery of the dorsal visual system. Blindsight is usually defined as a medical condition in which the person can respond to visual stimuli without consciously perceiving them. According to Weiskrantz (2007), the idea originally stemmed from work on the visual cortex of monkeys, where it was demonstrated that the animal, although technically blind, could still respond to various kinds of visual stimuli. Later studies demonstrated the phenomenon in humans (e.g., Humphrey, 1974; Weiskrantz et al., 1974).

Perhaps the most startling, and most convincing, evidence came from the study of two human neurological patients, TN and DB (the patients' initials). Following two successive strokes, TN had major neurological damage in his visual cortex, which rendered him blind in both eyes by all traditional measures of vision. Researchers took TN to a hallway and asked him to walk down the hallway without his usual cane. Unbeknownst to TN, researchers had placed several objects in the hall around which he would have to negotiate. To the researchers' amazement, TN avoided them all, even pressing himself against the wall to avoid a trash can. Patient DB, whose occipital cortex had been removed surgically because of a tumor, was also blind according to traditional measures of vision. Researchers used forced-choice tests, in which DB was asked to guess where, between two locations in front of him, an object had been placed. His guesses were considerably more accurate than chance, even though he could not see the objects. He was also sensitive to long or short object presentation intervals, to color, contrast, and motion, and to the onset and offset of the target's presence. Very clearly, both of these patients were "seeing" objects about which they were not consciously aware of (de Gelder et al., 2008; Weiskrantz et al., 1974).

These findings eventually were interpreted to mean that we possess two visual systems: a ventral system with access to consciousness (which DB and TN had lost completely) and a dorsal system that does not have access to consciousness (which was intact in DB and TN). (The anatomical pathways for these systems are illustrated in figure 4.4.) These observations involving patients, together with experimental evidence involving sighted individuals performing actions under visual illusion conditions (e.g., Bridgeman et al., 1981), demonstrate clearly that we can respond to objects in our environment unconsciously, guided by visual information of which we are completely unaware.

Exploring Further

1. Patients with optic ataxia and visual agnosia have been the focus of study by neurophysiologists. What information have these patients provided to researchers with regard to the distinction between ventral and dorsal visual streams?
2. What types of visual illusions have been used in research to separate dorsal and ventral stream processing?

into separate parts, particularly because it deals with the separate roles of the dorsal and ventral systems.

Despite the characterization of ventral vision as a system for object identification, it would be wrong to conclude that it has no role in movement control. Ventral vision has access to consciousness, so it is processed through the information-processing stages discussed in chapter 2, leading to action in much the same way as any other information source. In the conceptual model in figure 4.3, vision can be seen as just another source of information arising from action, so its only access to the loop would be through the stages of information processing. In one sense, this is obvious. You can look at and consciously identify an oncoming car, which would then lead to the decision to try to avoid it. Ventral vision is critically involved here, and failures to identify objects properly can lead to serious errors. This is particularly important in night driving, when the ventral system's accuracy (visual acuity) is degraded considerably.

Before realizing there could be a dorsal system for movement control, scientists believed that a conscious ventral system was the only way visual information could influence action. In this outdated view, a baseball batter watching a pitch come toward the plate relied only on the relatively slow processes in the information-processing stages to detect the ball's flight pattern and to initiate changes in movement control. This idea was supported by numerous experiments that seemed to show that visual control of action was particularly slow and cumbersome. However, recent information about the dorsal visual system, together with the ideas about optical-flow processes in vision, has markedly changed our understanding of visual information processing for action.

Ventral Stream in Movement Control

The ventral stream provides information about the "what" in motor control. An expert baseball batter knows that different types of pitches have different spins—rotations of the ball that help the batter to predict a pitch's trajectory. A dental assistant must know not only the difference between the shape of a sickle probe and a periodontal probe but also needs to be able to identify each with an associated verbal label when called upon. Thus, the ventral stream usually needs information presented in well-lit visual conditions in order to identify object information, which then can be used for conscious, decision-making processes for action.

Object identification, via the ventral stream, plays a crucial role in movement planning before the initiation of an action. For example, have a look at the objects in figure 4.5 and think about which grip you would use to pick up each object. For the juice glass (object *a*), a full-hand grip is needed. A three- or four-finger grip is needed for the beer mug (object *b*), but a thumb-and-finger grip is appropriate for the teacup (object *c*). The pen (object *d*) is usually picked up with a precision grip if the performer intends to use it to write something. However, if the performer intends to use the pen as a tool—say, to stab a hole in a cardboard box—then a power grip would be used. Thus, information provided by the ventral stream is combined with the action goal for further processing in the movement planning stages (see Rosenbaum et al., 2013, for a fuller treatment).

Dorsal Stream in Movement Control

James J. Gibson changed the way scientists theorized about the visual control of movement (e.g., Gibson, 1966). A particularly important concept promoted by Gibson was that of optical-flow patterns, and how this information was used by the dorsal visual system to control body movement (such as balance) and to provide information about the timing of events, such as the time to close a gap between the performer and an object.

For example, riding a bicycle along a busy path or street requires rapidly processing many sources of visual information. The cyclist needs be aware of traffic signs and signals, pedestrians crossing the street, cars turning away and into the oncoming path, and, of course, the dreaded opening of the driver's door of a parked car. As the cyclist looks into this textured environment, each

FIGURE 4.5 The ventral stream identifies the visual properties of an object for the purpose of advance grip planning of objects *a* through *d*. However, the visual properties of objects do not tell the whole story—intentions about what action will be performed with an object also determine which grip to use. For example, think about how you would grip object *d* if you were planning to write with it, and compare that to how you would grip object *d* if you planned to use it to stab a hole in a cardboard box (see Rosenbaum et al., 2013).

visible feature reflects rays of light, which enter the eyes at specific angles; collectively, this is called the **optical array**. Because the cyclist is moving, each object in the environment shifts its position relative to the cyclist continuously, causing a change in the information provided by the optical array. This change in information is termed **optical flow** and can be thought of as a flow of light across the retina. The important point is that optical flow provides numerous important kinds of information about the cyclist's movement through the environment, such as

- time before a collision between the cyclist and an object,
- direction of movement relative to objects in the environment,
- movement of environmental objects relative to the cyclist,
- stability and balance of the cyclist, and
- velocity of movement through the environment.

Time-to-Contact Information Figure 4.6 presents an example of how the optical array picks up information about an object first seen in the distance (say 25 m [meters] away—object A), then at a closer distance (15 m away—object B), then at a very close distance (5 m—object C). The angle of light given from the edges of the object at distance A is very small (α_1); it increases slightly as it gets 10 m closer (α_2), and then it expands at a much more rapid rate over the next 10 m (α_3).

The pattern of optical flow from an oncoming object, such as parked car, indicates the time remaining until the object reaches the plane of the eye (Lee & Young, 1985). The retinal image of an approaching object expands as the object approaches, and it expands more quickly as the object approaches more quickly. These changes in optical flow are picked up by the dorsal system, providing information about object distance, as well as the time until the object will contact the plane of the eye. This time-to-contact information, or **tau** (τ), which is defined as the retinal image size divided by the image's rate of change in size, is proportional to the time remaining until contact. Thus, τ is derived from optical-flow information and used by the dorsal stream to specify time-to-contact with the object. This timing information is critical in interceptive actions involving coincident timing, such as striking or catching a ball, driving, or preparing the body for entry into the water during a dive.

Direction of Movement of Objects One can run through a forest, avoiding trees successfully, by using optical-flow information about the relative rates of change in the visual angles of the trees. For example, assume that the objects shown in figure 4.7 are trees. For tree A, the angles of light from the left and

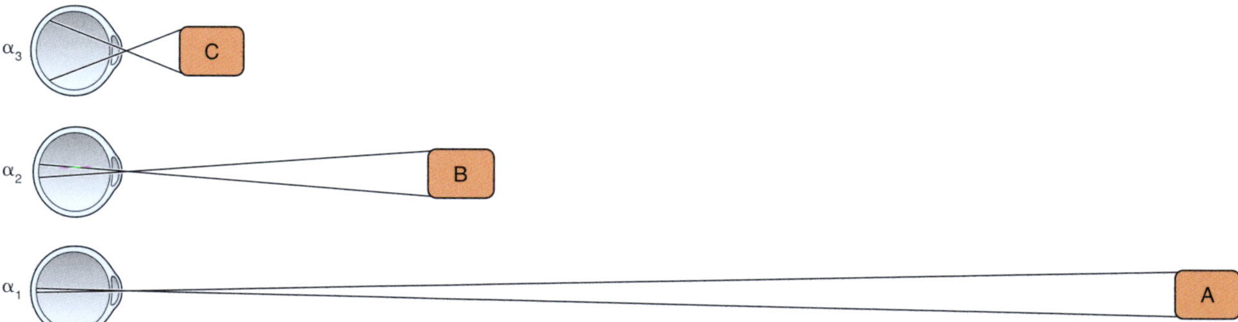

FIGURE 4.6 Objects A, B, and C are traveling at the same velocity in the right-to-left direction toward an eye (gray circles). The sizes of the object's optical image on the rear of the eye (the retina) at different distances are α_1, α_2, and α_3. Notice that when the object travels from A to B, the size of the retinal image changes at a slower rate than it does for the same distance covered from B to C. These changes in optical flow are picked up by the dorsal system, providing information about object distance and time until the object will contact the plane of the eye.

As a mountain biker navigates the trail, she processes a continuously changing stream of visual information about the environment. Describe one example each of information processed by the ventral and dorsal systems by this mountain biker.

right edges expand at the same rate from both sides, indicating that the eye is traveling directly toward tree A and will collide with it. For tree B, on the other hand, the angles of light from the right side are expanding systematically more slowly than those from the left side. This indicates that the eye will pass to the right of tree B.

Balance Maintaining balance has traditionally been the domain of proprioceptive information in detecting sway and loss of stability. For example, when the body sways forward, the ankle joint is moved and the associated musculature is stretched, producing movement signals from the muscle spindles and other proprioceptors. Also, receptors in the inner ear are sensitive to movements of the head, providing information about body sway and balance.

However, vision also plays a key role in balance control. Look straight ahead at an object on the wall. Without shifting your direction of gaze, move your head slightly forward and backward and pay attention to the changes in visual information. You will probably notice that the objects in peripheral vision seem to sweep rapidly back and forth and that these changes are dependent on your head movement. Could this peripheral information serve for balance control?

Lee and Aronson (1974) demonstrated that balance is strongly affected by varying the visual information, suggesting that the optical-flow variables in peripheral vision are critical to balance. In their experiment, the participant stood in a special small room surrounded by walls suspended from a very high ceiling; the walls did not quite touch the floor. The walls could be moved with the floor kept still, to

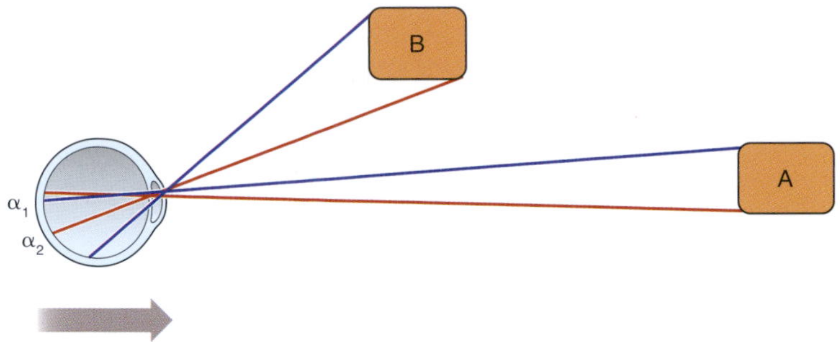

FIGURE 4.7 The observer, represented here by an eye, is heading toward object A, and will pass to the right of object B; in our example, A and B are trees. The dorsal system detects that the rays of light from both sides of tree A are expanding at about the same rate, whereas the light rays from the left side of tree B are expanding more quickly than are those from the right side. This indicates that if the observer doesn't change course she will collide with tree A and will pass to the right of tree B.

influence only the optical-flow information. Moving the walls slightly away caused the participant to sway slightly forward, and moving the walls closer caused the participant to sway backward. With a little child, an away movement of the walls could cause the participant to stumble forward, and a toward movement of the walls could cause a rather ungraceful plop into a sitting position (see figure 4.8).

Moving the wall toward the person generates optical-flow information that ordinarily means the head is moving forward—that is, that the person is out of balance and falling forward. The automatic postural compensation is to sway backward. Such visually based compensations are far faster than can be explained by conscious processing in the ventral system, with latencies of about 100 ms (Nashner & Berthoz, 1978). These experiments suggest that optical-flow information and the dorsal system are critically involved in controlling normal balancing activities.

This role of vision in balance control has strong implications for learned postures as well. In performing a handstand on the still rings, where it is important to remain as motionless as possible, the visual system can signal very small changes in posture, providing a basis for tiny corrections to hold the posture steady.

Processing Visual Feedback In some situations visual information can be used very rapidly (with latencies less than 100 ms) to

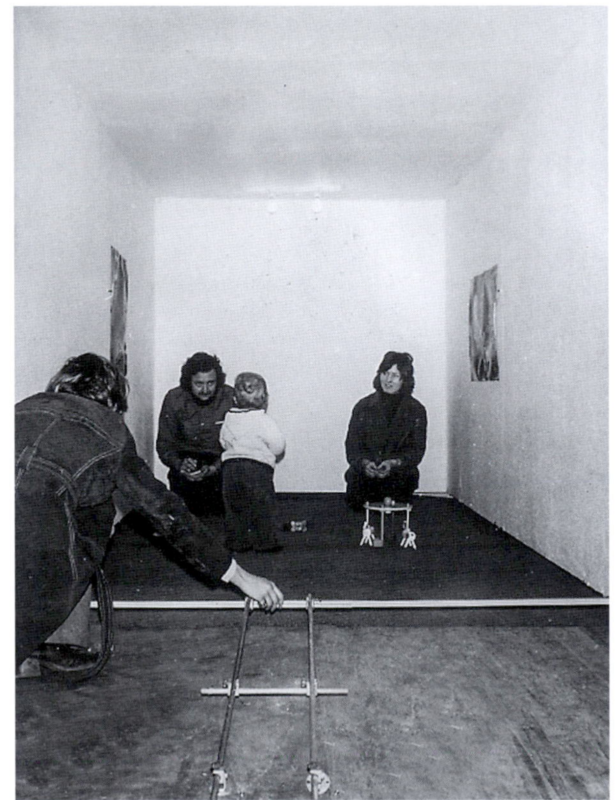

FIGURE 4.8 David N. Lee's moving room apparatus. Moving the walls forward (away from the camera) made the young child sway forward, and moving the wall backward caused the child to plop into a sitting position. This evidence suggests that vision is critical for balance. (David Lee is second from the left in this photo.)

make adjustments in the control of movement. In other situations, however, visually based corrections involve the relatively slow stages of information processing, and one line of the research has been to identify how much time is needed to conduct this processing activity.

Following the initial work by Woodworth (1899), a unique strategy was devised by Keele and Posner (1968) to measure the time to process visual feedback. The participant's goal was to complete an aimed hand movement to a target with minimal spatial and temporal error. The target distance was 15 cm, and there were four target goal MTs (150, 250, 350, and 450 ms). Thus, the movements were completed in times that ranged from very rapid (150 ms goal, but they were actually completed in 185–190 ms) to fairly slow (450 ms). Participants were given verbal feedback about their actual MTs after each trial to help them to move in the instructed MT. A critically important feature of the research design was that participants completed some of the trials in the dark—the ambient lights were suddenly, and *randomly*, extinguished on one-half of the trials just at the initiation of the movement. The prediction was simple: If visual feedback was used to guide the movement onto the target, then having the ambient lights on should produce more accurate aims than when the ambient lights were off. But if the movement was made too fast to *use* visual feedback, then no differences in accuracy would be expected.

Keele and Posner's results are presented in figure 4.9. The first thing to note is that as the MTs became longer in time, the accuracy in hitting the target improved, but mainly so for the movements made with the lights on. It is important to note that the accuracies with the lights on versus lights off were identical for the shortest MT, and the curves diverged as movements became longer in time. These data suggest that the minimum time to use visual feedback in these actions was approximately 190–250 ms. Thus, slower movements (> 250 ms) benefited from having the ambient lights on.

Estimates of the minimum time for visual information processing have provided more

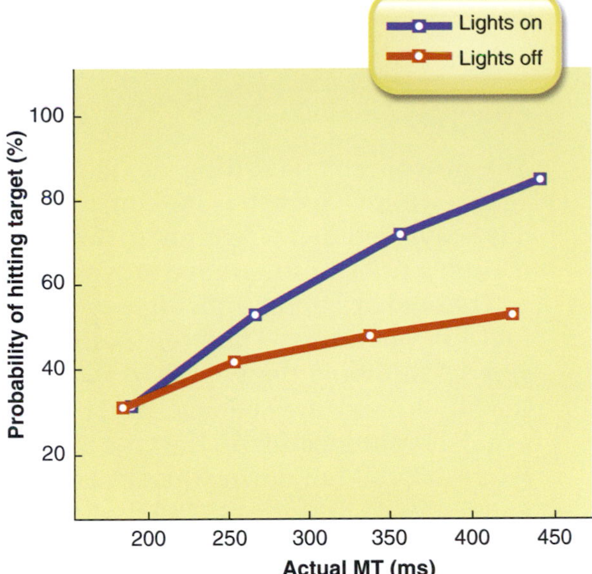

FIGURE 4.9 Movements completed in times less than 200 ms showed no improvement in accuracy with the ambient lights on (compared to lights off), but movements made in times longer than 250 ms did benefit from having the lights on.

clarity since the research of Keele and Posner. If the vision offset is unexpected, as in Keele and Posner's task, the amount of time needed to process the visual feedback is roughly similar to that for an RT-task. However, if the availability of visual feedback can be predicted, then the processing time is reduced considerably, perhaps to as low as 80–100 ms (Elliott, Hansen, & Grierson, 2010).

Visit the web study guide to read "Cool Papa Bell" and complete the self-directed learning activities.

Vision in the Conceptual Model

The distinction between dorsal- and ventral-stream visual processing has obvious implications for our conceptual model as presented in figure 4.3. Although ventral-stream processing would still occur as suggested in the model (through the slow processing stages, in the outer loop), dorsal-stream processing would be expected to be unconscious.

Focus on RESEARCH 4.2

Gaze Control

Eye-movement recording devices provide researchers with precise measures of gaze—where a person is looking during an action or perceptual event. These studies have revealed that we voluntarily control gaze using two different types of eye movements: smooth-pursuit eye movements and discrete-saccadic movements.

The goal of smooth-pursuit movements is to keep the target of our gaze fixed on the fovea of the retina. The eyes fixate on an object that is either motionless or moving slowly, allowing the viewer to pick up precise detail. Faster object movements, on the other hand, are characterized by brief fixations and rapid shifts (called *saccades*) to a different location in the visual environment. Information is picked up during the fixations, but not during the saccades between fixations. These rapid eye movements and fixations provide us with the capability to pick up information rapidly from a wide range of sources in our visual environment, for example as required when driving (looking out the front and side windows, checking the various mirrors, etc.).

Researchers have discovered something very interesting about the way highly skilled and less-skilled athletes use vision just before the onset of action. Expert performers keep their eyes fixated for a longer period of time just before movement onset than do non-experts. Moreover, individuals can improve their performance if they are trained to fixate their gaze for a longer period of time just before action. These findings have been replicated in many different types of activities (e.g., basketball free-throw shooting, target shooting, golf, juggling) and have been termed the **quiet-eye effect** (see Vickers, 2007, for a good review).

There remains considerable uncertainty regarding the mechanism(s) responsible for the quiet-eye effect. One hypothesis is that a prolonged gaze period might stabilize the perceptual system, facilitating movement processes dependent on them. Another view is that this period of inactivity provides an opportunity to shift attentional resources to an optimal-control focus (see focus of attention discussion in chapter 3). Although other possible reasons cannot be excluded, the generality of the quiet-eye effect suggests that these mechanisms accompany skill development.

Exploring Further

1. What are rods and cones of the eye, and what specific information do they contribute to vision?
2. What is the difference between looking and seeing? How does the activity known as parkour reveal that what traceurs and traceuses see is different from what the rest of us see?

Because dorsal-stream processing is nonconscious, relatively fast, and inflexible, it is fed back to relatively low levels in the central nervous system, considerably downstream from the processes that select and initiate movement but upstream from the muscles and the spinal cord. Thus, dorsal vision can be thought of as operating at intermediate levels of the system to make minor adjustments in already programmed actions, such as compensation for head movement in the golf swing and alterations in posture to maintain balance on the still rings. For this reason, we have added a feedback loop from the resulting movement to the level of the motor program in figure 4.10.

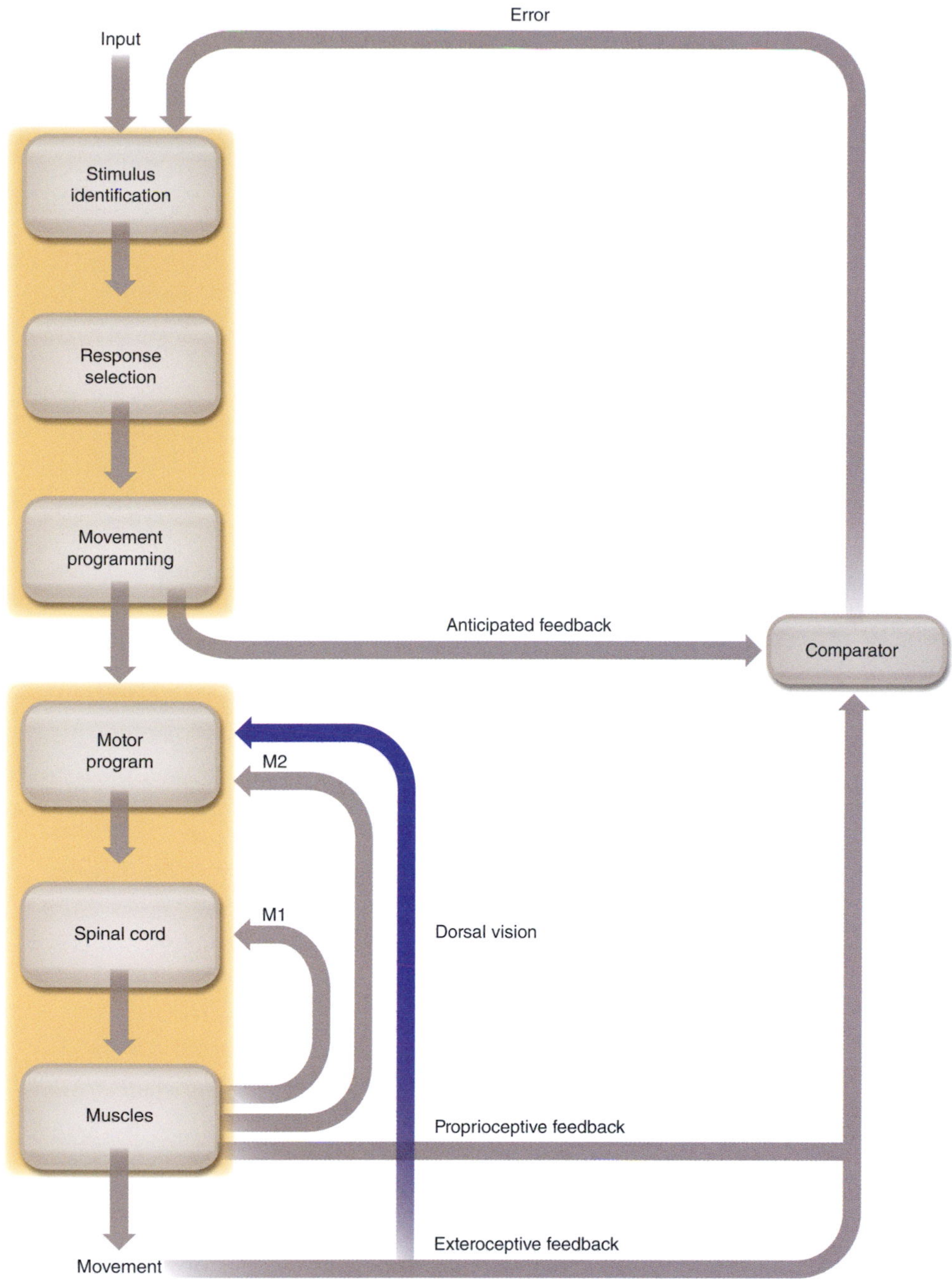

FIGURE 4.10 Conceptual model with the addition of dorsal-stream loop.

Audition and Motor Control

The role of auditory feedback in movement is less understood, perhaps because of the dominant role of vision and the attention given to it by researchers. Yet we know that audition can have profound effects on motor control. For example, a speaker who talks into a microphone at a large concert hall and hears his voice projected from the sound system at the very back of the hall will experience a delay in hearing the auditory feedback of his voice. Such delays are well known to increase speech errors and slowed rates of speaking. Auditory delays can disrupt other forms of movement control, such as playing a musical instrument (Pfordresher & Dalla Bella, 2011) or typing buttons on a phone that has briefly

Focus on
APPLICATION 4.2

Visibility in Nighttime Car–Truck Accidents

A not uncommon motor vehicle accident occurs at nighttime—the driver of a car going at the posted speed limit runs into the back of a vehicle that is stopped or moving very slowly (perhaps a truck on a hill). The driver of the car had no trouble seeing the taillights on the back of the parked or slowly moving vehicle. Rather, the problem was that the driver did not know what the lights were "doing." What could be going on here?

On a clear night, the driver can probably see the taillights from quite a long distance away (perhaps a mile or so). Presumably, the rate of visual expansion (in this case, the lights appearing to move farther apart) of the optical flow on the retina provides information that the vehicle ahead is stopped (or going very slowly), instead of going at the same speed as the driver in the car. But the problem is that the rate of expansion is so small (smaller than the threshold rate for detecting any expansion, which is 0.2 degrees/second). This means that the following driver cannot perceive the expansion until the car is about 400 ft (about 133 m) from the object, where it is just possible to detect that the optical array is expanding. The problem is that 400 ft is very close to the distance over which a car at 60 mph (about 95 kph) can be brought to a complete stop—and this is under ideal (i.e., dry, good visibility) conditions. Therefore, the following driver does not perceive that the truck is moving far more slowly than he is until it is almost too late. Unless the following driver is extremely alert, the car can easily strike the slow-moving truck.

Another issue is that, at a very far distance away, the visibility of taillights does not necessarily indicate to the driver that what she is approaching is actually a truck. It could be lights on two separate objects, such as road signs (spaced apart by a small distance), or two motorcycle taillights, or something other than a vehicle. Some proponents of vehicle safety have advocated placing additional retro-reflective material on trucks to make them more visible or conspicuous. But this really does not reduce the visual perception problem raised here, because the rate of visual expansion of the retro-reflective material is essentially the same as that of the lights. Therefore, when you are 500 ft (about 150 m) from the truck, you have the same problem of not being able to identify what the object is doing, speed-wise.

delayed sounds. Ironically, delayed auditory feedback is sometimes used in the treatment of stuttering, perhaps because it causes individuals to slow their speech (Lawrence & Barclay, 1998).

A good example of the important role of audition in sport is the controversy in tennis involving players such as Maria Sharapova and Rafael Nadal. The issue concerns the influence of loud grunts that coincide with the contact of the ball and racket. Some sport commentators have gone as far as to suggest that grunting represents a form of cheating. And they may have a valid argument. A study by Sinnett and Kingstone (2010) found that video clips of ground shots accompanied by a burst of white noise were responded to more slowly and less accurately than the same videos shown without the white noise. This finding might suggest that the sound of the ball–racket contact is a critical component of the perceptual process, and masking or interfering with the sound can disrupt the perceiver's performance. This finding is further

Focus on

APPLICATION 4.3

When Vision Distorts Performance

In chapter 3, we discussed the various properties of attention. Directing one's attention toward a specific external source is considered an important mechanism, and vision can provide information critical for effective performance. However, performers often find that visual control dominates the other senses and that visual information leads to an unavoidable capture of attention. In fact, many believe that vision tends to dominate all other sources for our attention, and this dominance does not always produce positive outcomes. In many activities, performers have a choice of the modes of control they use, such as the race car driver or pilot who can monitor the sounds of the engine or kinesthetic information as opposed to the visual information provided by numerous cockpit gauges or information seen through the windscreen. And sometimes this nonvisual information is more reliable than the information provided by vision.

Visual information is obviously very important in many situations, but in other situations an overreliance on vision can result in ineffective performance. A good example comes from sailboat racing, which is rich in visual information about the aerodynamic shapes of the sails and the way the wind is flowing over them. This visual information can yield relatively good performance. However, focusing on vision is ignoring other forms of information, such as the sounds the boat makes as it goes through the water, the action and position of the hull felt by the "seat of the pants," and forces on the tiller, all of which provide additional useful information about speed—but only if the person at the helm is attending to them. Some racing sailors have used blindfolded training methods in an attempt to learn to decrease their reliance on vision and share the attentional resources among other internal targets (senses) to optimize performance. The idea is that when vision is prevented for a long time, the sailors develop sensitivity to the less dominant sources of information.

Visual illusions provide a powerful demonstration of visual dominance effects. In the *size–weight illusion*, for example, two opaque containers, one much larger than the other, are filled with equal amounts of sand so that they are of identical weights. The participant is asked to lift both and judge which one is heavier. Vision (and experience) tells us that a larger container is usually heavier than a smaller one, and when proprioception fails to confirm that, we naturally conclude the opposite—that the *smaller* container must have more weight in it than the larger container. Here, visual information is overriding proprioception.

The McGurk effect reveals a vision–audition interaction. For example, a participant is asked to watch and listen to a video of someone speaking a word over and over again (e.g., "blow"). If you close your eyes and listen to the audio portion of the video it is obvious that the person is saying "blow." But the video is actually of someone mouthing the word "flow" over and over again, with "blow" being given on the audio. Most people who watch the video and also listen to the audio report that the person is saying "flow," even though what is actually heard is "blow." And sometimes people even report something completely different than either "flow" or "blow." Here, vision is distorting the (true) information provided by audition.

The McGurk effect and the size–weight illusion are just two examples of how visual dominance tends to overshadow the contributions made by the other senses.

supported by tennis research showing that predictive judgments of ball landing position corresponded to the loudness of the ball contact—the louder the contact, the further (deeper) into the court was the predicted landing position of the ball (Cañal-Bruland et al., 2018). Therefore, masking or distorting the quality of this auditory information with loud grunts could play a disruptive role.

Auditory information can also conflict with vision to create a distorted perception. For example, an outfielder in softball might be fooled into predicting that a line drive seen leaving a batter's bat will go over her head. In fact, the sound of the bat–ball contact correctly indicated that it was a softly hit ball requiring the outfielder to run in, rather than back. Here the visual information distorted the correct information provided by sound (see Gray, 2009, for more). The overshadowing of audition by vision is also illustrated in the McGurk effect, discussed in Focus on Application 4.3.

Visit the web study guide to read "Craps and Weighted Bats" and complete the self-directed learning activities.

Summary

The effectiveness with which a performer processes various forms of sensory information often determines overall performance level. Sensory signals from the environment are usually termed exteroceptive information, whereas those from the body are termed proprioceptive information. For human performance it is useful to think of these signals as operating in a closed-loop control system, which contains an executive for decision making, an effector for carrying out the actions, feedback about the state of the environment, and a comparator to contrast the environmental state with the system's goal.

In the conceptual model of human performance, closed-loop control is added to the stages of information processing discussed in previous chapters. This model is particularly effective for understanding how slower actions as well as continuous tasks (such as tracking) are performed. To the conceptual model are then added several reflex-like processes that account for corrections without involving the information-processing stages. In moving from the M1, M2, and **M3** (or voluntary reaction time), these responses show systematically increased flexibility and increased latency. Finally, vision is considered as a special case of closed-loop control. Two visual streams are introduced, a dorsal stream for motor control and a ventral stream for object identification, and the role of the dorsal stream in balance and in producing and correcting actions is considered. These sensory systems are then integrated into the conceptual model, which helps to show how these various sensory events can support or modify skilled actions and under what conditions they operate.

WEB STUDY GUIDE ACTIVITIES

The student web study guide offers these activities to help you build and apply your knowledge of the concepts in this chapter.

Interactive Learning

Activity 4.1: Identify the roles of the sensory organs involved in proprioception by matching each receptor with its location and function.

Activity 4.2: Identify which component of a closed-loop control system relates to each of a series of actions.

Activity 4.3: Indicate whether each in a list of characteristics applies to the dorsal or ventral visual processing stream.

Activity 4.4: Choose the labels for the conceptual model of motor control to review its stages, including closed-loop control pathways and visual stream information.

Principles-to-Application Exercise

Activity 4.5: The principles-to-application exercise for this chapter prompts you to choose an activity, identify sources of proprioceptive and exteroceptive information during the activity, and evaluate which sources of information are useful to the performer. You will also apply the concept of closed-loop control to the activity.

Motor Control in Everyday Actions Narratives

The Magnetic Hill

The Curling Draw

The Tickle

Cool Papa Bell

Craps and Weighted Bats

Check Your Understanding

1. Name the four distinct parts of a closed-loop control system. Describe how each of these parts might function for a child stacking toy blocks.
2. Explain how the pattern of optical flow can inform an outfielder attempting to catch a fly ball about when and where the ball will reach the height of the fielder's glove.
3. How does ventral-stream movement control play a role in movement planning when opening various doors throughout your day?

Apply Your Knowledge

1. Several sources of sensory information are available to a skier as she makes her way down an alpine ski run. Describe and provide examples of exteroceptive and proprioceptive information that she might receive during her run, and indicate why this information is important for movement.
2. How closed-loop control processes are used (if at all) is dependent on the task that is performed. Contrast the role played by closed-loop control processes for casting a fishing line and tracing a clothing pattern onto fabric. Would this role change if either of the tasks were sped up?

Suggestions for Further Reading

An overview of closed-loop control of movement is provided by Ghez and Krakauer (2000), with specific roles assigned to spinal reflexes presented by Pearson and Gordon (2012). Tresilian (2012, ch. 3) provides an exquisitely detailed review of the anatomy and roles of the various proprioceptors in motor control. Elliott and Khan (2010) edited an excellent book that provides many contributions regarding the various roles of vision in motor control. The contributions of ventral- and dorsal-stream processing are debated in Norman (2002). And a more comprehensive discussion of the various topics presented in this chapter can be found in chapter 5 of Schmidt at al. (2019). See the reference list for these additional resources.

5

Motor Programs

Motor Control of Brief Actions

KEY TERMS

central pattern generator (CPG)
deafferentation
generalized motor program (GMP)
invariant features
motor program
novelty problem
open-loop control
parameterized
parameters
reflex-reversal phenomenon
relative timing
sensory neuropathy
startle RT
storage problem
surface feature

CHAPTER OUTLINE

CHAPTER OBJECTIVES

Chapter 5 describes how motor programs are used in the control of movement. This chapter will help you to understand

- motor control as an open-loop system and the role of motor programs,
- experimental evidence for motor programs,
- limitations and problems in the simple motor program concept, and
- generalized motor programs and evidence for this expanded concept.

Watching a diver complete a rapid, complex, acrobatic maneuver while freefalling through space toward the pool leaves the impression of a single, fluid, coordinated motion. How does the skilled diver produce so many movements so quickly? What controls them, and how are they combined to form a whole? The skilled diver gives us the impression that these quick movements might be organized in advance and performed without much feedback control, or at least, not using the relatively slow kinds of feedback processing that we discussed in chapter 4.

This chapter investigates the idea of open-loop control, introducing the concept of the motor program as responsible for this kind of movement control. Then the various feedback pathways discussed in the previous chapter are examined as to their interaction with motor programs, giving a more complete picture of the interplay of central and peripheral contributions to movements. The chapter also focuses on the concept of a **generalized motor program (GMP)**, a theory that can account for the common observation that movements can be varied along certain dimensions—for example, playing the guitar or a piano sequence slower or faster (or louder or softer) without sacrificing its underlying structure (i.e., the rhythm).

In many actions, particularly quick ones produced in stable and predictable environments (e.g., springboard diving, hammering), most people would assume that a performer somehow plans the movement in advance and then triggers it, allowing the action to run its course without much modification of the individual elements. Also, the performer does not seem to have much awareness or conscious control over the movement once it's triggered into action; the movement just seems to "take care of itself." Perhaps this is obvious. Certainly you cannot have direct, conscious control of the thousands of individual muscle contractions and joint movements—all the *degrees of freedom* that must be coordinated as the skilled action is unfolding. There is simply too much going on for the limited-capacity attentional mechanisms (which we have discussed in chapters 3 and 4) to control any one of them individually.

If these individual contractions are not controlled directly by processes of which you are aware, how then *are* they controlled and regulated? In many ways, this question is one of the most fundamental to the field of motor behavior because it goes to the heart of how biological systems of all kinds control their actions. This chapter focuses on the ways the central nervous system is organized functionally before and during an action and how this organization contributes to the control of the unfolding movement. As such, this chapter is a close companion to chapter 4, which considered the ways sensory information contributes to movement production. This chapter adds the idea of centrally organized commands that sensory information may modify somewhat. A key feature of this idea involves the important concept of a **motor program**, which is the prestructured set of movement commands that defines and shapes the movement.

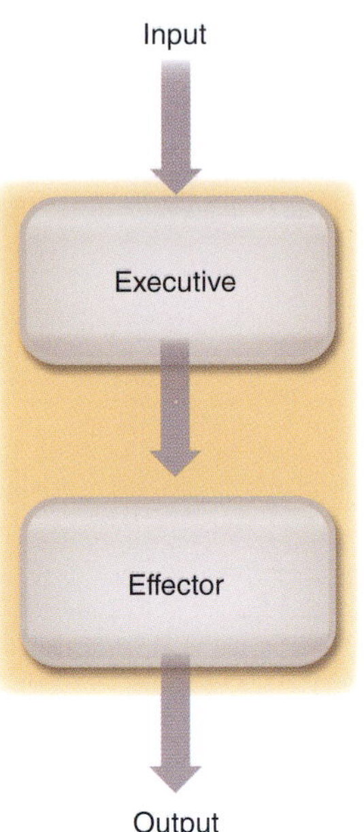

FIGURE 5.1 A basic open-loop system.

Motor Program Theory

The concept of the motor program, which is central to this entire chapter, is based on a kind of control mechanism that is in some ways the opposite of the closed-loop system discussed throughout chapter 4. This type of functional organization is called **open-loop control**.

Open-Loop Control

The basic open-loop system is illustrated in figure 5.1, and consists essentially of two parts: an executive and an effector. This open-loop structure has two of the main features used in closed-loop control (figure 4.1), but missing are the feedback and comparator mechanisms for determining system errors. Open-loop control begins with input about the desired state being given to the executive (or decision-making) level, whose task it is to define what action needs to be taken. The executive then passes instructions to the effector level, which is responsible for carrying out these instructions. Once the actions are completed, the system's job is over until the executive is activated again. Of course, without feedback, the open-loop system is not sensitive to whether or not the actions generated in the environment were effective in meeting the goal, and since feedback is not present, modifications to the action cannot be made while the action is in progress.

This kind of control system can be observed in many different real-world mechanisms. For example, an open-loop system is used in most traffic signals, where it sequences the timing of the red, yellow, and green lights that control the traffic flow. If an accident should happen at that intersection, the open-loop system continues to sequence the lights as if nothing were wrong, even though the standard pattern would be ineffective in handling this new, unexpected traffic flow problem. Thus, the open-loop system is effective as long as things go as expected, but it is inflexible in the face of unpredicted changes.

A microwave oven is another example of an open-loop system. The user places a frozen entree in the oven and programs it to defrost for 5 min, and then to cook on high power for another 2 min. Here, the program tells the machine what operations to do at each step and specifies the timing of each operation. Some microwave ovens are sensitive to the temperature of the item being cooked because a feedback mechanism (temperature sensor) has been added. But many are not, and without a feedback mechanism these latter machines follow the instructions without any regard for whether they will result in the desired state (an entree that is ready to eat).

Generally, the characteristics of a purely open-loop control system can be summarized as follows:

- Advance instructions specify the operations to be done, their sequencing, and their timing.
- Once the program has been initiated, the system executes the instructions, essentially without modification.
- There is no capability to detect or to correct errors because feedback is not involved.
- Open-loop systems are most effective in stable, predictable environments in which the need for modification of commands is low.

Motor Programs as Open-Loop Systems

Many movements—especially ones that are rapid, brief, and forceful, such as kicking and key pressing—seem to be controlled in an open-loop fashion, without much conscious control once the movement is under way. The performer in these tasks does not have time to process information about movement errors and must plan the movement in its entirety before movement initiation. This is quite different from the style of control discussed in the previous chapter, where the movements were slower (or longer in time) and were largely based on feedback processes of various kinds.

Open-loop control seems especially important when the environmental situation is predictable and stable. Under these circumstances, human movements appear to be carried out without much possibility of, or need for, modification. This general idea was popularized more than a century ago by the psychologist William James (1891) and has remained as one of the most important ways to understand movement control.

Consider a goal such as hitting a pitched baseball. The executive level, which consists of the decision-making stages of the system defined in chapter 2, evaluates the environment in the stimulus identification stage, processing such information as the speed and direction of the ball. The decision about whether or not to swing is made in the response selection stage. Then, the movement is programmed and initiated in the movement programming stage, in which details about the swing's speed, trajectory, and timing are determined.

Control is then passed to the effector level for movement execution. The selected motor program now carries out the swing by delivering commands to the spinal cord, which eventually directs the operations of the skeletal system involved in the swing. This movement then influences the outcome—resulting in the desired movement (hitting the ball squarely) or not (e.g., missing the ball, popping the ball up).

Although the decision-making stages determine what program to initiate and have some role in the eventual form of the movement (e.g., its speed and trajectory), movement execution is not actually controlled by the conscious decision-making stages. Therefore, the movement is carried out by a system that is not under direct conscious control. By this view, the motor program is the agent determining which muscles are to contract, in what order, when, and for how long.

Visit the web study guide to read "Moving Sidewalks and Beer Glasses" and complete the self-directed learning activities.

Open-Loop Control in the Conceptual Model

How does this concept of open-loop control and the motor program fit with the conceptual model of human performance? Figure 5.2 shows the conceptual model developed in chapter 4 (figure 4.10), now with the portions highlighted (light-green shading) that

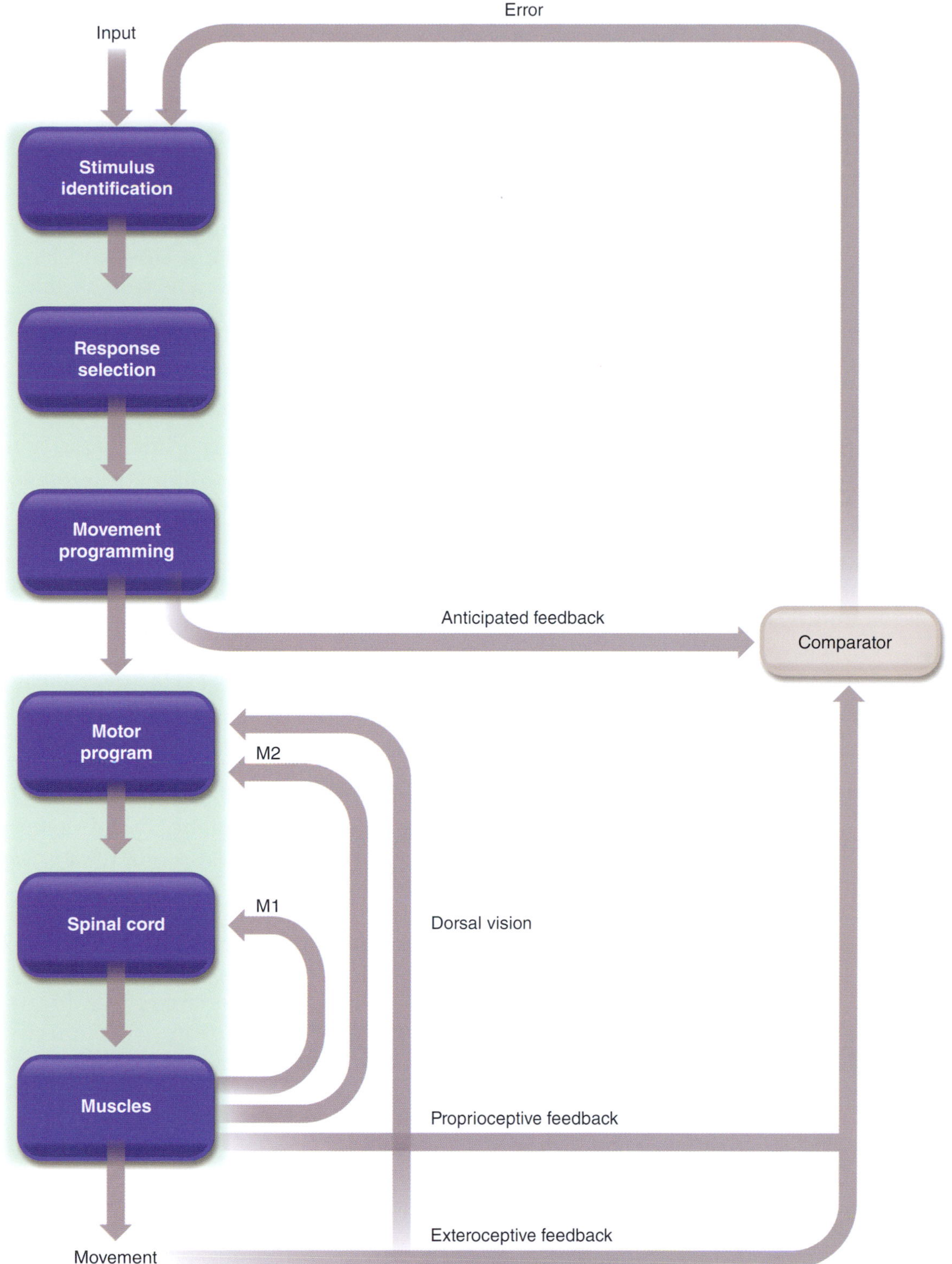

FIGURE 5.2 Conceptual model with the open-loop processes highlighted in light green.

comprise the open-loop components. The conceptual model here reflects motor performance as an open-loop control system with feedback added (the parts not shaded) to enable corrections through the other loops discussed previously. This more complete conceptual model has two basic ways of operating, depending on the task. If the movement is very slow or of long duration (e.g., threading a needle), the control is dominated by the feedback processes. If the movement is very fast or brief (e.g., a punch or kick), then the open-loop portions tend to dominate. *In most tasks, motor behavior is neither open- nor closed-loop alone but a complex blend of the two.*

For very fast or brief actions, the theory of motor programs is useful because it gives a set of ideas and a vocabulary to talk about a functional organization of the motor system. If a given movement is said to be a programmed action, it appears to be organized in advance, triggered more or less as a whole, and carried out without much modification from sensory feedback. This language describes a style of motor control with *central* movement organization, where movement details are determined by the central nervous system and are then sent to the muscles, rather than controlled by peripheral processes involving feedback. Of course, both styles of control are possible, depending on the nature of the task, the time involved, and other factors.

Evidence for Motor Programs

A number of separate lines of evidence converge to support the existence of motor program control. This evidence comes from some rather diverse areas of research: (1) studies of RT (reaction time) in humans, (2) experiments and case studies involving animals and humans in which feedback has been removed, (3) studies of central pattern generators, (4) the analysis of behaviors when humans attempt to stop or change an action, and (5) the impact on muscle activation patterns when movement is unexpectedly blocked.

Reaction-Time Evidence

In chapter 2 we discussed evidence that the RT duration was slowed when more information needed to be processed (e.g., Hick's Law), when processing was not natural (e.g., in S-R incompatible situations), and so on. Generally, RT was determined mainly by the processing undertaken in the stimulus identification and response selection stages. In this section we review evidence that RT is also influenced by the factors affecting the movement-programming stage.

Response Complexity Effects

Participants in RT experiments are typically asked to respond to a stimulus by initiating and carrying out a predetermined movement as quickly as possible (as discussed in chapter 2). Duration of the RT is measured as the interval from the presentation of the stimulus until the movement begins, so any added time for movement completion itself does not contribute directly to RT. However, beginning with the work of Henry and Rogers (1960; see Focus on Research 5.1), many experimenters have shown that RT is affected by several features of the movement *to be performed in the future*, presumably by influencing the complexity (and duration) of the movement-programming stage.

Henry and Rogers (1960) found that increases in the complexity of the upcoming movement to be performed also increased RT—that is, the time delay in initiating the response. This finding, plus much more research since the publication of Henry and Rogers' work, has produced the following set of findings (Klapp, 1996):

- RT is slower when additional elements in a series are added to the action (e.g., a unidirectional forward stroke in table tennis would likely be initiated with a faster RT than a backswing plus a forward stroke).
- RT is slower when more limbs must be coordinated (e.g., a one-handed piano chord would be initiated with a faster RT than a two-handed chord).

Focus on
RESEARCH 5.1

The Henry–Rogers Experiment

One of Franklin Henry's many important contributions was research that he and Donald Rogers published in 1960. The experiment was simple, as many important experiments are. Participants responded as quickly as possible to a stimulus by making one of three movements that were prepared in advance. Note that only one of these movements would be required for a long string of trials, so this was essentially a simple-RT paradigm (see chapter 2). The three different types of movements, designed to be different in complexity, were (1) a simple finger lift, (2) a simple finger lift plus a reach to slap a suspended ball, and (3) a simple finger lift followed by slapping a distant ball with the back of the hand, then moving to the push button, and then grasping a near ball (see Fischman, Christina, & Anson, 2008, for details). Each of these actions was to be done as quickly as possible.

Henry and Rogers measured the RT to *initiate* each of these actions—the interval from the presentation of the stimulus until the beginning of the required movement, which always began with a simple finger lift. (Remember that the RT does not include the time to complete the movement itself.) They found that the time to initiate the movement increased with added movement complexity. The simple finger-lift movement (1) had an RT of 150 ms, the intermediate-complexity movement (2) had an RT of 195 ms, and the movement with two reversals in direction (3) had an RT of 208 ms.

Notice that in each case, the stimulus to signal the movement (processed during the stimulus identification stage) and the number of movement choices (processed during the response selection stage) remained the same for all three movement complexities. Thus, because the only factor that varied was the complexity of the movement, the interpretation was that the elevated RTs were somehow caused by increased time for movement programming to occur before the action. This notion has had profound effects on the understanding of movement organization processes and has led to many further research efforts to study these processes more systematically (see Christina, 1992; Klapp, 2010). Most importantly, these data support the idea that rapid movement is organized in advance, which is consistent with the motor program concept.

Exploring Further

1. Analyze the differences in actions required for the three movements in the Henry and Rogers study. Describe at least three differences in the movements' requirements that might have led to increases in the complexity of the motor program.
2. What additional changes could be made to the action requirements of the most complex movement (3) that might be expected to increase movement programming time?

- RT is slower when the duration of the movement becomes longer (e.g., a 100 ms bat swing would be initiated with a faster RT than a 300 ms bat swing).

The interpretation of the various research findings is that when the to-be-produced movement is more complex in any of these ways (number of elements, number of limbs involved, the overall duration of the action),

RT is slower because more time is required to organize the motor system before the initiation of the action. This prior organization occurs, as discussed in chapter 2, in the movement programming stage. The effect on RT of the complexity of the to-be-performed movement provides evidence that at least some of the action is organized in advance, just as motor program theory would expect.

Visit the web study guide to read "Antilock Brakes" and complete the self-directed learning activities.

Startled Reactions

In the previous section we discussed the idea that RT becomes longer with increases in the complexity of the to-be-performed movement. Here, we focus on research showing that RT can be dramatically shortened under certain conditions.

We have all been in situations in which a completely unexpected event, such as a very loud noise, caused a severe reaction—we were startled. The response is often accompanied by contractions in the muscles of the face and neck and protective movements of the upper limbs. A very interesting property of the startle response is that these movements are initiated much faster than voluntary responses to a stimulus.

An innovative series of studies examined the **startle RT** as a paradigm to reveal insights about movement programming. In these studies (reviewed in Carlsen et al., 2011; Valls-Solé, Kumru, & Kofler, 2008), the participant is typically asked to prepare to make a rapid, forceful, sometimes complex response to a moderately intense stimulus (auditory or visual). Occasionally, the stimulus is accompanied by an extremely loud acoustic signal (e.g., 130 decibels [dB]; by comparison, the sounds of a chainsaw and music at a rock concert typically only reach 120 dB).The loud acoustic signal usually produces the typical startle indicators (clenched neck and jaw muscles, among other reactions). However, what also happens is that the movement is produced with an RT up to 100 ms faster than on the control trials, even though the movement itself remained unchanged.

These findings fit quite well with the motor program concept. The idea here is that the executive has prepared a motor program in advance of the stimulus to respond, which is normally released by a voluntary, internal go-signal from the executive to the effectors. The startle RT has the effect of hastening the release of this signal, by means of either speeding up the executive's processing time or perhaps even bypassing the executive altogether. The research is unclear at this point as to exactly *why* the same movement is initiated much faster on startled trials than on voluntary, unstartled trials, but the role of the motor program in carrying out the response is clearly implicated.

Deafferentation Experiments

In chapter 4, we mentioned that information from the muscles, the joints, and the skin are collected together in sensory nerves, which enter the spinal cord at various levels. A surgical technique termed **deafferentation** involves severing (via surgery) an animal's afferent nerve bundles where they enter the cord, so the central nervous system no longer can receive information from some portion of the periphery. The motor pathways are not affected by this procedure as information about motor activity passes through the (uncut) ventral (front) side of the cord. Sensory information from an entire limb, or even from several limbs, can be eliminated by this procedure.

What are experimental animals capable of doing when deprived of feedback from the limbs? Monkeys with deafferented upper limbs are still able to climb around, playfully chase each other, groom, and feed themselves essentially normally. It is indeed difficult to recognize that these animals have a total loss of sensory information from the upper limbs (Taub, 1976; Taub & Berman, 1968). The monkeys are impaired in some ways, however; they have difficulty in fine finger control, as in picking up a pea or manipulating small objects. On balance, though, it is remarkable how little impaired these animals are in most activities.

If the movement is quick enough, the motor program controls the entire action; the movement is carried out as though the performer were deprived of feedback. The capability to move quickly thus gives additional support to the idea that some central program handles the movement control, at least until feedback from the movement can begin to have an effect.

Case studies of humans also support this general conclusion. Lashley (1917) found that a patient with a gunshot wound to the back, who was without sensory feedback information from the legs, could still position his knee at a specified angle without feedback. And individuals who have lost much of their sensory feedback (so-called **sensory neuropathy** patients) are able to perform quite well in their environments as long as visual information is available (Blouin et al., 1996).

These studies show that sensory information from the moving limb is certainly not absolutely critical for movement production, and it is clear that many movements can occur nearly normally without it. This evidence suggests that theories of movement control must be generally incorrect if they *require* sensory information from the responding limb. Because feedback-based theories cannot account for these actions, many theorists have argued that the movements must be organized centrally via motor programs and carried out in an open-loop way, not critically dependent on feedback (e.g., Keele, 1968). In this sense, the deafferentation evidence supports the idea that movements can be organized centrally in motor programs.

Central Pattern Generator

The idea of motor programs is similar to that of the **central pattern generator (CPG)**, which was developed to explain certain features of locomotion in animals, such as swimming in fish, chewing in hamsters, and slithering in snakes (Grillner, 1975). A genetically defined central organization is established in the brainstem or the spinal cord. When this organization is initiated by a brief triggering stimulus from the brain, sometimes called a *command neuron*, it produces rhythmic, oscillating commands to the musculature as if it were defining a sequence of right–left–right activities, such as might serve as the basis of locomotion. These commands occur even if the sensory nerves are cut (deafferented), suggesting that the organization is truly central in origin.

The notion of the CPG is almost identical to that of the motor program. The main difference is that the motor program involves learned activities that are centrally controlled (such as kicking and throwing), whereas the CPG involves more genetically defined activities, such as locomotion, chewing, and breathing. In any case, there is good evidence that many genetically defined activities are controlled by CPGs (Zehr, 2005).

Inhibiting Actions

Another line of evidence to support motor program control can be found in experiments in which participants are required to inhibit or stop a movement after having initiated the process of making the action. This is the kind of activity that one sees quite frequently in baseball batting (see Focus on Application 5.1 on checked swings). A question asked by researchers concerns the point of no return—at what point after starting the processing stages that lead to a movement is one committed to making, or at least starting, the action? In other words, at what point is the signal released to send the motor program to the muscles?

The stop-signal paradigm is the method most frequently used to study action inhibition, and an early contribution to this research was provided by Slater-Hammel (1960), described in detail in Focus on Research 5.2. The findings of this study, which involved a very simple finger lift off a key (presumably with little biomechanical delay), suggested that the point of no return occurred about 150

The concept of a central pattern generator is used to describe simple, genetically defined activities such as walking, whereas motor program theory applies to learned skills such as riding a bicycle. List two other activities performed by animals that are likely controlled by CPGs.

to 170 ms before the time when the movement was initiated. However, an action such as a baseball swing is much more complex and has a considerably longer movement completion time than the finger lift used by Slater-Hammel. The evidence suggests that a motor program is released that is responsible for initiating and carrying out the entire action unless a second motor program is initiated in time to stop or change its completion (see Focus on Research 5.2; also Verbruggen & Logan, 2008).

Visit the web study guide to read "Point of No Return" and complete the self-directed learning activities.

Muscle Activity in Blocked Movements

The final line of evidence supporting the existence of motor programs comes from experiments in which patterns of muscle activity are examined during a brief limb action. Figure 5.4 shows integrated electromyogram (EMG) tracings from a quick elbow extension movement (Wadman et al., 1979). In the normal movement (red traces), first there is a burst of the agonist muscle (here, the triceps). Then the triceps turns off and the antagonist muscle (the biceps) is activated to decelerate the limb. Finally, the agonist comes on again near the end to stabilize the limb at the target area. This triple-burst pattern (agonist–antagonist–agonist) is typical of quick movements of this kind.

Occasionally, and quite unexpectedly, on some trials the lever was blocked mechanically by the experimenter so that no movement was possible. Figure 5.4 also shows what happens to the EMG patterning on these blocked trials (blue lines). Even though the limb does not move at all, there is a similar pattern of muscular organization, with the onset of the agonist and the antagonist occurring at about the same times as when the movement was not blocked. Later, after about 120 ms or so, there is a slight modification of the patterning, probably caused by the reflex activities (e.g., stretch reflexes) discussed in chapter 4. But the most important findings are that the antagonist muscle (biceps) even contracted at all when the movement was blocked and that it contracted at the same time as in the normal movements.

How could this essentially normal EMG activity be produced for a movement that is never made nor indeed even started? The feedback from the blocked limb must have been massively disrupted, yet the EMG patterning was essentially normal for 100 ms or so. Therefore, these data contradict theories arguing that feedback from the moving limb (during the action) acts as a signal (a trigger) to activate the antagonist muscle contraction at the proper time. Rather, these findings are some of the strongest data in support of

Focus on
APPLICATION 5.1

Checked Swings in Baseball

The bat swing in baseball is a good example of a motor program in action. The typical swing consists of a coordinated action involving a step with the lead foot toward the oncoming ball, followed by a rapid rotation of the trunk and shoulders, propelling the bat with a large angular velocity and minimum overall movement time. There is good reason to believe that the step and swing are part of a single motor program, initiated by elite batters on almost every pitch, but that latter parts of the swing are *inhibited* before a full execution on many of those pitches. How do batters do this, and how successful are they at doing it?

The physics of baseball tell us that there is very little time available for a major league batter to hit a baseball. For pitches in the range of 85 to 95 mph (137 to 153 kph), the ball takes less than a half second to reach the hitting zone after being released from the pitcher's hand. The batter typically prepares for the pitch and may initiate the step before the pitcher has actually released the ball. And at some point along the way, usually before the ball reaches the midpoint in its flight toward the plate, the batter must decide whether to proceed with the swing (including where to aim the bat for its intended collision with the ball) or inhibit its execution. The result is four different types of batter responses (see Gray, 2009, for much more on these ideas):

1. The batter successfully inhibits the motor program, and the swing is never initiated.
2. The batter starts the swing but inhibits the completion of the motor program, resulting in the bat stopping before it crosses the plate (which defines it as a "non-swing").
3. The batter starts the swing but fails to inhibit the motor program in time, resulting in a slowed velocity of the bat as it crosses the plate (resulting in a "completed swing," according to the rules of baseball).
4. The batter starts and completes the motor program without attempting to inhibit the swing—a classic example of a completed swing.

the motor program idea that the movement activities are organized in advance and run off unmodified by sensory information for 100 to 120 ms, or at least until the first reflexive activities can become involved.

Motor Programs and the Conceptual Model

Motor programs are a critical part of the conceptual model seen in figure 5.2, operating within the system, sometimes in conjunction with feedback, to produce flexible skilled actions. The open-loop part of these actions provides the organization, or pattern, that the feedback processes can later modify if necessary. The following are some of the major roles of these open-loop organizations:

- To define and issue the commands to musculature that determine when, how forcefully, and for how long muscles are to contract and which ones are to contract

Focus on
RESEARCH 5.2

Initiating a Motor Program

Before officiating was automated, races like the 100 m sprint were timed by hand, with a stopwatch. The timing judge started her stopwatch when she saw the smoke of the starter's pistol and stopped it when the she saw the runners cross the finish line. But let's consider *how* she stopped her stopwatch. If she stopped it when she *actually* saw the runner cross the line, then the clock would be stopped a short time later, because completing her action would be delayed by two factors: (1) the amount of time required to send the motor instructions to the hand holding the watch and (2) the biomechanical delays in pushing the button. Therefore, the problem for the judge in accurately timing the point when the sprinter actually crossed the finish line is that she must initiate her command signal by a duration that equals the sum of the two factors defined above *prior* to the arrival of runner at the finish line.

Our interest, of course, is the first concern—how long does it take to send the motor instructions? To answer this question, Arthur Slater-Hammel (1960) conducted an experiment that was similar to the example of the timing judge just presented. Participants held a finger on a key while watching an analog timer moving at one revolution per second; lifting off the key brought the sweep hand to an instantaneous stop. Participants were instructed to lift their finger from the key such that the clock hand would stop at exactly the point marked 800, or roughly at the 10 o'clock position on the clock (800 refers to a lapse of 800 ms after the start from the 12:00 position; see figure 5.3*a*). Note that in order to do this task accurately, similar to the timing judge, they would need to initiate the action at some point before the clock hand actually reached the 800 position.

A critically important aspect of the Slater-Hammel study was the insertion of special probe trials that occurred rarely and unpredictably. On these probe trials the experimenter would stop the clock hand at various locations before it reached 800.

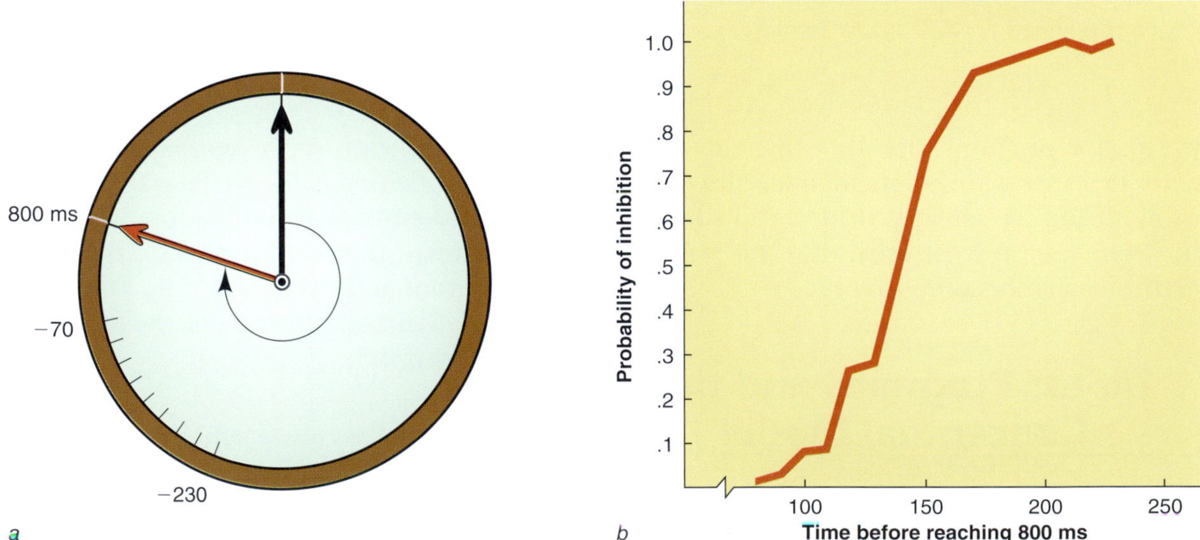

FIGURE 5.3 Slater-Hammel's (1960) task *(a)* and results *(b)*.

If this happened, the participant's job was simply to keep his or her finger on the key; thus, the probe trials required an *inhibition* of the normal task of lifting the finger to stop the sweep hand. The rationale was simple—if the motor program had not yet been sent to the muscles when they saw the sweep hand stop, then the participant should be able to inhibit the finger lift successfully. Conversely, there would be little chance of changing such a short, ballistic action if the sweep hand stopped after the motor program to lift the finger had already been sent.

Slater-Hammel plotted the probability of inhibiting the action successfully as a function of the time interval between 800 and where the clock hand had stopped. The data are shown in figure 5.3*b*. When the interval before the intended finger lift was relatively large (greater than the –230 point on the clock in figure 5.3*a*), seeing the clock hand stop resulted in inhibiting the movement successfully almost all the time (probability of inhibition > .9 in figure 5.3*b*). However, as this interval decreased, the participants would lift their finger more and more often, to the point that when the clock hand stopped at the –70 mark in figure 5.3*a* (70 ms before the 800 position), the participant could almost never inhibit the movement (probability of inhibition < .1 in figure 5.3*b*). Generally, when the clock hand was stopped about 130 to 150 ms before the intended finger lift, the participant could inhibit the movement successfully about half the time (corresponding to an average probability of inhibition = .5 in figure 5.3*b*). This finding can be interpreted to mean that the internal go-signal is issued about 130 to 150 ms before the intended action. This go-signal is a trigger for action, after which the movement occurs even though new information indicates that the movement should be inhibited.

Exploring Further

1. Slater-Hammel's estimate of the time required to anticipate the sweep hand's arrival at the 800 position is complicated by the fact that participants had a +26 ms constant error (CE) on the normal trials. What are the implications of this positively biased CE for the estimated time of when the internal go-signal is issued?
2. How could this stop-signal paradigm be adapted to examine the time required to make anticipatory actions in sport tasks such as batting a baseball?

- To organize the many degrees of freedom of the muscles and joints into a single unit
- To specify and initiate preliminary postural adjustments necessary to support the upcoming action
- To modulate the many reflex pathways to ensure that the movement goal is achieved

In the following sections we see research examples of how motor programs use anticipatory and feedback information to regulate movement control.

Anticipatory Adjustments

Imagine that you are standing with your arms at your sides and an experimenter gives you a command to raise an arm quickly to point straight ahead. What will be the first detectable EMG (muscular) activity associated with this movement? Most people would guess that the first contraction would be in the shoulder muscles that raise the arm. But, in fact, the EMG activity in these muscles occurs relatively late in the sequence. Rather, the first muscles to contract are in the lower back and legs, some 80 ms *before* the first shoulder

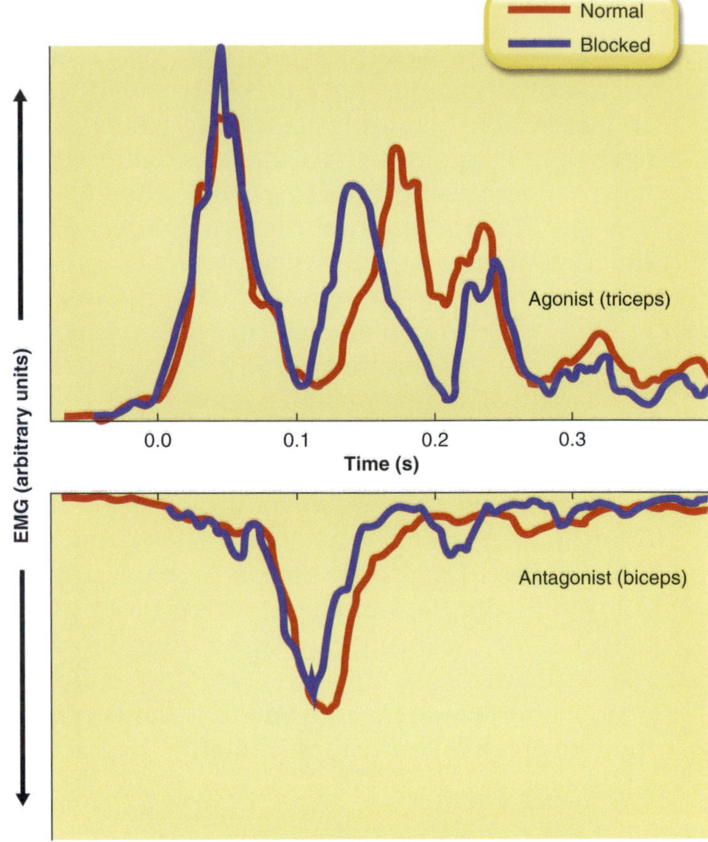

FIGURE 5.4 Electromyographic results from agonist (upper traces) and antagonist (lower traces) muscles when the participant actually produced the movement (normal trials—red lines) and when the movement was mechanically blocked (blocked trials—blue lines).

muscle contracts (Belen'kii, Gurfinkel, & Pal'tsev, 1967).

This order may sound strange, but it is really quite a smart way for the motor system to operate. Because the shoulder muscles are mechanically linked to the rest of the body, their contractions influence the positions of the segments connected to the arm—the shoulder and the back. That is, the movement of the arm affects posture. If no compensations in posture were first made, raising the arm would cause the trunk to flex, as well as to shift the center of gravity forward, causing a slight loss of balance. Therefore, rather than adjust for these effects *after* the arm movement, the motor system compensates before the movement through knowing what postural modifications will be needed.

There is good evidence that these preparatory postural adjustments are really just a part of the movement program for making the arm movement (W.A. Lee, 1980). When the arm movement is organized, the motor program contains instructions to adjust the posture in advance as well as the instructions to move the arm, so that the action is a coordinated whole. Thus, we should not think of the arm movement and the posture control as separate events; rather, these are simply different parts of an integrated action of raising the arm and maintaining posture and balance. Interestingly, these preparatory adjustments vanish when the performer leans against a support, because postural adjustments are not needed here.

Integration of Central and Feedback Control

Although it is clear that central organization of movements is a major source of motor control, it is also very clear (see chapter 4) that sensory information can modify these commands in several important ways, as seen in the conceptual model in figure 5.2. Thus, the question becomes how and under what conditions these commands from motor programs interact with sensory information to define the overall movement pattern. This is one of the most important research issues for understanding motor control.

Reflex-Reversal Phenomenon

In addition to the various classes of reflex mechanisms discussed in chapter 4 that can modify the originally programmed output (figure 4.10), another class of reflexive modulations exists that has very different effects on the movement behavior. Several experiments show how reflex responses are integrated with open-loop programmed control.

In one study, for example, the experimenter applies a light tactile stimulus to the top of a cat's foot while it is walking on a treadmill. If this stimulus is applied as the cat is just *placing* its foot on the surface of the treadmill (in preparation for load bearing), the response is to extend the leg slightly, as if to carry more load on that foot. This response has a latency of about 30 to 50 ms and is clearly nonconscious and automatic. If exactly the same stimulus is applied when the cat is just *lifting* the foot from the surface (in preparation for the swing phase), the response is very different. The leg flexes upward at the hip and the knee so the foot travels above the usual trajectory in the swing phase. Thus, the same stimulus has different (reversed) effects when it is presented at different locations in the step cycle.

These alterations in the reflex—reversing its effect from extension to flexion (or vice versa) depending on where in the step cycle the stimulus is applied—has been called the **reflex-reversal phenomenon** (Forssberg, Grillner, & Rossignol, 1975). It challenges our usual conceptualizations of a reflex, which is typically defined as an automatic, stereotyped, unavoidable response to a given stimulus: Here the same stimulus has generated two different responses.

Movement Flexibility

Complex reflex responses play an important role in the flexibility and control of skills. The cat's reflexes are probably organized to have an important survival role. Receiving a tactile stimulus on the top of the foot while it is swinging forward probably means that the foot has struck some object and that the cat will trip if the foot is not lifted quickly over the object. However, if the stimulus is received during the beginning of stance, flexing the leg would cause the animal to fall because it is swinging the opposite leg at this time. These can be thought of as temporary reflexes in that they exist only in the context of performing a particular part of a particular action, ensuring that the goal is achieved even if a disturbance is encountered. Analogous findings have been produced in speech research, where slight, unexpected tugs on the lower lip during the production of a sound cause rapid, reflexive modulation, with the actual responses critically dependent on the particular sound being attempted (Abbs, Gracco, & Cole, 1984; Kelso et al., 1984). The concern for the motor system in such situations is to ensure that the intended action is generated and that the goal is achieved (in this case, making the desired speech sound).

This adaptable feature of a movement program provides considerable flexibility in its operation. The movement can be carried out as programmed if nothing goes wrong. If something does go wrong, then appropriate reflexes are allowed to participate in the movement to ensure that the goal is met.

Problems in Motor Program Theory: Novelty and Storage

Open-loop control occurs primarily to allow the motor system to organize an entire, usually rapid, action without having to rely on the relatively slow information processing involved in a closed-loop control mode. Several processes must be handled by this prior organization. At a minimum, the following must be specified in the programming process in order to generate skilled movements:

- The particular muscles that are to participate in the action
- The order in which these muscles are to be involved
- The forces of the muscle contractions
- The **relative timing** and sequencing among these contractions
- The duration of each contraction

Most theories of motor programs assume that a movement is organized in advance by the establishment of a neural mechanism, or network, that contains time and event information. A kind of movement script specifies certain essential details of the action as it runs off in time. Therefore, scientists speak of running a motor program, which is clearly analogous to the processes involved in running computer programs.

However, motor program theory, at least as developed so far in this chapter, does not account for several important aspects of movement behavior. Perhaps the most severe limitations of motor program theory are (1) the failure to account for how novel movements are produced in the first place, and (2) lack of the efficiency that would be required to store in memory the massive number of motor programs that would be required in order to move.

This capability for producing novel actions raises problems for the simple motor program theory as we have developed it so far. To this point in the chapter we have provided evidence for the view that a given movement is represented by a program stored in long-term memory. Therefore, each variation in a tennis stroke, for example, associated with variations in the height and speed of the ball, the intended location of the ball placement, the distance to the net, and so on, would need a unique and separate program stored in memory because the instructions for the musculature would be different for each variation. Extending this view further suggests that we would need literally a countless number of motor programs stored in memory just to play tennis. Add to this the number of movements possible in all other activities of daily living, and the result would be an absurdly large number of programs stored in long-term memory. This leads to what has been called the **storage problem** (Schmidt, 1975), which concerns the capacity required for storing all of these separate programs in memory and made instantly retrievable when needed.

There is also the **novelty problem**. For example, when playing tennis, no two strokes, strictly speaking, are the same. That is, every stroke requires a very slight difference in the amount of contraction of the participating muscles. In this sense, then, every stroke the tennis player makes is novel, implying that the system would need a separate program for every shot. But that raises the novelty problem—if motor programs stored in memory are responsible for all such rapid movements, then how could something essentially new be based on something previously stored in memory? The simple motor program theory, as presented here to this point, is at a loss to explain the performance of such novel actions.

To summarize, these observations raise two problems for understanding everyday movement behavior:

1. The storage problem: How (or where) do humans store the nearly countless number of motor programs needed for future use and make these stored programs instantly retrievable from memory?
2. The novelty problem: How do performers produce truly novel movements, never performed previously, if the program for such an action is not represented in memory?

Many years ago the British psychologist Sir Fredrick Bartlett (1932), in writing about tennis, said this: "When I make the stroke, I do not . . . produce something absolutely new, and I never repeat something old"

(p. 202). What did he mean? The first part of his statement means that, even though a movement is in some sense novel, it is never totally brand-new. Each of his ground strokes resembles his other ground strokes, possessing his own style of hitting a tennis ball. The second part of Bartlett's statement conveys the idea that every movement is novel in that it has never been performed *exactly* that way before.

The novelty and storage problems for motor program theory discussed in the previous section, and indeed, in explaining Bartlett's keen insight regarding the tennis stroke, motivated a search for alternative ways to understand motor control. There was a desire to keep the appealing parts of motor program theory but to modify them to solve the storage and novelty problems. The idea that emerged was that motor programs must be *generalized* (Schmidt, 1975). This generalized motor program (GMP) consists of a stored pattern that is adjusted at the time of movement execution, allowing the action to be changed slightly to meet the current environmental demands.

Generalized Motor Program Theory

The quote from Bartlett captures the essence of GMP theory: Some features of the tennis stroke remain the same from shot to shot, and some features of the stroke are changed each time. According to GMP theory, what remains the same reflects the **invariant features** of a motor program—those features that make the pattern appear the same, time after time. Invariant features are the reason our unique writing style appears the same regardless of whether we are using a pen to write in a notebook, using a marker to write large enough on a whiteboard for everyone in a large class to read, or using our toe to write something in the beach sand.

The aspect that allows changes from stroke to stroke (in Bartlett's quote) is represented in GMP theory as the relatively superficial or **surface features** of the movement. If the pattern represents the invariant features of your writing style, then modifying what are called **parameters** determines how it is executed at any one time, representing its surface features. Writing something slow or fast, large or small, on paper or in the sand, and with a pen or a toe, represents how the GMP is executed at that particular time. The word *parameter* comes from mathematics, and represents numerical values in an equation that can be applied to the equation but do not change the *form* of the equation. For example, in a linear equation, whose general form is $Y = a + bX$, the values a and b are parameters—Y and X are related to each other in the same way for any values of a and b. The unique performance that occurs when certain parameters are changed does not alter the invariant characteristics of the GMP—the parameters change only how the GMP is *expressed* at any given time.

In GMP theory, movements are thought to be produced as follows. As determined via sensory information processed in the stimulus identification stage, a GMP for, say, throwing (as opposed to kicking) is chosen during the response selection stage. This GMP is then retrieved from long-term memory, much the same way that you retrieve your friend's telephone number from memory. The GMP is then prepared for initiation, or **parameterized**, during the movement programming stage.

One of the necessary processes here is to define *how* to execute this program. Which limb to use, how fast to throw, which direction to throw, and how far to throw must be decided based on the environmental information available just before action. These decisions result in the assignment (probably in the response selection stage) of movement parameters—characteristics that define the nature of the program's execution without influencing the invariant characteristics (that determine its form) of the GMP. Parameters include the speed of movement, its amplitude (overall size), and the limb used. Once the parameters have been selected and assigned to the program, the movement can be initiated and carried out with this particular set of surface features.

According to GMP theory, the key variables to consider are what constitute the invariant features of the GMP and what constitute the parameters, or surface features. These important issues are discussed in the next sections.

Invariant Features of a GMP

To understand the nature of GMPs, we need to know what features of the flexible movement patterns remain invariant, or constant, as the more surface features (such as movement speed, movement amplitude, and forces) are altered. When movement time is altered, for example, almost every other aspect of the movement changes too. The forces and durations of contractions, the speed of the limbs, and the distances the limbs travel all can change markedly as the movement speeds up.

However, what if some aspects of these movements could be shown to remain constant even though just about everything else was changing? If such a value could be found, scientists argued, it might indicate something fundamental about the structure of the GMP that serves as a basis for all of these movements, thus providing evidence for how motor programs are organized or represented in long-term memory. Such a constant value is termed an *invariance*, and the most important invariance concerns the temporal structuring of the pattern (the rhythm or relative timing).

Relative Timing

Rhythm, or relative timing, is a fundamental feature of many of our daily activities. Of course, rhythm is critically important in such activities as music and dance. But timing is also a key feature of many sporting activities (such as the golf swing) and work activities (e.g., typing, hammering). There is strong evidence to suggest that relative time is an invariant feature of the GMP. An example is the evidence provided in the Armstrong (1970) study, discussed in Focus on Research 5.3.

Generalized motor program theory suggests that the motor program for signing your name retains its invariant features, no matter what you are writing on.

The graph in figure 5.5 shows a sample trial in which one of Armstrong's (1970) participants produced a pattern from memory that was made too quickly. The red line in figure 5.5 illustrates a performed overall time of about 3.2 s, compared to the goal movement (blue trace), to be done in 4.0 s. But compare the peaks of the red line with the peaks of the blue line in this figure—you will notice that the *whole movement* appeared to speed up as a unit. That is, each of the peaks (movement reversals) occurred sooner and sooner in real time, but occurred at about the same time relative to the overall time of the pattern; hence the term *relative time* (see Gentner, 1987, or Schmidt et al., 2019, for more on these issues).

Relative timing is the fundamental temporal structure of a movement pattern that is independent of its overall speed or amplitude. Relative timing represents the movement's fundamental "deep structure," as opposed to the surface features seen in the easily modified alterations in movement time. This deep temporal organization in movements seems to be invariant, even when the actions are produced at different speeds or amplitudes.

More specifically, relative timing refers to the ratios of the durations of several intervals within the movement, as illustrated in figure 5.6. Consider two hypothetical throwing movements, with movement 1 being performed with a shorter movement time than movement 2. Imagine that you measure and record the EMGs from three of the important muscles involved in each action (in principle, nearly any feature of the movement could be measured, not only EMG). If you measure several of these contraction durations, you can define relative timing by a set of ratios, each defined as part of the action's duration divided by the total duration. For example, in movement 1, *a* refers to the total movement duration and *b*, *c*, and *d* refer to the durations of three measurable parts of the action. The ratios $b/a = .40$, $c/a = .30$, and $d/a = .60$ can then be calculated. This pattern of ratios is characteristic of this throwing movement, describing its temporal structure relatively accurately.

In movement 2, despite a longer duration, this set of ratios stays the same because the values of b/a, c/a, and d/a are the same as in movement 1. When this set of ratios is constant in two different movements, we say that the relative timing was invariant. Notice that movement 2 seems to be simply an elongated (horizontally stretched) version of movement 1, with all of the temporal events occurring more slowly in a systematic manner. This will always be found when relative timing is invariant. According to the GMP theory, movement 2 was produced with a slower timing parameter than movement 1, so the whole movement was slowed down as a unit, but its relative timing was preserved.

One of the important principles of movement control is that when a brief, rapid movement is changed these alterations seem to be made with an invariant relative timing. This occurs, for example, when changing the speed of the action (a fast versus a slow throw), the size of the action (making your signature large or small), or the trajectory of the action (throwing overarm versus sidearm). Relative timing is invariant across several different kinds of surface modifications, so the form of the movement is preserved even though the superficial features of it may change. There is some controversy about whether relative

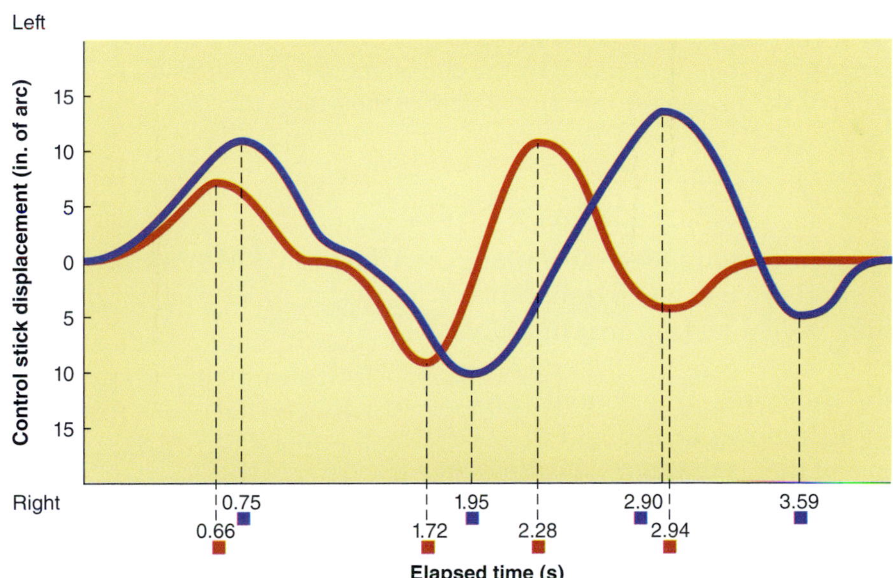

FIGURE 5.5 Participants learned to make a timed movement of a lever with their right arm. The goal movement pattern is depicted by the blue line. The trace in red represents a trial in which the movement is made too rapidly; the error in the timing of the reversals increases as the movement unfolds, which is what would happen if the red trace were simply a speeded-up version of the blue trace.

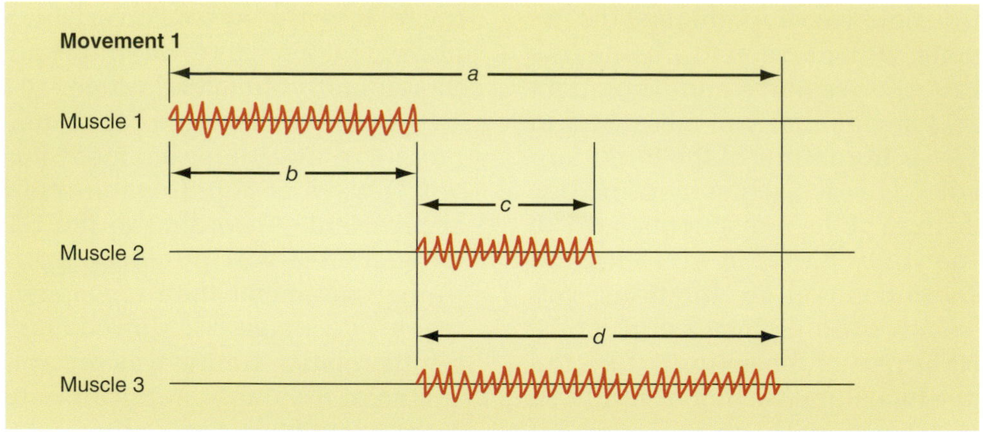

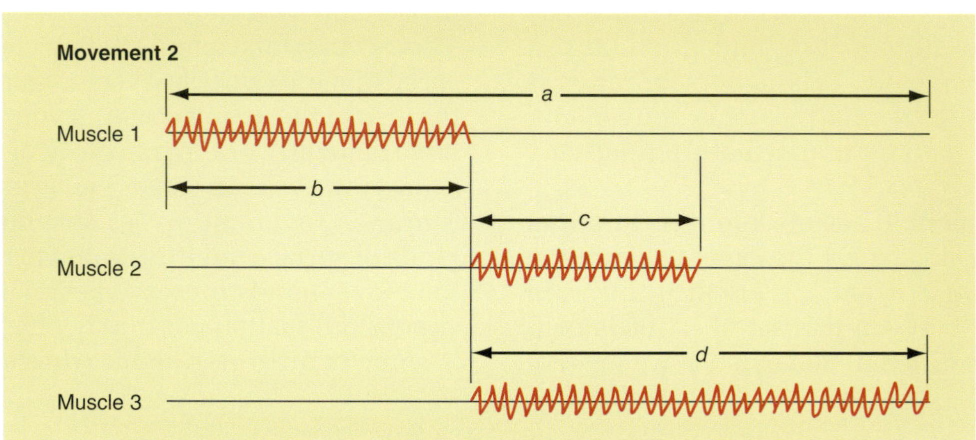

FIGURE 5.6 Hypothetical relative timing of EMG traces from three muscles for two hypothetical throwing movements. The relative-time ratios are computed by dividing the muscle EMG durations (i.e., *b*, *c*, and *d*) for each muscle (i.e., 1, 2, and 3) by the overall movement time (i.e., *a*). Notice that these ratios remain roughly constant when the movement time of the action changes (upper versus lower panel).

timing is perfectly invariant (Gentner, 1987; Heuer, 1988), but there can be no doubt that relative timing is at least approximately invariant.

Note that the relative timing actually produced by a performer can be thought of as a kind of fingerprint that is unique to a particular movement class. This pattern can be used to identify which of several motor programs has been executed (Schneider & Schmidt, 1995; Young & Schmidt, 1990). Focus on Application 5.2 provides more examples of how our GMPs reflect other kinds of biological "fingerprints."

Classes of Movements

An activity like overarm throwing represents a class of movements consisting of a nearly infinite number of specific activities (e.g., throwing various objects with different velocities and trajectories, etc.). The theory holds that the entire class is represented by a single GMP, with a specific, rigidly defined relative-timing structure. This program can have parameters in several dimensions (e.g., movement time, amplitude), making possible an essentially limitless number of combinations of specific throwing movements, each of which contains the same relative timing.

Focus on RESEARCH 5.3

Invariances and Parameters

An important contribution to the development of the GMP theory was made by Armstrong (1970) in analyzing the patterns of movements that participants made in one of his experiments. In Armstrong's experiment, learners attempted to move a lever from side to side in such a way that a pattern of movement at the elbow joint (defined in space and time) occurred, as depicted by the blue line in figure 5.5. This goal movement (blue line) had four major reversals in direction, each of which was to be produced at a particular time in the action, with the total movement occupying about 4 s.

Armstrong noticed that when the learner made the first reversal movement too quickly (red trace), the *whole* movement was also done too quickly. Notice that the red line's first peak (at reversal) was just a little early (at .66 rather than at .75). The discrepancy between the actual and goal reversal times increased roughly proportionally as the movement progressed (1.72 versus 1.95; 2.28 versus 2.90; and 2.94 versus 3.59). This gives the impression that every aspect of the movement pattern was produced essentially correctly but that the entire pattern was simply run off too quickly.

Armstrong's findings provided an early impetus to the development of the idea that the motor program can be generalized (Schmidt, 1975). Here, the program controlled the relative timing of the movement reversals. When an early reversal appeared sooner or later than the goal time, then all of the subsequent reversals sped up or slowed proportionally.

Exploring Further

1. In Armstrong's figure (figure 5.5), sketch a graph of how you predict an action with a 4.5 s overall movement time would look if the participant had preserved the same relative-timing structure.
2. Suppose Armstrong's participants had performed the pattern again, one month after the original sessions of practice. Which do you think would be remembered better, the overall timing or the relative-time structure of the pattern? Give reasons for your answer.

Locomotion represents another class of movements that could be considered to be controlled by a GMP. Research by Shapiro and colleagues suggests that, in fact, there are at least two separate GMPs for gait, each with unique relative timings—one for walking and another for running. Similar to the throwing example, however, we can speed up and slow down either the walking or running gait selectively without having to abandon the GMP.

Shapiro and collaborators (1981) studied the shifts in relative timing in locomotion. They recorded people on a treadmill at speeds ranging from 3 to 12 kph and measured the durations of various phases of the step cycle as the movement speed increased. When the treadmill speed ranged from 3 to 6 kph, all participants walked. Regardless of the speed, the relative time used for each phase of the step cycle remained about the same. When the treadmill speed was increased to 8 kph,

Focus on
APPLICATION 5.2

Relative-Timing Fingerprints

Identity fraud has represented a major threat to security for years. Forging someone's signature on a check and hacking into an account with someone's password are just two methods used by fraudsters to get illegal access to assets and information. However, the invariant features of one's GMP provide an important tool to combat the problem.

A person's signature is usually considered unique and different from anyone else's signature. Forging the spatial characteristics of a signature is not a difficult task. All the forger needs to do is obtain the target signature, compare the illegal and legal signatures, and continue to practice by making improvements on the imperfections until a realistic forgery is difficult to distinguish from the original. A password that is typed into an account on a computer is even easier to forge if the fraudster knows the characters to enter. All that is needed is to enter the correct sequence, and access is granted. However, relative timing is the missing ingredient in both of these cases of fraud.

Suppose, for example, that when you signed your name, the spatial *and* temporal recordings of each of the various loops and cursives in producing the letters, as well as the timing of your "t" crossings and "i" dottings and so on, were compared to a data bank in which a large number of your previous signature timings had been stored. According to GMP theory, the invariant characteristics of your signature would be repeated regardless of the tool you used to sign your name (e.g., familiar or unfamiliar pen), the surface on which you wrote it (e.g., paper or digital tablet), or the size of the writing. Most important though, the fraudster who had access only to the spatial characteristics of your signature would be completely at a loss to replicate its relative timing.

Typing your password also has a relative-timing characteristic that is uniquely yours, especially for those such as the authors of this book who are not trained typists. We each have our own unique style of typing—which letters are typically contacted with which fingers, how long each key is held down (dwell time), and the transition times that usually occur between particular letters. Once again, a data bank of previous executions of our passwords would give rise to a range of overall timings of these dwell and transition times, from which a relative-timing profile could be derived and to which the fraudster (hopefully) would not have access.

Fortunately for us, these methods of using digital knowledge of our GMPs are now a reality. A field of research that examines keystroke dynamics reveals an emerging technology and industry that is designed to improve security (Ahmad, Szymkowiak, & Campbell, 2013). In many ways you can think of your signature and typed passwords as relative-timing fingerprints that are unique to you.

---

however, where now all participants were running, the relative-timing pattern was completely different compared to walking. But as the running speed increased from 8 to 12 kph, there again was a tendency for these (new) proportions to remain nearly invariant.

The interpretation is that there are two GMPs operating here—one for walking and one for running. Each has its own pattern of relative timing and is quite different from the other. When the treadmill speed increases for walking, the parameter values are changed, which speeds up the movement with the same program while maintaining the relative timing. At about 7 kph, a critical speed is reached, and the participant abruptly shifts to a running program, but the relative timing of this activity is maintained nearly perfectly as running speed is increased further. (Note: we will discuss alternative interpretations of the walk-run transition in chapter 7.)

Visit the web study guide to read "Forensic Motor Control" and complete the self-directed learning activities.

Parameters Added to the GMP

In the previous section we discussed some of the features of movement that remain the same from one time to the next—the invariant features of the GMP. According to the theory, surface features need to be specified each time a movement is performed. That is, the GMP needs to be parameterized before it can be executed. What are some of these parameters?

Movement Time

Both the Armstrong study (Focus on Research 5.3) and the gait study by Shapiro and collaborators provided strong evidence that overall movement time could be varied without affecting the relative timing of the GMP. In Armstrong's study, the participant who accidentally sped up the movement pattern still retained that same timing of reversals in the movement. And the participants in the study by Shapiro and colleagues could vary speeds of walking and running without disrupting the relative timing of the step cycle. This also agrees with the common experience that we seem to have no trouble speeding up and slowing down a given movement, such as throwing a ball at various speeds, or writing more slowly or more quickly. These findings indicate that when movement duration is changed, the new movement preserves the essential temporal-pattern features of the old movement. Both movements are represented by a common underlying temporal (and sequential) pattern that can be run off at different speeds. Therefore, overall movement time is a parameter of the GMP.

For each of these photos identify one invariant characteristic of the movement and one parameter.

Movement Amplitude

The amplitude of movements can also be modulated easily in a way that is much like varying the time. For example, you can write your signature either on a check or five times larger on a blackboard, and in each case the signature is clearly "yours" (Lashley, 1942; Merton, 1972). Making this size change seems almost trivially easy.

The handwriting phenomenon was studied more formally by Hollerbach (1978), who had participants write the word "hell" in different sizes. He measured the accelerations of the pen (or, alternatively, the forces delivered to the pen) during the production of the words. These accelerations are graphed in figure 5.7. When the trace moves upward, this indicates acceleration (force) away from the body; a downward trace indicates acceleration toward the body. Of course, when the word is written larger, the overall magnitude of the accelerations produced must be larger, seen as the uniformly larger amplitudes for the larger word. But what is of most interest is that the temporal patterns of acceleration over time are almost identical for the two words, with the accelerations having similar modulations in upward and downward fluctuations.

This leads to an observation similar to the one just made about movement time. It is easy to increase the amplitude of the movements by uniformly increasing the accelerations (forces) that are applied, while preserving their temporal patterning. Therefore, the same word written twice with different amplitudes can be based on a common underlying structure that can be run off with scaled forces that govern the entire movement in order to produce different actions of overall different sizes. Therefore, overall amplitude of force is a parameter of the GMP.

Effectors

A performer can also modulate a movement by using a different limb—and, hence, different muscles—to produce the action. In the signature example, writing on a blackboard involves very different muscles and joints than writing on a check. In blackboard writing, the fingers are mainly fixed, and the writing is done with the muscles controlling the elbow and the shoulder. In check writing, the elbow and the shoulder are mainly fixed, and the writing is done with the muscles controlling the fingers. Yet the writing patterns produced are essentially the same. This indicates that a given pattern can be produced even when the effectors—and the muscles that drive them—are different.

These phenomena were studied by Raibert (1977), who wrote the sentence "Able was I ere I saw Elba" (a palindrome, spelled the same

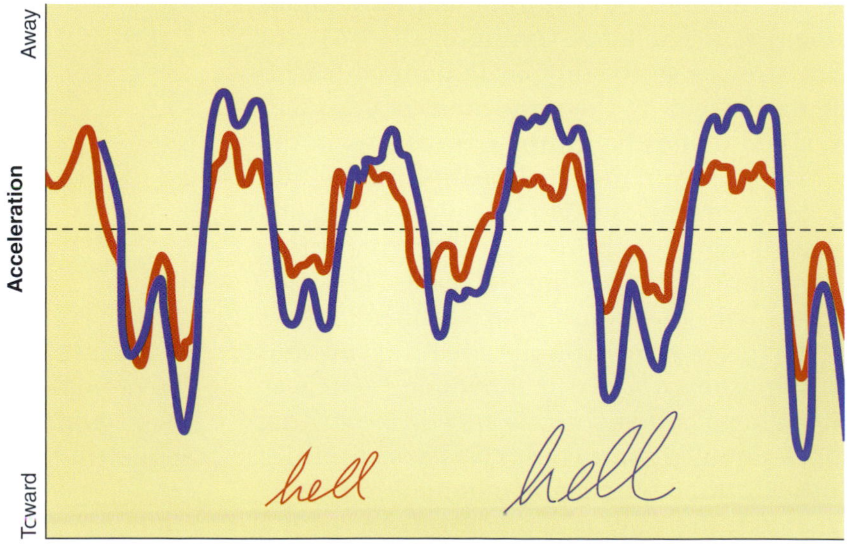

FIGURE 5.7 Acceleration-time tracings of two instances of writing the word "hell," once in small script (red) and again in larger script (blue). Although the amplitudes (which are proportional to the forces exerted on the pen) for the two traces are markedly different, the temporal organization of the patterning remains nearly the same in the two instances.

way backward as forward) with different effectors (i.e., limbs). In figure 5.8, line *a* shows his writing with the right (dominant) hand, line *b* with the right arm with the wrist immobilized, and line *c* with the left hand. These patterns are very similar. Even more remarkable is that line *d* was written with the pen gripped in the teeth, and line *e* used the pen taped to the foot! There are obvious similarities among the writing styles, and it seems clear that the same person wrote each of them, yet the effector system was completely different for each.

This all indicates that changing the limb and effector system can preserve the essential features of the movement pattern relatively easily. Therefore, the selection of effectors can be thought of as a kind of parameter that must be selected prior to action. There is some underlying temporal structure common to these actions, which can be run off with different effector systems while using the same GMP.

Summary of GMP Concepts

Some of these elements of the theory of GMPs can be summarized as follows:

- A GMP underlies a class of movements and is structured in memory with a rigidly defined temporal organization.
- This structure is characterized by its relative timing, which can be measured by a set of ratios among the durations of various events in the movement.
- Variations in movement time, movement amplitude, and the limb used represent the movement's surface structure, achieved by executing the action with different parameters, whereas relative timing represents its deep, fundamental structure.
- Even though a movement may be carried out with different surface features (e.g., duration, amplitude), the relative timing remains invariant.
- Whereas surface features are very easy to alter by parameter adjustment, the deeper relative-timing structure is very difficult to alter.

A good way to understand the invariant features of a GMP with certain added parameters is to consider movement as analogous to the various components of a stereo system (see Focus on Application 5.3).

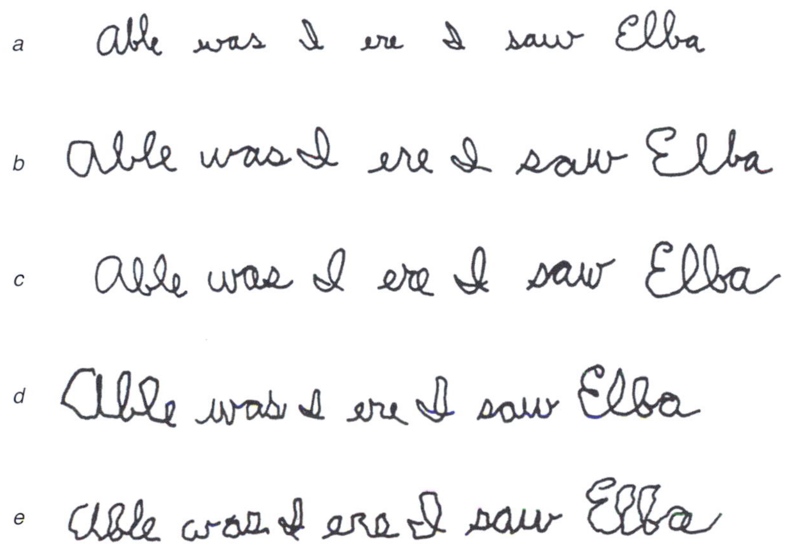

FIGURE 5.8 Five samples of writing a palindrome by the same participant, using (*a*) the dominant hand, (*b*) the dominant hand with the wrist immobilized, (*c*) the nondominant hand, (*d*) with pen gripped by the teeth, and (*e*) with the pen taped between toes of the foot.

Focus on APPLICATION 5.3

The Stereo System Analogy

A good analogy for GMPs involves the phonograph stereo system, in which a turntable sends signals from a record into an amplifier, whose output is delivered to speakers. In this analogy, illustrated in the top portion of figure 5.9, the phonograph record represents the GMP, and the speakers are the muscles and limbs. The record has all of the features of programs, such as information about the order of events (the guitar solo comes before the harmonica solo), the temporal structure among the events (i.e., the rhythm, or relative timing), and the relative amplitudes of the sounds (the first drumbeat is twice as loud as the second). This information is stored on the record, just as GMP theory says that the analogous information is stored in the program. Also, there are many different records to choose from, just as humans have many motor programs to choose from (e.g., throwing, jumping), each stored with different kinds of information.

Notice, though, that the record's output is not fixed (lower portion of figure 5.9): The speed of output can be changed if the speed of the turntable is increased. Note that the relative timing (rhythm) is preserved even though the speed of the music is increased. You can change the amplitude of the output by raising the volume; this

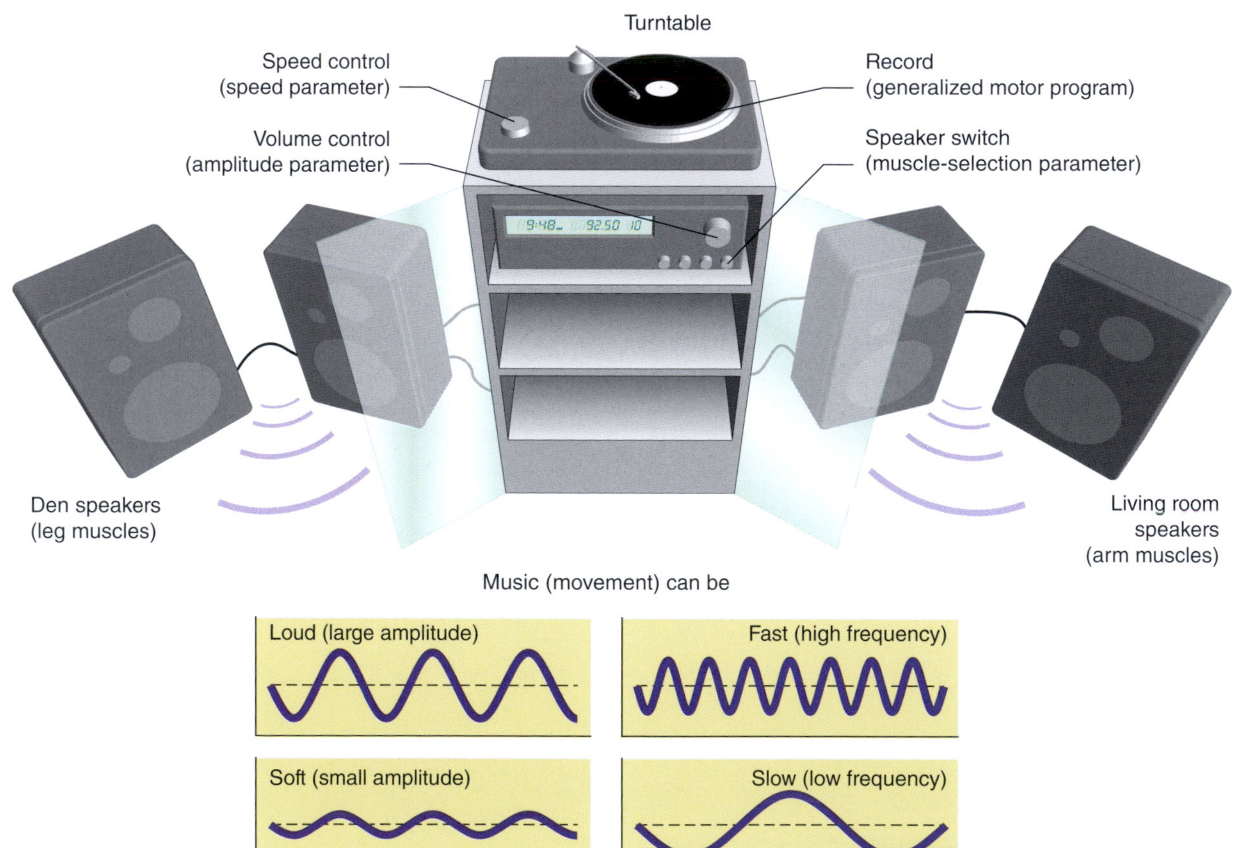

FIGURE 5.9 Illustration of the stereo system analogy.

increases the amplitudes of all the features of the sounds. Also, you have a choice of which effectors to use: You can switch the output from a set of speakers in the den to a second set of speakers in the living room; this is analogous to hammering either with the left hand or with the right, or with a different hammer, still using the same pattern.

Perhaps if you think of the theory of GMPs in concrete terms like a stereo system, you can understand most of the important features of the theory more easily. For example, when participants in the study by Shapiro and colleagues switched from walking to running, they first had to remove the walking "record" and replace it with a running "record." Then they had to parameterize it, like setting the volume, speed, and speaker controls. This analogy of the GMP and its parameters to the characteristics of a stereo system sometimes helps to understand the basic idea.

We started this section on GMPs by expressing dissatisfaction with the simple motor program views as developed earlier in the chapter. Two issues were considered to be especially problematic: the storage problem and the novelty problem. The GMP theory provides solutions to both of these problems. For the storage problem, the theory holds that an infinite number of movements can be produced by a single GMP, so only one program needs to be stored for each class of movement rather than an infinite number. And for the novelty problem, the theory suggests that a second memory representation, a *schema*, is the theoretical structure responsible for supplying parameters needed at the time of movement execution. Note that, by using a parameter not used before, the person can produce a novel action. Much more will be said about schema development in later chapters. But, for now, think of the schema as a mechanism responsible for selecting the parameters for the chosen GMP.

Summary

In very brief actions, there is no time for the system to process feedback about errors and to correct them. The mechanism that controls this type of behavior is open loop, called the motor program. This chapter is about motor programming activities. Considerable evidence supports the motor program idea: (1) Reaction time is longer for more complex movements but can be elicited much faster by startling stimuli, (2) animals deprived of feedback information by deafferentation are capable of strong, relatively effective movements, (3) some cyclical movements in animals are controlled by central pattern generators, (4) inhibiting behaviors are demonstrated when one attempts to stop or alter an action after it has been initiated, and (5) a limb's muscle activity patterns are unaffected for 100 to 120 ms when the limb is blocked by a mechanical perturbation.

Even though the motor program is responsible for the major events in the movement pattern, there is considerable interaction with sensory processes, such as the organization of various reflex processes to generate rapid corrections, making the movement flexible in the face of changing environmental demands. Finally, motor programs are thought to be generalized to account for a *class* of actions (such as throwing), and parameters must be supplied to define the way in which the pattern is to be executed (such as throwing either rapidly or slowly). The schema concept and how a schema is acquired with experience is discussed extensively in chapter 10.

WEB STUDY GUIDE ACTIVITIES

The student web study guide offers these activities to help you build and apply your knowledge of the concepts in this chapter.

Interactive Learning

Activity 5.1: Indicate whether each in a list of statements applies to simple motor program theory or general motor program theory.

Activity 5.2: Determine whether motor skills are controlled by open-loop or closed-loop processes, or a combination of both.

Activity 5.3: Review the conceptual model of motor control by identifying which elements are associated with open-loop control processes only, closed-loop control processes only, or with open- and closed-loop processes.

Principles-to-Application Exercise

Activity 5.4: The principles-to-application exercise for this chapter prompts you to choose a skill and identify components of the movement that a person would control using open-loop and closed-loop processing as well as situations in which both types of control would be important.

Motor Control in Everyday Actions Narratives

Moving Sidewalks and Beer Glasses

Antilock Brakes

Point of No Return

Forensic Motor Control

Check Your Understanding

1. Name the two distinct parts of an open-loop control system. How does an open-loop control system differ from a closed-loop control system? Describe how each part of an open-loop control system might function for a child tossing toy blocks into a bin.
2. Research evidence for the existence of motor program control comes from diverse research areas. List the six types of research evidence and discuss how two of these areas provide evidence for movements being planned in advance.
3. Though there were appealing parts of motor program theory, a desire to modify motor program theory to solve the storage and novelty problems arose. What idea emerged from this desire? How does it help to explain novel movements? How does it deal with the storage problem?

Apply Your Knowledge

1. A student is packing her lunch for school. List three movements (or components of movements) involved in packing a lunch that would be controlled using open-loop processes and three that would be controlled using closed-loop processes. Choose one of the open-loop controlled movements and describe a parameter of the generalized motor program that the student could modify.
2. A woodworker is building a piece of furniture that includes large, small, simple, and complex pieces. Describe two GMPs that may be used in building the furniture, and discuss two parameters that the woodworker might need to modify throughout the project for each GMP.

Suggestions for Further Reading

Keele (1968) has provided a historical review of the motor program concept. Selverston (2010) reviews CPGs in invertebrate models. The effects of response complexity on RT are reviewed by Christina (1992). More on the startle RT paradigm can be found in Carlsen et al. (2011). Schmidt introduced the concept of GMPs (1975) and later reviewed the evidence for them (1985). A more thorough treatment of all of the issues discussed in this chapter can be found in chapter 6 of Schmidt et al. (2019). See the reference list for these additional resources.

Principles of Speed, Accuracy, and Timing

Controlling Simple Movements

KEY TERMS

amplitude
effective target width (W_e)
Fitts' Law
index of difficulty
Schmidt's Law
speed–accuracy trade-off
width

CHAPTER OUTLINE

CHAPTER OBJECTIVES

Chapter 6 describes various principles and laws of simple and coordinated actions. This chapter will help you to understand

- the speed–accuracy trade-off in simple aiming movements,
- logarithmic and linear relationships between speed and accuracy,
- and the relationship between timing accuracy and movement time.

The construction worker is pounding nails into the shingles of a new roof when she notices a storm approaching. She quickens her pace, but in so doing, notices that her aims are missing the nail more and more often—something that occurs rarely when working at her normal pace. Why is this happening? How does working at a faster pace and swinging her hammer with more force contribute to more frequent misses?

This chapter addresses questions such as these about movement control. Some of the most fundamental principles of movement production—analogous to the simple laws of physics—are shown to govern the relationship between speed, accuracy, and timing. Along the way, we reveal some of the underlying causes of movement errors and discuss ways to minimize these errors. These laws of movement production are considered as they apply in the control of relatively simple movements. In the next chapter we discuss some of the ideas related to the performance of more complex movements.

One of the most fundamental principles of rapid movement concerns the relationships among the speed of a movement, its amplitude, and the resulting accuracy. Everybody knows that when you do things too quickly, you tend to do them less accurately or effectively. The old saying "Haste makes waste" suggests that this idea has been prevalent for many centuries. Woodworth (1899) studied these phenomena early in the evolution of motor skills research, showing that the accuracy of line-drawing movements decreased as their length and speed were increased. A major contribution to our understanding of this problem was provided by the psychologist Paul Fitts, who described for the first time a mathematical principle of speed and accuracy that has come to be known as Fitts' Law.

Fitts' Law

Fitts used a paradigm in which the participant tapped alternately between two target plates as quickly as possible. The separation between the targets (termed *A*, for movement **amplitude**) and the width of the targets (termed *W*, for target **width**) could be varied in different combinations (see figure 6.1). The movement time (MT) taken to complete these rapid taps increased systematically with

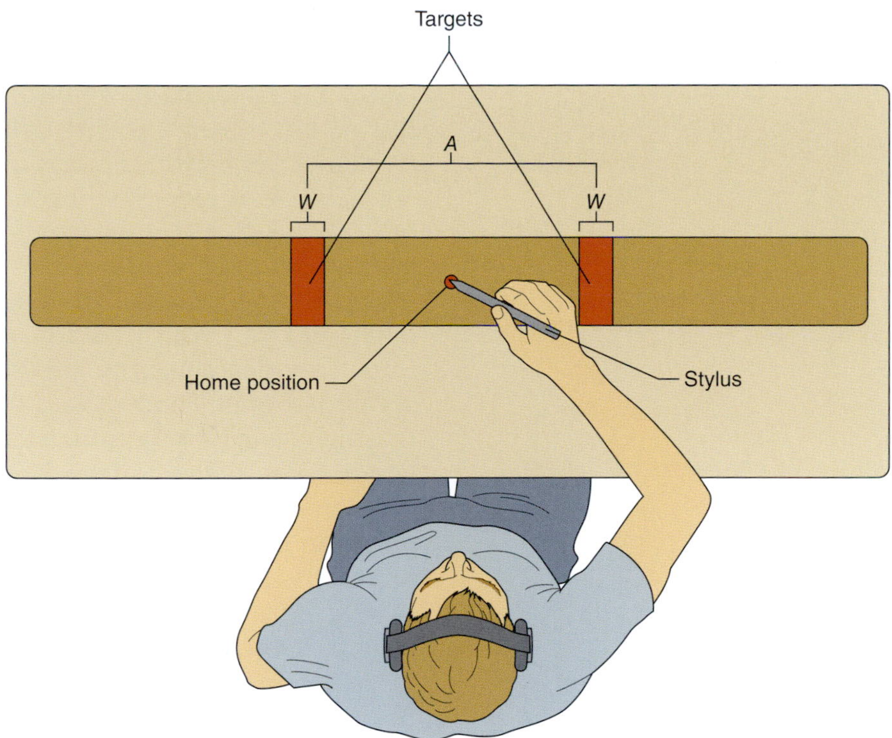

FIGURE 6.1 Illustration of a participant performing a Fitts tapping task. The participant taps between two targets of varying width (*W*) and with varying amplitude between them (*A*), attempting to move as rapidly as possible while keeping the number of target misses to a minimum.

either increases in the movement amplitude (due to a larger distance between the targets) or decreases in the target width (due to a smaller target-landing area). These relationships were combined into a formal mathematical statement that is now known as Fitts' Law (see Focus on Research 6.1).

Fitts' Law states that MT is constant whenever the ratio of the movement amplitude (*A*) to target width (*W*) remains constant. So, very long movements to wide targets require about the same time as very short movements to narrow targets. In addition, Fitts found that the MT increased as the ratio of *A* to *W* increased by either making *A* larger, making *W* smaller, or both. He combined these various effects into a single equation:

$$\mathrm{MT} = a + b\,[\mathrm{Log}_2(2A/W)]$$

where a (the MT-intercept) and b (the slope) are constants, and *A* and *W* are defined as before. The relationships between *A*, *W*, and MT are plotted in figure 6.2 for one of Fitts' data sets. The term $\mathrm{Log}_2(2A/W)$ is referred to as the **index of difficulty** (abbreviated ID), which seems to define the difficulty of the various combinations of *A* and *W*. Therefore, Fitts' Law says that MT is linearly related to the $\mathrm{Log}_2(2A/W)$, or simply, that MT is linearly related to the index of difficulty (ID).

An important point is that Fitts' Law describes the tendency for performers to trade speed for accuracy. In what has now become the typical Fitts tapping task, participants are told to minimize the number of target misses. In other words, they are instructed to adjust MT so that the errors are acceptably small. Thus, when the target size is increased, the accuracy requirements are relaxed and MTs are smaller than when narrow targets are used. This has led to the general notion of a **speed–accuracy trade-off**—the tendency for people to sacrifice or trade off speed in order to maintain acceptable levels of accuracy—as one of the most fundamental principles of movement behavior.

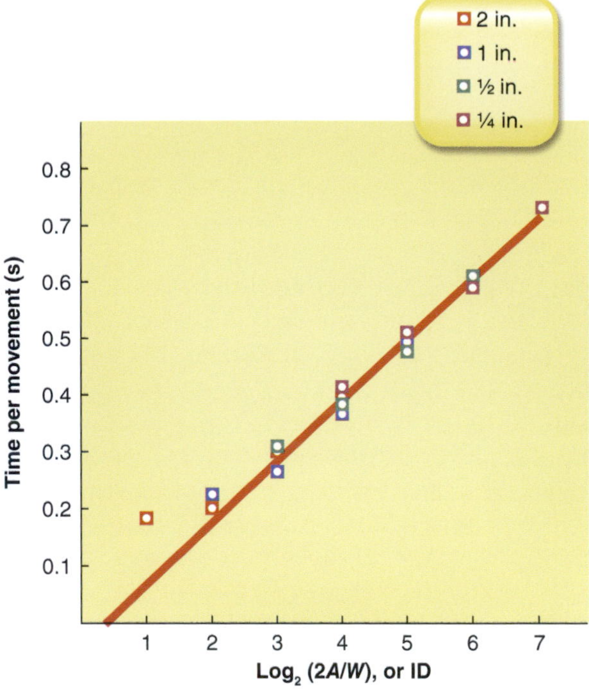

FIGURE 6.2 Average movement time (MT) as a function of the index of difficulty (ID).

Fitts' Law, which describes MT as a function of the movement distance and the accuracy requirements of a task, has been found to hold under many different environmental conditions (e.g., tapping underwater or in outer space), for many different classifications of people (e.g., children, older adults, individuals with neurological impairments), and for movements made with different effectors (e.g., handheld, foot-held, head-mounted pointing devices) (see Schmidt et al., 2019; Plamondon & Alimi, 1997). Fitts' Law also applies to how movement speed is controlled in many tasks of everyday living (see Focus on Application 6.1).

Visit the web study guide to read "The Calculator" and complete the self-directed learning activities.

The movements studied with the Fitts tapping task are almost always blends of programmed actions with feedback corrections added near the end to land on the target. That is, in these movements the performer generates a programmed initial segment of the action toward the target, probably processes visual feedback about the accuracy of this action during the movement, and initiates one (or sometimes more) feedback-based corrections to guide the limb to the target area (Elliott et al., 2017). As discussed in chapter 4, such visual compensations are probably processed through the dorsal visual stream and might not be controlled consciously. Thus, Fitts' Law describes the effectiveness of the combined open- and closed-loop processes that operate in these common kinds of actions, where potentially all of the open- and closed-loop processes shown in the conceptual model in figure 4.10 are operating together.

Finally, it is reasonable to suspect that slower movements are more accurate, at least in part, because there is more time available to detect errors and to make corrections (as discussed in chapter 4), and that MT lengthens when the number of corrections to be made increases. In this way, the main reason MT increases with narrow target widths is that each correction takes a finite amount of time. Meyer and colleagues (1988) and Elliott et al. (2017) have developed formal models of the processes involved in the speed–accuracy trade-off that extends our understanding of Fitts' principles.

Wishing to extend their ideas to tasks that are more typical and realistic, Fitts and Peterson (1964) used the same idea and variables as in the reciprocal-tapping task (figure 6.1), but used them with movements in which a single action was required from a starting position to a single target. Similar to the reciprocal-tapping task, these targets were located various distances (*A*) from the starting position and were of different sizes (*W*). Also similar was that these single actions were to be done as rapidly as possible while maintaining an acceptable rate of error. The independent variables *A* and *W* and the dependent variable MT were related to each other in essentially the same way as they were in the reciprocal task. That is to say, the equation for Fitts' Law also applied to the single-movement paradigm, which increases our confidence that Fitts'

Focus on RESEARCH 6.1

The Fitts Tasks

In his most well-known experiment, Fitts (1954) asked participants to make movements of a handheld stylus between two target plates. In this task, which is now typically known as the Fitts tapping task (see figure 6.1), the widths (*W*) of each target and the amplitude (*A*) between the targets were varied in different combinations, and the participant's goal was to alternately tap each target as quickly as possible while making as few errors as possible (missed targets < 5%). The experimenter would measure the number of taps completed in, say, a 20 s trial, and then compute the average time per movement, or movement time (MT).

However, this target-tapping paradigm was not the only way that Fitts studied rapid aiming. Figure 6.3 illustrates two other tasks used in Fitts (1954) research. In figure 6.3*a*, the participant's task was to move small metal discs with holes in the center (like carpenters' washers) from one peg to another. In figure 6.3*b*, the task was to move small pins from one hole to another. In both of these task variations, Fitts redefined target width (*W*) in terms of the tolerance between the discs and target pegs (figure 6.3*a*) or the diameter of the holes in the plate in relation to the diameter of the pin (figure 6.3*b*). With ID defined in this manner, Fitts found that the same equation—$MT = a + b$ (ID)—held well in accounting for the effects of the task parameters of movement speed.

How do all of these experimental tasks converge to define Fitts' Law? The first part is easy—amplitude is the distance-covering portion of MT and is common to each task. The effect of target size is more complicated. In the aiming task, this is essentially just target width. However, in the disc-transfer (figure 6.3*a*) and pin-transfer tasks (figure 6.3*b*), the target size is operationalized as the difference between sizes of the object and the target. For example, in the pin-transfer task, a large hole only represents an easy ID if the pin being inserted is relatively narrow. If the pin is wide, then the task becomes more difficult because there is less tolerance for error. Thus, all three of these tasks converge upon the central problem of the speed–accuracy trade-off—how the task parameters cause the participant to vary MT in order to make the end product of the aimed movement accurate.

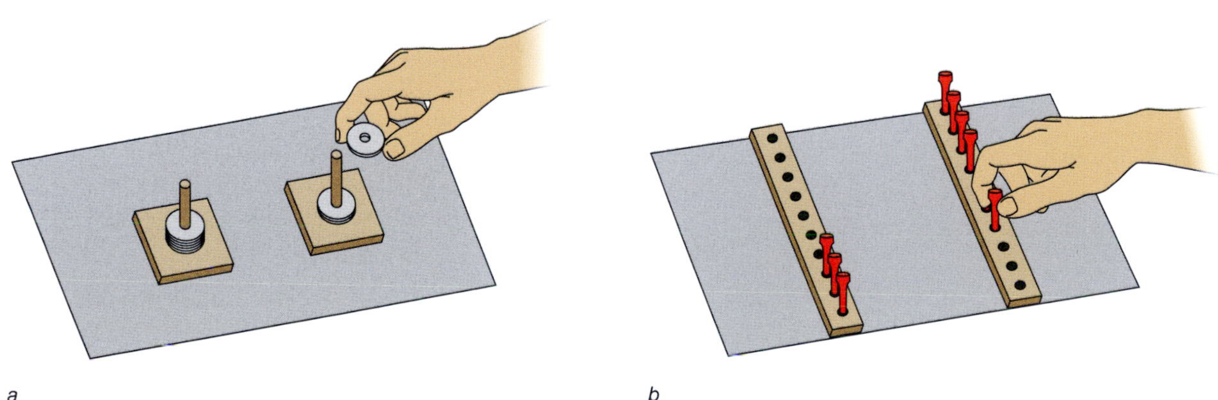

FIGURE 6.3 Alternative reciprocal-movement tasks used by Fitts (1954): *(a)* disc-transfer task, *(b)* pin-transfer task.

> *continued*

> The Fitts Tasks *continued*

Exploring Further

1. What would be the ID for a tapping task that had $W = 4$ and $A = 16$?
2. What changes in the foot's travel time from the accelerator to the brake pedal would you expect to see if you doubled the size of the brake pedal?

Law is one of the truly fundamental laws of motor behavior.

In brief, Fitts' Law tells us the following:

- Movement time (MT) increases as the movement amplitude (*A*) increases.
- MT increases as the aiming accuracy requirement increases, that is, as target width (*W*) decreases.
- MT is essentially constant for a given ratio of movement amplitude (*A*) to target width (*W*).
- These principles are valid for a wide variety of conditions, participant variables, tasks or paradigms, and body parts used.

However, a number of other questions remained unanswered. What about movements that are completed in a *very* short period of time, where presumably no feedback is involved during the movement? How can MT depend on the number of corrections when there is not enough time to make even a single correction? Some of these questions are answered in the next section.

Schmidt's Law

In the previous section we discussed Fitts' Law, which described the effects of target distance and size on MT when errors are kept at a constant rate. In this section we turn the discussion around and describe the effects of MT and distance on how errors are made.

Suppose that you were to make a quick action to move your hand or an object, as in the example of swinging a hammer at the start of this chapter. How does your accuracy change as the time for the movement and the distance of the movement vary? Such factors have been studied in aiming movements, where the participant directs a handheld stylus from a starting position to a target, with MT and movement distance being varied experimentally. The participant is instructed to move with a given MT (e.g., 150 ms) and receives feedback after each movement to help maintain the goal MT. One set of results from this kind of task is shown in figure 6.4, where accuracy is expressed as the amount of spread or inconsistency of the movement end points about the target area. This measure, called **effective target width (W_e)**, is the standard deviation of the target end points (the calculation of W_e is similar to how VE was calculated in chapter 1). The term *effective target width* means it is a measure of the target size the participant actually used in making the action with the required MT. Thus, W_e as used here is analogous to Fitts' *W*.

It is important to note from the legend in figure 6.4 that these movements are *very* fast, all with MTs of 200 ms or less. From the previous chapters, you would expect that such actions are controlled primarily by motor programming processes, with negligible vision-based feedback corrections. Yet, despite the absence of corrections, there is a gradual increase in the spread of the endpoint errors as the movement amplitude increases. That is, endpoint inaccuracy increases with movement amplitude for each of the different MT conditions (e.g., compare the W_e for the 140 ms MT condition for the three different amplitudes). Similarly, the inaccuracy of the movement increases as the MT is reduced at each of the amplitudes (e.g., compare the W_e for the three MT conditions at the 30 cm

Focus on
APPLICATION 6.1

Fitts' Law in Everyday Actions

Fitts' Law has many obvious applications in sport, in the design of industrial workspaces, and in the organization of controls in automobiles, aircraft, and so on. One example, of which you might not be aware, is the design of keyboards and calculators. Have a look at the keyboard on your computer, cell phone, or other data-input device. If the layout uses the principles consistent with Fitts' Law, you will notice that some keys are larger than others. For example, the space bar on most keyboard layouts is much larger than any of the other keys. Having larger keys means that we can make the faster movements to more frequently used keys with reduced risk of aiming errors (the Backspace, Shift, and Enter keys are also often larger in size). In other words, we can sacrifice a considerable amount of precision and still be accurate if we aim at a relatively large key. This feature allows us to move very quickly to these often-pressed keys. What other keys on your keyboard are afforded the same privilege? Does your calculator or cell phone keyboard layout have similar advantages for one or more keys? What about other data-input devices?

Navigating a cursor around a computer monitor also uses the principles of Fitts' Law, as noted in some pioneering work by Card, English, and Burr (1978). For example, the size of an icon affects the time to acquire it. Therefore, icons that increase in size as the cursor approaches are designed to reduce MT and aiming error. The size and distance of pop-up menus have obvious implications for time and errors when we are aiming the cursor at them.

Some designs use Fitts' Law in the opposite way too. For example, the next time you navigate to a website with a pop-up advertisement that can be closed by clicking the "x" icon in one of the corners, note how small the "x" is and whether it is moving or stationary. Presumably, the longer it takes for you to get your cursor over the "x" icon, the longer the information on the screen will have been there for you to process it (perhaps unwillingly). In this way, the design uses Fitts' Law purposely to *reduce* the size of the target in order to make the user spend more time on the screen. How many other applications can you think of in which the designer's intention is to make you move *more slowly* in order to be accurate?

---

distance). These two effects are more or less independent, as if the effects of increased amplitude can be added to the effect of reduced MT to produce aiming errors.

The importance of these effects of movement distance and MT on W_e suggest that open-loop processes necessary to produce the movement are also subject to the speed–accuracy trade-off. That is, the decreases in accuracy when MTs are short are not due simply to the fact that there is less time to process visual feedback; these effects of MT occur even in movements too brief to have any feedback modulations at all. Decreases in MT also seem to have effects on the consistency of the processes that generate the initial parts of the movement—that is, on the open-loop processes necessary to produce quick movements.

This finding is consistent with the ideas from Fitts' Law. In that situation, if the participant tries to make movements of a given distance too quickly, the result will be too many failures to hit the targets (which is

How can Fitts' Law help to explain the varied sizes of keys on a keyboard? What keys in this photo take advantage of Fitts' Law? How would you redesign this calculator to take advantage of Fitts' Law in general? Provide an example of how it might be redesigned for a specific purpose.

unacceptable in terms of the experimenter's instructions that generally demand errors on less than 5% of the movements). So the participant must slow down to comply with the experimenter's instructions, decreasing the variability in the movements and hitting the target more often.

These separate effects of movement amplitude and MT can be combined into a single expression, more or less as was done by Fitts. The amount of movement error (W_e) was linearly related to the movement's average

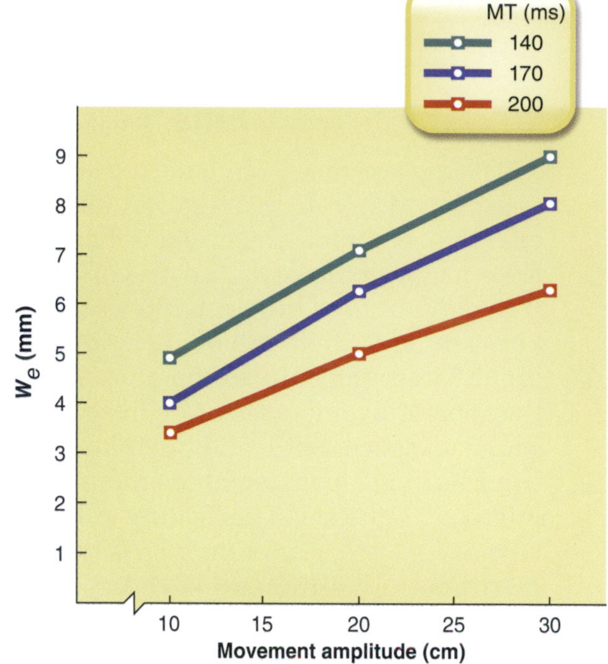

FIGURE 6.4 Variability of movement end points (defined as the standard deviation of the produced movement distances, or effective target width, W_e) in a rapid aiming task as a function of MT and distance.

velocity—that is, to the ratio A/MT (Schmidt et al., 1979). For example, in figure 6.5 the variability in hitting the target is plotted against the movement's average velocity (in centimeters per second, or cm/s), showing that, as the movement velocity increased, aiming errors increased almost linearly as well. In the present edition of this book we now follow others (e.g., Jagacinski & Flach, 2003) in naming this principle **Schmidt's Law**, which describes the *linear speed–accuracy trade-off.* Schmidt's Law suggests that aiming errors are about the same for various combinations of movement amplitude and MT that have a constant ratio (that is, a constant average velocity). Thus, increases in movement amplitude and decreases in MT can be traded off with each other to maintain movement accuracy in these rapid tasks.

Visit the web study guide to read "The Gimme Putt" and complete the self-directed learning activities.

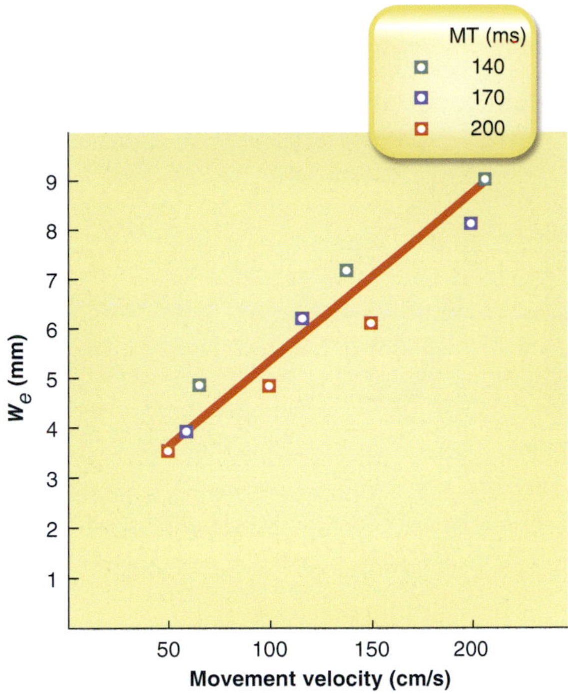

FIGURE 6.5 Variability of movement end points (W_e) in a rapid aiming task as a function of average movement velocity (A/MT).

Understanding Schmidt's Law

Why do very rapid movements, in which there is little time for feedback processing and corrections, produce more errors as the movement distance increases or the MT decreases? The answer seems to lie with the processes that translate the motor program's output into movements of the body part. In chapter 5 we discussed how motor programs are responsible for determining the ordering of muscle contractions and the amounts of force that must be generated in the participating muscles. How might these sources of error contribute to movement inaccuracy?

It has been known for a long time that even if the performer attempts to produce the same force over and over on successive trials, the actual force produced will be somewhat inconsistent. This variability is thought to be caused by the relatively "noisy" (i.e., inconsistent) processes that convert central nervous system impulses into the activation of muscle motor units, which ultimately exert forces on bones, thus causing movements. Also, there is variability in the contractions generated by various reflex activities.

The presence of these noisy processes in the system means that the forces actually produced in a contraction are not exactly what were intended by the motor program. Noise in the system can be thought of in terms of the phonograph record analogy presented in chapter 5. By this analogy, noise can be introduced in several places in the stereo system, such as scratches on the record, quality of the turntable needle and speakers, and imperfections in the electronics and wiring of the system. These deviations from perfect fidelity in the stereo system make the sounds we hear be slightly different than the sounds as originally recorded.

In movement control, these noisy processes are not constant; they change as the amount of contraction force changes. This has been studied using tasks in which the participant is asked to produce brief (ballistic) force applications to an apparatus handle; these force applications are such that the peak force produced on any contraction matches a (submaximal) goal force. Figure 6.6 illustrates a typical set of results. Notice that as the contraction force increases, there is more variability in these forces, as if the noisy processes were becoming larger as well. In the figure, the variability in these forces (i.e., the within-participant standard deviation of the force productions), which is interpreted as the size of the noise component, is shown as a function of the size of the contraction, expressed as a percentage of the performer's maximum force. The noise component generally increases as the amount of force increases, up through about 70% of the participant's maximum. However, when the contractions are very large, approaching maximal values, the amount of force variability appears to level off again, with perhaps a slight decrease in the force variability in nearly maximal contractions. These findings have been reported in both laboratory tasks (Sherwood, Schmidt, & Walter, 1988) and with real skills such as an overarm throwing task in which participants threw balls at 40% to 100% of their maximum velocities (Urbin et al., 2012).

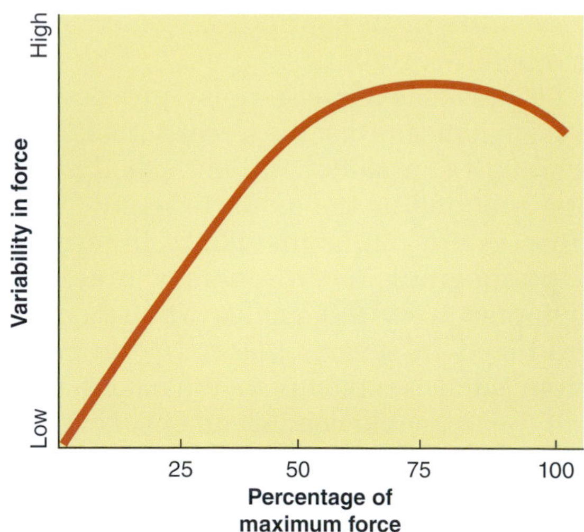

FIGURE 6.6 The relationship between the variability in force produced as a function of the percentage of maximum force used.

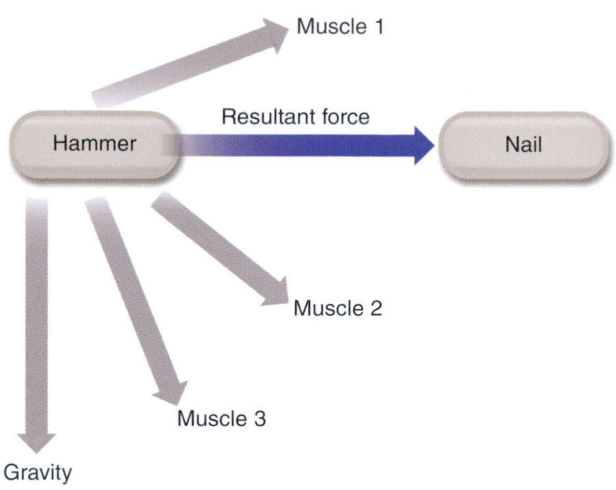

FIGURE 6.7 A hammer, swung at a nail on a vertical board by an arm and hand, is influenced by many forces.

How does this information help in understanding error generation? To extend the example discussed at the beginning of the chapter, consider a movement like hammering a nail into a wall by swinging the hammer with the arm and hand. In such a movement, many muscles operate on the hands, arms, and upper torso to produce forces against the bones, which direct the hammer toward the nail. The direction of action of some of these muscles may happen to be lined up with the intended movement, but most of them are not; rather, the muscles are aligned at various angles to the action, as shown in figure 6.7. And, in many actions such as this, gravity acts as one of the contributing forces as well. To complete such an action perfectly, the various muscles must contract with just the right amounts of force, in coordination with each other, so that the *resultant* force is in line with the intended movement. Of course, if any of these forces is substantially in error—for example, if the contraction of muscle 1 is too great—the movement's direction will be in error as well, with the movement missing the target.

Now, what happens when a given movement is made more rapidly? Of course, as the MT decreases, the forces exerted against the bones of the arm must increase. When these forces increase (up to about 70% of maximum) the noisiness of these forces increases as well (figure 6.6). This has the effect of adding a slight error component (with the variations in muscle force being independent) to the contraction of each of the involved muscles, causing them to contract slightly differently from how the motor program intended. If these forces are no longer perfectly coordinated with each other, the movement will tend to miss its target. Thus, the movement's inaccuracy increases as MT decreases, primarily because of the increased noise involved in the stronger muscle contractions.

In summary, this is why increasing the speed of a rapid movement contributes to its inaccuracy (Schmidt's Law):

- The relative contraction forces of the various participating muscles are a major factor in determining the ultimate trajectory of the limb.
- The inconsistency in these forces increases with increased force.
- When MT decreases, more force is required.
- When amplitude increases, more force is required.

- More force generates more variability, which causes the movement to deviate from the intended trajectory, resulting in errors.

Speed–Accuracy Trade-Off Exceptions

As common as the speed–accuracy trade-off seems to be for movement behavior, there are a few situations in which it does not appear to hold, or at least in cases in which the principles are somewhat different from those indicated in the previous sections. These situations involve cases in which (1) extremely rapid and forceful actions are involved, (2) targets are imbedded in a visual illusion, and (3) timing accuracy is the movement goal.

Very Forceful Movements

Many human movements, especially those in sport, require extremely forceful contractions of muscles, leading to nearly maximal movement speeds, as in kicking a football or hitting a golf ball. Making the movement at near-maximal speed is often only a part of the problem because these actions often must be performed with great precision in space and time. As it turns out, alterations in movement speed affect these nearly maximal actions somewhat differently from many of the less forceful actions discussed so far.

Consider a rapid, horizontal, straight-arm movement in which a handheld pointer is aimed at a target as if it were a ball to be hit. What would happen to the spatial accuracy if the required MT decreased, so the movements would be closer and closer to the performer's maximal force capabilities? This is similar to your swinging of a hammer harder and harder, with the limit being your own force capabilities. As you might expect from Schmidt's Law, movements with shorter MTs are less spatially accurate but only up to a point, as seen in figure 6.8. Participants in this study by Schmidt and Sherwood (1982) produced MTs of about 160 ms (slowest) to 80 ms (fastest), which represented a range of force production capabilities between 21% and 84%. As seen in figure 6.8, by reducing MT there were increases in the percentage of maximum force produced from 21% to 32% and 50%. The result was a rapid increase in force variability. However, when the MT was reduced further, the percentage of maximum force rose from 50% to 84% and resulted in a *decrease* in the force variability (see figure 6.6). Thus, very rapid and very slow movements have the most spatial accuracy, and moderate-speed movements have the least accuracy. This set of data goes against the strict interpretation of Schmidt's Law, in which faster movements are always less spatially accurate.

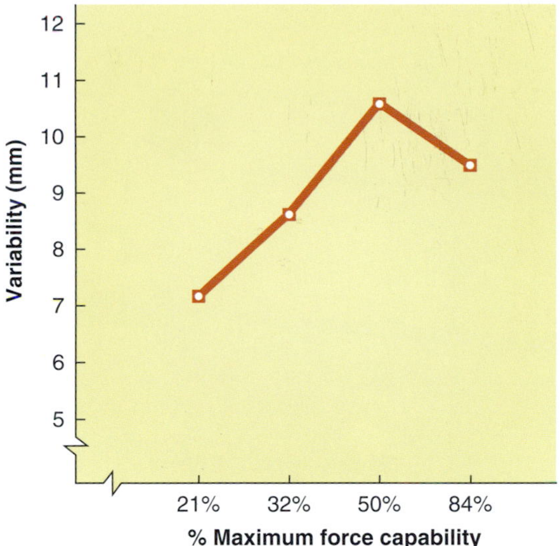

FIGURE 6.8 The effect of force on the positional variability in horizontal arm swing movements. The percentage values on the x-axis are the percentages of the participant's maximum force produced, and correspond to increasingly smaller MTs (i.e., 21% = 158 ms mean MT; 32% = 130 ms; 50% = 102 ms; 84% = 80 ms).

How can these near maximally forceful movements be made so rapidly yet be so spatially accurate? These movements are very much like those illustrated in figure 6.7, where several muscles operate in coordination to determine the limb's trajectory. Also recall that, when the forces are very large,

Very forceful movements performed at nearly maximal speed are an exception to the speed–accuracy trade-off. At what percentage of maximum velocity might you expect performance to be most variable?

approaching maximum, the force-variability levels off and actually decreases slightly, as seen in figure 6.6 by the small downturn near the highest levels of force. Therefore, the nearly maximal movements in figure 6.8 are operating in a range where the forces are becoming *more consistent* with increases in force. This low-force variability allows these very forceful actions to be very consistent spatially.

In summary, here's how the theory attempts to explain what happens when a movement requires very high levels of muscular contractions (greater than about 70% of the participant's capabilities):

- Increasing speed by reducing MT can decrease spatial and timing error.
- Because a greater muscular force requirement actually increases accuracy in this range, adding inertial load to the movement can decrease error, up to a point.
- An inverted-U relationship exists between spatial accuracy and force requirements, with least accuracy at moderate levels of force.

Visual Illusions

Aiming at targets, such as throwing darts at a bull's-eye, putting a golf ball toward a hole, or kicking a soccer ball toward a goal, can be influenced greatly by its immediate visual environment. Consider the figures presented in figure 6.9 for example. Three target circles are illustrated in figure 6.9*a*—one has no surrounding environment (the lone circle in the middle of the figure), one is surrounded by a ring of small circles (array on the left), and one is surrounded by a ring of large circles (array on the right). Many perceptual experiments have been performed with these stimuli, and the typical finding is that the target circle surrounded by ring of small circles is judged to be larger than the target circle surrounded by the ring of large circles. The perceived size of the control target usually falls in between.

Another visual illusion is the Müller-Lyer illusion (figure 6.9*b*). When participants are asked to judge the length of the straight line, the figure on the left, with the inward-pointing arrows, is judged to be longer than the control line in the middle, and much longer than the line on the right, with the outward-pointing arrows.

The actual sizes of the targets in figure 6.9 are exactly the same—the middle circles all have the same diameter, and the lines are all the same length. And yet, when targets like these are used in manual aiming experiments, their surrounding visual environments have an impact on movement control. For example, participants in Elliott and Lee (1995) made a ballistic aiming movement from one end of a Müller-Lyer target toward the other end of the line. Consistent with the perceptual illusion, the aiming errors were largely overshoots (positive CE) in the lines that appeared to be longer (left side of figure 6.9*b*) and undershoots (negative CE) for the lines that appeared to be shorter (right side of figure 6.9*b*).

Similar findings have been shown with circles, as in figure 6.9*a*, in which a golf ball was putted toward the target circle. In studies by Witt et al. (2012) and Wood et al. (2013), participants hit golf balls toward targets that were projected onto a putting surface that were surrounded by rings of smaller or larger circles. Similar to the perceptual judgments, the putts were more accurate when made toward targets that appeared to be bigger (figure 6.9*a*, left side) than target holes that appeared smaller (figure 6.9*a*, right side).

Should these findings be considered as speed–accuracy trade-off exceptions? It depends. In the case of the Ebbinghaus-Titchener illusion, motor performance differences were found for targets that in actuality were identical in size. In the case of the Müller-Lyer illusion, differential aiming errors were found for lines of identical lengths. So, in one sense, these are exceptions because the *actual* target dimensions did not predict the observed outcomes. On the other hand, perhaps they might not be considered as speed–accuracy trade-off exceptions because the aiming errors in these studies were influenced in a manner that was consistent with the participants' *perceptions* of the targets.

Of special interest with these visual illusions, however, are some potential implications for sport performance. For example, Chauvel et al. (2015) found that participants who putted toward a hole surrounded by a ring of small circles (making the hole seem bigger) improved their performance more during a practice session than did a group of participants who putted toward a hole surrounded by a ring of large circles. Importantly, when retested a day later in which the surrounding circles were no longer present for either group, the group that had previously practiced with the perceptually larger hole maintained an advantage in performance. As we will discuss in later chapters, such

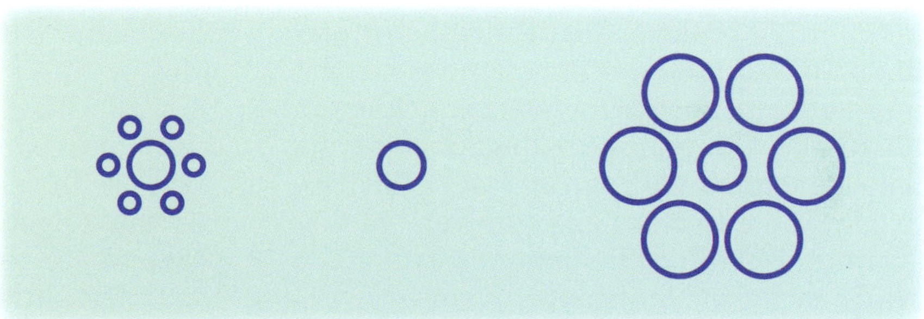

a Ebbinghaus-Titchener illusion: The circle in the middle appears larger when surrounded by smaller circles (figure on the left) than when surrounded by larger circles (figure on the right). Both are the same size as the lone circle in the center.

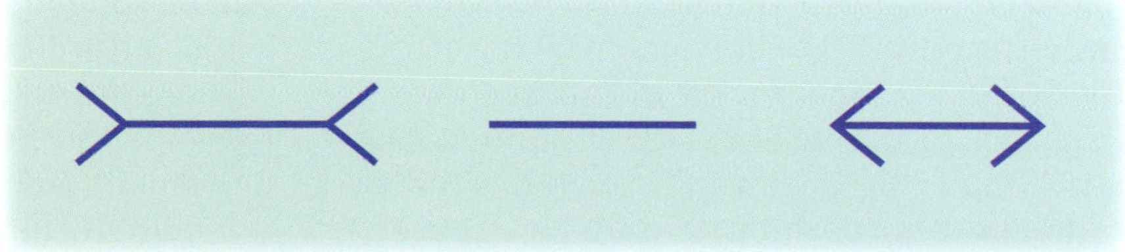

b Müller-Lyer illusion: The line connecting the two inward-pointing arrows (figure on the left) appears to be longer than the line connecting the two outward-pointing arrows (figure on the right) even though the two lines are the same length as the line in the middle.

FIGURE 6.9 Two visual illusions used in aiming studies: (*a*) the Ebbinghaus-Titchener illusion, and (*b*) the Müller-Lyer illusion.

differences, when found in tests of retention, are strong evidence for learning effects. In this case, practice with the perceptually larger holes produced better learning than with the smaller-looking holes.

Movement Timing

In previous sections of this chapter the concern was with situations in which spatial accuracy was the major goal, and we showed how this changes as movement velocity changes. However, for many skills the main or additional goal is *temporal accuracy* (e.g., batting a baseball). In such skills a movement must be timed so that some part of it is produced at a particular moment (e.g., the bat must cross the plate at the same time the ball is there). The timing accuracy is critical to the success of the movement. For example, a perfectly struck chord on the guitar only makes a contribution to the music when it is timed right.

Still other skills have both temporal and spatial goals, intermixed in complicated ways. Of course, batting a pitched baseball requires accuracy in terms of where to swing to meet the ball (spatial) as well as when to swing (temporal). But an important skill in batting demands that the performer be able to time the *duration* of the swing. Knowing or predicting the duration of the swing is critical in order for the batter to determine when to initiate the swing so the bat arrives over the plate coincident with the arrival of the ball. So being able to make a fast movement that occupies a predictable amount of time is a critical factor in batting effectiveness.

In this section we are concerned with the temporal component of such skills, discussing the factors that affect timing accuracy. The temporal component can be isolated somewhat in the rapid task in which the performer makes a fast movement, whose goal is to produce a particular MT as accurately as possible. Timing accuracy is studied as a function of changes in MT, as well as other variables. It turns out that skills with purely temporal goals seem to follow somewhat different principles than those having purely spatial goals (Schmidt et al., 1979).

What happens when participants are asked to produce movements of a given distance but with the MT goal reduced from 300 ms to 150 ms? One might expect that because the velocity of the movement is larger, it would have more error, as was found in figures 6.4 and 6.5 (Schmidt's Law). Not so. Decreasing the MT (i.e., movements made faster) has the effect of *decreasing* the timing error, making the movement more accurate in time, not less. This can be seen in figure 6.11, in which variability in timed actions increases almost linearly with increases in goal MT; halving the goal MT (within limits) almost tends to halve the timing errors. An additional finding is that this relationship for MT and timing variability holds not only for discrete, single-action movements but also for repetitive movements (Wing & Kristofferson, 1973). Therefore, for skills in which timing error has to be reduced, the main factor is the MT, which is quite different from the situation for skills with spatial goals as demonstrated in figures 6.4 and 6.5 (see Schmidt et al., 1979).

These findings about timing errors are not as strange as they seem at first, as you will see if you do the following simple demonstration. Use the timer function on a cell phone and, without looking at it, start and stop the timer in order to generate exactly 10 s. Do this 10 times in total and record the amount of error you make on each trial. Then use the error scores on the individual 10 trials to generate average constant error (CE) and variable error (VE) (see chapter 1). Next, do 10 trials of the task again, but this time try to generate 5 s. Compare the error measures generated from the 10 trials on the two tasks. You will likely find that the amount of error you make in estimating 5 s will be about half the amount of error for 10 s (especially VE). Why? A probable reason is because the system that generates these durations (including both the stopwatch and arm movement tasks) is "noisy" or variable, and the amount of this variability increases or accumulates as the duration of the event to be timed increases.

Applying the Principles: Baseball Batting

It may seem from the previous section that sometimes contradictory principles are involved in these rapid actions. To help in understanding, it will be useful to apply these principles to a familiar task like batting in baseball. This task requires several of the processes discussed so far, such as anticipation and timing, prediction of the ball's spatial trajectory and its arrival time at the coincidence point, and rapid movements that must be both forceful and accurate, so the principles can be applied to various parts of this action. To examine the effects of altering the MT of the swing of the bat, let's assume that some factors are held constant, such as the nature of the pitch and the situation in the game.

A few facts about the timelines involved in hitting a baseball are summarized in figure 6.10. In elite skill–level baseball, a 90 mph (145 kph) pitch requires about 460 ms to travel from the pitcher to the plate, and the MT of the swing of the bat is about 160 ms (Hubbard & Seng, 1954). Evidence presented earlier showed that the internal signal to trigger the swing occurs about 170 ms before the movement starts (Slater-Hammel, 1960; review figure 5.3*b* and Focus on Research 5.2). With these process durations combined, the signal to trigger the action must be given about 330 ms before the ball arrives at the plate—that is, 170 ms to prepare the swing plus 160 ms to carry it out. Therefore, the decision about whether or not to swing at the ball must be made well before the ball has traveled even halfway to the plate, or after only 130 ms of ball travel. Although some

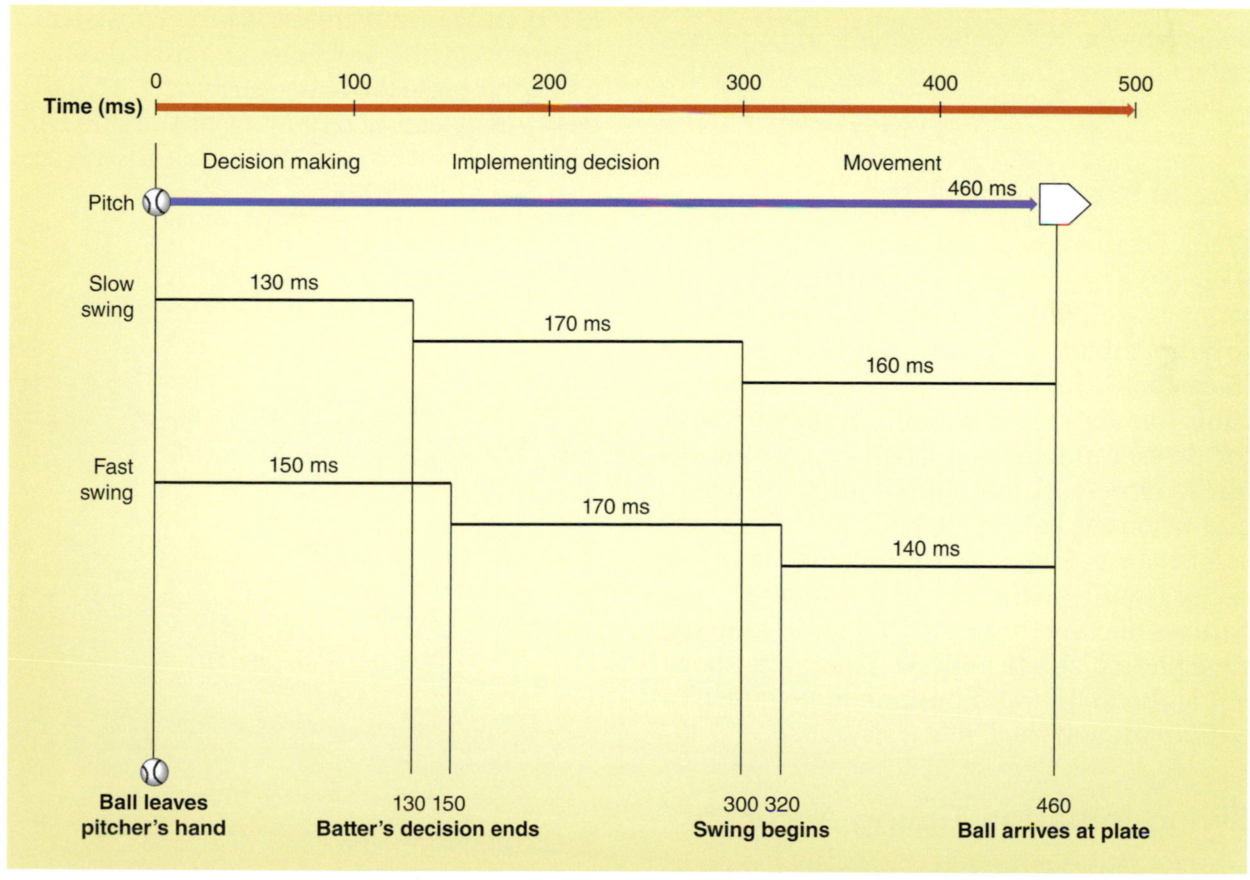

FIGURE 6.10 Timeline of events as a baseball leaves the pitcher's hand and arrives at the plate. The pitch is traveling at a velocity of 90 mph. A fast swing (140 ms) has 20 ms less MT than a slower swing (160 ms).

late, visually based corrections in the movement are possible, as discussed in chapter 4, the majority of the action must be planned in advance and initiated by the central nervous system some 330 ms before the ball arrives. Making decisions relative to the occurrence of these critical times plays a decisive role in a batter's success in hitting a pitched ball and also in making changes to an initial decision to swing (see Focus on Application 5.1 for more on checked swings).

An important consideration, given the previous discussion of speed and accuracy processes in the chapter, is this: What would happen if the batter could speed up the swing, say from 160 ms to 140 ms? The bat swing's MT could be made shorter through instructions or training to make the actual movement faster, through shortening the movement distance by reducing the backswing (a very slight effect), through using a lighter bat, or through changing the biomechanics of the movement in various ways. Reducing the bat swing MT by 20 ms would have important implications for several separate factors discussed in the previous few sections.

Visual Processing Time

Figure 6.10 shows that shortening the MT delays the beginning of the swing, hence the point at which the details of the action have to be specified, to a position several feet later in the ball's flight. This provides additional time for viewing the ball's trajectory and for determining time to contact, and should allow more accurate anticipation of where and when the ball will arrive. And this extra information comes at a point that is maximally useful—when the ball is closer to the batter—making these extra 20 ms of viewing time particularly beneficial. Therefore, shortening the MT should provide more effective anticipation of the ball's trajectory.

Swing-Initiation Timing Accuracy

If the swing of the bat is speeded up, the decision about when to initiate the movement is made later and is more temporally accurate. In an experiment on a simulated batting task, shortening the MT stabilized the initiation time of the movement, as if the batter were more certain of when to start the swing (Schmidt, 1969). Starting the swing at a more stable time therefore translates into a more stable time for the movement end point at the plate, which yields greater movement timing accuracy.

Movement Timing Accuracy

One process the batter must go through in planning the swing is to estimate the duration of his *own* movement. Poulton (1974) termed this "effector anticipation." Therefore, the batter selects a MT, then initiates this action at such a time that the middle of the movement coincides with the arrival of the ball at the plate. If the actual MT is different from the one predicted, the middle of the movement will be too early or late, causing timing errors in hitting the ball. Because reduced MT increases movement timing consistency (figure 6.11), the movement's actual duration will be closer to the batter's estimate. This will result in greater accuracy in hitting the ball, particularly in terms of the timing aspects (see also Schmidt, 1969).

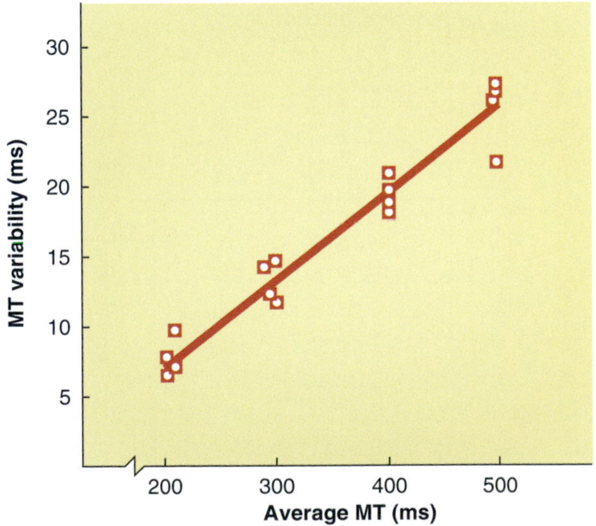

FIGURE 6.11 The effect of average MT duration on the variability of timing. As MT decreases (i.e., movements are made faster), the variability of timing decreases (i.e., becomes more stable).

Movement Spatial Accuracy

Making the movement faster also influences spatial accuracy, as discussed earlier. If the movement is already relatively slow, instructions to decrease the MT have a detrimental effect on accuracy in hitting the ball. However, most bat swing movements are already quite fast, near the performer's limits in producing force. Recall that when movements are very fast and forceful, reducing the MT tends to increase—not decrease—accuracy (figure 6.11), because the force variability decreases in this range with decreases in MT (figure 6.6). Therefore, reducing the MT when it is already quite short results in improved spatial accuracy, giving more frequent ball contact.

Ball Impact

Finally, of course, a faster swing gives more impact to the ball if it is hit—a critical factor in the particular game of baseball. Increasing the load by having a heavier bat can improve spatial accuracy (Schmidt & Sherwood, 1982) and would have only minimal negative effects on movement speed. Clearly, both added bat mass and a faster MT contribute to greater impact with the ball if and when it is hit.

Nearly every factor associated with decreased bat swing MT discussed here would be expected to influence the chances of hitting the ball. Perhaps understanding these factors makes it clearer why professional batters seem to swing with near maximal speeds.

Speed of Initiating Movement

A curious phenomenon occurs in Western action movies in which the combatants duel in a gunfight—the person who draws first almost always loses (figure 6.12). According to Kelso (1995), this curiosity was first noted by the famous physicist Niels Bohr, who famously took his research team to see old Western movies to lighten up the tension in the lab. Could this result really happen? Why would starting to move before the other person be a bad idea?

Making the first move provides an obvious head-start advantage. But can that advantage be overcome by moving faster? If so, why? Such questions were the premise of studies that compared the speed to self-initiate movement compared to the speed of reactive movements. One paradigm saw pairs of research participants play a friendly but competitive game in which the simple goal was to complete an upper-arm movement faster than the opponent (Welchman et al., 2010). Many trials were completed and scored on the basis of who started their movement first. As Bohr had anticipated, Welchman et al. found when a participant moved first they did so more slowly than when they were reacting to their opponent (who had moved first), especially when kinematics such as peak velocity and the time to reach peak velocity were measured (LaDelfa et al., 2013). Nicknamed the "gunslinger effect" by LaDelfa et al., this somewhat surprising finding has being replicated in experiments using more complex actions, such as a karate punch (Martinez De Quel & Bennett, 2014), as well as when the participants performed as a cooperative unit rather than in competition (Weller et al., 2018).

The gunslinger effect raises some fundamental questions about the differences in self-initiated and reactive movements. Studies of brain activity during movement suggest that self-initiated (or willed) actions involve a different neural pathway than do reactive responses (Weller et al., 2018). This finding may also help to further our understanding about why individuals with certain neurological disorders, such Parkinson's disease, have more difficulty in self-initiating movements than responding with similar actions to environmental stimuli.

The implications of the gunslinger effect for the information-processing model in figure 4.10 are not entirely clear at this time. Presumably the motor program would still need to be sent to the spinal cord and muscles, but perhaps so using different neural mechanisms for self-initiated and

FIGURE 6.12 In the lore of Western movies, the person who draws first usually loses.

reactive movements. Regardless, as we have seen throughout this chapter, the speed of completing—and in this case, initiating—simple movements is influenced importantly by a number of task-related factors. As we will see in the next chapter, the complexity of the discussion increases as we consider how actions are coordinated.

Summary

The accuracy of rapid movements controlled by motor programs is influenced by speed and amplitude variations, and these actions display a typical speed–accuracy trade-off. Increases in speed (decreases in MT) usually degrade spatial accuracy unless the movements are very rapid and forceful. On the other hand, decreasing the MT usually enhances *timing* accuracy. These effects are caused by relatively noisy low-level processes in the spinal cord and the muscles that make the contractions differ slightly from those originally intended. Movements that are self-initiated are started more slowly than reactive movements, perhaps reflecting different neural structures in their process.

WEB STUDY GUIDE ACTIVITIES

The student web study guide offers these activities to help you build and apply your knowledge of the concepts in this chapter.

Interactive Learning

Activity 6.1: Identify the correct equation for Fitts' Law.

Activity 6.2: Select the type of movement to which each statement applies to better understand the speed–accuracy trade-off and exceptions to it.

Principles-to-Application Exercise

Activity 6.3: The principles-to-application exercise for this chapter prompts you to identify a skill that involves rapid movement and requires accuracy, then to explore how the speed–accuracy trade-off phenomenon applies to the skill you have chosen and explain the sources of error in rapid movements.

Motor Control in Everyday Actions Narratives

The Calculator

The Gimme Putt

Check Your Understanding

1. Distinguish between temporal and spatial accuracy. Give an example of an activity (e.g., a game of tennis) where both might be important. Describe a situation where temporal accuracy is important and explain why this is so, and then do the same for a situation where spatial accuracy is important.
2. Explain what Fitts' Law tells us about motor control and speed–accuracy trade-offs.

Apply Your Knowledge

1. Your friend has come up with a silly competition: At the driving range you race to see who can go through a bucket of golf balls the fastest, while keeping score for accuracy in hitting a middle distance on the range. The winner is determined by a combined score of time and error (distance from the target). Discuss two strategies that you might use to win the competition. Would your strategies change if the winner were determined by time and the combined distance of your shots? What if the competition got even sillier and the accuracy in timing between the shots mattered?

Suggestions for Further Reading

Woodworth's legacy on speed and accuracy research is presented by Elliott, Helson, and Chua (2001). Further details on sources of error in motor control for aiming movements have been reviewed by Meyer et al. (1988) and Elliott et al. (2017), who provide elegant theories of these processes that applies to many different kinds of limb movement situations. Meyer et al. (1990) and Elliott et al. (2001) have also written historical reviews about speed–accuracy trade-off effects. Urbin et al. (2011) review later-day work on Schmidt's Law. Wing (2002) provides a detailed account of timing variability from an information-processing viewpoint. See the reference list for these additional resources.

7

Performance of Complex Movements

From Abilities to Coordination Dynamics

KEY TERMS

ability
anti-phase
control parameter
coordination dynamics
differential method
general motor ability
individual differences
in-phase
prediction
relative-age effect
relative phase
self-organization
skill

CHAPTER OUTLINE

CHAPTER OBJECTIVES

Chapter 7 describes differing approaches to understanding how complex motor skills are performed. This chapter will help you to understand

- the nature of abilities and how they are distinguished from skills,
- two approaches to conceptualizing the "all-around athlete,"
- the difficulty in predicting future successes in motor performance,
- how Fitts' Law is affected when moving two limbs to separate targets,
- why horses, and humans, change gaits,
- how two oscillating limbs spontaneously coordinate, dissolve, and recoordinate in measurable patterns.

The first six chapters of this book have described the study of motor performance by deconstructing the movement process, illustrated by the conceptual model (see figure 5.2). Focus was directed at research concerning the performance of relatively simple skills, such as speeded reactions or aimed limb movements. However, skilled performance in sport, music, performance arts, and indeed, most activities of daily living, are characterized by skills that are much more complex in nature. Look at the photo on the first page of this chapter, for instance. The juggler is balancing on a unicycle, moving by alternating the actions of each leg, catching and releasing knives in a coordinated fashion, and doing it all while playing the bagpipes. In this chapter we consider different approaches to understanding how complex movement skills like these are performed.

Three different approaches to the study of complex movement are described in this chapter. Early in motor skills research there was a heavy emphasis on skills and abilities—how individuals could be defined by the set of skills and abilities they possessed and how these differentiated individuals from one another. Later research abandoned this differential approach for one designed to understand movement processes that applied to everyone. These investigations were carried out initially with discrete skills. Later on, the focus shifted to coordination of continuous skills and with it came a completely new theoretical focus—how performance changed as a function of time and interactions with the environment.

Traditional Approaches to Studying Complex Movement

The traditional approach, which dominated motor skills research into the 1960s, concerned the differences between and among people on measures of performance. This approach used techniques referred to as the **differential method**, concerned with the fact that none of us are the same and focused on how and why we differ from one another. The differential method contrasted markedly with the experimental method, using alternative ways of thinking and conducting research. As a result, research about **individual differences** tends to look very different from the experimental research that was described in the first six chapters.

Consider the conceptual model presented in figure 5.2 as illustrating all the ways in which individual differences could occur. Essentially, every one of the processes we discussed in the earlier parts of the book is a candidate for having individual differences in its functioning. The study of individual differences actually involves two rather distinct emphases: the study of abilities and the study of prediction.

Abilities

A typical question asked by an individual-differences researcher might be this: Why is Bonnie such a standout surgeon? One answer, on which we focus in part II of the book, concerns practice and learning. That is, the standout surgeon has devoted many hours to practicing her craft, which has made a large contribution to her skilled performance. Another answer suggests that the surgeon inherited some special abilities—a certain fundamental characteristic that allows her to perform at a high level. An **ability** is a characteristic that underlies particular skills, is largely inherited genetically, and is not modifiable by practice.

Prediction

The second aspect of individual-differences research concerns what is called **prediction**. The car insurance industry charges us rates that are dependent, in part, on the likelihood that we will have an accident, and uses historical data to determine these numbers. The insurance company knows that there is a relationship between certain fundamental features of the drivers (e.g., the driver's age, accident record) that are relatively strongly related to (or correlated with) future accident propensity. These driver features can be thought of as abilities—the insurance company is predicting the likelihood of an accident based on some measure of your abilities. Of course, the company cannot accurately predict whether or not you will have an accident next year. But if you are in a younger age group (16–25), the likelihood of having an accident is larger than that of someone in an older age group, and thus your premium rates are higher.

Prediction is all around us. Universities typically use various test measures (e.g., the SAT) as estimates of which applicants are most likely to succeed in their programs. Some dental schools use various "spatial abilities" tests as a means to screen applicants for admittance into their programs. The gymnastics coach may screen out who will not become a collegiate gymnast on the basis of, say, body configuration. People who are over 6 ft tall and weigh more than 220 lb are less likely to be successful gymnasts than others with slighter physical dimensions. Others may attempt to predict who will be a successful athlete based on more movement-based ability measures (e.g., strength, speed).

Abilities Versus Skills

Of critical importance to individual differences research area is the distinction between the concepts of ability and skill. In common language, these words are used more or less interchangeably, as in "Buddy has good ability (or skill) at guitar." However, as defined earlier, abilities are genetically determined and largely unmodifiable by practice or experience. An ability, therefore, is part of the basic "equipment" people inherit and use to perform various tasks. **Skill**, on the other hand, refers to one's proficiency at a particular task, such as shooting a basketball. Skills, of course, can be modified by practice, are countless in number, and represent the person's potential to perform those particular activities. Thus, one could say "Eric has good visual acuity," implying that he has the ability to see very well. But Eric has developed the specific skill of identifying patterns of motion

Name two potential visual abilities and perceptual skills demonstrated by a professional goalkeeper.

in football through considerable practice, and this *skill* has Eric's visual acuity as an underlying *ability*.

It is helpful to think of ability as a factor that sets limits on performance. Some people will very likely never become linemen in professional football, regardless of how much time they devote to practice, because they do not have the proper body-configuration for this skill. The requisite ability (or abilities) required for a particular task act as constraints to limit the level of skill that a particular individual can eventually attain. On the other hand, if a novice does not perform very well on a particular task, this might lead to the suspicion that she does not have the requisite ability to develop the skill. However, much of this deficit can often be erased through effective practice. Notice that even though measures of the skill can change with learning, the ability underlying this skill would not change with practice (because it is stable and enduring). Appreciating the differences between the terms *ability* and *skill* is important in applying the differential method to understanding issues such as individual differences and prediction.

Defining Individual Differences

Individual differences are defined as stable, enduring differences among people in terms of some measurable characteristic or performance of some task. Two people can differ on a given performance in at least two different ways. First, if the test involves a very stable measure such as body weight, after a single measurement we might conclude that one person is really heavier than the other. Although the scales might have some small degree of variability, the *repeatability* of the measure is very good. This is an example of a measured characteristic that reveals a stable, enduring difference between two people.

A second difference between people, however, can also occur when no stable enduring difference is really present. For example, if one person rolls a strike in bowling on one attempt and another person rolls a gutter ball, it might not be wise to conclude immediately that the first person is a better bowler than the second person based on this one measurement. This is because almost anything can happen on a particular performance attempt by chance alone, and individual differences must be based on stable, enduring differences. In the first example (weighing people on scales), you are relatively confident of stable, enduring differences in the measured trait, whereas in the second example you are not.

Understanding the "All-Around Athlete"

One of the long-lasting controversies in the individual-differences literature concerns the so-called all-around athlete. Most of us have known a kid from school who was a star athlete on the football, baseball, and basketball teams, and who also won medals in track and field. And then there were those other kids—the all-around *non*-athletes. They seemed to have no proficiency in motor skills whatsoever. How do we understand these apparent all-around athletes and non-athletes? Two hypotheses, quite different in their approach to answering this question, have been proposed.

Visit the web study guide to read "The Babe" and complete the self-directed learning activities.

General Motor Ability Hypothesis

One view held that all motor performances are based on a single ability called the **general motor ability**. By this view, the all-around athlete is one who possesses a strong general motor ability—a single capability that underlies motor performance. Conversely, the all-around non-athlete is the person who lacks a strong general motor ability and thus succeeds in essentially no skilled physical activities.

The idea of a general motor ability shared many similarities with ideas popular in the early 20th century about the structure of cognitive skills. This kind of thinking was the basis for the idea of general intelligence, which attempted to explain a person's supposed potential for cognitive activities in terms of an overall, unitary value—the IQ. Further, general cognitive ability (IQ) and general motor ability were thought to be relatively separate, with intelligence not contributing very much to movement skills and vice versa.

Henry's Specificity Hypothesis

In contrast to the general motor ability hypothesis, Henry (1958/1968) proposed that motor abilities are *specific* to a particular task or skill. This idea had three important assumptions. Henry suggested that humans possess many separate abilities rather than just one ability. Also, these abilities were assumed to be independent of each other—thus the strength of one ability was completely unrelated to the strength of any other ability. Lastly, any specific skill we learn or task we perform depends on a *set* of abilities, with each skill or task comprised of a different set. The last assumption was the most critical of the specificity hypothesis, as it predicted that the performance of any two tasks (such as running speed versus skating speed) would be unrelated. Since the abilities that underlie any two skills might have few, if any, abilities in common, the specificity view predicted that there would be little likelihood of a common basis for similar performance outcomes.

At this point it might be a good idea for the reader to review the information related to correlation analyses that was presented in chapter 1. In short, a correlation analysis would result in a high correlation if each individual performed similarly on two separate tasks (figure 1.3*a*). A low correlation would exist if there was no relationship between each individual's scores on the two tasks (figure 1.3*b*). Thus, researchers used this strategy to examine both field and laboratory data to determine whether high or low correlations among motor skills would be found.

There are numerous data sets in the literature, but one by Drowatzky and Zuccato (1967) makes the point particularly well (see Marteniuk, 1974, for a full review). Drowatzky and Zuccato examined a large group of participants on six tests of balance, and the correlations between each pair of tests were computed (15 correlations in all). These values are shown in the matrix in table 7.1, which contains the correlation of every test with every other test. The highest correlation in the entire matrix was between the tests named "bass stand" and "sideward stand" ($r = .31$). All of the other correlations were numerically lower than this, ranging from .03 to .26. Even the highest correlation of .31 means that there was only $.31^2 \times 100 = 9.6\%$ in common (or shared variance) between these two tests; over 90% of the abilities underlying the two tests were different (i.e., $100\% - 9.6\% = 90.4\%$). Based on these data, it is impossible to argue that there was some single, underlying general motor ability that accounted for individual differences in all of these tests. Rather, these findings, plus many other studies, provided strong support for the specificity hypothesis.

Abilities as a Basis for Prediction

As mentioned earlier, a large part of the traditional work on complex movement concerned prediction of performance or skill. We discussed the insurance company's attempt to predict the possibility that you will have a vehicle accident on the basis of certain characteristics. In many movement-based skills, attempts to predict the potential for future performance have often been based on the measurement of current abilities. In baseball, for example, it would save time and specialized training if individuals could be reliably identified as future elite pitchers, catchers, or outfielders.

As promising as this idea sounds, however, the prediction of success in movement skills is not very effective. There are two important reasons why this is so. First, effective prediction for the desired or goal activity (e.g., pitching) would require a full understanding of the requisite abilities, which is poorly understood. Research underscoring Henry's specificity hypothesis showed quite clearly that the single ability was untenable. But how many abilities are there and how specific might they be? The Drowatzky and Zuccato study (table 7.1) showed that six separate tests of balance ability were uncorrelated, suggesting that at the very least, there could be many abilities alone that underlie processes involved in balancing. There is no way to know which of these might be most important for pitching, for example, and how they would be identified in tests.

Even if the underlying abilities for the desired activity were known, there is the further problem that the contribution of relative abilities for a task shifts with practice. At one level this is obvious. For beginners, considerable cognitive activity is involved in deciding

Table 7.1 Correlations among Six Tests of Balance

	Stork stand	Diver's stand	Stick stand	Sideward stand	Bass stand	Balance stand
Stork stand	–	.14	–.12	.26	.20	.03
Diver's stand	–	–	–.12	–.03	–.07	–.14
Stick stand	–	–	–	–.04	.22	–.19
Sideward stand	–	–	–	–	.31	.19
Bass stand	–	–	–	–	–	.18
Balance stand	–	–	–	–	–	–

The Relative-Age Effect

Here is an interesting phenomenon. Assume that you are examining the statistics on high-level hockey players in Canada (i.e., those playing on Junior A or professional teams). These statistics, used mostly for promotional purposes, include such things as each player's height, weight, position played, hometown, and birthday. If you examine the birthdays of these players, you will find that hardly anyone on the team was born in the late months of the year, and that a disproportionate number were born in January, February, and March. Why should it be the case that most high-level hockey players were born early in the year? Could it be that being born early in the year leads to a better general hockey ability?

Beginning with the research of Barnsley, Thompson, and Legault (1992), popularized in the mainstream press by Gladwell (2008), and studied in many investigations since (reviewed by Cobley et al., 2009, and Smith et al., 2018), there is one very compelling and reasonable explanation. And it is not a "better general ability" explanation.

Nearly everyone knows that in Canada hockey is a very special and traditional sport. Seemingly, most kids would like to see themselves succeed at the highest level possible in hockey. As a result, Canadian hockey is structured so that many age-group teams are available to join, starting at a very early age (as young as 5 years old). In the leagues in which they play, players are typically assigned to teams on the basis of calendar-year age groupings. This procedure creates a very interesting bias. For example, in 2019, a child born on January 1, 2010, would play on the 9-year-old team, whereas a child born just one day earlier, on December 31, 2009, would play on a team of 10-year-olds.

We know, of course, that especially in young boys and girls, one year of age makes a big difference in terms of maturation, body size, and so on; older boys and girls (i.e., those with a birth date earlier in the calendar year) tend to be bigger, faster, and stronger, other things being equal. In many cases, coaches of these age-group teams focus more attention on the most effective players, setting the stage for a "rich-get-richer" phenomenon. As a result these older kids improve more than teammates born later in the year, which carries over to the next age-group team: Now they have an advantage because (1) they are still older than the kids born late in the year, and (2) they had the extra coaching and attention during the previous year because they were older—and so forth.

This phenomenon has been labeled the **relative-age effect** because the players who are born early in a given year are relatively older than the players born late in that year, even though, by traditional methods, they are categorized as the same age and play in the same league. In a way, this argument goes against the idea that champion players are born with the right abilities. Rather, this argument suggests that those players who were lucky enough to be born early in the year have an advantage over their late-in-the-year counterparts because of the enriched coaching, playing time, and so on.

Exploring Further

1. Suppose sport teams in school were based on school-year birth dates rather than calendar-year birth dates. Which children (born in which months) would be the beneficiaries and losers in this luck of the draw?
2. Aside from hockey skills, name two motor skills that might be similarly affected by this relative-age effect and two motor skills that you might anticipate would be unaffected.

what to do, remembering what comes after what, and trying to figure out the instructions, rules, task scoring, and the like. Therefore, someone with strong cognitive abilities (*if* these could be accurately identified and measured) might be a good candidate for selection for some task. But with some experience, as one learns the intellectual parts of the task, the role of these cognitive abilities in performance might be replaced by abilities related more to movement control. Therefore, strong abilities that were identified among novice performers might not be the strong abilities required in later stages of expertise.

Prediction for future success in sport sounds wonderful in principle, but there are difficulties in actual practice. For example, in various attempts to predict success in activities such as military pilotry during World War II, participants were measured on a large number of predictor tests, which were presumed to be measures of various underlying abilities. The relationship between this battery of predictor tests and the criterion task of pilotry was computed using a statistical technique called multiple regression. This technique identifies and applies weights (indicating importance) to various predictors in such a way that the weighted sum of the predictor variables correlates maximally with the criterion. The results of studies using a predictor test battery revealed that at best, only about 50% of the abilities underlying the criterion pilotry task were being measured by the test battery; the remaining abilities underlying pilotry remained unknown (Adams, 1953, 1956; Fleishman, 1956). The situation is even more dismal in sport because this problem has received almost no systematic study, whereas the prediction of pilotry had considerable research support. The result is that prediction in sport situations is not very effective. Fortunately, this does not end our interest in the development in skilled performance. The second part of this book is devoted to the study of methods by which training effectiveness and efficiency are influenced by a number of important factors that are under the direct control of the instructor and learner.

Visit the web study guide to read "Websites and Silly Walks" and complete the self-directed learning activities.

Coordinating Discrete Movements

The traditional approach to the study of complex motor performance focused on the measurement of abilities and individual differences—how abilities are combined to define an individual and how a set of abilities makes us different from each other. The process-oriented approach, as we have described in chapters 1 through 6, treats individuals as basically the same in terms of how movements are performed. This section and the remainder of this chapter extend the process-oriented approach by considering how movements made with two or more degrees of freedom are performed at the same time.

In chapter 6 we presented various factors related to the speed and accuracy in making rapid, mainly single-limb, aiming movements. Much of that discussion focused on actions such as moving a limb to a target (e.g., positioning a cursor on an icon, or a foot on the brake pedal), or using two limbs together to move a single object (e.g., swinging a baseball bat to hit a ball, or an ax to split a block of wood). The principles discussed in chapter 6, such as Fitts' Law and Schmidt's Law, appear to describe speed–accuracy trade-offs very well for these types of movements.

But consider now what happens when we coordinate limbs not with the purpose of moving a single object (e.g., a bat or an ax) but rather with distinct goals for each limb. For example, a guitarist will press on specific strings at specific locations with the left hand while the right hand runs a pick across the strings; a typist presses the Ctrl and Alt keys with the left hand and presses the Delete key with the right; and a carpenter squeezes a nail with two fingers on one hand while swinging a hammer with the other. Are these types of actions explained by the same principles as previously discussed, or are unique principles required to explain them?

Bimanual Tasks

Simultaneously performing two tasks that each require spatial precision combines topics discussed in several previous chapters. In chapter 4, we discussed closed-loop processes—if MT is sufficiently long, then end-point precision is facilitated because the limb can be visually guided toward the target. In chapter 3, we said that attention is limited to producing and controlling only one motor program at a time. And in chapter 6, we discussed how Fitts' Law and Schmidt's Law described speed–accuracy trade-offs for these types of movements. Putting these discussions together, then, how is the simultaneous, visually guided control of two separate limbs achieved when moving to separate targets? As we will see in the following sections, speed and accuracy become a much more complex issue when two or more limbs have distinct spatial goals.

Bimanual Fitts Aiming

The bimanual Fitts task is a variation of the single-limb task. A bimanual version of the continuous task (Fitts, 1954) was first used by Robinson and Kavinsky (1976), and a bimanual version of the discrete task (Fitts & Peterson, 1964) was introduced by Kelso, Southard, and Goodman (1979). In the discrete version, the limbs could be assigned various combinations of tasks. For example, the limbs could be assigned to perform identical tasks, both with either low IDs (figure 7.1*a*) or high IDs (figure 7.1*b*). However, the limbs could also be assigned to different (incongruent) tasks, say, one with a low ID and one with a high ID (figure 7.1*c*). According to Fitts' Law, MT is a function of the task parameters, width (*W*) and amplitude (*A*)—the MT for any particular task should be simply a function of its ID (review chapter 6 for more details). Therefore, a strict prediction of Fitts' Law would be that each limb would arrive at its target in an MT that was consistent with that task's ID. For congruent tasks, MTs should be similar; for incongruent tasks, MT should be less for the limb moving to the smaller ID.

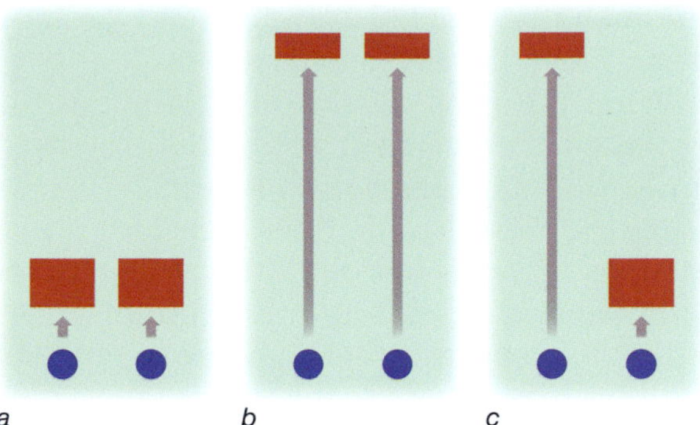

FIGURE 7.1 Three variants of the bimanual Fitts task: (*a*) Both limbs move to a low-ID task (large target, small amplitude); (*b*) both limbs move to a high-ID task (small target, large amplitude); and (*c*) incongruent limb-ID assignment, here the right hand performs a low-ID task and the left hand performs a high-ID task.

The studies by Kelso and colleagues (1979) found that, in general, when both limbs moved to targets of the same ID, the MTs were within the expected values as predicted by Fitts' Law. However, for limbs moving to targets with incongruent IDs, the results failed to support the strict predictions of Fitts' Law. For example, when paired with a limb moving to a high ID, the MT of the limb moving to a low-ID task was considerably slower than would be expected. The set of findings from this research is rather complex, but in general, the overall conclusion was that Fitts' Law failed to accurately predict the MTs when two limbs were moving to targets with incongruent IDs.

Now consider another bimanual aiming study in which both limbs moved to congruent targets. In this study, the trajectory of one limb had to rise above a physical barrier in order to move from the starting point to the target; there was no barrier for the movement of the other limb (Kelso, Putnam, & Goodman, 1983). Interestingly, Kelso et al. found that the unimpeded limb, even though not physically required to do so, was elevated as if it too were going over the barrier. It is important to note in this study that the trajectories of the limbs were not mirror images of each other. That is, the effect of the barrier *influenced* the kinematics of the unimpeded limb, but not so much that it acted identically to the limb being moved over the barrier.

What do these results suggest about the process of movement coordination when multiple goals are complementary versus when they are incompatible? One idea is that the executive issued one generalized motor program to control both limbs; another idea is that two separate motor programs, one for each limb, were sent to the musculature. The evidence from studies using the incongruent bimanual task conditions suggest that the two limbs failed to act independently, offering some evidence to support a single generalized motor program view. Some additional support for this view is provided next using a different kind of bimanual task.

The γ–V Experiment

Try this simple experiment for yourself. Draw small figures that represent the Greek letter gamma (γ) on a tablet, whiteboard, or sheet of paper taped to your desk. Draw the γ relatively quickly, without modification during its production. The figure must cross over near the center and have a rounded bottom. When you can do this effectively, use the other hand to draw regular Vs. The procedure is the same as before except that now the figure must not cross over itself and must have a pointed bottom. Based on chapter 5, each figure is represented by its own motor program because the temporal structures for the two figures are different: down–up for the V and down–over–up for the γ. Most people do not have any trouble producing these figures when each is drawn on its own, as in the left side of figure 7.2 (unimanual).

Now try to produce these two figures together, using the same hands as before. You will find, as Bender (1987) did, that doing both tasks at the same time is very difficult, with results such as those shown in the right side of figure 7.2 (bimanual). Most people make the same figure with both hands or at least they produce certain features of one of the different figures with both hands (e.g., a rounded bottom). Clearly, the fact that the participants could produce these actions unimanually was evidence that there was a separate motor program available for each. But, even after considerable practice, most people cannot do this dual task effectively. This demonstration indicates that, even with separate programs for producing a V and a γ, these programs cannot be executed independently at the same time.

These findings, together with the results from Kelso and coauthors (1979, 1983) presented in the previous sections, can be interpreted to suggest that the motor system can produce only a single motor program at one time. This is an extension of the idea expressed earlier that the movement programming stage could organize only a single movement at a time, after completion of the other stages. But now the focus is on the production of the movement itself. When two

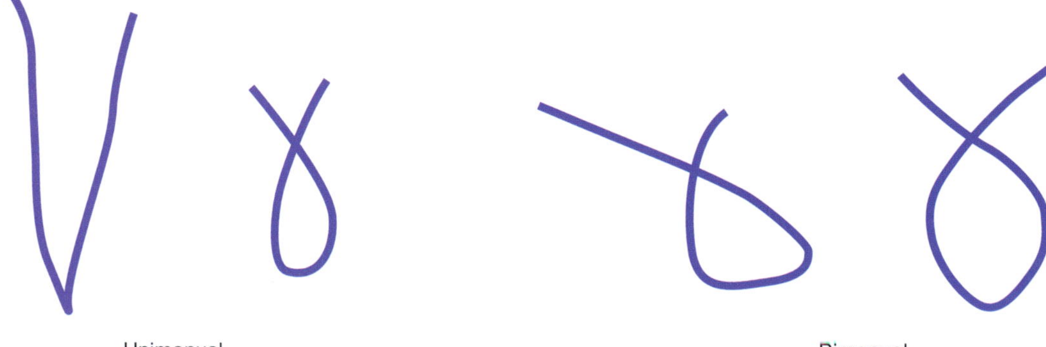

FIGURE 7.2 The γ–V task. Participants are asked to produce the capital letter V with the left hand and the Greek letter gamma (γ) with the right hand. In unimanual trials only one letter is written at a time; in the bimanual trials both letters are written simultaneously.

Focus on RESEARCH 7.1

Coordination in Golf Putting

Almost every golf instructor contends that body sway during the golf putt is detrimental to accuracy—the golfer should keep the lower body, torso, and, most importantly, the head as still as possible and simply rotate the shoulders to move the putter and strike the ball. But, for a number of reasons, this is very difficult to do. For example, a putting study by Lee and coauthors (2008) showed that both novice and expert golfers moved their heads considerably during a putt. However, they did so in fundamentally different ways.

Figure 7.3*a* illustrates 60 putts taken by one of the novices in the study, and figure 7.3*b* shows 60 putts by one of the experts. The blue lines show the movement velocities of the head during a putt, and the red lines show the velocity profiles of the putter during the same time period. Note that although both the novices and experts moved their heads during each and every putt, the novice moved the head in the same direction as the movement of the putter, the expert moved the head in the *opposite* direction of the putter.

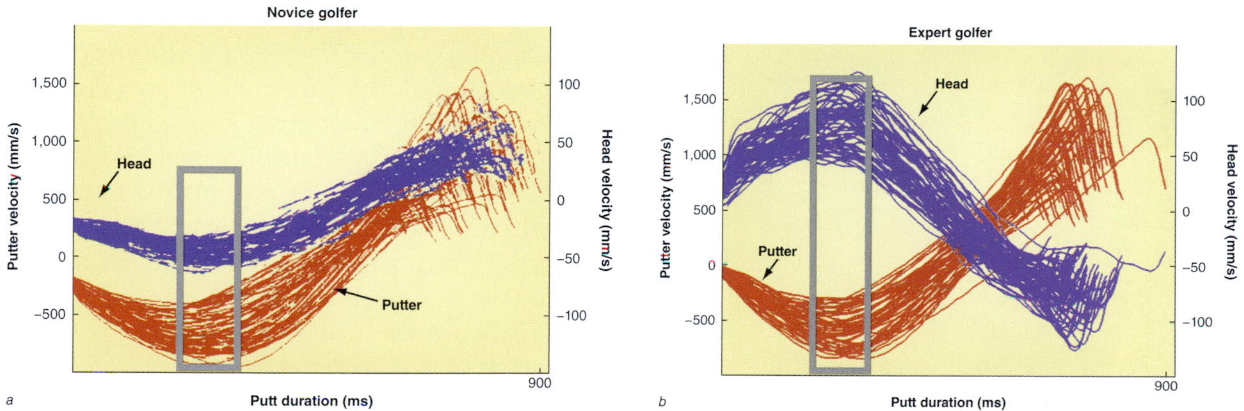

FIGURE 7.3 Velocity profiles of 60 putts made by a novice golfer (*a*) and an expert golfer (*b*). Each line represents the kinematic timeline of one putt (blue lines are head velocities, red lines are putter velocities). Both novices and experts moved their heads during the putts, but with different coordination patterns. The novices moved their head and putter in the same direction; experts moved them in the opposite directions.

Regardless of the direction of head movement, have another look at both graphs. Do you notice some similarity between the two? The point at which the putter velocity traces reversed their direction in the graphs coincided generally with the reversal of the head velocity (the areas inside the boxes in each figure). We take this evidence as suggesting that the timing of the movements of both the putter and head are the result of the common motor program. The novices dealt with the "head problem" by moving it in the same direction as the motion of the putter; the experts dealt with it by moving their head in the opposite direction as the movement of the putter.

independent programs would be best suited for the upcoming task requirements, instead, the system responds with a hybrid solution that attempts to control both limbs similarly.

Complex Bimanual Patterns

A more complex version of the γ–V experiment by Heuer, Schmidt, and Ghodsian (1995) revealed additional evidence for this single motor program view. Participants were given extensive practice in performing a single-reversal arm movement of a lever with the left arm (flexion, then extension), together with a double-reversal lever movement of the right arm (flexion, extension, flexion). Analysis of the movement kinematics revealed a tight coupling of the temporal occurrence of specific landmarks of each limb pattern, suggesting again that such a complex coordination was being governed by a single motor program. Also, participants found it almost impossible to move one limb faster than the other if asked to do so. The evidence of a strong coupling between the arms, provided more support for the idea that a common motor program can be applied to the control of both arms to control a coordinated, simultaneous action (see also Focus on Research 7.1).

Analysis of the head movements of novice and expert golfers during a putt showed different coordination patterns between the movements of the golfer's head and the putter.

Bimanual Object Manipulation

A casual observation by Rosenbaum led him on a long journey to describe why individuals choose flexible movement plans based on end-state goals (e.g., Rosenbaum, 2010). He observed that waiters in outdoor cafes (where unused glasses sit upside down on tables) would grasp a glass using an inverted (thumb-down) posture in order to pick it up, invert it, and pour water into it. A series of experiments later confirmed that end-state comfort ruled the grasp choice decision—initial awkward postures are adopted in order that end-state comfort is achieved. For waiters, it was simply a decision made out of efficiency and effectiveness, but one that had a determining influence on movement planning and motor control.

To demonstrate the waiter dilemma described above, imagine how you would turn over an hourglass, as illustrated in figure 7.4*a*. As predicted by Rosenbaum's end-state comfort ideas, you would likely grasp the hourglass in the middle using an inverted, thumb-down posture, so that when you inverted it the glass would be placed on the table with the hand in a thumb-up posture. Now imagine inverting two hourglasses, as illustrated in figure 7.4*b*. Here the likely initial posture for each limb would be thumbs-down, but symmetrical, with the back of each hand facing the other. Control of such a coordination pattern could be achieved with a single motor program that specified symmetrical commands to each limb.

But now consider the action required in figure 7.4*c*—here the initial postures likely would be asymmetrical. Experiments performed on reaching and turning objects like

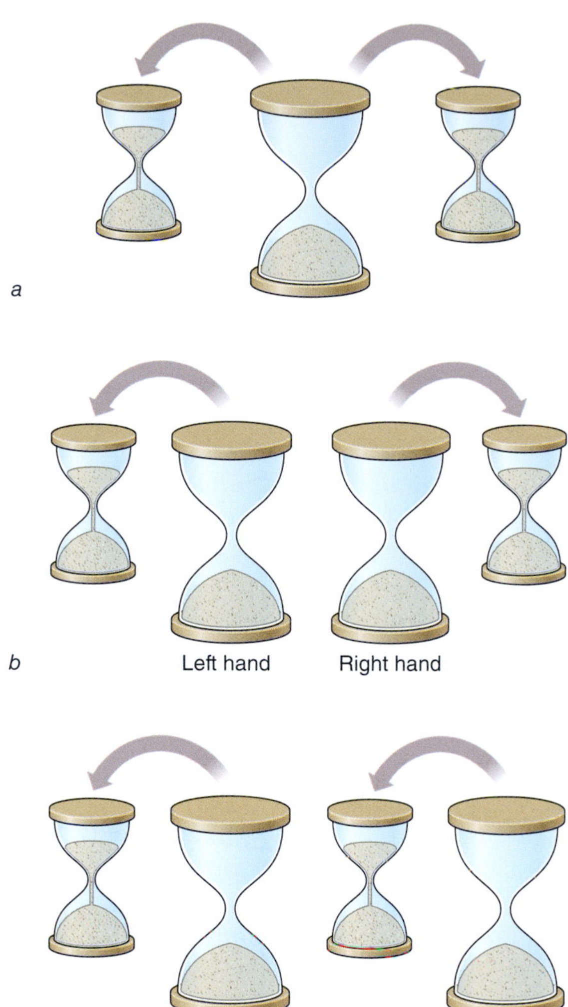

FIGURE 7.4 Imagine how you would grip the middle of the hourglass in 7.4*a* in order to turn it over to the left or to the right. How would you grip two hourglasses in 7.4*b* and 7.4*c* to achieve the results as shown? In all cases initial awkward grips likely would be chosen to maximize the most comfortable end-position of placing the object.

these revealed a markedly slowing in the time to make decisions about the initial postures and transport in situations like figure 7.4*c*. This result was likely due to the interference created by specifying different reach-and-grasp specifications for each limb (e.g., Janssen et al., 2010; Kunde & Weigelt, 2005). Although the relative timings of the reach portion of the two limbs could be specified by a generalized motor program, other commands related to the spatial orientations of the reach and grasp components would need to be specified for each limb, resulting in the general slowing.

Coordinating Continuous Movements

In many ways, controlling the continuous movement of two or more effectors represents quite a different problem for the movement system, and one that requires some additional assumptions for the generalized motor program approach to the problem. As a result, there have been a number of different ways to conceptualize both the manner in which the research is conducted and how the results are interpreted. We start with one of the basic questions facing researchers who study both animal and human motor control.

Locomotion

Bipedal animals, like humans, typically use one of two gaits to move around—walking or running. Although we can hop and skip, and locomote using other types of gait, walking and running are the two most common. Why is this so? And why, when you are on a treadmill, do you choose to walk at some speeds yet run at other speeds?

Animal Locomotion

One answer to these questions has come from studying the behavior of horses on a treadmill (Hoyt & Taylor, 1981). Horses, being quadruped, have more gait options than bipeds (Alexander, 2003). When allowed to freely choose a gait, horses typically walk at speeds between at 1–2 m/s (4–7 kph), trot at speeds of 3–4 m/s (11–14 kph), and gallop at speeds greater than 5 m/s (>18 kph). Hoyt and Taylor found that horses naturally changed gaits at speeds that corresponded to optimal energy expenditure. And when trained to extend gaits into non-normal speeds, horses did so at an energy cost. For example, trotting at slow speeds, where horses would naturally walk, and at high speeds, where

Relative Phase: An Index of Coordination

An oscillating object, such as a pendulum, can be characterized as a repeating 360° cyclical trajectory. Any single point within its cycle can be identified as a specific phase angle. When two oscillating objects are paired, how much they are synced together can be described in terms of a measure called **relative phase**. In motor coordination experiments, the oscillating objects may be two fingers, two legs, or even two limbs of different people. In the two-finger example, relative phase provides a single value that describes the position of one finger within its 360° oscillation cycle relative to the position of the other finger within its cycle. In performing an in-phase pattern, for example (see text for description), the goal is to maintain the same relative position (their phase angles) of both fingers within their own respective cycles. For example, if at some point both fingers are at 120° through the oscillation cycle, then the relative phase is the difference between the right finger's phase angle (120°) and the left finger's phase angle (120°). Therefore, the in-phase relative phase goal is a relative phase of 0° (i.e., 120°–120°=0°). For an anti-phase pattern, the goal is to coordinate the fingers to be in opposite positions within their cycle (e.g., 120° versus 300°), always offset by a relative phase of 180° (300°–120°=180°).

By sampling the relative phase throughout a trial, adding the measures and dividing the total by number of measures taken, an average (or mean) relative phase of the general coordination tendency is provided. Since human performance is never perfect, the mean relative phase for an in-phase pattern usually approximates 0° relative phase; an anti-phase pattern approximates 180° mean relative phase, when being performed accurately. The standard deviation is calculated in a similar way as variable error, described in chapter 1. The standard deviation captures the degree to which each individual sample is unlike the mean of all the samples. In other words, it describes how reliable is the approximate value of the mean. When all of the individual samples are tightly arranged around the mean, then the standard deviation is small; when they are scattered widely around the mean, then the standard deviation is large.

Taken together, both the mean relative phase and the standard deviation are important indices of coordination. The mean indicates *what* pattern is being performed (in-phase, anti-phase, or some other pattern) and the standard deviation describes how *well* (or stable) it is being performed.

Exploring Further

1. Describe the difference between the coordination patterns made by the upper arms in the front crawl versus the breaststroke in swimming.
2. How would fatigue affect the performance of swimming strokes in terms of the relative phase measures?

they would naturally gallop, were associated with elevated levels of energy consumption when compared to the preferred gaits at the same speeds. Hoyt and Taylor concluded that minimizing energy costs was a likely explanation for why horses selected the gaits they did (and by extension, perhaps why you choose walking or running gaits at certain treadmill speeds), and when horses (and you) transition from one gait to another.

Human Locomotion

As discussed previously, energy efficiency is one explanation for why some gaits, and coordination patterns in general, are preferred over others. However, there is an alternate view, more in line with a motor-control perspective. Consider the findings of a study of gait transitions in humans by Diedrich and Warren (1995). Their participants walked on a treadmill at speeds that were above and below what is considered normal and comfortable (which is ~ 3.6 kph or 2.2 mph). They also ran at speeds that were normal for running and at speeds that were much slower than typical running gait speeds.

Figure 7.5 illustrates some very interesting results of this experiment, but needs some explanation. First, speed of locomotion is expressed on the horizontal axis as a Froude number, which is a dimensionless scale that accounts for individual differences in a person's size and stride length. In general, the range of Froude numbers represent walking speeds ranging from 3.2 to 9.0 kph (2.0–5.6 mph) and running speeds ranging from 5.4 to 13.0 kph (3.4–8.1 mph). The vertical axis expresses the standard deviation of the relative phase of the ankle and knee angles—a measure of the stability of the gait pattern's relative phase (see Focus on Research 7.2). The shaded vertical box in the figure represents the average speeds at which the participants freely chose to change from a walking to a running gait (or from a run to a walk) as the treadmill was sped up or slowed down by the experimenter. These transitions occurred at speeds ranging from 6.8 to 8.4 kph (4.2–5.2 mph).

What is most interesting to note in figure 7.5 is that the stability of the walking gait's relative phase became weakened when walking was slower or faster than at the normal transition points (i.e., to the left or right of the gray box). Similarly, the running gait was destabilized when participants ran at speeds where they would normally walk (i.e., to the left of the shaded box). The Diedrich and Warren findings are critically important for they suggest that we choose to change from walking to running gaits (and back again) not because of energetic reasons, but rather as a means to achieve the more efficient and effective coordination pattern for the current locomotion speed. In this case, the standard deviation in relative phase of the pattern was the key impetus for making the decision to change gaits.

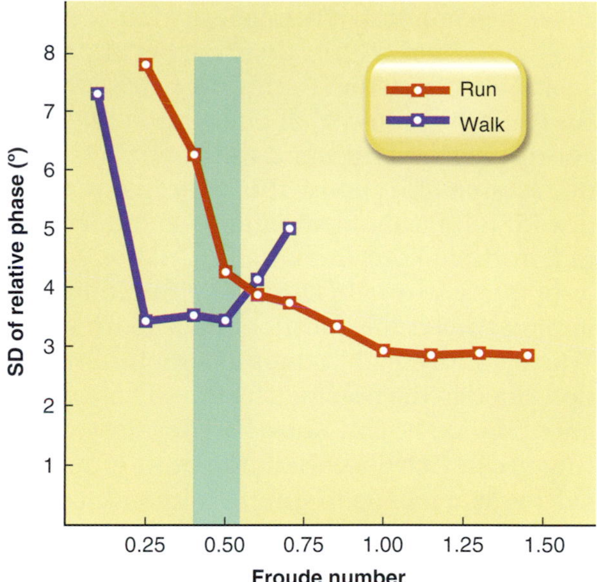

FIGURE 7.5 The stability (standard deviation) in the ankle-knee relative phase at various walking and running speeds. The shaded area illustrates the normal transition speeds for changing gaits. Walking variability was found to be destabilized above and below these preferred speeds.

Visit the web study guide to read "Party Tricks" and complete the self-directed learning activities.

Bimanual Timing

Try this simple experiment: Point your index fingers on both hands straight ahead of you, as if you were pointing two pistols at a target, then just oscillate both fingers. Even with these very simple instructions, most people spontaneously do this task by oscillating each finger toward their midline, then away, oscillating back and forth using what researchers call an **in-phase** mode of coordination. Here, in-phase means that right-finger flexion and the corresponding left-finger flexion occur at the same time within their cycles and with relatively consistent timing. Considering the limitless ways in which one could choose to coordinate both fingers at the same time, why do most people choose this pattern and what does it tell us about spontaneous tendencies to coordinate our limbs?

In many ways, this finger-oscillation problem resembles the question that Diedrich and Warren addressed in their locomotion study, described in the previous section. That is not a coincidence—Scott Kelso had developed this finger-oscillation paradigm about a decade earlier as a means to mimic human locomotion (Kelso, 1984). As well, Kelso's interpretation of the results influenced how Diedrich and Warren conceptualized the impetus for gait transitions (see Kelso, 1995, for more on the development of the paradigm). The next sections describe some of the questions addressed by Kelso and others, and how this research paradigm evolved into a new way of thinking about problems of continuous movement coordination.

Coordination Dynamics

The spontaneous in-phase coordination described in the previous section is one of two coordination patterns that you can easily perform with your oscillating fingers. The other is called an **anti-phase** coordination pattern, in which both fingers point to the right and then to the left, like the movements of windshield wipers on many cars. The in-phase and anti-phase coordination patterns are the most natural and stable timing relations that can be performed with the upper limbs (Yamanishi et al., 1980). All other timing patterns are much more errorful and difficult to perform (but can be learned with practice and feedback).

In a landmark study by Kelso (1984; Kelso, Scholz, and Schöner, 1986), participants moved their fingers in either an in-phase or an anti-phase pattern by keeping pace with a metronome that began at a low speed (1.25 Hz; slightly faster than one complete cycle per second), and increased in speed at regular intervals. The results of their study are illustrated in figure 7.6.

Figure 7.6 looks rather complicated, but the explanation of the results is straightforward. Means (figure 7.6*a*) and standard deviations of relative phase (figure 7.6*b*) (see Focus on Research 7.2) illustrate how the in-phase and anti-phase patterns were performed as the metronome speed was increased. As expected, the in-phase pattern started near a mean of 0°, and remained there as speed increased. Also as expected, the anti-phase pattern started near a

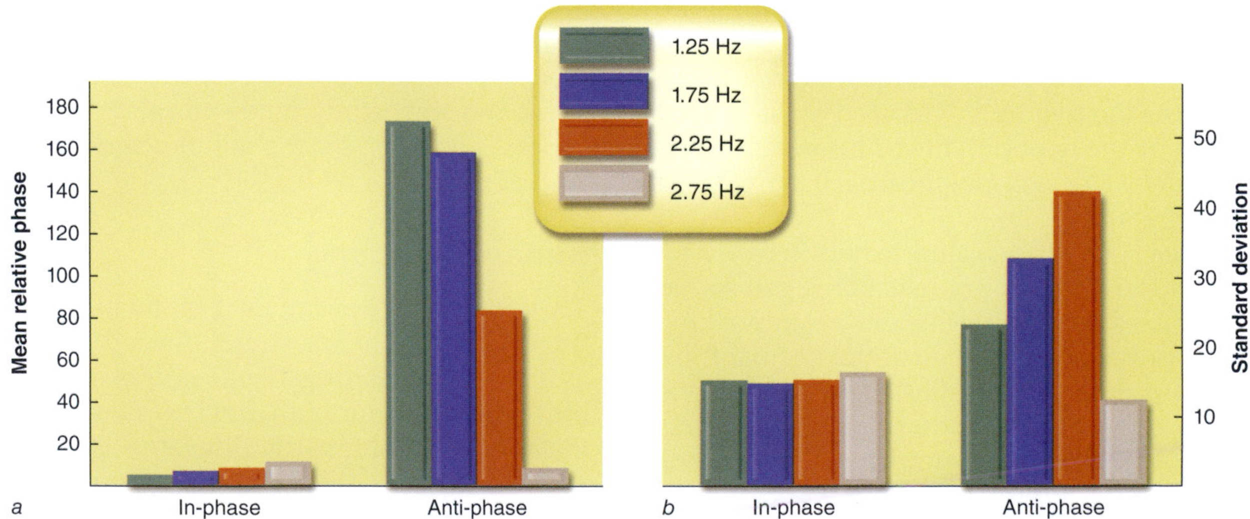

FIGURE 7.6 Mean relative phase (*a*) and standard deviation of relative phase (*b*) for coordination patterns starting as in-phase or anti-phase, as a function of metronome pacing speed.

mean of 180°. However, with increased speed, the fingers originally coordinating in the anti-phase pattern had completely switched to an in-phase pattern by the time the metronome reached a speed of 2.75 Hz. The standard deviation data help us to understand why this happened. Although the in-phase remained stable as speed increased, the anti-phase pattern became increasingly destabilized with increasing speed. Normal stability was regained by the time the pattern had completely switched to an in-phase relative phase.

Visit the web study guide to read "Disappearing Act" and complete the self-directed learning activities.

The Kelso et al. (1986) findings are important because they capture the essence of two-finger **coordination dynamics**. The essential features of these dynamics are the existence of a naturally stable, two-pattern state that is subject to destabilization and shift to a state where only one pattern remains stable. In the language of coordination dynamics (a branch of physics) the metronome speed served as a **control parameter** that led to the change in states. A follow-up study by Kelso, Scholz, and Schöner (1988) showed how *intention* could also be considered a type of control parameter, revealing other features of the system's coordination dynamics.

In this later study, Kelso et al. (1988) asked participants to begin in one coordination pattern (either in-phase or in anti-phase) and then, on command, to switch into the other pattern as quickly as possible. This is easy to demonstrate for yourself. What you will find is that in order to achieve the switch, you must destabilize the pattern you are currently performing before you can make the switch into the other pattern. Based on the previous study, described above, what we know is that in-phase is the more stable of the two patterns. Therefore, it should take longer to destabilize the in-phase pattern before you can completely switch to anti-phase. And this is exactly what Kelso et al. found—the switching took longer to stabilize into the new pattern when going from in-phase to anti-phase than it did from anti-phase to in-phase.

Some have criticized the oscillating, two-finger research as too experimental or lab-oriented to relate to real or complex motor skills. But as we have discussed throughout the book, and will continue to do in the chapters that follow, the importance of these studies with simple skills is not what they say about performing these tasks per se. Rather, their importance is what is revealed about the processes that underlie human motor performance and learning. The initial work on the coordination dynamics of two oscillating fingers, and the theory development that followed (Haken, Kelso, & Bunz, 1985; Kelso, 1995, 2009), has led to new perspectives, research, and theorizing about activities such as drumming (e.g., Fujii et al., 2010), swimming (e.g., Seifert et al., 2014), and cross-country skiing (Cignetti et al., 2009), among many other real skills and activities.

Coordination Dynamics Versus Motor Programs

Investigators from the **self-organization** perspective hold that the regularities of movement patterns are not represented in programs but rather emerge naturally (that is, through physics) out of the complex interactions among many connected elements, or degrees of freedom (Turvey, 1977). This is analogous to the ways in which many complex physical systems achieve organization and structure without having any central program or overarching set of commands, such as the sudden transformation of still water to rolling patterns as it begins to boil. Researchers argue that it is incorrect to think that complex patterns of continuous motor activity are controlled by central commands, just as it would make little sense to postulate a central program for governing the patterns in boiling water. Kelso and Engstrøm (2005) provide a useful analogy here. Think of the motor program perspective as an orchestra whose actions are under the supervision of a conductor, and the self-organization perspective as a conductor-less orchestra. Both

The self-organization perspective views human movement as analogous to a conductor-less orchestra. Describe the role that a conductor plays from the motor program perspective.

achieve a coordinated activity but do so in different ways.

A scientific debate about these issues has been continuing for several decades and has sometimes (incorrectly in our view) pitted the validity of one view against the other. The two sides of the debate tend to study different tasks (e.g., rapid, discrete movements versus continuous, oscillating motions), so there is little basis on which to compare theoretical predictions. In the end, it is likely that neither theoretical perspective will be correct in all aspects, which should lead to the development of new theories with stronger predictive powers. And this is a good thing, as such is the fate of a healthy science.

Interpersonal Coordination

The orchestra example used in the last section was not by accident, as the dynamic interactions among musicians combine to produce a musical score that is much greater than the sum of the collective parts. Orchestras are just one example of two or more people working together to produce a coordinated action. Rowing, dancing, cheerleading, and tugs-of-war are a few more examples where people must work together as a unit in order to maximize group output—be that maximum force, velocity, or some other end result.

The coordination dynamics of two people acting as independently moving oscillators can share some of the same qualities as we have described in the last sections. Perhaps this is not surprising because (in most cases) the two people share similar information—they can often see and hear what the other is doing and may be able to get similar haptic and proprioceptive information as well (such as when dancing or carrying a load together). For example, in a study by R.C. Schmidt et al.

FIGURE 7.7 In this interpersonal coordination task the goal is for the duo to coordinate the motions of their legs either in the same direction or in opposite directions.

(1990), two participants each swung one of their lower legs either in the same direction (flexing and extending at the same time) or in opposite (alternate) directions (see figure 7.7). The results were much like the bimanual results discussed earlier. Coordinating in the same direction was more accurate and stable, and when oscillation speed increased there was a tendency to switch from the alternate to the same direction pattern.

These spontaneous interpersonal coordination tendencies are fascinating for they suggest that humans tend to synchronize motor behaviors as functional units in social contexts. This tendency has been documented in situations as simple as two people walking side by side (van Ulzen et al., 2008) and as complex as the spontaneous coordinated clapping by an audience at the end of a concert (Néda et al., 2000; see Oullier & Kelso, 2009, for a review). Note that instances of interpersonal coordination do not mean that people are walking or clapping in unison throughout the entire episode. Rather they exemplify cases where periods of coordinated behavior far exceed what would be anticipated if the individual actions were completely independent.

Perhaps one of the more fascinating demonstrations of spontaneous, unintentional interpersonal coordination was described by Varlet and Richardson (2015) in their analysis of the men's 100-m sprint final in 2009. The much-anticipated showdown between Usain Bolt and Tyson Gay resulted in a world record performance by Bolt, who ran the race in a time of 9.58 s, shaving an incredible 0.11 s off the world record—a record that, historically, is typically bettered by hundreds of a second, not by over a tenth of a second! The analysis of the race by Varlet and Richardson revealed that Gay's performance might have influenced Usain's remarkable time.

Figure 7.8 illustrates the relative phase for each pair of strides taken by the two sprinters. Since Bolt is much taller than Gay, the length of his stride is longer but is less frequent. As a result there is a continuous drift of the relative phase of the two sprinter's cycles during the race. The continuous drift is shown clearly in their semifinal races (in which they competed in separate heats), as shown in figure 7.8*a*. The drift is also apparent for a large portion of the final race too (figure 7.8*b*). However, there were four periods of time during the race when the strides of Bolt and Gay were locked at 0° relative phase for 3–4 strides. These periods of phase-locking were not an accident and revealed a spontaneous interpersonal

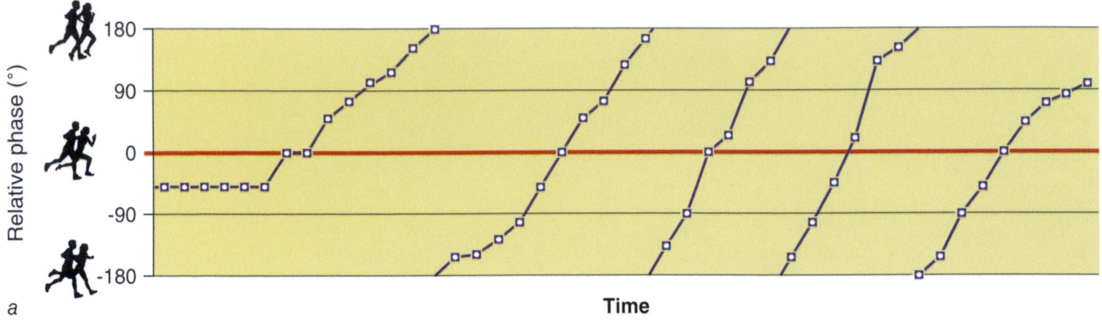

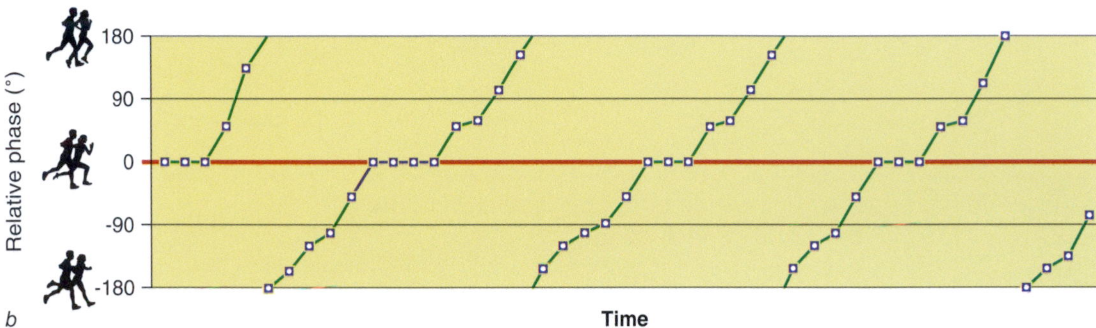

FIGURE 7.8 Analysis of the Usain Bolt–Tyson Gay relative phase drifts during their semifinal (*a*) and final (*b*) 100-m races. Each blue dot represents a relative phase value of coordinated stride cycle each time Bolt's right foot touched down. The semifinal (in which they appeared in separate races) shows no evidence of phase-locking, whereas in the final (in which they were in adjacent lanes) they phase-locked in synchronous timing (0° relative phase) for 3–4 strides at regular intervals throughout the race.

coordination that likely benefited both sprinters to excel, which at the time, were personal best race times for *both* sprinters.

Summary

There are many interesting aspects of understanding complex skills in people and approaches to their study. A critical concept is an ability, which is defined as a stable, enduring trait that underlies the performance of various tasks. An ability is distinguished from a skill, which is proficiency in some particular task. Henry's research tells us that the old concept of a general motor ability, with one ability thought to underlie all motor proficiency, is simply incorrect. Generally, the relationships between skills are low, suggesting that abilities are very specific to particular tasks. Predicting success in some future activity is a critical individual-difference consideration and is based on the notion of abilities. However, prediction is not very effective, probably because of the incomplete understanding of the fundamental abilities that underlie performance, and this is particularly so in sport.

A different approach to the study of complex skills is focused on movement coordination. Initial study in this area examined the bimanual performance of discrete tasks. Research found that coordination required more than applying the laws found for simple movements. Instead, understanding coordination required an appreciation of how movement requirements were modified to accommodate two or more degrees of freedom. Research blossomed when coordination of continuous movements were examined, as the dynamics of coupled oscillators became a dominant theory in research and application.

WEB STUDY GUIDE ACTIVITIES

The student web study guide offers these activities to help you build and apply your knowledge of the concepts in this chapter.

Interactive Learning

Activity 7.1: Explore the distinction between an ability and a skill by indicating which in a list of descriptions applies to each.

Activity 7.2: Test your understanding of the correlations between skills by interpreting two correlation graphs and how their performance skills would most likely correlate.

Activity 7.3: Describe how the mean and standard deviation of relative phase would be determined for the right feet of two cyclists.

Principles-to-Application Exercise

Activity 7.4: The principles-to-application exercise for this chapter prompts you to identify a sport or activity and analyze the abilities and skills that would affect its performance, as well as consider the issues that would arise when predicting who would be successful in the sport or activity and what challenges might arise.

Motor Control in Everyday Actions Narratives

The Babe

Websites and Silly Walks

Party Tricks

Disappearing Act

Check Your Understanding

1. How were statistical correlations used to examine abilities? What did researchers find out about correlations among skills? What does this tell you about the concept of a general motor ability?
2. Describe three components involved in attempts at prediction of a future skill level on a criterion task. How effective is skill prediction in a sport setting?
3. Describe both a single-limb and a bimanual Fitts' task. Explain, in general terms, how findings using the bimanual Fitts' task were different than those using the single-limb task.

Apply Your Knowledge

1. Explain the differences between an ability and a skill. How would you illustrate these differences to a friend who has told you that she would like to train quickness in her young field hockey team? What might you suggest to include in practice to improve on skills requiring speed?
2. What difficulties might a talent scout for a high-level swim team encounter

when predicting which young children at a swim camp are likely to do well at an elite level? How might the abilities needed to perform well as a novice differ from those needed after several years of training?

3. Your band is trying a new song in which a critical guitar part comes in "off the beat" of the drummer. Why might the guitarist find this difficult to do?

Suggestions for Further Reading

Additional reading on early thinking about individual differences in motor control can be found in Henry (1958/1968), Marteniuk (1974), and Adams (1987). A more general discussion of the history and nature of motor abilities can be found in Schmidt and Lee (2011, ch. 9). Turvey (1977) provides an excellent introduction to (then) new ways of thinking about coordination. Kelso's 1995 book provided an excellent summary of the coordination dynamics research, which was updated and extended by Swinnen and Wenderoth (2004) and Kelso (2009).

PART II

Principles of Skill Learning

To this point in the text, our focus has been on understanding some of the factors that underlie motor behavior, such as the principles of movement control. Most of the major variables that determine the quality of movement output have been introduced and discussed. In addition, we have developed a conceptual model of motor behavior that illustrates most of the important factors that influence movement. By this point, then, you should have a reasonably good overall concept of how skills are performed and what some of the limiting factors might be.

The concepts and terminology in part II should be familiar, as they are mainly the same as those used in part I. A major focus in part II concerns the ways in which the components of the conceptual model can change with practice and experience, as well as the research-based principles that govern such changes. So, as in part I, a major emphasis is on research indicating how certain features in practice contribute to the future capability for movement. As you will see, many of these features of practice are available to the coach or instructor to use directly with learners; hence this discussion includes many ways in which practice can be varied in real-world settings to optimize learning. Another related issue concerns the extent to which skills are retained over time so they can be helpful to the performer in the future. The practically oriented reader should find this section of the text useful.

8

Introduction to Motor Learning

Concepts and Methods in Research and Application

KEY TERMS

capability
far transfer
learning curves
motor learning
near transfer
performance curve
retention test
transfer of learning
transfer test

CHAPTER OUTLINE

CHAPTER OBJECTIVES

Chapter 8 introduces the concept of motor learning and describes fundamental principles regarding how it is studied. This chapter will help you to understand

- a clear definition of motor learning and how it differs from motor performance,
- temporary and "relatively permanent" effects of practice variables,
- transfer designs and their importance in learning research, and
- the measurement of transfer of motor skills.

Imagine that you are an instructor in a two-day cardiopulmonary resuscitation (CPR) course, charged with teaching a set of skills to a group of adults. For grading, you want to measure skill levels at the end of the course but are puzzled about how to do it. Would the best measure of skill take into account the students' levels of proficiency at the start of the class? Would you measure the amount learned at the end of a course, when fatigue might influence the results? Or would you measure skill at some time later, after the course has finished, by which time some forgetting might have occurred? What skills should you ask learners to perform as a test—the same as practiced earlier or slight variations of them? And under what conditions would the test be conducted—in the stress-free conditions in which the skills were taught, or in the heightened levels of excitement that would no doubt put the skills to the test in a real emergency, or something in between?

This chapter concerns motor skill learning, the remarkable set of processes through which practice and experience can generate large, nearly permanent gains in human performance. The initial focus of the chapter is understanding the concept of learning, establishing some basic ideas about how learning is defined and conceptualized. Then we turn to how, and with what standards, one can measure and evaluate the effectiveness of practice, both in laboratory and in practical settings with relevance to teaching. Finally is a discussion of transfer of learning, by which the skills acquired in one situation can be applied to another.

The capability to learn is critical to biological existence because it allows organisms to adapt to the particular features of their environments and to profit from experience. For humans, this learning is most critical of all. Think how it would be to go through life equipped only with the capabilities inherited at birth. Humans would be relatively simple beings indeed without the capability to talk, write, or read, and certainly without the capability to perform the complex movement skills seen in sport, music, or industry. Although learning occurs for all kinds of human performances—cognitive, verbal, interpersonal, and so on—the focus here is on the processes that underlie learning the cognitive and motor capabilities that lead to skills as defined earlier.

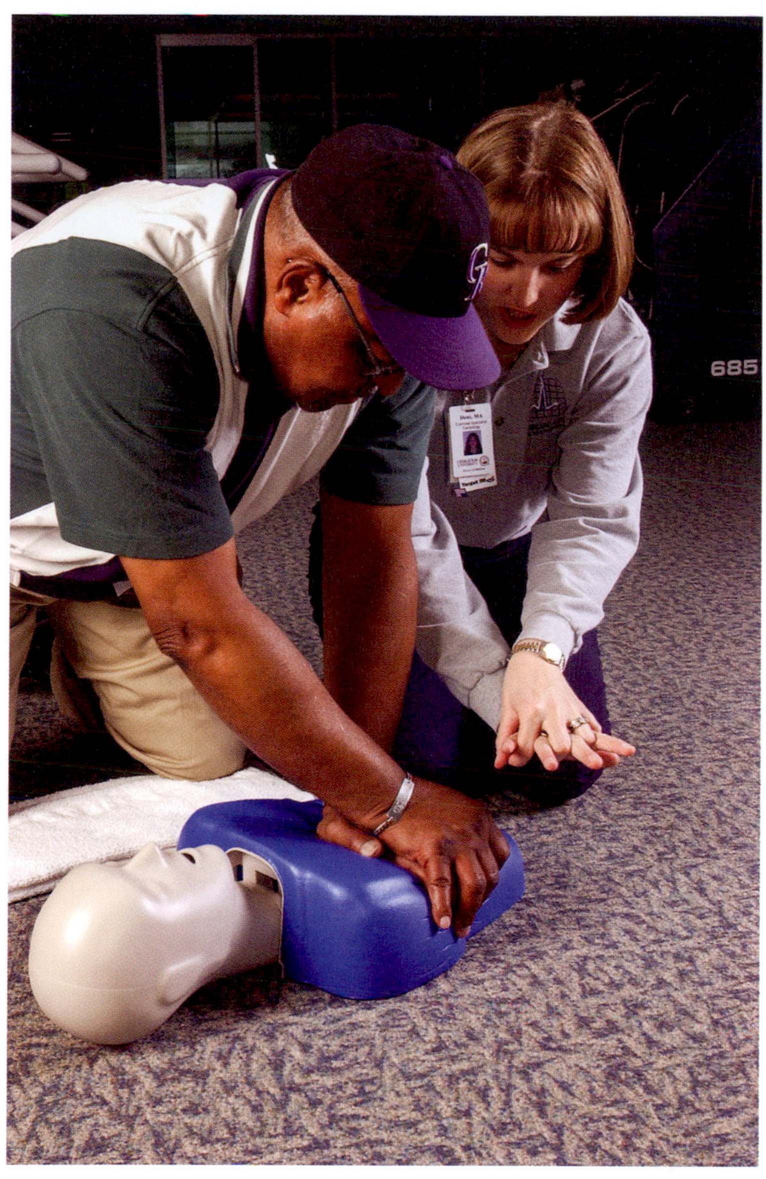

Describe one fundamental difference between performance and learning for students learning CPR.

Learning seems to occur nearly continuously, almost as if everything you do today generates knowledge or capabilities that affect how you do other things tomorrow and beyond. However, this book takes a more restricted view of learning, in which the focus is on situations involving *practice*—deliberate attempts to improve performance of a particular skill or action. Practice, of course, often takes place in classes or lessons, either in groups as might be seen in the CPR example provided earlier, or individually, as in private ski lessons or physical therapy sessions. Usually, but certainly not always, there is an instructor, therapist, or coach to guide this practice, to evaluate the learner's progress and give feedback about it, and to decide about future activities to maximize progress. This focus on practice with an instructor defines an important class of human activities and requires investigation of the many factors—such as the nature of instructions, evaluation, and scheduling—that collectively determine the effectiveness of practice.

Instructors are in an important position to influence learning if they have a solid understanding of the fundamental processes underlying practice settings. A critical starting point is understanding the nature and definition of learning.

Motor Learning Defined

When a person practices, the usual result is almost always an improved performance level, which can be measured in a number of ways, such as a lower golf score, reduced time to complete a simple surgical operation, or a larger number of roofing shingles nailed in a 20 min period. But there is more to learning than just improved performance. Researchers have found it useful to define learning in terms of the gain in the underlying *capability* for skilled performance developed during practice, with the improved capability leading to improved performance.

But be aware that improved performance does not by itself define learning. Rather, improved performance is an indication that learning *may* have occurred, which represents an important distinction. This idea can be formalized by a definition:

> **Motor learning** is a set of processes associated with practice or experience leading to relatively permanent gains in the capability for skilled performance.

There are several important aspects to this definition, which are discussed in the next sections.

Learning Affects Capability

The term **capability** for performance may seem odd, but it simply reflects the fact that any *single* performance may not reflect the skill level that underlies the performance. Just as the fastest runner does not always win the race and the more skilled tennis player does not always win the game, any performance may exceed or fall short of its theoretical true capability. So we are interested in measuring the underlying capability for performance, being mindful that on any given occasion the learner might not, for various reasons, perform up to her capability.

Learning Results From Practice or Experience

Everyone knows there are many factors that improve the capability for skilled performance. However, learning is concerned with only some of these factors—those related to practice or experience. For example, the performance capabilities of children increase as they mature and grow. However, these growth factors are not evidence of learning because they are not related to practice. Similarly, gains in cardiovascular endurance or strength could occur in training programs, leading to more effective performance in activities like soccer, but these changes are not related to practice as considered here.

Learning Is Not Directly Observable

During practice there are many alterations to the central nervous system, which some refer to as *brain plasticity*, where the term *plasticity* refers to a brain that is changeable under various conditions (Kantak & Winstein, 2012). Some of these alterations help establish relatively permanent changes in movement capability. These processes are generally not directly observable, though, so their existence must usually be inferred from the changes in performance they presumably support. It is useful to think of these changes as occurring to the fundamental decision-making and movement-control processes, discussed in the previous chapters, that are brought together in the conceptual model of human performance. Figure 8.1 shows the conceptual model again, this time highlighting some of the human performance processes thought to be influenced by practice.

Some examples of changes to these processes are (1) increased automaticity, together with speed and accuracy, in analyzing the environmental and movement feedback information (during stimulus identification), (2) improvements in the ways actions are selected (during response selection) and parameterized (in movement programming), (3) building more effective generalized motor

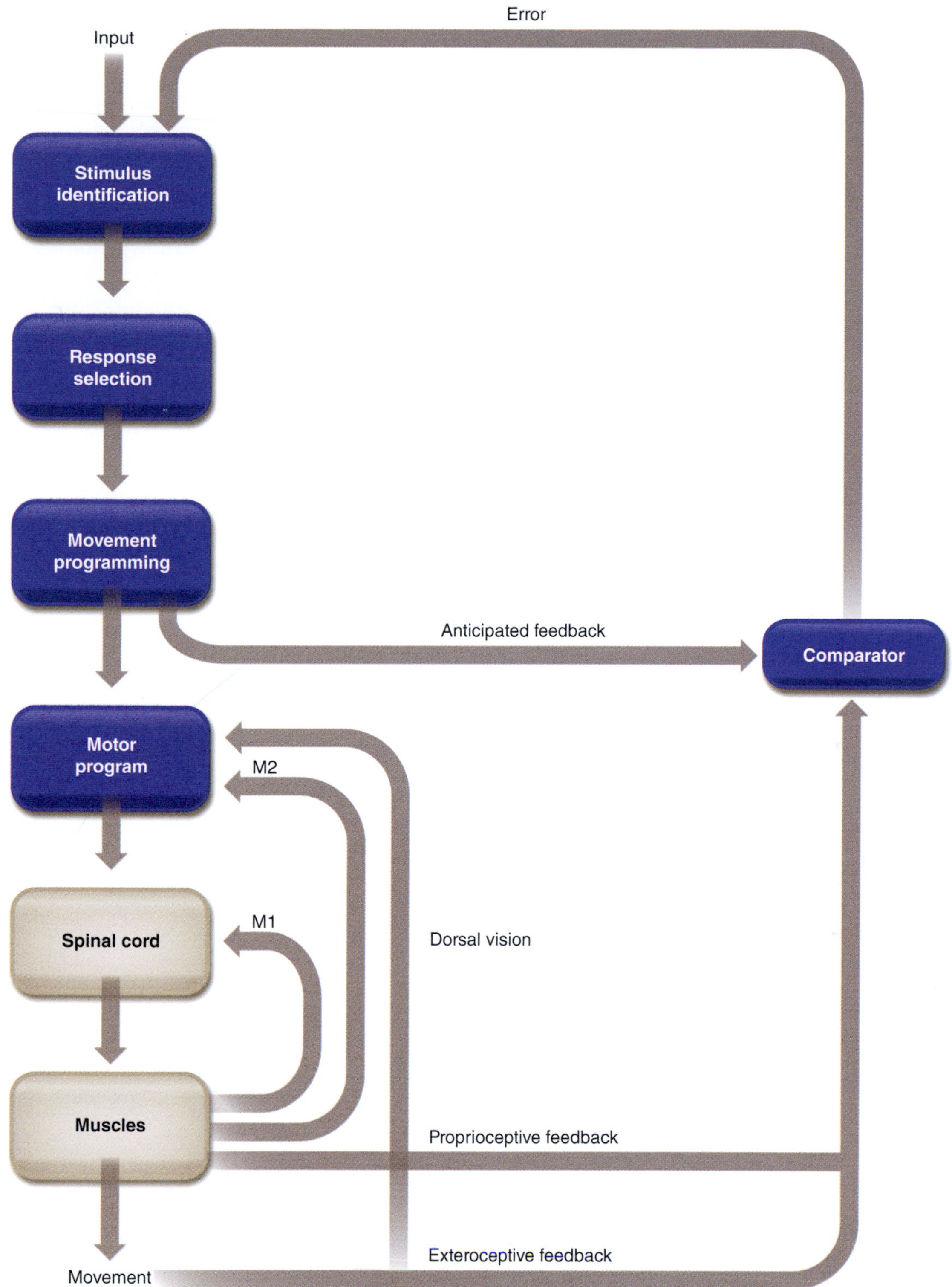

FIGURE 8.1 Conceptual model with the processes that improve with practice highlighted in dark blue.

programs and effector processes, (4) providing more accurate and precise feedback in several ways, and (5) establishing more accurate references of correctness to aid in, for example, balance. In fact, learning can occur at all levels of the central nervous system, but the levels highlighted in figure 8.1 account for the biggest changes. Of course, all of these processes have been discussed before; we now simply add the notion that they can be improved in various ways through practice, leading to more effective performance.

Even though the underlying processes are not directly observable, we can usually observe and measure the products of the learning process by measuring changes in skill. Changes in underlying processes lead to more effective capability for skill, which then allows more skillful performances. Therefore, evidence about the development of these processes can be gained by examining carefully chosen performance tests. The performance gains on these tests are usually assumed to result from gains in skill.

Learning Requires Relatively Permanent Changes

One important qualification must be added to the previous section. In order for a change in skilled performance level to be regarded as due to learning, the change must be *relatively permanent*. Many different factors affect the momentary level of skilled performance, some of which are temporary and transient. For example, skills can be affected by drugs, sleep loss, mood, stress, motivation, and many other factors. Most of these variables alter performance only temporarily, and their effects soon disappear. Consider caffeine, for example; the performance gains from the caffeinated state to the decaffeinated state are not due to learning because the changes are transient and reversible by adding caffeine again. There are many variations of practice that can be shown to affect performance greatly, but often these effects gradually wear off, allowing performance to return to its previous level. These changes were clearly not relatively permanent.

In studying learning, it is important to understand those practice variables that affect performance in a relatively permanent way. This changed capability is then a relatively permanent part of the person's makeup and is available at some future time when the given skill is required.

An analogy might be useful. When water is heated to a boil, there are changes in its behavior (analogous to performance). But these are not permanent changes because the water returns to the original state as soon as the effects of the variable (heating) dissipate. These changes therefore would not be analogous to learning changes because they are not relatively permanent. However, when an egg is boiled, its internal state is changed. This change is relatively permanent because cooling the egg does not reverse its internal state to the original. The relatively permanent changes in the egg are analogous to changes in the human due to learning. When people learn, relatively permanent changes occur that survive the shift to other conditions or the passage of time. After learning, you are not the same person you were before, just as the state of the egg is not the same as before.

The realization that performance alterations due to learning must be relatively permanent has led to special methods for measuring learning and evaluating the effects of practice variations. Essentially, these methods allow scientists to separate relatively permanent changes (due to learning) from temporary changes (due to transient factors). We return to this idea in a subsequent section.

To emphasize the features of the definition of learning, the following statements are important to keep in mind:

- Learning results from practice or experience.
- Learning is not directly observable.
- Learning changes are inferred from certain performance changes.
- Learning involves a set of processes in the central nervous system.
- Not all changes in performance are due to learning.

- Learning produces an acquired capability for skilled performance.
- Learning changes are relatively permanent, not transitory.

Visit the web study guide to read "How You Get to Carnegie Hall" and complete the self-directed learning activities.

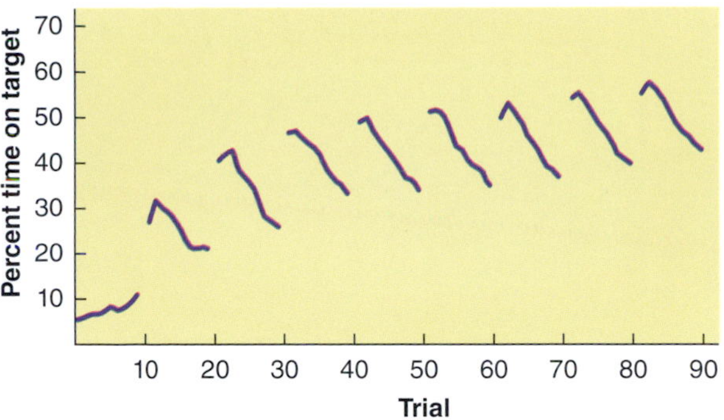

FIGURE 8.2 Performance curve for a group of participants practicing a rotary pursuit tracking task. The score reflects the proportional amount of time in contact with the object to be tracked during a 1 min trial. Participants in this experimental group performed nine blocks of 10 consecutive trials with no rest (i.e., 10 min of continuous tracking), each block followed by a 20 min rest period (i.e., rest after trial 10, trial 20, and so on).

How Is Motor Learning Measured?

For both the experimental effects of learning in the laboratory and the practical effects of learning in applications of daily living, measuring learning and evaluating progress are conducted in line with the same general principles. Some of these are presented in this section.

Performance Curves

By far the most common and traditional way to evaluate learning progress during practice is through **performance curves**. Assume that a large number of people are practicing some task, and performance measures for each of their attempts (called *trials*) have been collected. From these data, a graph of the average performance for each trial can be drawn, as in figure 8.2. These data were generated from a rotary-pursuit tracking task, in which participants attempted to keep a handheld stylus in contact with a constantly moving target. The measure of performance, percent time-on-target (the proportion of time in contact with the target during a 1 min trial), illustrates a number of interesting details about performance changes during practice (Ammons & Willig, 1956).

The data plotted in figure 8.2 illustrates the performance of one group of participants (who were part of a larger experimental design). This group performed nine blocks of trials in a massed practice format (see chapter 10 for more on the effects of massed versus distributed practice). Each participant practiced the tracking task for 90 trials, each trial being 1 min in length. Trials for this group were organized such that 10 trials in a block were performed consecutively, with no rest intervals. A 20 min rest was provided after the 10th trial in each block had been performed. Performance was assessed using time-on-target (TOT) scores, a measure of the participant's accuracy. As you might expect, 10 min of continuous performance would result in the accumulation of considerable fatigue, both physically and mentally. The performance illustrated in figure 8.2 is a classic representation of the effects of this kind of practice on performance: (1) starting from trial 11 and onward, performance within each 10-trial block showed some initial improvement, then a deterioration in performance, and (2) following each 20 min rest period there was a considerable improvement in performance (e.g., from trial 10 to 11, from 20 to 21, etc.). In other words, the entire practice curve showed a tendency for some dramatic performance improvements as well as performance decrements.

But notice two other trends that are illustrated in these data. The fact that performance deteriorated due to accumulating fatigue within each 10-trial block did not overshadow an important observation that steady

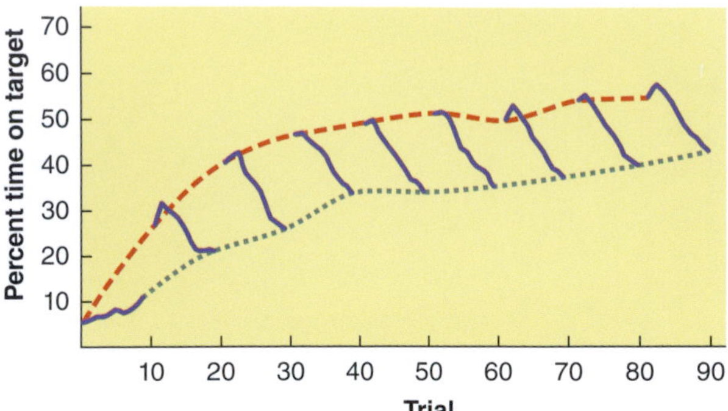

FIGURE 8.3 This figure illustrates the same data as shown in figure 8.2 but with two performance curves added. The red dashed curve connects the data points from the first trial in each 10-trial block. The blue dotted curve connects the data points from the last trial in each block. Despite the changes that occur within each block of continuous tracking trials, both curves demonstrate what is typical of performance curves when practicing a new motor task.

improvements were achieved throughout, as illustrated by two curves presented in figure 8.3. One curve (the red dashes) connects the data from the first trial in each of the nine 10-trial blocks. The blue dotted curve connects the data from the last trial in each block. The shape of each of these curves illustrates what is classically known as a *typical* performance curve—illustrating that the largest improvements occur early in practice, with smaller improvements occurring later on.

Be aware that the shape of the performance curves in figure 8.3 reflect performance improvements that are moving upward relative to the *y*-axis. For practice with some other tasks the typical curve slopes downward, such as those in which time or errors are the performance measures. In this case, typical performance would be reflected by a lower score on the *y*-axis, with rapid lowering of scores occurring early in practice, then more gradually being reduced later in practice.

Regardless of whether the improvements are shown as moving higher or lower on the *y*-axis, the general form of performance curves—steep at first and more gradual later—is one of the most common features of learning any task and reflects a fundamental principle, sometimes called the *law of practice* (Snoddy, 1926). The mathematical form of these curves and how they change with various features of the task and the nature of the learners have been discussed in some detail by numerous writers in the skill area (e.g., Newell, Liu, & Mayer-Kress, 2001, 2009).

The major points so far about performance curves can be summarized as follows:

- Performance curves are plots of individual or average performance against practice trials.
- Such curves can either increase or decrease with practice, depending on the particular way the task is scored.
- The law of practice says that improvements are rapid at first and much slower later—a nearly universal principle of practice.

Limitations of Performance Curves

There are many useful ways to use performance curves, such as to display a given learner's performance gains or to chart the progress of a group of individuals. At the same time, several potential difficulties require caution in drawing interpretations from these curves.

Performance Curves Are Not Learning Curves

As useful as performance curves are for illustrating learners' progress, several characteristics limit their usefulness. First, these are not **learning curves**, as if they somehow charted the progress of learning. These curves are simply plots of (usually the average of many participants') performance over practice trials, which (as seen in the next sections) do not necessarily indicate much about progress in the relatively permanent capability for performance, as learning was defined earlier (see also Focus on Research 8.1).

Focus on RESEARCH 8.1

Learning Curves: Facts or Artifacts?

In an important early article, Bahrick, Fitts, and Briggs (1957) identified a number of artifacts of so-called learning curves. Participants practiced a tracking task in which hand movements of a lever were used to follow a variable cursor presented on a screen. The researchers recorded the performances for analysis and later scored them in three different ways. First they defined performance accuracy in terms of a very narrow band of correctness around the track (5% of the screen's width) and counted the number of seconds out of each 90 s trial the participant was on that target (time-on-target, or TOT). Next, Bahrick et al. estimated TOT using a band of correctness that was somewhat larger or more lenient (15% of the screen's width), and then they did it again for a very large target band of correctness (30% of the screen's width). Then they plotted these various TOT scores for each trial, giving the three curves shown in figure 8.4.

Remember that these curves came from the *same* performances from the same participants, who were not aware of the scoring that Bahrick and colleagues did afterward. If you were to consider the shapes of these curves as indicators about learning, you would be forced into three contradictory conclusions: (1) The learning gains were rapid at first and slower later (30% curve); (2) the learning gains were linear across practice (15% curve); and (3) the learning gains were slow at first and more rapid later (5% curve). In fact, only one improvement rate was experienced by each participant, but it was estimated in three different ways, which led to three different conclusions about the changes with practice. These differences are caused by so-called scoring artifacts. When the performance maximum is reached, this is called a *ceiling effect* because a higher performance score is not possible. In this study, 100% time-on-target represents the ceiling. Performance minima can also represent a scoring artifact. If tracking error had been measured in this study (say, using root-mean-square error, or RMSE), then zero error would be the minimum score possible and would

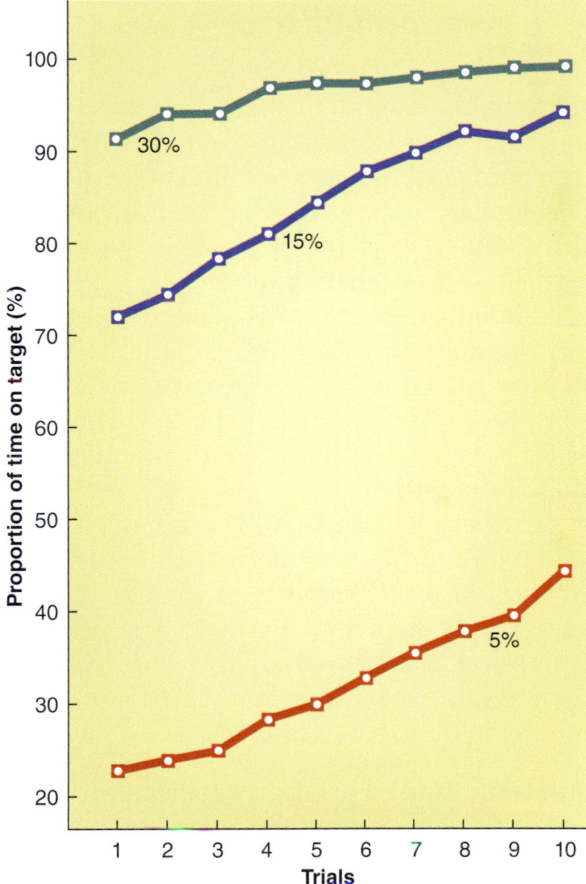

FIGURE 8.4 Proportion of time-on-target for a group of participants practicing a tracking task, scored with three different criteria. Performance was considered to be on target whenever the participant's tracking was near the cursor within 5%, 15%, or 30% of the screen's width.

> *continued*

> Learning Curves: Facts or Artifacts? *continued*

be called a *floor effect*, because a lower performance score than this is not possible. In general, these artifacts occur whenever the measured scores become less sensitive to the gains in the internal capability for responding. The Bahrick et al. experiment warns of the difficulties in using performance curves and the potential errors that can be made in making conclusions from these curves. This might give some clue as to the origin of the title for their article, "Learning Curves—Facts or Artifacts?"

Exploring Further

1. Think of another motor learning task; describe how changes in the criterion for success could be made and how these changes might affect the shape of the performance curve over practice trials.
2. Provide an example of a floor effect and a ceiling effect in the task described for question 1.

Between-Participant Effects Are Masked

One of the main reasons for using performance curves is that they average or "smooth out" the discrepant performances of different learners. Through averaging of a large group of people together, performance changes in the (mythical) average participant can be seen and, it is hoped, inferences can be made about changes in general proficiency. This is particularly useful in research settings, where the difference between two groups of participants is studied as a function of different practice methods, for example.

The drawback is that this averaging process hides any differences between people, termed *individual differences* in chapter 7. Because of this, the averaging method gives the impression that all participants improve at the same rate, or in the same way, which we know is not correct in most cases.

Within-Participant Variability Is Masked

A third drawback to performance curves is that the performance fluctuations *within* a single person tend to be obscured by averaging procedures. When examining smooth performance curves, such as those in figures 8.3 and 8.4, it is tempting to assume that the individual learners' performances contributing to the curves progressed smoothly and gradually as well. What we will see often in later chapters, however, are figures in which performance plots represent not just a single trial but rather a block of trials. What this means is that multiple separate trials for any single participant are averaged to produce a single score, which is then averaged over the group of participants in an experimental condition. Thus, the averaging process produces a curve that masks both within-participant and between-participant variability.

Distinguishing Learning From Performance

Critically important, not only for the experimental study of learning but also for evaluating learning in practical settings, is the distinction between learning and performance. According to this view, practice can have two different kinds of influences on performance—one that is relatively permanent and due to learning, and another that is only temporary and transient.

Temporary and Relatively Permanent Effects of Practice

One product of practice is learning—the establishment of a relatively permanent improvement in the capability to perform. A relatively permanent change in the person (which really could be the result of changes in a collection of processes, as seen in figure 8.1) allows the individual to perform a particular action in the future and endures over many days or even many years. Essentially, the concern of researchers who study motor learning is the discovery of practice conditions that maximize the development of these relatively permanent changes, so that these conditions can be used in various practical settings to enhance learning.

It is important to remember, however, that many practice conditions have temporary effects as well as relatively permanent ones. Some effects are positive and contribute to increased performance levels (e.g., motivation), whereas others are negative and can degrade performance (e.g., fatigue). A key concern is identifying what these effects are and distinguishing their impact on performance versus learning.

For example, various kinds of instructions or encouragement during practice elevate performance due to a motivating or energizing effect. As we will see in chapter 11, giving the learner information about how performance is progressing during the practice of a task can have an elevating effect. Providing guidance in the form of physical assistance or verbal directions during practice can also benefit performance. Various mood states can likewise elevate performance temporarily, as can certain drugs. Other temporary practice factors can be negative, degrading performance temporarily. For example, sometimes practice generates physical or mental fatigue, which can depress performance relative to rested conditions (e.g., see figure 8.2). Lethargic performances can result if practice is boring or if learners become discouraged at their lack of progress; this effect is more or less opposite to the energizing effects just mentioned. Numerous other factors associated with practice could exert similar effects.

Practice can have numerous important effects on the learner:

- Relatively permanent effects that persist across many days, even years
- Temporary effects that vanish with time or a change in conditions
- Simultaneous temporary and relatively permanent effects that can influence performance markedly

Separating Temporary and Relatively Permanent Effects

Suppose that you are interested in trying out a new teaching aid for improving the alignment skills of a golfer when setting up to make a putt. (The device is not legal for actual competition and can be used only during practice sessions.) Your evaluation of the benefit of this new alignment aid for learning will be based on whether or not it enhances performance in a relatively permanent way—that is, after the device has been removed (perhaps as in a golf game). After all, if the positive effects of the alignment aid disappear as soon as it is removed, the aid cannot have had much advantage as a learning tool.

Whenever learners practice, and especially when instructors intervene to enhance learning (e.g., by giving instructions and feedback), it is important to have a way to separate the relatively permanent effects from the

Identify one negative and one positive benefit on either performance or learning that might occur with practice using this training aid.

temporary effects. Frequently in research settings, and sometimes in practical settings as well, learners are divided into two separate classes or groups. For example, let's suppose that one group of golfers practices trying to make 6 ft (1.8 m) putts with the alignment aid, and another group practices without the aid. The two groups might practice under these two different conditions for a period of time, perhaps over 10 sessions, with records of the percentage of putts made. You might average all of the golfers' scores for each group separately and plot performance curves, essentially as was done in figures 8.2 and 8.3. Such a plot might look like the one in figure 8.5, where the average percentage of putts made from 6 ft away is plotted for the 10 sessions.

Which condition is more effective for learning—practice with the alignment aid or without it? This might seem like a silly question on the surface. Looking at the graph in figure 8.5 reveals that the group of golfers who used the alignment aid improved their performance in practice more rapidly than did the group who practiced without the aid. It would seem obvious that practice performance with the alignment aid was more accurate than without it, and the difference *might* be due to learning, which would be most interesting and valuable to know. As argued in the previous section, however, the difference between these two groups might be only a temporary performance effect, which could disappear as soon as the alignment aid was removed.

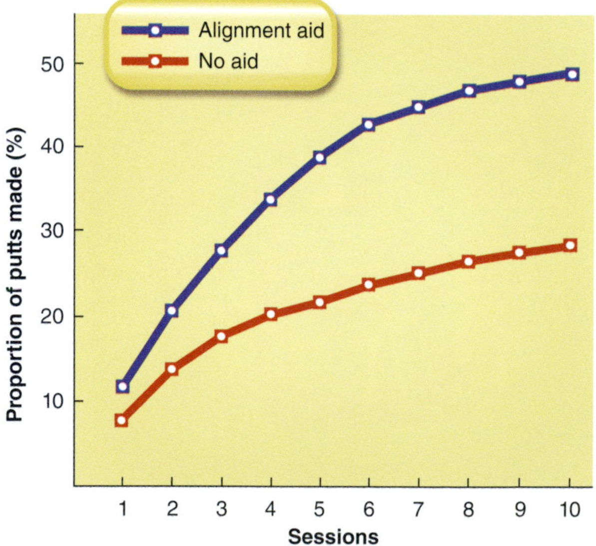

FIGURE 8.5 Hypothetical performance curves for two groups practicing the golf putt with or without an alignment aid.

The problem can be posed more systematically in the form of hypotheses about the two conditions:

> *Hypothesis 1:* The group that practiced with the alignment aid learned more than the group that practiced without it (a stronger relatively permanent capability for performance had been developed).
>
> *Hypothesis 2:* Although the group that practiced with the alignment aid performed more accurately during the practice sessions than the group that practiced without it, they were no better in the relatively permanent capability for performance.

Which of these two hypotheses is correct? The answer, based only on the data in figure 8.5, is unknown. The information presented gives no way to tell whether the advantage of the alignment aid group is due to some relatively permanent (learning) effect or to some temporary (performance) effect that is likely to disappear once the alignment aid is no longer available. This is a critical problem because there is no real basis for deciding which learning method is better. Fortunately, additional procedures are available that permit separation of learning and performance effects.

Transfer Designs

A so-called transfer design can analyze whether a change that improves performance in practice also improves learning by separating the relatively permanent and temporary effects of a variable. This method has two important features. First, the temporary effects of the variable must be allowed to dissipate. In our golf example, the temporary effects of the alignment aid (if any) might be informational or physical (a type of guidance), operating mainly during actual performance, so very little time for dissipation would be needed. As a result, any other temporary effects (such as increased motivation) would dissipate relatively quickly,

Focus on APPLICATION 8.1

Self-Assessments of Learning

In most activities of daily life, the learner is responsible for making the decisions about how to practice, such as scheduling the frequency of sessions and their duration. Practice for a motor skills competition is no different than other types of studying—you determine how to practice and the practice duration, and stop practicing when you feel competent or confident in your *predicted* capability to perform when it counts, just as one does in preparation for an examination. The critical question is this: What is the basis for making this prediction?

A common problem is that most learners interpret temporary indicators of performance as permanent indicators of learning or remembering. This is especially problematic when a temporary boost to performance is (mistakenly) used as an indication of learning. Motor skills practice can also result in a similar feeling of overconfidence. One of the factors that is addressed in chapter 10 concerns blocked versus random (or interleaved) practice scheduling. Drill-type or blocked-ordered practice generally produces better skilled performance than randomly ordered practice trials. And, if asked to predict what their performance would be in a delayed **retention test**, participants engaged in blocked practice predict that they will have achieved far more learning compared to participants engaged in random practice (Simon & Bjork, 2001). However, the reality is much different (the opposite, actually; see chapter 10 for details). This research illustrates that self-assessment judgments of learning can be quite unreliable, especially when they are based on *current* indicators of performance during practice. A good review of the research and applied nature of these memory and learning issues is provided by Soderstrom and Bjork (2015).

---

and certainly would dissipate before the next session. Second, the learners in both groups must be tested again under common conditions in a transfer (or retention) test, both groups performing either with or without the alignment aid. This is done to equalize any temporary effects that the test conditions themselves might have on retention performance. Otherwise, the results would be difficult to interpret.

In general, the term **transfer test** usually refers to a change of task conditions, whereas a *retention test* usually refers to a test given after an empty period without practice (in reality, though, the terms are often used interchangeably). The tests could be given a day or more after the last practice session or several minutes after the last session. Because the interest in the golf alignment aid example is mainly in the effect of the alignment aid on transfer performance when the aid is no longer available (analogous to a game), the decision is to test both groups without the aid. The logic that underlies a transfer or retention test is this: If the temporary effects have dissipated by the time of the test then any differences observed in the test should be due to the relatively permanent effects acquired through training with the aid during the practice sessions. In this way, the learning effects of the alignment aid are not evaluated during practice, but rather in the transfer or retention test, when the temporary effects have disappeared, leaving the relatively permanent effects behind to be revealed on the test.

The essential features of a transfer design can be summarized as follows:

- Allow sufficient time (rest) for the supposed temporary effects of practice to dissipate. The amount of time will vary depending on the particular nature of the temporary effects.

- Evaluate learners again in a transfer or retention test, with all groups performing under identical conditions.
- Any differences observed in this transfer test are due to a difference in the relatively permanent capability for performance acquired during earlier practice—that is, in learning.

Consider the possible transfer test outcomes of the hypothetical alignment-aid experiment just described. Four of these possibilities are shown in figure 8.6, labeled A, B, C, and D in the right (transfer) portion of the figure. In transfer outcome A, the performances of the two groups are different by approximately the same amount as was present at the end of the practice sessions (compare performance on session 10 with transfer outcome A). In this case, the appropriate conclusion would be that all of the difference between groups achieved by the last session of practice was due to a relatively permanent effect because allowing the temporary effects (if any) to dissipate did not change the groups' relative status at all. Conclusion: Practice with the alignment aid was more effective for learning than was practice without the aid.

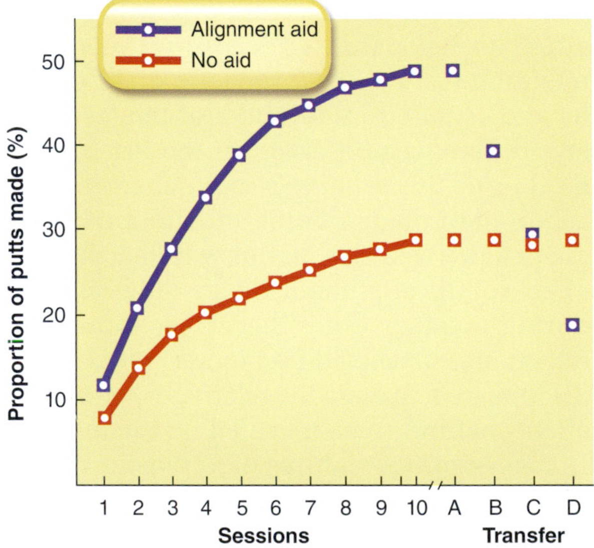

FIGURE 8.6 Hypothetical effects on transfer tests of two groups practicing the golf putt with or without an alignment aid. Four different possible outcomes on the transfer test are illustrated in transfer outcomes A, B, C, and D.

Now consider transfer outcome B in figure 8.6, where the transfer performance of the group practicing with the alignment aid is more accurate than that of the other group, but the difference is not as large as it was in the last practice session. From these test results one could argue that some of the difference between the performances of these groups in the practice session was due to temporary effects because dissipation reduced the difference somewhat. However, not all of the practice session difference was temporary because some of it remained in the transfer test, after the temporary effects dissipated. Conclusion: Practice with the alignment aid elevated performance temporarily, but it also produced some lasting effects on learning, compared to practice without the aid.

Next, examine transfer outcome C in figure 8.6, where the transfer performances of the two groups are essentially the same but at the level of the no-aid group at the end of practice. Here, when the temporary effects have dissipated, all of the differences that had accumulated between the groups during practice dissipated as well. This leads to the conclusion that the effect of the practice aid was entirely due to some temporary elevating change, and none of it was due to learning. Conclusion: Practice with the alignment aid elevated performance compared to performance without the aid, but it had no effect on learning.

Finally, examine outcome D, where the performance of the group that had practiced with the alignment aid resulted in transfer performance that was *less* accurate than that of the group that had practiced without the aid. This is a rather odd and counterintuitive result, for it reveals that not only did all performance advantages of the alignment aid disappear when the temporary effects dissipated but that the alignment aid resulted in a learning effect that was smaller than practice without it. Conclusion: Practice with the alignment aid elevated performance during practice but had a degrading effect on learning compared to the group that practiced without the aid. (Note: We will see some results that look like this in chapters 10 and 11, including the effects of training aids.)

Visit the web study guide to read "Learning to Win from Losing" and complete the self-directed learning activities.

Measuring Learning in Practical Settings

The issues just discussed may seem, at first glance, to relate mainly to the evaluation of learning in research situations. However, transfer designs form the basis for the evaluation of learning in many teaching situations as well. For example, when a learner practices some skill, for example, producing the proper amount of pressure in cardiopulmonary resuscitation (CPR), the proficiency level reached at the end of a practice session may not reflect the actual performance capability achieved. Because practice and various factors involved in it may also affect performance temporarily, they may mask the underlying acquired skill capability.

Practice conditions may also not reflect accurately the emotional conditions under which some skills are required. For example, CPR skills are usually needed in emergency situations, where the emotional stress may be elevated quite dramatically compared to the situations under which practice is typically conducted. Therefore, various types of retention and transfer tests may be required to assess the true level of skills learned during practice.

A related issue concerns evaluation for the purpose of grading. If a learner's grade in some activity is related to the *amount* learned, then basing the grade on performance toward the end of some practice session would be unwise. The learning level would tend to be masked by various temporary practice effects. A far better method would be to evaluate the learner's performance in a delayed retention or transfer test, administered sufficiently long after practice so that the temporary effects of practicing have dissipated.

Transfer of Learning

The term *transfer* is closely related to learning although it is used in a slightly different way than the term *transfer test*. Transfer refers specifically to the learning that is seen when practice on one task contributes to performance capability in some other task. Transfer can be positive or negative, depending on whether it enhances or degrades performance on the other task, usually when compared to a no-practice control condition. An important variation of the ideas about learning addressed thus far requires further discussion—**transfer of learning**. As the name implies, this concept involves the learning achieved in one task or in one practice setting when it is applied to the performance of some other task, or in some other setting, or both.

A good example involving transfer of learning is the handgun skills of a police officer. Transfer is a particularly important notion for instructors of police officers because the conditions under which practice is conducted are often quite different than the conditions in a real situation in which handgun involvement is required. However, for the safety of the public and the people involved, the skills acquired in practice must be maximally transferrable to the broadest range of transfer conditions possible. Therefore, teaching for transfer, or organizing practice and instruction to facilitate transfer of learning, is an important goal for most instructional programs.

Role of Transfer in Skill Learning Settings

Transfer is assumed whenever the skills learned in one task are applied successfully to the performance of some other task version. Consider police officers who undertake handgun shooting practice, for example. Shooting at targets at a practice range under rested, nonstressful conditions perhaps assumes that this experience will transfer to shooting in a life-or-death situation. In this situation, the transfer from practice to the transfer task skill situation must be substantial. If it is not, practicing the drills could be largely a waste of time.

Visit the web study guide to read "Zero-Sum Training" and complete the self-directed learning activities.

Transfer is also assumed when instructors modify skills to make them easier to practice. For example, relatively long-duration, serial skills, such as doing a gymnastics routine, can be broken down into their elements for practice. Practicing the stunts in isolation must benefit the performance of the whole routine (the *criterion task*), which is made up of the individual stunts. However, in more rapid skills, such as a tennis serve, it is usually not so clear that breaking down the skill into ball-toss and ball-strike portions for part practice will be effective for transfer to the whole task. The principles of transfer applicable to such situations are described in chapter 9.

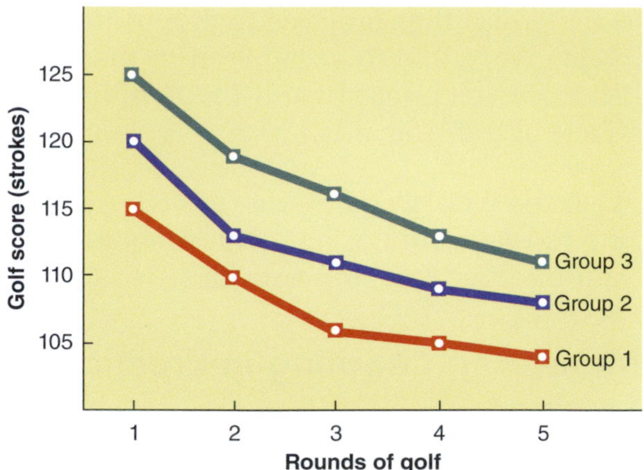

FIGURE 8.7 Hypothetical average scores for a round of golf as a function of prior practice experiences. Earlier, group 1 (red line) practiced at a driving range, group 3 (green line) practiced miniature golf, and group 2 (blue line) received no practice. The differences between groups 1 and 2 demonstrate positive transfer from practice at the driving range. The differences between groups 2 and 3 reveal negative transfer from practice at miniature golf.

How Is Transfer Measured?

Issues concerning the measurement of transfer are closely related to the learning measurement issues discussed earlier. Essentially, we want to estimate the performance level of the criterion task, with the relatively permanent effects of learning separated from any temporary performance effects. However, rather than asking how practice variations of a given task affect learning, transfer concerns how performance on the transfer task is influenced by practice on some other task.

Suppose you want to know whether practicing golf at the driving range transfers to the actual game of golf. Consider three hypothetical groups of participants with different kinds of practice experiences. Group 1 practices for 4 h at the driving range, group 2 does not receive any practice, and group 3 practices for 4 h at a miniature-golf course. After these various practice activities, all groups transfer to (are tested on) five rounds of golf on an actual golf course. The results of this hypothetical experiment are shown in figure 8.7, where the average scores for the five rounds of golf are plotted separately for the three groups. Assuming that the groups are equivalent at the start of the experiment, the only reason for the groups to be different on the first (and subsequent) rounds of golf is that the previous experiences have somehow contributed to, or detracted from, actual golf skill. Therefore, the focus for transfer would be on the relative differences among the groups on the criterion task.

Figure 8.7 shows that group 1, which had practiced at the driving range before the five rounds of golf, performed more effectively than group 2, which received no previous practice. In this case, we would have said that the driving range experience transferred *positively* to golf because it facilitated golf performance over and above no practice. If this were an actual experiment, you might conclude that the skills developed on the driving range were applicable in some way to those on the golf course

Transfer can also be negative, as you can see by comparing groups 2 and 3 in figure 8.7. Notice that group 3, which had practice only on the miniature-golf task, performed more poorly on the five rounds of golf than group 2, which had no prior practice at all. In this case, miniature-golf experience transferred *negatively* to golf performance. If this had happened in an actual experiment, you might conclude that the skills learned in miniature golf not only were different from those required on a golf course but in fact led to disruption in the learning of those skills needed in the golf game.

How much positive transfer occurred, and how can we put a measurement number on it? One way is through so-called percentage transfer. A means of doing this is to provide an estimate of the total amount of improvement of the group that had no prior practice on any task—in this case, group 2—and then compare that to the initial performance of the group that had the type of practice being evaluated. Simply taking the initial performance score of the no-practice group (120 strokes) and subtracting the final performance score (109 strokes) shows an improvement from 120 to 109 = 11 strokes. Then we see that group 1 (driving range practice) and group 2 (no prior practice) differ by about five strokes on the first session; that is, of the total 11 strokes of improvement that group 2 realized, five of them were gained in driving range practice. Researchers often describe these changes in terms of percentages—here, 5/11 = 45% transfer.

Alternatively, some researchers represent transfer in terms of a "savings score," where the amount of savings (here, in practice time) generated on the criterion task is the result of having practiced at the driving range. In this example, referring to figure 8.7 again, if we were to draw a horizontal line from group 1's initial performance (115 strokes) until it intersected the trend line for group 2, and then dropped a perpendicular line to the *x*-axis, we could compute a savings score—in this case about 1.7 rounds of golf for group 1. That is, as a result of having practiced on the driving range, group 1 "saved" about 1.7 rounds of golf practice.

Be aware, however, that these measures of amount of transfer are clearly confounded or flawed by concepts discussed already in this chapter. One of the fundamental ideas is that performance curves and their shapes are often arbitrarily defined by choices the experimenter makes before the study (e.g., the size of the target; see figure 8.4 and the related discussion). So, in terms of the percentage transfer measurement, basing the measurement of transfer on the changes that the no-prior-practice group produced is also arbitrary, producing an arbitrary percentage transfer score. A similar argument can be made for the savings score; as figure 8.7 shows, the initial shape of group 2's performance curve is also somewhat arbitrary. About the best we can say is that these measures provide useful ways of describing transfer results in relative terms.

Specific Transfer

The previous sections on measuring learning have perhaps left the impression that the only way to measure the relative amount learned is by performance on some delayed retention test. This is probably the most important way to estimate learning, but other ways are possible, and some are even preferable in some situations.

The essential issue is what we want learners to be able to do after training. In some cases, learners are trained to be proficient at a specific task with a limited range of variations. For example, basketball players take foul shots using a set shot from a distance of 15 ft (4.6 m) to the basket (i.e., from the free-throw line). So, it seems perfectly reasonable to devote considerable set-shot practice from the free-throw line because the set shot is a specific type of basketball skill that is normally not performed at any other location on the court. Many closed tasks share these characteristics.

Generalized Transfer

One critical aspect of many training settings is the extent to which the practice transfers to different, yet very similar settings in the real world. This is sometimes termed **near transfer**, the learning goal being a task relatively similar to the training task. A good example that contrasts nicely with the free throw is the jump shot in basketball. The jump shot can be taken from an infinite number of places on the court and under a variety of game situations. Being able to perform in such varied and unpredictable conditions is one mark of a highly skilled performer. Therefore, tests of transfer in which performance is measured on some variant of the task that is similar, yet different, from those in the practice conditions would be a reasonable test of generalized transfer.

Sometimes instructors want to train learners to develop more general capabilities for a wide variety of skills, only a few of which are actually experienced in practice. This is usually termed **far transfer** because the eventual goal is quite different from that in the original practice setting. For example, elementary school children are taught to throw, jump, and run; the main concern is the extent to which these activities transfer to future activities involving throwing, jumping, and running but occurring in very different settings.

In all these situations, the evaluation of training effectiveness is not based exclusively on how well the learners master the skills during actual practice. Rather, if transfer to relatively different activities is the goal, the most effective training program will be the one that produces the best performance on some transfer test performed in the future—one that may involve quite different skills from those actually practiced. Here, the effectiveness of a training program is measured by the amount of transfer to some different activity.

Summary

Motor learning is defined as a set of processes associated with practice. As such, the emphasis is on the determinants of this capability, which supports or underlies the performance. Hence, factors that affect performance only temporarily need to be distinguished from the factors affecting this underlying capability, which makes the use of learning curves somewhat risky for evaluating learning.

However, temporary and learning effects can be separated through the use of transfer or retention tests. In some experiments on learning, groups of learners practice under different conditions in acquisition; after a delay, they are tested on the same task but under conditions that are identical for all the groups. This procedure focuses attention on the relative performance in the retention tests as measures of learning.

WEB STUDY GUIDE ACTIVITIES

The student web study guide offers these activities to help you build and apply your knowledge of the concepts in this chapter.

Interactive Learning

Activity 8.1: Using a figure from the text, interpret the findings of a transfer design study to understand the effects of a mechanical aid on learning.

Activity 8.2: Review the types of learning transfer by matching terms with their definitions.

Activity 8.3: Check your understanding of the definition of motor learning through a fill-in-the-blanks exercise.

Principles-to-Application Exercise

Activity 8.4: The principles-to-application exercise for this chapter prompts you to choose a skill and examine the effects of practice for a person learning that skill. You will identify the possible temporary and permanent effects of practice and consider how you could collect evidence to distinguish temporary from permanent effects.

Motor Control in Everyday Actions Narratives

How You Get to Carnegie Hall
Learning to Win from Losing
Zero-Sum Training

Check Your Understanding

1. Define motor learning and indicate why each of the following terms is important to that definition.
   - Capability
   - Practice and experience
   - Performance
2. Distinguish between near transfer and far transfer and between positive transfer and negative transfer. Give one example of each.
3. List and describe two limitations of using performance curves to evaluate learning progress.

Apply Your Knowledge

1. List three essential features of a transfer design. How would these features be included in an experiment to examine if the use of a pole to aid in balance during a one-foot stance task is beneficial to learning to perform the one-foot stance task without the pole?
2. Describe one practical setting where the proficiency level reached at the end of a practice session may not reflect the actual performance capability achieved under the conditions where the skill will eventually be required. How could you assess the true level of skills learned during practice?

Suggestions for Further Reading

Important cautions about the learning–performance distinction are provided by Kantak and Winstein (2012) and Cahill, McGaugh, and Weinberger (2001). An analysis of so called learning curves is given by Stratton and coauthors (2007). More information on the measurement of learning can be found in Schmidt et al., (2019, ch.11) and also on the retention and transfer of learning (ch. 14). See the reference list for these additional resources.

9

The Motor Learning Process

Skill Acquisition, Retention, and Transfer

KEY TERMS

autonomous stage
cognitive stage of learning
constraints
constraints-led approach
criterion task
degree of freedom
degrees of freedom problem
deliberate practice
error-detection capability
fixation (associative or motor) stage
forgetting
gearshift analogy
lead-up activities
part practice
physical fidelity
psychological fidelity
repetition
set
simulator
specificity of learning
transfer
warm-up decrement
whole practice

CHAPTER OUTLINE

CHAPTER OBJECTIVES

Chapter 9 describes the processes that influence motor learning—skill acquisition, retention, and transfer. This chapter will help you to understand

- basic principles of the skill acquisition process,
- two conceptualizations of learning stages during skill acquisition,
- factors that influence the retention of skills after periods of no practice, and
- factors that influence the transfer of skills to new tasks or performance situations.

Playing the guitar provides a good example of how practice leads to the development of motor skill. Consider the beginning chords of the classic rock song, "Rumble," by Link Wray. The first three chords are D, D, and E. For a right-handed guitarist, the D chord is achieved by pressing down on the third fret of the second string and the second fret of the third string with the left hand while strumming the second, third, fourth, and fifth strings with the right hand. The D chord is played twice; then the fingers on the left hand shift to make an E chord, which requires fingers on the left hand to press the first fret of the third string and the second fret of the fourth and fifth strings while the right hand now strums all six strings.

The beginner guitarist is faced with a number of problems to be solved simultaneously, such as knowing which fingers are placed where, having to avoid strings that should not be touched, remembering what positions compose what chords and which strings the right hand should strum, then moving the hand and fingers to create a whole new chord. And this does not even consider the timing structure that must underlie these chords. It is very impressive, indeed, that anyone can learn to play the guitar given what we've just said; yet many do, and many do it very, very well.

Learning to play the guitar is a good example of the topics presented in this chapter. Typically, the beginning guitarist goes through changes in skill progression, called stages of motor learning. Certain principles of learning apply to almost all motor learning, and these principles result in the acquisition of a specific set of subskills that support performance. But that is not the whole story about motor learning. Time away from playing the guitar has an impact on future performance because the retention of skills is expected to be different for different types of tasks, so being able to classify guitar playing as a member of one of several classes of skills is important. And lastly, motor learning would be very inefficient if we had to progress through the entire skill acquisition process for each and every guitar that we might play and under different circumstances in which we find ourselves (e.g., standing versus sitting). We expect our playing skills to generalize (or transfer) to different guitars, situations, and environments; therefore, information about the factors that are expected to affect transfer constitutes a critical component of any discussion of the learning process.

Skill Acquisition

Quite simply, the single most important factor leading to the acquisition of motor skill is practice. However, *practice* is also probably one of the most poorly understood and misused terms when applied to the concept of learning. In this section we describe some principles of practice, how they affect learning, and what occurs as the result of practice.

Basic Principles of Practice

It almost goes without saying that the most important variable for learning is practice itself. There's no easy way around it, and as a general rule, more practice produces more learning. A considerable amount of interest in practice and learning was generated by the book *Outliers*, by Malcolm Gladwell, in which he popularized the idea that achieving expertise required 10,000 hours of practice—a concept that had arisen from some research conducted by Anders Ericsson and his colleagues (read Ericsson & Pool, 2016, for a great overview). Unfortunately, this so-called 10,000-hour rule misrepresented the findings of Ericsson's work. The amount of practice *time* was not Ericsson's main concern because not all practice methods are equal in their impact on learning. In this section we describe the basic principles of effective practice, and what might and might not lead to effective and efficient skill acquisition.

Practice Is More Than Just Repetition

The term *repetition* is often incorrectly substituted for *practice*, and many well-intentioned instructors and coaches confuse the two concepts. To us, the term **repetition** invokes the idea of repeating a movement, again and again and again. The concept brings to mind the idea that repetitions somehow groove or stamp in a memory, with more repetitions leading to a deeper groove or more durable stamp in memory. The metaphor causes one to think (incorrectly, in our view) of learning as a concept similar to muscle hypertrophy that results from repetitious exercise.

Consider the following quotes from two very influential theorists as counterpoints to the traditional view of practice as repetition.

> **Bartlett:** When I make the [tennis] stroke, I do not . . . produce something absolutely new, and I never repeat something old. (Bartlett, 1932, p. 202)
>
> **Bernstein:** The process of practice towards the achievement of new motor habits essentially consists in the gradual success of a search for optimal motor solutions to the appropriate problems. Because of this, practice, when properly undertaken, does not consist in repeating the *means of* solution of a motor problem time after time, but in the *process of solving* this problem again and again by techniques which we changed and perfected from repetition to repetition. It is already apparent here that, in many cases, "practice is a particular type of repetition without repetition" and that motor training, if this position is ignored, is merely mechanical repetition by rote, a method which has been discredited in pedagogy for some time. (Bernstein, 1967, p. 134)

The conceptual model that we have developed throughout the book highlights the most important components of the human information-processing system that are involved in movement control. These components fluctuate due to temporary factors, improve with development, and regress with advancing age. Importantly, though, the components of the processing system become more effective and efficient with learning. In our view, the most effective learning occurs when a repetition activates as many of the individual components of the processing system as possible. In this way, practice is successful to the degree that it engages the entire conceptual model presented in figure 8.1.

Ericsson's use of the term **deliberate practice** captures the essence of engaging the conceptual model (Ericsson & Pool, 2016). Deliberate practice is effortful, oriented toward goal attainment, and actively uses augmented feedback to improve performance. Research has shown, for example, that skilled athletes engage in more of the behaviors typified by the term *deliberate practice* than do less-skilled athletes (Coughlan et al., 2014). The idea has been a useful construct in many different fields of training, including the development of expertise in music, sport, and medicine.

Specificity of Learning

Although transfer is a hallmark of learning (discussed in more detail later in this chapter, and in chapter 11), a consistent finding in the literature is that motor learning is quite specific. In general, **specificity of learning** suggests that what you learn depends largely on what you practice. Specificity effects are wide-ranging. This example might make the idea more clear: If you want your soccer team to perform well in the dark, in the rain, and in front of many noisy fans, then the most effective practice would be done in the dark, in the rain, and in front of many noisy fans. Practicing in a particular environment or workspace often leads to better performance mainly in (sometimes only in) that workspace, compared to a different or altered workspace (this is perhaps one of the bases of the so-called home-field advantage; Carron, Loughhead, & Bray, 2005). Another important finding is that the sensory feedback (e.g., visual, auditory, tactile) resulting from performance during specific types or locations of practice becomes part of the learned representation for skill, such that later performance is more skillful when that *same* sensory information is available, compared to situations in which one or more of these feedback channels is altered (Proteau, 1992). Thus, while an important goal of practice is to facilitate transfer (i.e., performance enhancement for unpracticed situations or contexts), it is important to recognize that specificity of learning is the dominant characteristic.

Learning Versus Performance during Practice

Perhaps it is obvious that when learners acquire a new skill, they are doing something different than they had done earlier. The processes leading to learning require that the learner change something in the movement patterning, usually such that the performance becomes more effective and efficient. Yet, when assisting learners during practice, many instructors encourage learners to "do your best" on each practice attempt. This generates two conflicting practice goals: performing as well as possible in practice versus learning as much as possible in practice by attempting to explore new techniques, strategies, and movement patterning.

In our assessment of the research literature, the old adage that "if you make errors in practice you will learn to make errors" could not be farther from the truth. The learner who attempts to always perform as well as possible in practice tends to avoid modifying (experimenting with) movements from attempt to attempt, which detracts from learning. The approach for maximizing performance, repeating the most effective pattern discovered so far, is not effective for learning in part because it discourages such experimentation. One way to separate these conflicting practice goals is to provide two fundamentally different activities during practice—practice sessions and test sessions.

First, provide practice sessions in which you instruct the learners simply to avoid repeating what they did earlier. Tell the learner to explore different styles of movement control to discover some more effective pattern of action. Self-discovery of new skill techniques is a hallmark of motor learning, and the effective instructor can use various means to help the learner make these discoveries (Davids et al., 2008; Newell, 1986).The learner should know that performance quality is not critical during this practice period, and that the only goal is to discover some new way to execute the skill that will be more effective in the long term.

Of course, the measure of the effectiveness of this learning progress is a test of some kind.

After several minutes in the practice session, the instructor could announce a switch to a test session, in which the next five attempts are treated as a test. In the test session the learner is to perform as well as possible, using the best estimate gained so far of the movement pattern for the most proficient performance. After the test session, the learner has some idea of his progress and can return to the discovery practice mode to continue searching for more effective movement patterning and skill technique. Such tests could be formally evaluated and graded, but they can also be effective if given only for the student's own information. Evaluating progress by asking learners to compile their own test scores is an excellent method to help them assess their own progress; it is both motivating and educational (we will have much more to say about feedback and evaluation in chapter 11).

Benefits of Practice

Obviously, a major goal of practice is effective performance, which can be thought of as developing the capability to perform some skill on future demand. However, there are several other benefits of practice that leave the learner with capabilities not so directly related to actual task proficiency. Actually, the term *motor learning* is a bit of a misnomer, as what results from practice is much more than just "motor" learning. In this section we briefly describe some of the benefits to be expected from practice.

Perceptual Skills

The game of chess provided an unlikely beginning for this important research area. DeGroot (1946) and Chase and Simon (1973) showed chessboards to experts and nonexperts. In one condition the pieces were arranged according to a partially played game of chess; in another condition the pieces were arranged randomly on the board (i.e., a grouping of chess pieces that was unlikely to occur in an actual game). After viewing the board for about 5 s, the participants were asked to recreate the scene they had just viewed on another board. As expected, the experts were much better than the nonexperts at recreating the board, but *only* for the board that had a game structure. There was no difference between experts and novices when they tried to recreate the randomly arranged board. This study provided important evidence that the experts did not have a better memory, in general, for briefly presented information. Rather, the experts' capability to remember the chessboard information was specific to their skills of observation and perception, acquired over many years of practice.

From these chess studies emerged a research paradigm that has addressed the perceptual advantage in athletes that is gained with practice and experience. Different methods are used to assess this advantage. One example is showing videos of specific activities (as in sporting events) in which a critical portion of the video is blocked from view (e.g., the information about a baseball pitcher's arm motion and grip on the ball; see Focus on Research 2.3). Participants (usually a mix of experts and nonexperts) are asked to predict something about the result of the blocked action (e.g., something about the ball's flight; see Williams, Ward, & Smeeton, 2004, for a review). Another research strategy is to monitor the eye and head movements made by performers of differing skill levels to assess whether the active search for information is changed as the result of practice or experience (e.g., Vickers, 2007). Results from this research tend to support the original findings with chess players—that expertise is quite specific to the nature of the skill that has been practiced. The research also shows that experts tend to seek out more specific and narrowly focused information in a perceptual display, and to pick up that information much earlier in the action than nonexperts (see Abernethy et al., 2012, for an excellent review).

Research also suggests that practice and the development of skill fundamentally change the way in which experts view the world. Anecdotally, this has been claimed by many involved in high-level sports. For example, NHL hockey players are often reported as seeing the game being played more slowly

Traceurs and traceuses, who are skilled in the activity of parkour, see obstacles in the environment as challenges to act upon. Describe a different parkour activity in which the object is viewed as something different than might normally be viewed.

than do the fans. Another example is the activity known as parkour, in which participants move in an environment by climbing, jumping, or crawling through, over, or under any obstacles in the way. Participants who become skilled in parkour tend to view things as objects to be acted upon, rather than as obstacles, as most of us would view them. In one study, Taylor et al. (2011) found that traceurs judged walls to be shorter than nontraceurs, adding validation to the idea that expertise changes perception of the environment that involves that skill.

Visit the web study guide to read "Wayne Gretzky" and complete the self-directed learning activities.

Attention

Attention was a major focus of chapter 3. We presented several different concepts of attention, which can now be considered from a learning perspective—the effect of practice on these concepts of attention. We consider two of these in this section.

Reduced Capacity Demands One of the fundamental concepts from chapter 3 was that most tasks demand some attention for their performance, and performance suffers when the overall demand exceeds the available attentional capacity (e.g., see the discussion on distracted driving in Focus on Research 3.2). Thus, one benefit of practice is the reduced attention that is demanded by tasks that have been well learned. A wonderful study by Leavitt (1979) illustrates this concept well. In his study, Leavitt compared young hockey players of different ages, and of different playing abilities within each age, in the performance of a skating task (which was the main task), done either without a stick

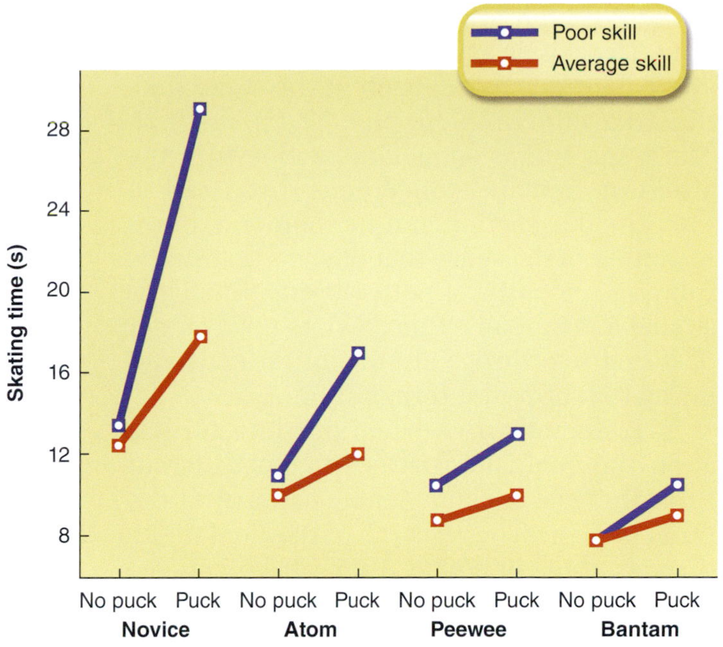

FIGURE 9.1 Skating times measured when participants were skating alone (the "no-puck" condition) and when they were skating and stick-handling (the "puck" condition) simultaneously. (Novice = 7.9 years of age on average; Atom = 10.1 years; Peewee = 11.3 years; Bantam = 14.1 years.)

and puck or when stick-handling a puck. (Ice skating without controlling a puck simultaneously is a much less attention-demanding task compared to skating and stick-handling a puck at the same time.) The time required to skate over a fixed distance was measured.

Leavitt's results are illustrated in figure 9.1. The graph is somewhat complex, so we will highlight a few key points. First, as expected, skating times with the stick and puck, in general, are longer than when skating without the stick and puck. Second, also as expected, the time when skating with the puck becomes progressively shorter as children become older (i.e., as they advance from the Novice to Atom to Peewee to Bantam age groups). And, lastly, within each age group, average-skilled players suffered less decrement in time when skating with the puck than did the poorly skilled players. Together, these findings point to the conclusion that as hockey skill improves there is less attention demanded by either the skating or stick-handling (or both), allowing them to be performed together with reduced decrements to performance.

Driving an automobile while engaged with an electronic communication device was another topic that we discussed in chapter 3. A large amount of research evidence has now been published clearly demonstrating that communicating on a cell phone (handheld or hands-free), texting (verbally or manually), plus many other forms of distraction are hazardous to driving performance (see Ishigami & Klein, 2009, and Caird et al., 2018, for reviews). But, given the findings discussed in the previous paragraph from Leavitt (1979), one might wonder if the decrement is the same for all drivers or more pronounced with individuals who have less experience (or skill) in either driving or using the communication device. To date, however, the research findings are mixed. In one study, for example, practice that involved both simulated driving and a secondary task improved performance but failed to eliminate the distraction deficit (Cooper & Strayer, 2008). And yet, in another study, a small proportion of the participants examined (2.5%) were identified as "supertaskers," showing no deficit to driving performance at all while engaged in various secondary tasks (Watson & Strayer, 2010). How and why these skills emerged and how (or if) they can be learned remains unknown.

Reduced Effector Competition Another important concept of attention is the interference that can arise when a task requires us to do two or more different things at the same time. The classic example of patting your head and rubbing your stomach at the same time illustrates the problem here (see figure 9.2). The issue shares some similarities with the attention-demand concept, as discussed in the previous section and in chapter 3, but it is unique in the sense that one has no trouble rubbing (or patting) both the head and the stomach at the same time. So it is not a matter of doing two things at once but a matter of doing two *different* things at once.

Interference arises when one effector has a movement goal or pattern that is different from the goal (or movement pattern) of the other effector. The research of Bender (1987), discussed in chapter 7, illustrates nicely the problem and the benefits that result from practice. She found that producing the English letter "V" with one hand and the Greek letter "γ" with the other hand was nearly impossible when these actions were to be performed at the same time. However, effector competition was reduced (but not eliminated) with considerable practice, perhaps due to the development of a single motor program that was responsible for controlling the two limbs as if they were a single limb (i.e., with a single motor program; see also Schmidt et al., 1998). The difficulty seems to be that the system is attempting to run two different programs at the same time and practice moves the learner closer to having a single motor program that governs both actions.

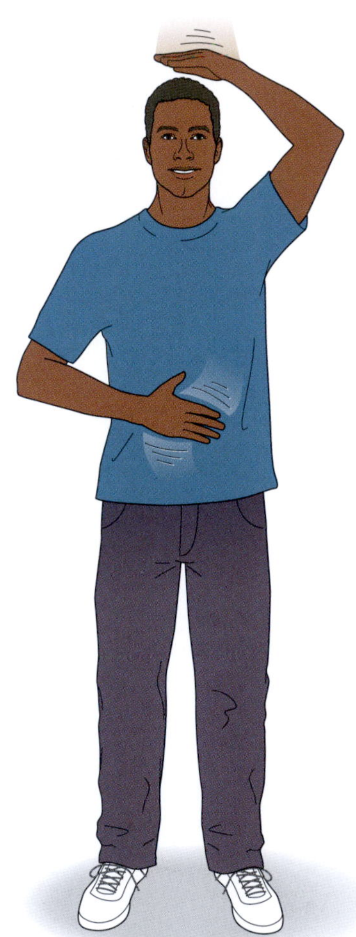

FIGURE 9.2 A typical coordination problem that can be solved with practice.

Motor Programs

A prominent theme in the motor learning literature suggests that many motor skills are learned through developing motor programs, as discussed in detail in chapter 5. How are these motor programs learned? The **gearshift analogy** provides a useful way to answer this question. When first learning to shift the gears of a standard-transmission car, the beginning driver goes through each of the seven steps illustrated in figure 9.3, the movement for each of these steps presumably being controlled by separate motor programs. As some proficiency is gained, some of these steps are combined into larger motor programs that are capable of controlling the movements for two of more of the individual steps. At the highest level of skill (e.g., with a race car driver) all seven steps are controlled by a single motor program.

Whether or not a sequence of actions is controlled by one, two, or perhaps more motor programs in sequence has been addressed by research designed to identify units of action. Imagine that a kinematic analysis of a movement allowed the measurement of the time of certain kinematic features (e.g., time of peak acceleration, time of maximum velocity). Since these kinematic features of movements are highly correlated in time over many individual trial executions (within participants), then we assume that these actions were run

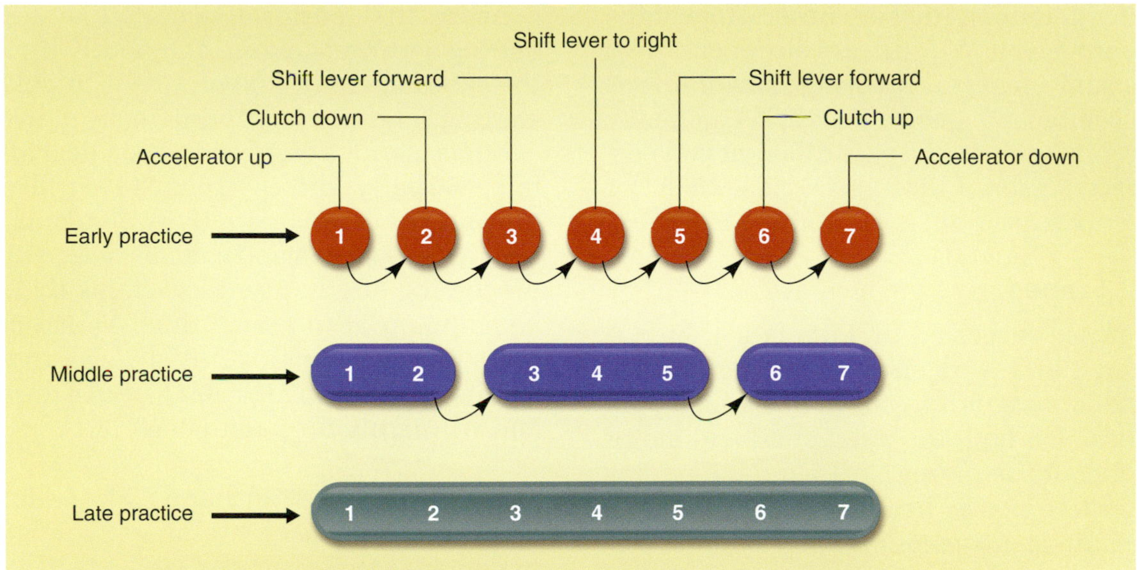

FIGURE 9.3 The gearshift analogy, using the example of shifting a standard-transmission car from second to third gear. Practice results in the reorganization of seven individual motor programs into one program.

off with a single motor program. A low correlation in time between any pair of such landmarks is evidence of separate programs (Schneider & Schmidt, 1995). This type of research can have many applications. For example, using this rationale, researchers analyzed childproof butane lighters and provided evidence that more than one motor program was required to complete all of the steps of igniting the lighter (Schmidt et al., 1996)—demonstrating that the safety feature was likely to be effective.

Error Detection

Error-detection capability represents another goal of practice. For example, the instructor is usually present during practice when a student is learning cardiopulmonary resuscitation (CPR) skills. Therefore self-detection of errors is not critical because the instructor is there to point them out and suggest corrections. However, the instructor will not be available to provide this corrective information when the learner attempts to perform this skill in an actual emergency. The learner who is able to detect and analyze her errors independently and thus make corrections in the moment will be a far more skilled provider of CPR. This error-detection and correction capability tends to make the learner self-sufficient, which is one overall goal of practice. We will have much more to say in chapter 11 about how the development of error-detection skills are promoted (or discouraged) by the manner in which augmented feedback is presented.

Tasks differ with respect to the saliency of different types of sensory information, of course. The sound of the engine is particularly important to the race car driver, and the sound of the instrument is obviously important to the musician. Visual information is critical to the dentist, although when provided by a mirror, that information requires special translation skills. People who have lost their sight can become particularly adept at tactile discrimination using movement (e.g., using Braille). The point here is that the detection and use of sensory information is a process that requires learning.

Stages of Learning

It is useful to consider learning as a series of relatively distinct stages (or phases) that can be identified in the skill acquisition process. These stages should not be confused with the information-processing stages discussed in chapter 2. Rather, they are descriptors of the different levels of skill development. Two important stages-of-learning contributions have been made, one by Fitts and another by Bernstein, each from a very different perspective (see Anson, Elliott, & Davids, 2005, for further discussion).

Fitts' Stages

The stages suggested by Fitts (1964; Fitts & Posner, 1967) were specifically designed to consider *perceptual–motor* learning, with emphasis on both the perceptual and motor components involving skill acquisition. This perspective places heavy emphasis on how the cognitive processes invested in motor performance change as a function of practice.

Fitts' Stage 1: Cognitive Stage As the stage name implies (**cognitive stage of learning**), the learner's first problem is cognitive, largely verbal (or verbalizable). The dominant questions concern goal identification, performance evaluation, what to do (and what not to do), when to do it, how to do it, and many other things. As a result, verbal and cognitive abilities dominate at this stage. Figuring out what to look at in the environment (or listen to, or feel, and so on) and generating an appropriate movement attempt are critical.

Instructions, demonstrations, videos, and other verbalizable information are also particularly useful in this stage. One goal of instruction is to have the learner transfer information from past learning to these initial skill levels. For example, many skills have similar stance requirements, so instructions that bring out already known stances should be useful for teaching a new one (e.g., "adopt an athletic stance "). Often, several previously learned movements can be sequenced together to approximate the desired skill (e.g., to shift gears, *push* in the clutch, *move* the gearshift down, and *let out* the clutch while gently *pressing* the accelerator) and can provide a start for later learning. Gains in proficiency in this stage are very rapid and large, indicating that better strategies for performance are being discovered, resulting in massive performance improvements. It is not of much concern that performance at this stage is halting, jerky, uncertain, and poorly timed to the external environment; this is merely the starting point for later proficiency gains.

Some learners engage in a great deal of self-talk, verbally guiding themselves through actions. However, this activity demands considerable attention and can interfere with the processing of other sensory events that may be going on at the same time. Verbal activity is effective for this initial stage, though, facilitating a rough approximation of the skill, and will likely drop out later.

Fitts' Stage 2: Fixation Stage The performer next enters the **fixation stage** (sometimes called the associative stage). Most of the cognitive problems dealing with the environmental cues that need to be attended to and the actions that need to be made have been solved. So now the learner's focus shifts to organizing more effective movement patterns to produce the action. In skills requiring quick movements, such as a tennis stroke, the learner begins to build a motor program to accomplish the movement requirements. In slower movements, such as balancing in gymnastics, the learner constructs ways to use movement-produced feedback.

Several factors change markedly during the fixation stage, associated with more effective movement patterns. Performance improves steadily. Some inconsistency from trial to trial is seen as the learner attempts new solutions to movement problems. Inconsistency gradually decreases, though; the movements involving closed skills begin to be more stereotypic, and those involving open skills become more adaptable to the changing environment (Gentile, 1972). Enhanced movement efficiency reduces energy costs, and self-talk becomes less important for performance. Performers discover environmental regularities to serve as effective cues for timing. Anticipation develops rapidly, making movements smoother and less rushed. In addition, learners begin to monitor their own feedback and detect their errors. This stage generally lasts much longer than the cognitive stage.

Fitts' Stage 3: Autonomous Stage After considerable practice, the learner gradually enters the **autonomous stage**. This is the stage usually associated with the attainment of expert performance—perceptual anticipation (chapter 2) is high, which speeds the processing of environmental information. The system generally programs longer movement sequences; this means that fewer programs need to be organized and initiated during a given interval of time, which decreases the load on attention-demanding movement initiation processes.

The decreased attention demanded by both perceptual and motor processes frees the individual to perform simultaneous higher-order cognitive activities, such as making decisions about strategies in sport, expressing emotion and affect in music and dance, and dealing with stress and chaos in emergencies. Self-talk about the actual muscular performance is almost absent, and performance often seems to suffer if self-analysis is attempted. However, self-talk could continue in terms of higher-order strategic aspects. Self-confidence increases and the capability to detect and correct one's own errors becomes more fine-tuned.

It is important to remember that performance improvements in the autonomous stage are slow, because the learner is already very capable when this stage begins. Learning continues however, as shown in many studies (see Focus on Research 9.1, for example).

Bernstein's Stages

In contrast to Fitts' emphasis on the information-processing aspects of perceptual and motor components of skill, Bernstein identified stages of learning from a combined motor control and biomechanical perspective.

Bernstein's Stage 1: Reduce Degrees of Freedom The initial problem facing the learner is what to do with all of the possible degrees of freedom of movement that are available for the body. A single **degree of freedom**, in Bernstein's view, refers to just one way (out of all of the ways) in which the various muscles and joints are free to move. In the initial stage of learning, Bernstein considered that the solution to the so-called **degrees of freedom problem** (i.e., explaining how all of the degrees of freedom are controlled) was to *reduce* the movement of nonessential or redundant body parts—in essence, by *freezing* these degrees of freedom. In some ways, this solution achieved the same goal as Fitts' first stage of learning—since the number of degrees of freedom that need to be controlled is reduced, there are fewer motions of the body that require conscious control, which allows attention to be devoted to the few degrees of freedom that provide maximal control of the rudimentary aspects of the action.

Bernstein's Stage 2: Release Degrees of Freedom As control of a minimum number of degrees of freedom in stage 1 begins to result in some initial successes, the typical learner attempts to improve performance by *releasing* some of the degrees of freedom that had initially been frozen. This release of degrees of freedom would seem to be particularly useful in tasks that require power or speed, as the degrees of freedom that have been released could allow for faster movement and greater accumulation of forces.

Bernstein's Stage 3: Exploit Passive Dynamics In Bernstein's final stage, the performer learns to exploit the passive dynamics of the body—essentially, the energy and motion that come "for free" with the help of physics (such as gravity, spring-like characteristics of muscle, and momentum). Thus, in Bernstein's final stage, the movement becomes maximally skilled in terms of effectiveness (achieving the end result with maximum assuredness) and efficiency (minimum outlay of energy).

Limitations of Fitts' and Bernstein's Stages

One thing that is important to keep in mind about both the Fitts and the Bernstein perspectives is that neither was meant to describe learning as a series of discrete, nonlinear, and unidirectional stages. The progression from one stage to another is not categorical, such as leaving one room of a house and entering another. In many ways, these stages were

Focus on
RESEARCH 9.1

Learning Never Ends

The shape of the classic skill acquisition profile, sometimes erroneously termed a “learning curve,” is illustrated by rapid gains early in practice, improvements slowing down as some proficiency is gained, then a gradual slowing to an eventual point where no further improvements in skill are detected. So, would it be correct to say that learning has ended as this point? Two classic studies in the motor learning literature suggest that the answer is no.

Bryan and Harter (1897, 1899) studied the perceptual–motor skill of telegraphy—involving the language of sending and receiving Morse code. They studied telegraphers of varying levels of experience and discovered many important findings. For example, the perceptual skill of receiving Morse code became faster and more efficient with practice. However, this was achieved not only through quantitative improvements (speed of letter detection) but also by means of qualitative change—as skill developed, telegraphers progressed by perceiving individual letters at first, then groupings of letters, then whole words, and then common phrases or groupings of words. The timing of dots and dashes is a critical component of sending Morse code, and Bryan and Harter found that the consistency in movement timing continued to improve over many years of experience (see Lee & Swinnen, 1993, for more analysis). In sum, there was no evidence that improvements stopped being made in either perceptual or motor skill. Rather, performance became more efficient and less variable with continued practice.

Crossman (1959) presented a very different type of analysis of a motor skill. He tracked the performance of cigar rollers who used a machine to combine leaves of tobacco into a finished product, a cigar. Crossman found that improvements in performance time leveled off only after seven years of experience (or 10 million cigars!) had been accumulated. However, the plateau in performance was not due to a limitation in human performance. Rather, performance leveled off because the limits of the cycle time of the machine had been reached. Presumably the cigar rollers would have continued to improve if they had not reached the machine’s limit.

The illusion that learning has ended is almost always caused by the limits reached in the sensitivity of the measurement tool in revealing further changes. New measurement tools continue to be developed and to reveal the process of motor learning in more detail. For example, recent studies of motor learning have revealed markedly different effects of transcranial magnetic stimulation (TMS) on performance, depending on whether it was applied early (after 5 sessions) or late (after 16 sessions) in practice (Platz et al., 2012a, 2012b). These changes in the brain to TMS are indicative of structural adaptations as the direct result of practice. We suspect that future studies using these and other measures of brain plasticity will provide clearer evidence that learning never stops.

Exploring Further

1. Consider a skill such as archery, which can be measured in terms of performance outcome (such as accuracy and consistency) and movement proficiency (e.g., steadiness). How might these different measures change at different rates as a function of practice?
2. Think of another motor task and describe how expertise might continue to evolve with continued practice. What measurement systems would be required to observe these continued changes?

In the photo, this girl is learning to use chopsticks to pick up her sushi. Note that her parents have tied a rubber band around the tops of the two chopsticks. Describe what effect this would have from (1) Fitts' perspective and (2) Bernstein's perspective.

meant to be considered as generic descriptions of performance capabilities and tendencies at any one time in the learning process, with the proviso that these capabilities change as learning progresses.

There are a number of other aspects of these two schemes that need to be considered. For example, Fitts considered performance change to be *regressive* as well as progressive, in the sense that performance, under conditions of high arousal or after a long layoff from practice, was expected to produce performance tendencies characteristic of a previous stage (Fitts et al., 1959).

Task differences also play an important role in the stage views of both Fitts and Bernstein. For instance, automaticity in Fitts' final stage might be achieved for some tasks but never achieved for other tasks. As one example, responding automatically to a specific stimulus with a specific response can be learned with many hours of devoted practice (e.g., Schneider & Shiffrin, 1977), although it might be impossible to ever develop automaticity for a novel, complex, serial, or continuous movement task.

Similarly, the nature of the task might limit the application of Bernstein's stages (Newell

Focus on
APPLICATION 9.1

Fitts and Bernstein on Learning to Play Ice Hockey

One way to conceptualize the different stages of learning perspectives proposed by Fitts and by Bernstein is with an example. Ice hockey involves two main tasks: skating (whole-body movements using two boots fitted with sharp blades that cut into the ice) and stick-handling (using a hockey stick to pass, shoot, and manipulate a flat rubber disk). What follows is an analysis regarding how the stages of learning might proceed according to Fitts and Bernstein.

Fitts' Stage 1

From Fitts' perspective, the process of maintaining balance is a primary concern, requiring massive amounts of attentional resources just to stay upright. Holding the stick is highly verbalizable, and doing so correctly is an important consideration. For right-handed players, the left hand holds the stick near the top of the shaft and the right hand holds it partway down the shaft. Shooting, passing, and manipulating the puck require considerable conscious resources since each of these activities perturb balance and pose a threat to the learner's posture.

Bernstein's Stage 1

For Bernstein, the same problem of staying upright and striking the puck is solved by reducing body motion. A steady base is critical; therefore movements that would destabilize that base, such as taking a long stride during the act of shooting or passing a puck, are largely avoided or reduced in magnitude. The motions of the body during skating are rather rigid, again to avoid destabilizing balance. The stick is used as a crutch during this stage to help maintain balance.

Fitts' Stage 2

Rudimentary skill has been achieved by the start of this stage—the learner has acquired the basic motor patterns to skate, shoot, pass, and manipulate the puck, although these require considerable cognitive resources to coordinate at the same time. Attention to skating and stick-handling has been reduced, however, allowing the learner to attend to other perceptual attributes of the situation, such as locating members of the opposing team and anticipating the movements of teammates.

Bernstein's Stage 2

For Bernstein, the learner's skating skills have improved dramatically due to the release of the body's degrees of freedom. Rather than appearing to walk on skates, the learner makes a sideward push with one skate and glides forward on the other skate. Considerably more trunk rotation is used to move, resulting in much faster skating speed. Control of the puck has also improved through more involvement of the wrist, forearm, and shoulder muscles. The result is greater force production and accuracy in receiving, shooting, and passing the puck, as well as more effective stick-handling control.

> *continued*

> Fitts and Bernstein on Learning to Play Ice Hockey *continued*

Fitts' Stage 3

In Fitts' autonomous stage, very little attention is given to the processes involved in skating and puck control or even the simultaneous coordination of these skills. Now the learner's cognitive involvement is invested in higher-order activities of the game—detecting patterns of game flow by members of both teams, planning strategic plays whereby the learner goes to locations on the ice that could provide an offensive or defensive advantage, or taking advantage of perceived weaknesses of the opponent.

Bernstein's Stage 3

Bernstein's final stage exploits the energy that comes with the fast and dynamic play of the game. Players learn to stop, turn, accelerate, and decelerate with precision and use the passive dynamics not only of their own body but also the energy obtained from on-ice objects, both animate (other players) and inanimate (e.g., the rink's wall, or boards). Modern skates and sticks are manufactured with composite materials, which are designed to be fully exploited by only the most highly skilled players.

Summary

This analysis represents just one example of how Fitts' and Bernstein's stages of learning might characterize the ways in which skill development proceeds. As you can readily tell from this comparison, the Fitts and Bernstein perspectives should not be seen as competing with each other. Rather, they represent two different theoretical approaches conceptualizing somewhat different sets of processes that change with practice.

& Vaillancourt, 2001). We can think of two common examples of skills whose learning would seem to contradict Bernstein's stage 2 characterization. One of these involves doing a handstand on the still rings in men's gymnastics. The learner seems to begin learning this task using nearly all of the available degrees of freedom (e.g., maintaining balance with hip and trunk movements, using the arms). When the learner is clearly past the initial stage, rather than releasing degrees of freedom, the learner seems to *freeze* them. All of the wild hip and arm movements seem to drop out, leaving behind control of balance by the wrists only: this would seem to be just the opposite order from Bernstein's views, where the learner seems to gain proficiency by freezing, then freeing, degrees of freedom. Another example concerns the skill of learning to windsurf. At first, the learner uses wild hip, knee, and arm movements to maintain balance on the board, much as the gymnast does on the still rings at this stage. Then, when clearly past the first stage, the learner seems to freeze the hip and knee movements so that the body is still and rigid, and control is due to very small movements of the sail with small elbow and wrist movements, again with freezing proceeding freeing. Konczak, vander Velden, and Jaeger (2009) found that, similar to these gymnast and windsurfer examples, expert violinists developed their skill by learning to reduce rather than release motions of their bowing arm.

In sum, we believe that the stage ideas of both Fitts and Bernstein retain considerable merit, and their longevity as descriptive analyses of the learning process attests to a continued prominence in the motor learning literature. However, one must not lose sight of the fact that these are rather generalized descriptions, not firm theories about the learning process.

Constraints-Led Approach to Learning

An alternative view, one that does not highlight stages of progress, makes a different emphasis about the learning process. The idea places importance on the concept of **constraints** to performance—that certain features serve to contain or act as boundaries on performance. For example, Higgins (1977) suggested that movement coordination was constrained by the interaction of environmental, biomechanical, and morphological constraints. A related idea was proposed by Newell (1986), who suggested that motor development involved an interaction of organismic, environmental, and task constraints that are shaped across the aging process.

The idea of constraints as a construct that shapes the learning process was more fully explored by Davids, Button, and Bennett (2008) and is illustrated by the model presented in figure 9.4. By this model, motor learning is a process of *exploration* whereby the interaction of various constraints shapes the discovery process. Organismic constraints are those factors unique to the individual learner, and include body dimensions, cognitive resources, and perceptual–motor abilities. Environmental constraints are the physical realities of the world in which we move, including gravity, bases of support (e.g., land, water, space, ice, etc.), and perceptual affordances. Task constraints are more specific to the engaged activity, such as the dimensions of the tools used in a sport (e.g., size, height, weight, and shape of bats, balls, sticks, etc.) and the rules that guide specific motor behavior. The concept of learning as an *interaction* of these constraints means that it is not one constraint alone that influences learning. Rather, it is how the three types of constraints combine that determines the progress of learning.

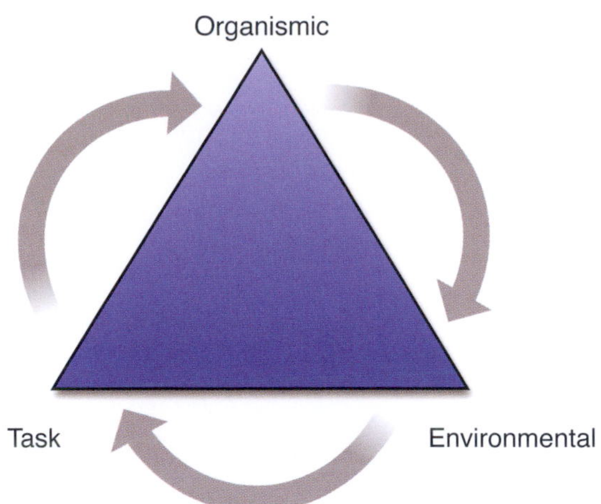

FIGURE 9.4 Motor learning, as conceptualized by the interaction of organismic, environmental, and task constraints.

Exploration and discovery learning are critical to the constraints-led approach, which differs from (and is perhaps opposite to) traditional methods of coaching and instruction that emphasize rigid drills and prescriptive guidelines for how movements should be made. Instead, the constraints-led approach considers the learner's perception and action needs as the critical components of practice. The goal of the coach or instructor is to determine how to change the task and environmental constraints in order to meet those needs. The approach is receiving increasing interest among coaches and instructors as a viable option to structuring learning environments (see also Focus on Research 9.2).

Skill Retention

This section concerns the fate of motor skills after a period of time during which no further practice is undertaken, during which time **forgetting** may occur. This interval of time is often termed the *retention interval*. As we will discuss, the absence of practice often is detrimental to skilled performance.

Forgetting

One of the truisms of life is that some skills seem never to be forgotten whereas others are lost rather quickly. An often-repeated example of the former is riding a bicycle, a skill that we

Focus on RESEARCH 9.2

A Constraints-Led Approach to Baseball Batting

The effects of a **constraints-led approach** to coaching and instruction is illustrated nicely in a study by Gray (2018), who compared three different strategies to increasing a baseball batter's launch angle in a simulated batting task. One group of batters was given different types of internal focus of attention instructions (such as "get your hands under the ball") that prescribed how to control movements in order to increase launch angle. Another group was given external focus instructions (such as "drive the ball over the infield"), which were also prescriptive in nature but focused on the end result of the movement rather than the movement itself (see chapters 3 and 10 for more on focus of attention). The third group was given no explicit instructions about how to increase launch angles. Instead, they were told just to try to hit each simulated pitch over a barrier, located just past the infield, which required a launch angle of 19° or more to exceed.

Six weeks of practice were followed by a retention test. As expected, performance following external focus of attention instructions was better than following internal focus instructions for variables such as ball exit velocity (force of ball contact) and in reducing pop-ups. The constraints-led group was also better than the internal focus group in these variables, but was also superior to the both attentional-focus groups in average launch angle.

To us, the most important finding in the experiment can be seen in figure 9.5. This figure shows how the angle of the bat was adjusted over the 6 weeks of practice (three sessions per week are illustrated). The idea here is that more adjustments—representing more explorations and changes in strategy to try to increase launch angles—would *increase* the batter's variability in bat path angles. As is clear in this figure, internal focus instructions led to few changes in variability, external focus instructions led to

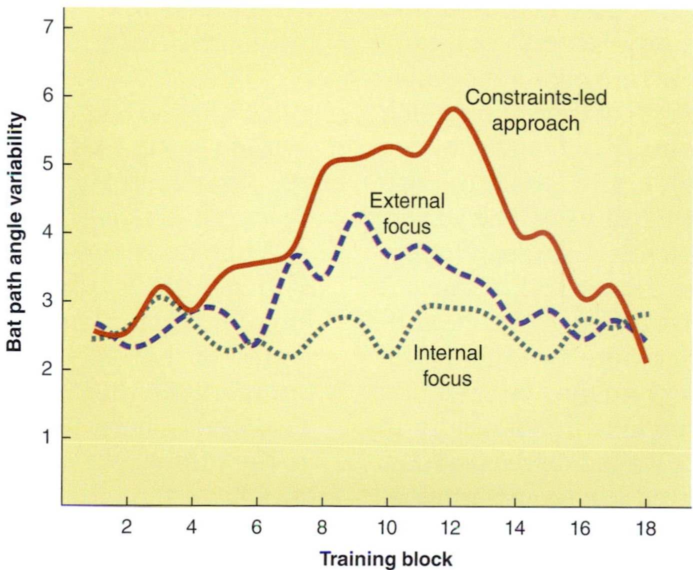

FIGURE 9.5 Variability in bat path angles were largest for the constraints-led approach, indicating increased explorations in self-discovery of methods to increase batting launch angles.

> *continued*

> A Constraints-Led Approach to Baseball Batting *continued*

some changes, but the constraints-led approach was the most successful in encouraging the batters to explore ways in which launch angles could be increased. Gray argued that this dynamic, goal-directed exploration process was responsible for the enhanced performance in various batting statistics seen later in the retention test.

Exploring Further

1. Think of another sport task in which a constraints-led approach could be used as an alternative to prescriptive style of instruction. In what measure of performance might you expect the variability to be increased, relative to prescriptive styles of learning?

seem to retain for very long periods of time during which we experience no intervening practice. In contrast, some memories are forgotten quite quickly, such as your hotel room number just days after you checked out.

Consider the following two studies that are representative of this contrast. In the first study, conducted many years ago by Neumann and Ammons (1957), experimenters asked participants to learn to match the locations of a series of eight paired switches and lights. This task seemed to have a relatively heavy verbal memory component to it, in that participants had to learn and remember which switch went with which light. Practice continued until participants performed two errorless trials, which, as illustrated in figure 9.6, required about 63 trials, on average. At that point the participants were split into five subgroups, each defined by the length of time after which the retention test would be performed—retention intervals of 1 min, 20 min, two days, seven weeks, or a full year. The results illustrated in figure 9.6 are very clear. Retention performance was dramatically affected by the length of the retention interval, with one year of no practice both producing the least skilled performance on the first retention trial and returning this group essentially to the level at which they started on the first day. This decrement required the largest number of trials (as compared to the other groups) to regain the criterion of two errorless trials. It is of interest to note here that the rate of improvement after one year of no practice was somewhat faster than it was in original practice, suggesting that perhaps not all of the skill had been lost during this retention interval.

Now contrast the results from Neumann and Ammons study (figure 9.6) with the findings reported by Fleishman and Parker (1962), presented in figure 9.7. The task required production of complex tracking movements involving movement of the hands in the *X* (left-right) and *Y* (forward-backward) dimensions and movement of the feet in the *X*-dimension, using an aircraft-type stick and rudder controls. Retention tests were performed after nine months or one or two years. As illustrated in figure 9.7, the retention loss was remarkably small, even after *two years* of no practice. It is clear that the type of task influences retention performance.

Visit the web study guide to read "Like Riding a Bicycle" and complete the self-directed learning activities.

What does the difference in the results of these two studies mean? We argue that long-term retention depends largely on the nature of the task—discrete tasks are forgotten relatively quickly, especially those with a relatively large cognitive component such as the one used in Neumann and Ammons' study. On the other hand, continuous tasks, exemplified by the task in the Fleishman-Parker study, are retained very well over long periods of no practice. Of course, the amount of original practice will have much to say about the relative amount of retention

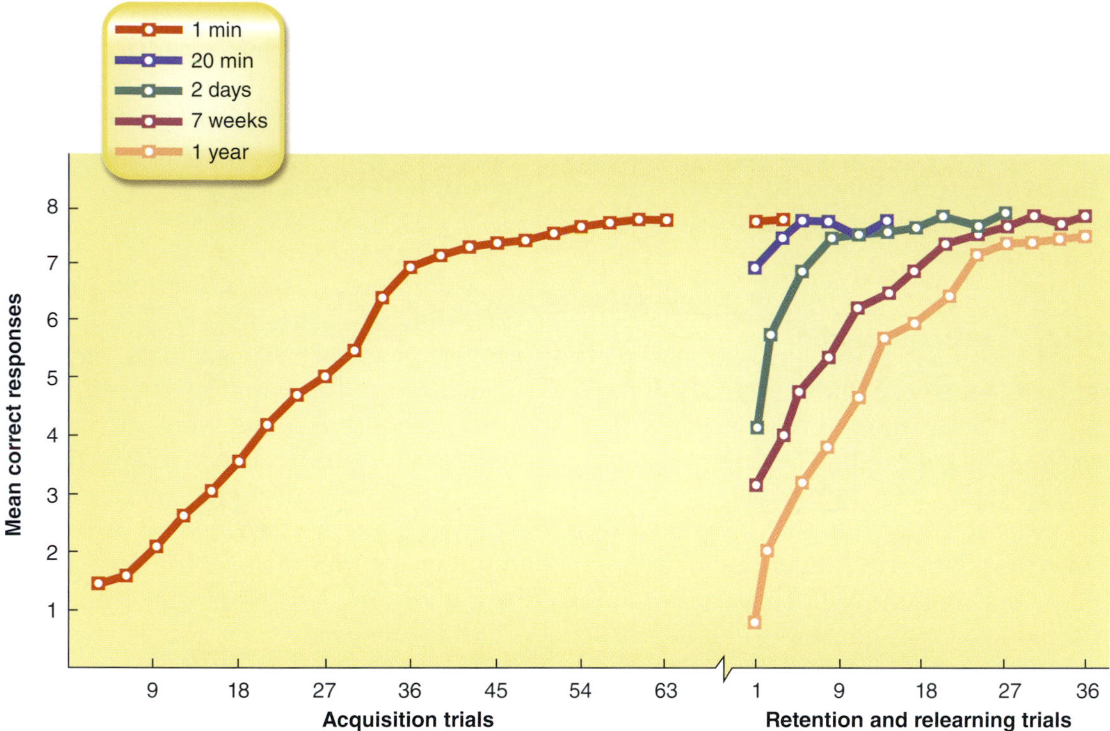

FIGURE 9.6 Forgetting of a discrete task (learning light switch combinations) occurred rapidly, and more additional practice trials were needed to reacquire the original criterion as the retention interval increased.

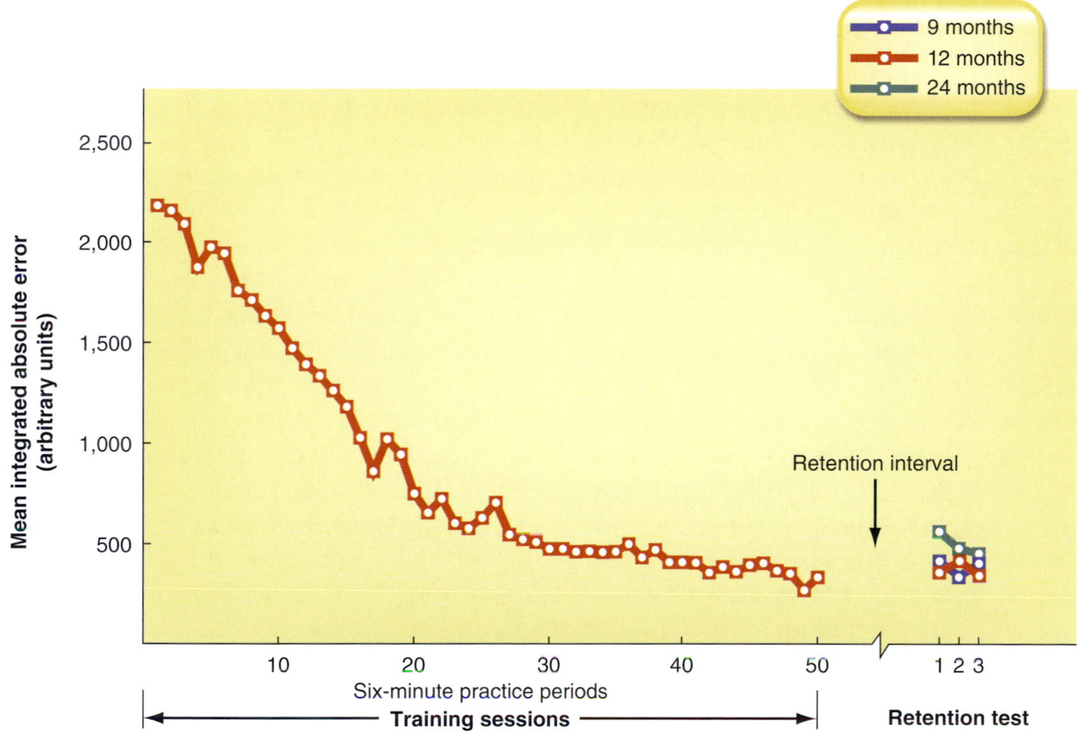

FIGURE 9.7 Results from Fleishman and Parker (1962). Motor skill tracking performance was retained well for periods of up to two years following original practice.

for these tasks (e.g., Ammons et al., 1958). But, in general, continuous tasks, like riding a bicycle, are retained for much longer periods of time than are discrete tasks.

Visit the web study guide to read "The Keypad" and complete the self-directed learning activities.

Warm-Up Decrement

The initial depression in motor activity at the very start of a performance represents what many researchers believe to be a different kind of retention deficit (Adams, 1961). Many examples exist. A musician may have trouble getting into the proper rhythm or mood to support optimal performance; a hockey goalie who is substituted late in the game may not be mentally prepared for the speed of play. In these cases the learner typically suffers a relatively large performance decrement and is temporarily prevented from performing at maximum capability. This disturbance to performance is eliminated quickly once a few trials of practice are experienced—essentially as with the 20 min retention-interval condition in Neumann and Ammons' study (figure 9.6). Still, the fact that these decrements to performance are relatively large, and that they appear reliably in so many different tasks and under so many different circumstances, have earned this research area its very own term: *warm-up decrement.*

Note that "warm-up" is not used here in the same sense as warming up physiologically to run a race, for example. Rather, **warm-up decrement** is considered a psychological factor that is brought on by the passage of time away from a task and is eliminated when performance begins again. Many consider warm-up decrement the result of a loss of the "set" (a kind of tuning or adjustment process not related to memory for the task itself) that had facilitated performance before the retention break and that, having been lost over the retention interval, now prevents a return to maximum performance potential for a short period of time. These decrements have a large role in tasks for which the performer must respond as well as possible on the very first attempt after a layoff of a few minutes (e.g., free-throw shots in basketball).

Visit the web study guide to read "Shooting Two from the Line" and complete the self-directed learning activities.

Set, when referring to warm-up decrement, has very specific meaning (Adams, 1961). According to researchers, **set** is a collection of psychological activities, states, or processes (for example, the target of attentional focus, one's perceptual focus, and postural adjustments). These processes are appropriate for and support performance while an activity is ongoing but are lost when a different set is adopted to support the activities undertaken during rest (e.g., a set of adjustments appropriate for resting).

One explanation for the occurrence of warm-up decrement is that it simply represents a type of motor forgetting. That explanation has not received much support from researchers, however, because so-called set-reinstating activities that do not influence memory for the task, undertaken near the end of the retention interval, have been shown to reduce or eliminate warm-up decrement. In contrast, activities (such as maximum-grip-force tests) that are deliberately designed to interfere with set for a task (such as delicate positioning of a lever on a trackway) produce increases in warm-up decrement (Nacson & Schmidt, 1971). These findings seem to argue against the idea that warm-up decrement is simply a memory loss (forgetting) of the main task.

Reinstatement of set before undertaking performance can eliminate much of the warm-up decrement that accrues over a retention interval, even a brief one. This finding likely helps to explain some of the benefit that occurs due to the pre-shot routine seen in many types of sporting events when an athlete performs a highly individualized set of behaviors just before the "real" action. These may involve bouncing the basketball a certain way or following a set of procedures before hitting a golf ball. But most high-level athletes do these activities in a similar way each time. Successful performance has much to do with these pre-shot routines, and research suggests that overcoming the negative effects of warm-up decrement is part of the reason for this success (Boutcher & Crews, 1987).

Skill Transfer

Transfer, which is sometimes called *generalization*, is an important goal of practice. It refers to the idea that learning acquired during practice of a given task can be applied to or transferred to other task situations. An instructor should not be satisfied if the students can perform only those task variations they have specifically practiced. The instructor wants them to be able to generalize specific learning to the many novel variations they will face in the future. The concern is how to organize practice to maximize generalization.

What Skills Will Transfer?

Transfer is defined as the gain or loss in the capability to perform one task as a result of practice or experience on another task. Transfer is positive if it enhances performance in the other skill, negative if it degrades it, and zero if it has no effect at all. The issues surrounding transfer, and particularly maximizing transfer by adjusting teaching methods and styles, are far-ranging and discussed briefly here.

Transfer and Similarity

An old idea in psychology and motor learning is that transfer of learning between two tasks increases as the similarity between them increases. One idea was that of identical elements (Thorndike & Woodworth, 1901), according to which learning certain elements in one situation transferred to another skill because the second skill used the same elements. As simple as this idea might sound, there have always been problems with it. One is that the concepts of "similarity" and "identical elements" are never explicitly defined. For example, is throwing a baseball more similar to passing a football than shooting a basketball? What exactly are the elements that are involved? As a result, this particular view of similarity has not been popular in the motor learning literature. However, other views of similarity and transfer have been supported by research.

Fundamental Movement Patterning Many have suggested that the so-called overarm pattern underlies throwing a baseball, serving in tennis, spiking a volleyball, and many other actions requiring forceful overarm movements to strike or throw an object. All these involve rotation of the hips and shoulders and ballistic actions of the shoulder–arm–wrist, ending finally with wrist–hand action to accomplish the particular goal. An analogous idea common among gymnasts is that certain fundamental actions (e.g., the sharp hip extension in a kip) can be applied to many apparatus events. In both these examples, if practice is given at one variant of the class of movements sharing the same general pattern, then the learner should be able to transfer the learning to any other variant using this same pattern. Of course, practicing a kipping action would not transfer to an overarm action or vice versa, because these skills use very different patterns, belonging as they must to separate movement classes.

Perceptual Elements Similarity is also evident in the numerous perceptual elements underlying many tasks. For example, learning to intercept flying balls of various kinds (baseballs, footballs, tennis balls, and so on) depends on learning the common features of ball flight, which are based on the principles of physics. In a similar way, police trainees must be attuned to the perceptual cues that alert them to a dangerous situation. Learning to react appropriately to such cues in one situation facilitates transfer to other situations in which the perceptual elements are similar.

Strategic and Conceptual Similarities Similar strategies, rules, guidelines, or concepts are present in many different activities. For example, driving behaviors, signs, traffic lights, and general rules of the road are common within a restricted population or community, which facilitates driving performance when you travel to parts of the country that are new to you. However, one would expect much less transfer, or perhaps even some negative transfer, when the rules of the road differ dramatically, as when tourists drive on the opposite side of the road in a foreign country (e.g., Americans driving in Australia).

Overall, the concept of similarity among skills involves several classes of common features:

- Common movement patterning
- Common perceptual elements
- Common strategic or conceptual elements

Motor Transfer as Learning Progresses

The transfer principles apply best when just beginning to learn a skill. In early practice an overarm throw and a tennis serve do seem similar, and relating them might help the novice get the idea critical to initial attempts. However, a tennis serve and an overarm throw are not the same thing, and at higher levels of proficiency the two skills become more distinct. What, then, are the principles of transfer for later stages of learning?

Motor Transfer Is Small Between two reasonably well-learned tasks that merely appear somewhat similar, there is usually very little transfer. The transfer that does appear is usually low-positive, the skills generally facilitating each other to some small extent. But the amount of transfer is generally so low that transfer ceases to be a major goal of practice; this is in contrast to the situation in the earliest practice stages, where transfer was a major goal. Therefore, teaching a particular skill A (which is not of major interest) simply because you would like it to transfer to skill B (which *is* of major interest) is not very effective, especially when one considers the time spent on skill A that could have been spent on skill B instead. Transfer is fine when received "for free" in early practice, but it usually requires too much time in later practice.

The principle just mentioned also applies to using various **lead-up activities**. These actions are usually not of interest in themselves but are considered only as means to another goal—the transfer to another skill. For example, learning to suture wounds by starting with grapes is a cost-effective lead-up activity to working with more realistic simulators or patients. In general, however, learning such preliminary activities tends to transfer to the degree that they are effectively similar to the goal conditions, which we will discuss in more detail shortly.

No Transfer of Basic Abilities A common misconception is that a fundamental ability (see chapter 7) can be trained through various drills or other activities. The thinking is that, with some stronger ability, the learner will see gains in performance for tasks having this underlying ability. For example, athletes are often given various "quickening" exercises, with the hope that these exercises will train some fundamental ability to be quick, allowing quicker responses in their particular sports. Coaches and physical therapists often use various balancing drills with the goal of increasing general balancing ability, eye movement exercises are used with the goal of improving general visual abilities, and there are many other examples. Such attempts to train fundamental abilities may sound logical, but they simply do not work (e.g., Abernethy & Wood, 2001; Lindeburg, 1949). Resources (time, money) would be better spent practicing the eventual goal skills.

There are two correct ways to think of these principles. First, there is no "general ability" to be quick, to balance, or to use vision, as discussed in chapter 7. Rather, quickness, balance, and vision in various tasks are each based on many diverse abilities, so there is no single quickness ability, for example, even if it could be trained. Second, even if there were such general abilities, these are by definition essentially genetically determined and are not subject to modification through practice. Therefore, attempts to modify an ability with a nonspecific drill are usually ineffective (e.g., see Giboin et al., 2018). A learner may acquire additional skill at the drill (which is, after all, a skill in itself), but this learning does not transfer to the main ability of interest.

Visit the web study guide to read "Sport Snake Oils" and complete the self-directed learning activities.

Transfer of Part Practice to Whole Performance

Some skills are enormously complex, such as playing a musical instrument or performing a gymnast's routine. Clearly, in such situations the instructor cannot present all aspects of the skill at once for practice because the student would be overwhelmed and would likely grasp almost none of it. A frequent approach is to divide the task into meaningful units that can be isolated for separate part practice. The goal is to integrate these practiced units into the whole skill for later performance. This is not as simple as it may sound because there are several factors that make integrating the learned units back into the whole skill somewhat difficult.

The question is how to create subunits of skills and how they can be practiced for maximum transfer to the whole skill. It is a simple matter to divide skills into parts. You could separate a gymnastics routine into the component stunts; you could divide the left and right hands of piano practice into separate components for practice. And each subpart could be divided even further. But the real question is whether these parts, practiced in isolation, will be effective for learning the whole skill, which is the overall goal. Thus, **part practice** is based on the transfer-of-learning principles defined earlier: Will the subunit transfer to the whole task that contains it? How much (if any) time should be spent on part practice, and would this time be more effectively spent practicing the whole task?

At first glance the answers to these questions seem obvious. Because the part of the task practiced in isolation seems the same as that part in the whole task, the transfer from the part to the whole task would seem to be almost perfect. This may be so in certain cases, but there are many other situations in which transfer is far from perfect. These differences in part-practice effectiveness depend on the nature of the skill.

Serial Skills of Long Duration

In many serial skills, the learner's problem is to organize a set of activities into the proper order, as with the gymnast who assembles a routine of stunts. Practicing the specific subtasks is usually effective in transferring to whole sequences. Part transfer works best in serial tasks of very long duration and in cases in which the actions (or errors) of one part do not influence the actions of the next part. That is, part practice is most effective for skills in which the parts are performed relatively independently. The learner can devote more practice time to the troublesome parts without practicing the easier elements, making practice time more efficient.

However, in many serial skills in sport, performance on one part frequently determines the movement that must be made on the next part. If the ski racer comes out of a turn too low and fast, this affects the approach for the next turn. Small positioning errors on the beam in one move determine how the gymnast must perform the next one. If a part-to-part interaction is large, as it might be if the sequence is run off quickly, modifying a given action as a function of performance on a previous action is an important component of the skill. However, these interactions between parts of the whole skill cannot be practiced and learned in isolated part practice; **whole practice** is necessary. The gymnast might be able to do all of the individual stunts in her routine, but she still might not be able to perform an effective routine in a meet because she never learned to modify each component movement based on the previous one.

Discrete Skills of Short Duration

Any skill is, in some sense, serial because certain pieces of it come before other pieces, such as hitting a baseball, which contains step, hip turn, and swing elements. At some point, though, these individual parts, when viewed separately, cease to be parts of the whole skill. Dividing a golf swing into smaller and smaller arbitrary parts destroys a critical aspect that allows the parts to be characterized as a component of a swing; that is, the division seems

A gymnast putting together a routine (here, coauthor Richard Schmidt, when he was an NCAA gymnast at Cal) must become skilled at performing the routine as a whole, since each movement must be modified in response to the previous movement. Describe another serial task in which discrete parts are put together into a whole.

to disrupt the essential features of the action. Practice at these subparts could be ineffective, even detrimental, to learning the whole task.

Several experiments suggest that practicing parts of a discrete task in isolation transfers little if at all to the whole task (e.g., Lersten, 1968; Schmidt & Young, 1987), especially if the task is rapid and ballistic. This is probably related to the fact that the components in rapid tasks usually interact strongly, which means less effective transfer. In fact, transfer from the part to the whole can even be negative in certain cases, so practicing the part in isolation could be worse for the whole task than not practicing at all!

This evidence suggests that when very rapid skills are broken down into arbitrary parts, these parts become changed from the same parts in the whole task so that the part practice contributes very little to the whole. In tasks like the slap shot in ice hockey, for example, practicing the backswing separately from the downswing changes the dynamics of the action at the top of the backswing, which

FIGURE 9.8 An aircraft cockpit simulator.

is dominated by actively lengthening muscles whose spring-like properties allow the downswing to be smooth and powerful. Therefore, practicing the backswing in isolation, which eliminates the role of these spring-like muscle properties, is quite different from performing the same backswing in the context of the whole skill.

The principles of part practice can be easily summarized:

- For very slow, serial tasks with no component interaction, part practice on the difficult elements is very efficient.
- For very brief, programmed actions, practice on the parts in isolation is seldom useful and can even be detrimental to learning.
- The more the components of a task interact with each other, the less the effectiveness of part practice.

Simulation and Transfer

Transfer principles are commonly used in the area of simulation. A **simulator** is a practice device designed to mimic features of a real-world task. Simulators are often very elaborate, sophisticated, and expensive, such as devices to train pilots to fly aircraft (figure 9.8). But simulators need not be elaborate at all, such as wireless video game consoles (e.g., Levac, Rivard, & Missiuna, 2012). Simulators can be an important part of an instructional program, especially when the skill is expensive or dangerous (e.g., learning to fly a jetliner), where facilities are limited (e.g., cycling on a treadmill instead of in a velodrome), or where real practice is not feasible (e.g., using artificial patients rather than real humans for surgery practice).

Evaluating Simulator Effectiveness

Of course, a simulator must provide positive results in order to justify its use. Therefore, the amount of transfer resulting from the time spent in a simulator is an important consideration in determining its effectiveness and efficiency. Consider figure 9.9, showing the hypothetical performance curves on a novel motor learning task for two groups of participants. The simulator group begins practice on the **criterion task** after having 3 h of practice on a simulator task, designed to provide positive transfer to the criterion task. The no-simulator group receives no prior practice on the simulator.

Figure 9.9 illustrates performance of both groups on the criterion task. Note that the point on the axis corresponding to 0 h of practice refers to the first trial on the criterion task for both groups (this point occurs after 3 h of

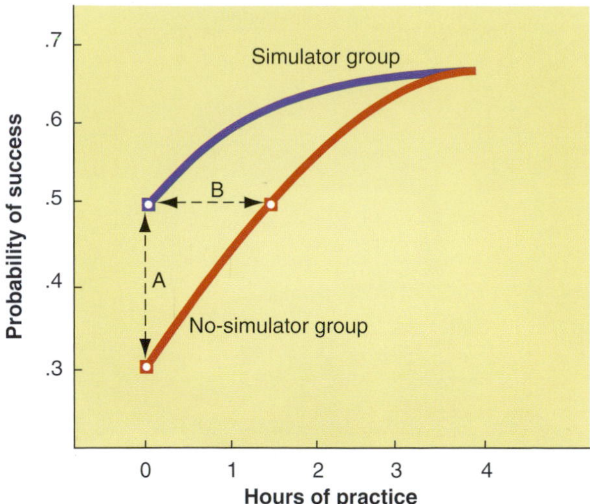

FIGURE 9.9 Hypothetical performance curves of two groups of learners on a novel motor learning task. The simulator group practiced a simulation task for 3 h before initial practice on the criterion task, whereas the no-simulator group had no previous practice.

practice on the simulator task for the simulator group). From figure 9.9 we can see that there is considerable positive transfer from the simulator to the criterion task, seen as the gain in probability of success from .30 to .50 (the difference labeled A in figure 9.9). Now look at the difference labeled B in figure 9.9. This difference suggests that the simulator group started at a level (.50) that took the no-simulator group 1.5 h of practice on the criterion task to achieve. So, in some respects, the simulator experience saved about 1.5 h of practice on the criterion task.

However, there is another way to look at this result. Remember that the simulator group had already spent 3 h of practice on the simulator. Since the simulator group spent 3 h of practice on the simulator but the no-simulator group "caught up" in 1.5 h, the simulation actually *cost* 1.5 h of real (sometimes very expensive) simulator time. Viewed in this way, the simulator was not effective at all in reducing the time of training.

Time is not the only relevant factor here, though. The effectiveness of a simulator sometimes must also be judged in relation to the relative financial costs of simulator practice and criterion task practice, the availability of resources and facilities, safety, and so on. Relative to practice cost in a flight simulator, practice cost in an actual jetliner would be staggering, and there are obvious concerns for the safety of people, equipment, and so on. Thus, the evaluation of simulators in an instructional setting can be complicated, and it must take into account a number of important factors in making decisions about their use and effectiveness.

Physical versus Psychological Fidelity

Remember that the overall goal of simulation is for the learning in the simulator to transfer to the criterion task. Scientists who conduct research in this area refer to the quality of the simulation in terms of *fidelity*—the degree to which the simulator mimics or is faithful to the criterion task. Two different types of fidelity constructs have been examined in the literature. **Physical fidelity** refers to the degree to which the physical or surface features of the simulation and criterion tasks themselves are identical. In contrast, **psychological fidelity** refers the degree to which the behaviors and processes produced in the simulator replicate those required by the criterion task. Although these seem like similar constructs, in fact they are quite different and have the potential to result in quite different effects on transfer (e.g., Kozlowski & DeShon, 2004).

Because transfer is expected to increase with task similarity, this idea has naturally led to the notion that physical fidelity should be as high as possible. Aircraft-cockpit simulators (figure 9.8, for example) replicate the cockpit of a real aircraft very closely (although doing so is often very expensive). Another example is cardiopulmonary resuscitation (CPR) mannequins, which are designed to be as anatomically correct as possible for the purpose of training lifesaving skills. Physical fidelity refers to the degree to which the simulator replicates the physical features of the criterion task—possessing as much of the look, sound, and feel of the criterion task as possible.

Psychological fidelity is less concerned with the physical similarity between the simulator and criterion tasks and more concerned with the target skills and behaviors required to perform the criterion task. In the case of CPR mannequins, for example, simulator training might emphasize the perceptual and decision-making processes that are presented in an emergency situation, under high levels of stress, and perhaps under environmental challenges (e.g., extreme heat or cold). Psychological fidelity is concerned with training the skills that will be required of the end user in the criterion task.

Physical and psychological fidelity should be seen as complementary, not competing goals, according to Kozlowski and DeShon (2004). Still, situations can arise in which too much faith is placed in the physical fidelity, without enough attention devoted to the psychological processes. Returning to our CPR example, some mannequins provide very exacting physical fidelity—the sights, sounds, and proprioceptive feedback that would appear to promote excellent perceptual and motor skill transfer. Yet just using the mannequin without considering how to structure the practice conditions and how to provide augmented feedback would be a major mistake, as the behaviors practiced during training would ultimately be expected to affect transfer to real emergency situations.

These issues of training motor skill behaviors are the major focus of the next two chapters. As we will see, how practice is structured and how feedback is augmented during practice determine the quality of motor learning that results from practice.

Summary

Motor learning is a fundamental necessity that we often take for granted, yet it is required for just about every facet of our daily existence. As people practice, they generally pass through stages of learning that describe the current state of their skill proficiency. Although some debate exists concerning how to best characterize these stages, practice results in some basic principles regarding how new motor skills are acquired and a specific set of benefits that result.

But periods of no practice are also a fact of life, and the retention of learned skills after a lengthy time away from them represents a critical area of research. Retention of skills is affected greatly by their classification; continuous skills are generally retained much more completely, and for longer periods of time, than discrete skills. Warm-up decrement refers to a specific type of retention deficit due to the loss of an activity set. Being able to perform a learned activity in a new situation concerns the issue of skill transfer. Simulators of various kinds can efficiently mimic important elements of a skill when practicing the actual skill would be too costly, dangerous, or impractical.

WEB STUDY GUIDE ACTIVITIES

The student web study guide offers these activities to help you build and apply your knowledge of the concepts in this chapter.

Interactive Learning

Activity 9.1: Indicate whether a given understanding of a stage of learning fits with Fitts' or Bernstein's model of skill acquisition.

Activity 9.2: Distinguish the goals of practice and test sessions by indicating whether each in a series of statements applies to practice or testing.

Activity 9.3: Review the terminology of skill acquisition, retention, and transfer through a matching exercise.

Principles-to-Application Exercise

Activity 9.4: The principles-to-application exercise for this chapter prompts you to choose a movement skill, identify the goal of practice for this skill, and explore additional ways that practice might affect performance of this skill.

Motor Control in Everyday Actions Narratives

Wayne Gretzky
Like Riding a Bicycle
The Keypad
Shooting Two from the Line
Sport Snake Oils

Check Your Understanding

1. Contrast Fitts' and Bernstein's stages of learning. Name each stage and provide a brief description. Name one limitation of each of these perspectives.
2. Define warm-up decrement and explain how its effects can be reduced.
3. Distinguish between performance and learning during practice. How can they have conflicting goals, and how might this be overcome?

Apply Your Knowledge

1. List four benefits of practice discussed in this chapter and provide an example of how each might be illustrated by a karate student and a truck driver.
2. Your neighbor tells you that he will be learning to lead climb at a local rock-climbing gym. He tells about how lead climbing can be difficult because there are many parts to placing the safety gear properly while climbing and the decisions made can influence the next movement. From what he tells you about the lessons, it seems like the instructor will be using part practice. Why might the instructor have chosen this method? What alternatives would the instructor likely have considered, and why were these not chosen?

Suggestions for Further Reading

Specificity of learning, which remains an enduring topic in motor skills, was reviewed from different perspectives by Marteniuk (1974) and later by Proteau (1992). The development of expertise was the topic of a series of chapters in a volume edited by Starkes and Ericsson (2003). Differing views on stages of learning were described by Anson, Elliott, and Davids (2005). And a range of topics on transfer of learning was reviewed by various authors in the book edited by Cormier and Hagman (1987). See the reference list for these additional resources.

10

Organizing and Scheduling Practice

How the Structure of Practice Influences Learning

KEY TERMS

blocked practice
constant practice
contextual-interference effect
demonstration
distributed practice
elaboration hypothesis
forgetting hypothesis
goal setting
massed practice
mental practice
modeling
observational learning
random (interleaved) practice
schema theory
self-regulation
variable practice

CHAPTER OUTLINE

CHAPTER OBJECTIVES

Chapter 10 describes the influence of the ways in which practice is structured and various conditions under which practice is conducted. This chapter will help you to understand

- key factors that occur while undertaking physical practice,
- basic concepts regarding the nature of practice,
- practice schedule organizations and their impact on performance and learning, and
- the role of practice variability in motor learning.

Imagine you are in charge of designing a plan for teaching a group of learners a particular set of skills. They may be prospective chiropractors learning different manipulation techniques, or a high school woodworking class learning to use a lathe, or perhaps a physical education class learning a set of tumbling exercises. Or maybe there is no teacher involved at all, and you, the learner, are wondering how best to structure your music practice. How would you organize your time? How would you intersperse physical practice with periods of rest? In what order will you practice various skills, how much variation in skills would you introduce into your practice, and how much practice will you allow on one task variation before moving to the next? Questions like these affect the effectiveness of practice and, subsequently, learning. This chapter presents the principles that help you solve these problems concerning how to maximize quality of practice.

Practice can occur at many different times and places, under varying conditions, and it can be either almost unintentional or highly guided and structured. In experiments, many features of practice settings can be varied systematically, and these factors have been found to make practice more or less effective; many of these are under the direct control of the instructor. Of course, being armed as you are with principles of movement performance and learning will facilitate such decisions, equipping you to make wise choices about structuring practice to produce the most effective outcomes—usually the maximization of learning.

Motivation for Learning

Instructors often have the impression that the learner's motivation is not a problem—that a student would obviously want to learn a particular skill. However, students do not always share their instructors' enthusiasm for learning. An unmotivated learner is not likely to practice, and the result can be little or no learning. A motivated student devotes greater effort to the task, with more serious practice and longer practice periods, leading to more effective learning. How can instructors influence this motivation to learn?

Intrinsic motivation for learning concerns the learner's internalized drive—here, a drive to learn a skill. Considerable research has been conducted to understand how intrinsic motivation affects the learner in a wide variety of situations and skills, and has resulted in important advances in theory (e.g., Deci & Ryan, 2000) and application (e.g., Weinberg & Gould, 2019). For our purposes, however, we consider specifically the tools and techniques that may influence a learner's intrinsic motivation.

Deci and Ryan (2000) suggest that an individual's intrinsic motivation is largely determined by three basic needs: autonomy (control of one's own destiny), competence (mastery of the skill), and relatedness (being accepted within a social context). Of course, the importance of each of these basic needs will differ in every individual. Therefore, as an instructor, becoming familiar with the individual, and understanding how the acquisition of a motor skill fits into the individual's needs, goes a long way in determining how best to respond in a learning context. The following sections discuss how motor learning may be affected by specific factors that influence motivation.

Goal Setting

An important motivational method is **goal setting**, whereby learners are encouraged to adopt specific performance goals. This method has had numerous applications, particularly in industry, and it has strong implications for learning in sport and physical education (Locke & Latham, 1985). In one experiment involving learning to shoot a rifle, Boyce (1992) set specific goals for some participants, instructed others to set their own specific goals, or simply told participants to "do your best." Performance of the three groups over a five-session practice period in which these goal-setting methods were given is presented in figure 10.1, along with the results in a retention test, where the goal-setting instructions were no longer applied. The findings clearly showed that adopting a specific goal improved performance compared to the "do your best" group. Moreover, this effect was maintained in a retention test. This is one of the few studies to demonstrate effects of goal-setting instructions on both performance (i.e., during practice) and learning (i.e., on a test of retention—see chapter 8 for a discussion of the use of retention tests to distinguish between performance and learning).

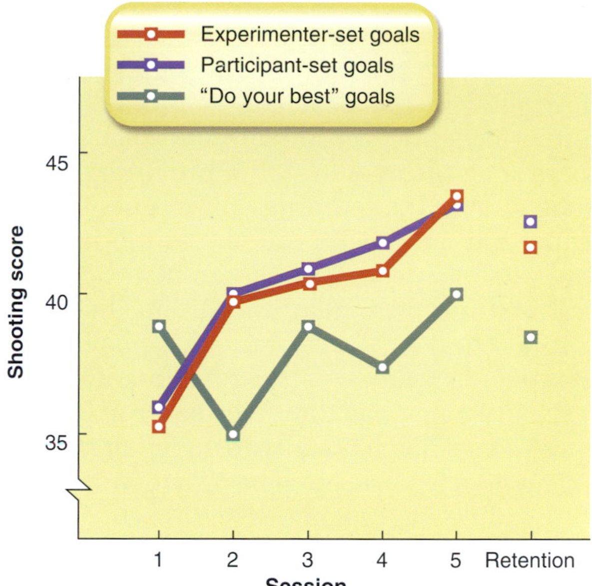

FIGURE 10.1 Results of the Boyce (1992) study in which learners practiced a shooting task after different goal-setting assignments.

These results suggest that instructors encourage their learners to set realistic goals, ones that can be reasonably achieved with practice and effort. The learner can become discouraged by not even approaching goal levels that are too high. Yet goals that are too easily met can result in boredom and reduced motivation. Being encouraged to commit oneself to a specific, challenging (but not impossible) goal is strongly motivating and has positive benefits on performance and learning.

Self-Regulated Practice

Although Boyce's participant-set-goal group described in the previous section did not outperform the experimenter-set-goal group, there is ample evidence that providing some control over the learning environment is an important factor that influences motivation and enhance learning. Researchers call this **self-regulation**; it refers to giving learners ownership over some of the components of practice. In studies of this type, learners are typically told that they can control factors such as how much practice to undertake, when augmented feedback will be provided, or how to organize the practice schedule (reviewed by Sanli et al., 2013).

An important component in the experimental design of these studies is the inclusion of yoked control groups that provide the same conditions of practice as the self-regulated group. These yoked conditions are determined entirely in advance and are not under the control of the learner, but in all other ways are identical to the conditions of the self-regulated practice group. For example, in Wulf and Toole (1999), some participants were allowed to choose the exact trials when they would use ski poles as assistance devices in a simulated slalom skiing task. The remaining trials were performed without the poles. Each participant in the yoked group was paired with a participant in the self-regulated group and used the poles on exactly the same trials as self-regulated counterpart. The only difference was that the yoked participant had not made the decision regarding whether to use to pole or not. Following two days of practice, performance in retention was far superior for the self-regulated group compared to the control group, even though both groups had received exactly the same schedule of practice. The inclusion of the yoked group, therefore, allowed the researchers to be confident in their conclusion that self-regulation—giving the learners ownership of their practice regime—had positively influenced the quality of learning.

Social-Comparative Information

Although augmented feedback—information that is provided to the learner from an external source—is the focus of the entire next chapter, it also serves an important goal as a motivator. Lewthwaite and Wulf (2012; also Wulf & Lewthwaite, 2016) reviewed a rapidly growing body of evidence suggesting that positive augmented feedback can provide a boost to motor learning, even if that feedback is not entirely true.

For example, in one study by Lewthwaite and Wulf (2010, see figure 10.2), using a balance task, participants in one group (red bars in figure 10.2) were told that their performance was 20% more accurate than the average performance of others who had participated in the experiment (termed *false-positive normative feedback*). Their performance was compared to that of another group (blue bars in figure 10.2) given *false-negative normative feedback*—they were told that their performance was 20% less accurate than the average participant. A third (control) group (green bars) was provided only their actual results, with no mention of normative standing. The results of these feedback conditions illustrates clear benefits for the false-positive normative feedback group by the end of the first day of practice, throughout the second day of practice, and in retention. Interestingly, there were no (significant) differences between the false-negative group and the control group, suggesting that the normative feedback provided a boost to learning when positive, but did not degrade learning reliably when it was negative.

The Lewthwaite and Wulf findings have also been replicated in an applied setting. Eliasz (2016), using a similar experimental protocol with first-year medical students, found that learning a surgical task was benefited by the provision of false-positive normative feedback—again, even though the feedback itself was bogus.

In all, the collective findings from studies on goal-setting, self-regulation, and positive-normative feedback are very persuasive evidence favoring the beneficial role of

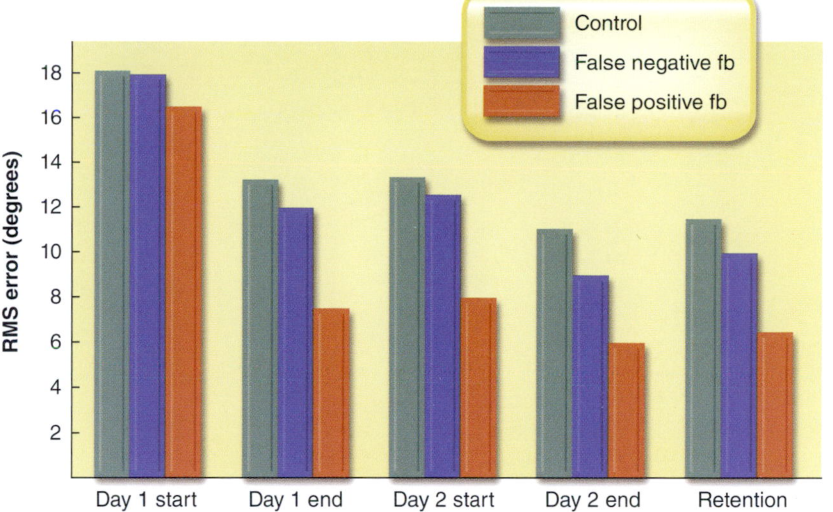

FIGURE 10.2 Results of the Lewthwaite and Wulf (2010) study, using a balance task. One group received false-positive normative feedback about their performance (red bars), another received false-negative normative feedback (blue bars), and a control group received only true feedback (green bars).

motivation in motor learning. According to Wulf and Lewthwaite (2016), motivating experiences increase an individual's confidence and expectations for future performances. When applied in practice, these motivational experiences also contribute to enhanced learning.

Attentional Focus

Earlier, in chapter 3, we discussed the effects on performance of directing a performer's attentional focus through verbal instructions. For most performers, instructing them to pay attention to the intended *result* of an action (an external focus) produces more skilled performance than an instruction to pay attention to the movement itself (an internal focus). This basic result has been replicated for many different sport activities, such as golf, baseball, basketball, and volleyball as well as other activities such as jumping and balancing (see Lohse, Wulf, & Lewthwaite, 2012, and Schmidt et al., 2019, ch. 11, for reviews). Importantly, for our discussion here, this effect has also been extended to *learning* a new skill.

For example, groups of learners in a study by Wulf and colleagues (2003) practiced a balancing task while standing on a teeter-totter type of balance board (called a stabilometer) and holding a cylindrical tube in their hands. A control group (red bars in figure 10.3) of participants was given no instructions about where to direct their attentional focus while balancing. The other groups were instructed to balance while maintaining a specific focus—either to keep their hands held horizontal (an internal-focus instruction; blue bars in figure 10.3) or to keep the tube horizontal (an external focus; green bars). The beneficial effect of external-focus instructions can be seen by superior reduction in balance error over two days of practice and in tests of retention (where no attentional-focus instructions were given) and transfer (where none of the participants held the tube). This finding is quite remarkable given that instructing someone to hold their *hands* horizontal is only subtly different than instructing them to hold the *tube* horizontal (because the hands hold the tube), and yet the two different instructions had vastly different effects on performance and retention.

The findings illustrated in figure 10.3 could be interpreted from two perspectives: (1) that external attentional focus instructions *facilitated* performance (during the practice trials) and learning (as measured in the retention and transfer tests), or (2) that internal attentional focus instructions *degraded* performance and learning. Or perhaps the findings indicate

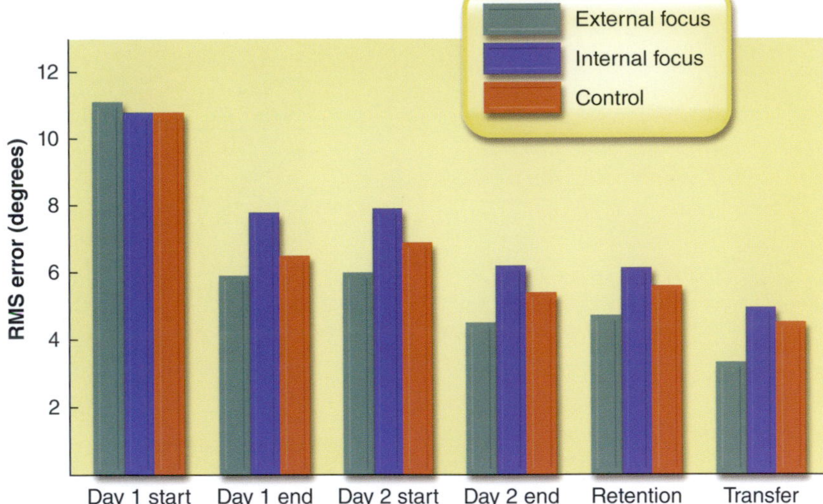

FIGURE 10.3 Effects of attentional focus over two days of practice and in retention and transfer tests. RMS = root-mean-square (see chapter 1).

some combination of these facilitation and degradation effects. Regardless, the impressive amount of evidence in favor of external-focus instructions on motor performance and learning has many implications for both practical application as well as theory.

Demonstrations and Modeling

Not all pre-practice instruction can or best be provided verbally, so actions, strategies, and anticipated perceptual experiences are sometimes more effectively illustrated visually than described in words. In such cases visual aids, such as images, videos, and live **demonstrations** by an instructor or by the learners themselves (sometimes called **modeling**) are often used. This procedure comes under the general heading of **observational learning**, in which the learner gains information by watching another's performance.

The modeling process has been studied by researchers quite intensely over the past several decades. The result is a complex set of moderating variables that influence the observational learning process. The decision about how to maximize the effectiveness of a model seems to depend on a number of factors, which are summarized well by Ste-Marie et al. (2012). How observational learning works without active movement on the part of the learner is a question that has raised plenty of debate. But there is little doubt that a considerable amount of learning, particularly early in practice, comes from scrutinizing others' actions. Important questions such as who should be the model (e.g., another learner versus a skilled performer), when observation should be scheduled relative to physical practice, and what additional information should be provided during the observational process, have drawn the attention of researchers. The literature review by Ste-Marie et al. (2012) is an excellent starting point for the interested reader.

Visit the web study guide to read "Bend It like Becker" and complete the self-directed learning activities. 

Mental Practice

One useful addition to the collection of activities in a practice session is to ask the learner to mentally rehearse skills to be learned, without actual, overt physical practice. In **mental practice** the learner might think about the skills being learned, rehearse each of the steps sequentially, imagine doing the actions that would result in achieving the goal, or anticipate the sensations (e.g., auditory or proprioceptive) that may occur as a result of performing an action.

Can this method actually contribute to learning? For many years, scientists and educators in the motor learning field had very much doubted that motor learning could be accomplished through mental practice. The understanding of practice and learning at the time held that some cognitive aspects of a skill could be learned through mental practice, but that overt physical action was essential for the motor aspects of learning. Many researchers believed that motor learning could not occur without movement, active practice, and feedback from the movement to signal errors.

However, evidence from various experiments has demonstrated convincingly that mental practice procedures actually generate motor learning. Although mental practice does not result in as much learning as the same amount of physical practice, mental practice does result in far more improvement than in no-practice control groups (see Feltz & Landers, 1983, for a review). Figure 10.4, from Hird et al. (1991), provides results from two separate tasks, the pegboard and pursuit rotor tasks. The fact that mental practice generated learning in the pursuit rotor task (for example), which does not seem to have a high cognitive component beyond the first few trials, suggests strongly that the learning of motor control must be involved with mental practice.

How Does Mental Practice Work?

There are several views regarding how mental practice generates new-task learning. One idea focuses on the cognitive aspects of the task—that mental practice facilitates the learning of "what to do" (Heuer, 1985). For example, a tennis player could decide what shot to take, a baseball player might think about how to grip the bat, and a skier could rehearse the sequence of turns in the ski run. These cognitive elements are thought to be present only in the early stages of learning (the cognitive stage discussed in chapter 8). Thus, according to this view, mental practice effects are predicted to apply only to early learning since these cognitive components of learning drop out after being acquired in the first stage (see chapter 9). Although learning cognitive elements is undoubtedly a major factor in mental practice, evidence such as that illustrated in figure 10.4 (and in Focus on Application 10.1) suggests that there is more to mental practice than just this. Beyond these early

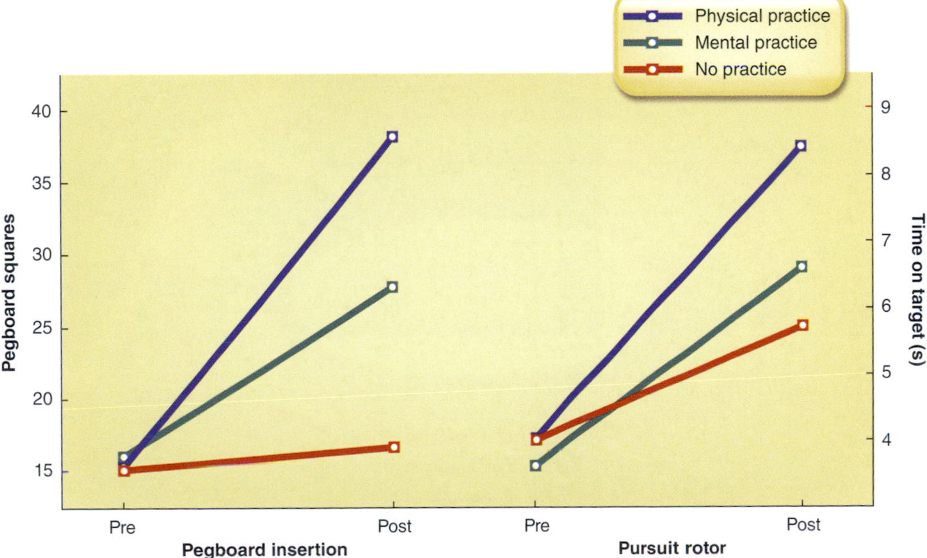

FIGURE 10.4 Effects of physical practice (blue) and mental practice (green) compared to no-practice control conditions (red) on groups learning a pegboard-insertion task (left) and a pursuit-rotor task (right).

stages of practice, both the pegboard-insertion task and the pursuit-rotor task involve considerable learning of movement control, as these tasks seem largely devoid of cognitive or conceptual components. Rawlings et al. (1972) also studied mental practice with the rotary-pursuit task, and their results were very similar to those of Hird et al. Clearly, mental practice is not just cognitive or symbolic learning.

One account for the role of mental practice in acquiring the motor aspects of skill learning has origins that can be traced back to the 1800s. Mental practice, according to this older view, causes the motor system to produce minute contractions of the participating musculature, with these contractions being far smaller in amplitude than those necessary to produce action. By this view, the movement is carried out in the central nervous system, providing practice even without overt body movement. Although EMGs (electromyograph recordings of the muscles' electrical signals) do show some evidence of weak activities during mental practice, the patterning of these EMGs does not resemble that of the actual movements very closely, making it difficult to understand how these

Mental practice does contribute to learning, though the exact way it does this is still unclear. One way may be allowing the learner to practice decision making, such as a tennis player's choosing what shot to take.

Focus on
APPLICATION 10.1

Mental Practice in Stroke Rehabilitation

The application of mental practice as a method to improve motor skills has been a part of sport for years. In some sports the facilities are restricted to seasons of the year, therefore mental practice would be a perfect fit for practicing sport in the off-seasons when facilities are not available. When research on mental practice, such as that shown earlier in this chapter, began to reveal positive effects on motor learning, instructors and therapists began to use these methods in their teaching and therapies, respectively—notably, they were justified in using these methods in stroke rehabilitation.

Stroke is a medical condition that results in damage to the brain. Often the damage is to one side (hemisphere) of the brain, resulting in motor control impairments to the opposite side of the body. One goal of rehabilitation is to regain function by repairing the brain through goal-directed movements. Continued activations, from active physical practice, can lead to partial or full restoration and compensation.

But, there are limitations to the amount and frequency of rehabilitation treatments involving a therapist. Active movement outside therapy times may be encouraged but, unless specified and monitored, may not always be wise (for various reasons). Fortunately, recent research has shown that mental practice (and imagery) generates neural activations of the brain that are similar to actual movement (Garrison, Winstein, & Aziz-Zadeh, 2010). Since mental practice cannot replace physical rehabilitation as an effective therapeutic technique, the combination of physical and mental practice is more effective than either form alone (Cha et al., 2012; Dickstein & Deutsch, 2007; Nilsen, Gillen, & Gordon, 2010). There appears to be little doubt that mental practice serves as an effective addition to the occupational and physical therapists' arsenal of rehabilitation tools.

---

electrical activities alone could be the basis for enhanced learning. The idea that mental practice produces minute muscular contractions has not generated much research support.

A more recent view of this account of mental practice does hold more promise. By this view, mental practice (or imaging) produces anticipated sensory consequences of an action (also called feedforward information). As discussed earlier (see chapter 4), feedforward information is a critical component of movement control, which allows one to anticipate the results of an action if it was performed as expected, and to make rapid corrections if the feedback information does not match the feedforward (expected) signals. The idea is that by producing those anticipated sensations during mental practice, the learner builds what some have called a "forward model" of the action in memory. In this way, some motor learning can occur in the absence of movement, but further refinements require physical practice to learn how the forward model compares with actual sensory feedback resulting from movement (e.g., Gentili et al., 2010).

When and How to Use Mental Practice

The learner needs to be instructed carefully in the methods of mental practice. It is not enough simply to suggest that the learner go somewhere and "practice mentally"; systematic procedures are necessary. Weinberg and Gould (2019) provide additional tips for maximizing the use of imagery and mental practice, such as performing imagery and mental-practice activities in as many different settings as possible. Because mental practice and imagery require no apparatus, large groups of learners can practice at the same time. The clever instructor will find ways to interleave the two practice modes to provide maximal gains, for example, by urging mental practice during the rest phase between trials of a fatiguing task or to break up a long string of repetitious physical practice trials.

Organizing Practice and Rest Periods

Scheduling practice is a major concern in designing a program of instruction. This includes how many days per week skills should be practiced, whether to provide layoff days, how much to practice on each day, and how much rest to provide during the practice period so fatigue does not become a problem. Some of these questions have been studied in the laboratory and in applied settings, revealing interesting and useful implications for skills learning.

There are countless ways to organize practice, of course, but how these variations affect learning and trade off with each other is complicated. Several common features of practice sessions have been well-studied, and we will discuss two research streams in this section: (1) research studying the effect of rest among periods of practice, and (2) research on mental practice and observation given during the intervals between periods of practice.

How Often to Practice

One of the first decisions concerns how often the learners will practice. On the one hand, a major goal of an instructor is usually to facilitate maximal learning before the first opportunity to perform the skills in a real situation. Most training schedules involve a limited period of time in which certain skills are practiced (e.g., a fixed number of weeks).

One frequent solution to the scheduling problem is to provide as much practice as possible, concentrating it to maximize the practice time. However, as shown by Baddeley and Longman (1978) with keyboard skills, there is likely some upper limit to the amount of practice per day that is effective for learning. In this study, postal workers were retrained for a total of 80 h of practice time (60 h only for one group). The practice was varied in terms of the amount of practice time per session (1 or 2 h) and the number of sessions per day (one or two). Among the three groups that received 80 h total of training, two groups completed the training in 40 days (either spread over two 1 h sessions per day or one 2 h session per day) and one group completed the 80 h in 20 days (with two 2 h sessions per day). The group that received 60 h total of training completed the training in 60 days (one 1 h session per day). The data in figure 10.5 present the results for the last part of the training period for all four groups, plus the results for three retention tests conducted months later. (Note that one peculiarity of this study was that the group having the least concentrated practice [1 h, once per day] received 20 h less total practice time than the other three groups.)

A consistent finding in figure 10.5 throughout practice and in retention was the relatively poor performance of the most concentrated practice group—the individuals who practiced for 4 h a day (2 h sessions, twice per day, red trace). Distributing practice over long periods (40 or 60 days), produced superior performance over the practice periods and in all of the retention tests. But one other interesting finding in the Baddeley and Longman study must be noted. The practice schedule that produced the poorest performance during practice as well as the least learning (2 h, twice per day, red trace) was voted as the most popular practice condition among the trainees. This illustrates an important consideration: Learners do not always know which procedures work most effectively in terms of the overall goal of learning. (We will see more evidence of this poor understanding of the learning process later in this chapter.)

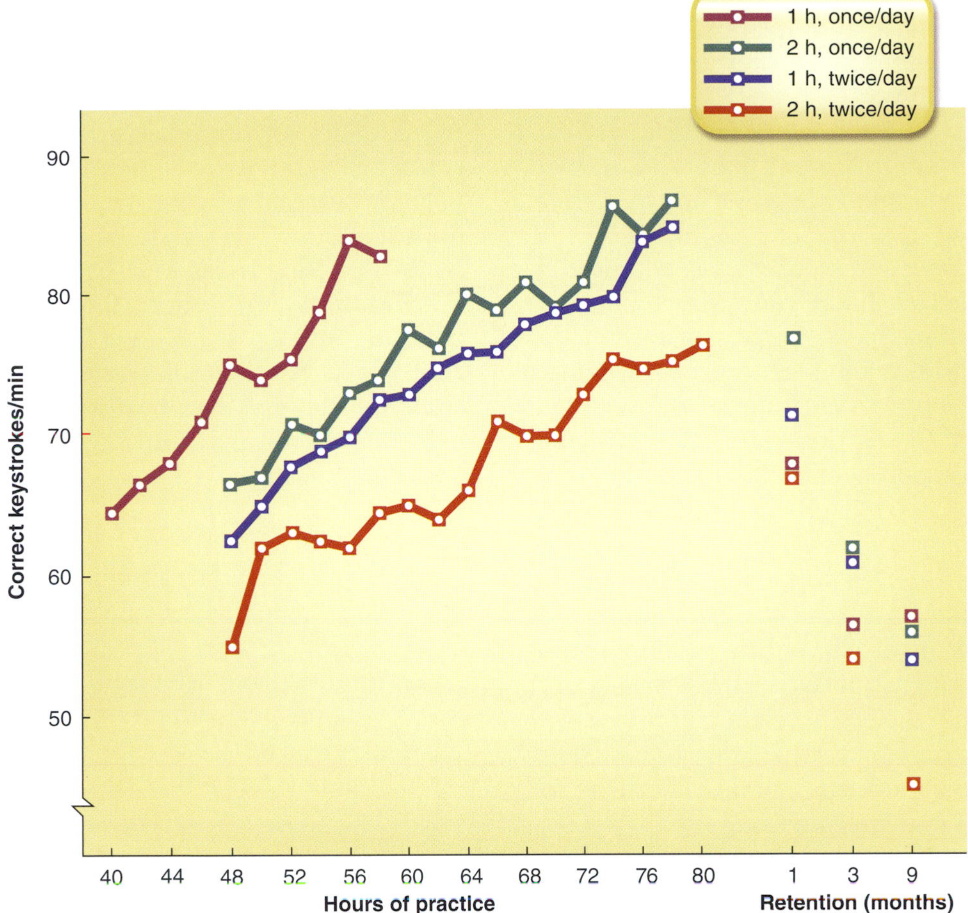

FIGURE 10.5 Results of the Baddeley and Longman (1978) study of retraining postal workers on keyboard tasks under different distributed-practice conditions.

The trainees' dissatisfaction with the longer practice distribution schedules highlights an important concern regarding the issue of practice *efficiency* versus practice *effectiveness*. The Baddeley and Longman study clearly demonstrated both: Although practicing 4 h/day was the least effective schedule in terms of learning, it was the most efficient in terms of total practice time (i.e., the fewest number of days spent in the practice environment). The decision to trade off effectiveness versus efficiency when determining how to distribute work and rest periods across days is not a simple one, and must take into account other factors, such as the likely motivational deficits that might occur with extended periods of practice and the fatigue-producing effects of the task.

Work and Rest Periods During a Practice Session

Unlike the questions concerning practice scheduling over a week, issues concerning organizing practice and rest during a single practice session have been studied a great deal in the laboratory. For the purposes here, we can define two classes of practice distribution, based on the relative amounts of practice and rest provided, typically called massed and distributed practice in the literature.

Massed practice provides relatively little rest between trials. For example, if a task has practice trials each of 30 s in duration, a massed-practice schedule might call for rest periods between trials of only 5 s or perhaps no rest at all (so-called continuous practice).

On the other hand, **distributed practice** calls for much more rest, perhaps with a rest period between trials that is as long as a trial itself (30 s in this example). There is no fixed dividing line between massed and distributed practice, but massed practice is generally defined as having considerably less rest between trials than distributed practice.

Researchers interested in massed and distributed practice have generally been concerned with the effects of physical and mental fatigue-like states on learning effectiveness (see Lee & Genovese, 1988, for a review). For a given number of practice trials, decreasing the amount of rest between trials reduces the time available for dissipation of fatigue, degrading performance on the next practice trial and perhaps interfering with learning. Many experimenters have used a fixed number of practice trials in an acquisition session, varied the amount of rest between these trials, and then measured learning on a retention test. These work and rest schedules have different effects on performance and learning for discrete and continuous tasks.

Discrete Tasks

A few of the distribution-of-practice experiments have used relatively rapid discrete tasks. Generally, when the task involves performance trials that are only a few tenths of a second, as in a throw or a kick, it is very difficult to make the rest periods short enough to affect performance. In the laboratory, even when the rest periods were made as short as 300 ms, seemingly far shorter than for any real-world practice session, the result has been either no decrement in performance or learning or perhaps even slight advantages for massed conditions (see Carron, 1967; Lee & Genovese, 1989). It may be best to conclude that, for discrete tasks, there is no evidence that reducing the rest time through massed practice affects learning.

Continuous Tasks

By far, most massed- and distributed-practice research has involved continuous skills analogous to real-world tasks such as swimming or typing. In these tasks, fatigue-like states have much more opportunity to build up within a trial, so decreasing the rest between trials has larger effects. This can be seen in a study by Bourne and Archer (1956), in which groups of participants performed 30 s trials on a pursuit-rotor task that were separated by differing periods of rest between trials—either 0, 15, 30, 45, or 60 s. The results of the performance in the practice trials and in a retention test are illustrated in figure 10.6. Three general conclusions can be drawn from this figure, and these conclusions typify the results seen generally with distribution-of-practice experiments using continuous tasks (Lee & Genovese, 1988):

1. Longer rest periods generally lead to better performance during practice (i.e., distribution of practice has a performance effect).
2. The positive effect of longer rest intervals on performance remains large on a retention test (i.e., distribution of practice has a learning effect).
3. The size of the differences between groups is generally reduced after a retention interval (i.e., the magnitude of the learning effect is generally smaller than the magnitude of the performance effect).

Implications of Practice Distribution Effects

The effects of rest between trials have considerable importance when viewed from the standpoint of practice effectiveness versus practice efficiency. Clearly, longer rest periods have positive effects on both performance and learning. However, these effects come with a cost, because essentially the rest periods are lost time. In economic terms, the cost of introducing rest periods into a training application (e.g., in an airplane cockpit simulator) might outweigh the benefits to learning. Fortunately, there are alternatives to resting that can make the time between physical practice trials more effective *and* efficient from a learning standpoint. Two of these—mental practice and observation—were discussed earlier in this chapter. We

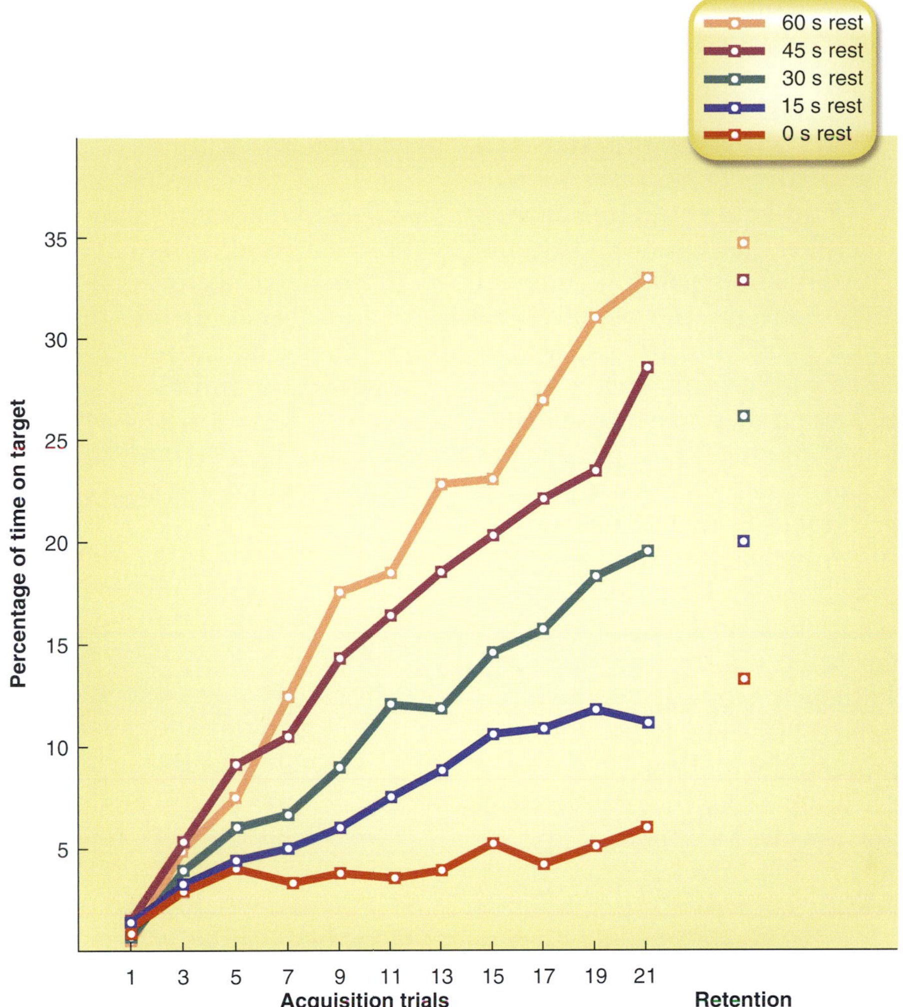

FIGURE 10.6 Results of the Bourne and Archer (1956) study examining the effects of rest intervals of differing length, inserted between 30 s periods of practice on a pursuit-rotor task.

consider these alternatives again in the next sections as a means to improve both practice effectiveness and efficiency (Ong & Hodges, 2012).

Inserting Mental Practice and Observation

An important practical issue arising from the previous section concerns the costs versus benefits of distributed practice—although relatively long rest periods are efficient for performance and learning, they are inefficient from a time-management perspective. For example, in the Baddeley and Longman (1978) postal-worker retraining study, the most-distributed practice groups (1 h sessions, once a day) would have required four times longer to complete the same amount of practice as the most-massed group (2 h sessions, twice a day). Therefore, to increase both effectiveness and efficiency, it would make sense from a theoretical and practical viewpoint to insert periods of mental practice or observation during the rest between trials or sessions. Rather than seeing rest as lost time, one can use these intervals productively to enhance motor learning at the same time the learners are recovering from fatigue. In effect, this strategy would make distributed practice both effective and efficient compared to massed practice because both intervals of physical practice *and* mental practice or demonstrations would contribute positive effects to learning.

A second perspective concerns how rest during periods of physical practice can encourage self-evaluation of performance outcomes, which would contribute to learning. One of the principles that we discuss in the next chapter concerns how using augmented feedback allows learners to become self-sufficient in their capability to assess their own performance and to learn to help themselves through error corrections. Interspersing periods of mental practice, demonstrations or observations, or both between periods of physical practice encourages learners to assess and better understand what makes their own performance more or less effective.

Finally, mixing physical practice with periods of demonstration, observation, or mental practice would likely have positive effects on motivation as well. These periods provide time for reflective thinking about the positive things that occurred during physical practice and about how the negative aspects might be improved upon in the next opportunity to perform. All of these factors are known to contribute positively to learning and inserting them into otherwise empty intervals of rest would benefit learning.

Variable and Constant Practice

Ultimately, the goal of practice is to prepare a learner to perform to the highest possible level of skill when it really counts—such as applying CPR (cardiopulmonary resuscitation) skills in an emergency. An obvious problem that arises in emergency or criterion-task situations, especially so in CPR situations, is that practice is usually undertaken in relatively sterile environments—stress-free, unrestricted working environments that provide excellent lighting, warm climates, and so on—which may be quite unlike the environment and conditions under which CPR is applied in an emergency. Practice, in these cases, must prepare the learners to be highly adaptable to such that they can perform in a way they have never performed before. How does one prepare for these different criterion tasks, and, more importantly, what are the features of practice that enable one to perform in such novel situations with skill and dexterity? One way to think about practice from this perspective concerns an idea discussed earlier, regarding the process of adding parameters to generalized motor programs, and how the capability for this process is learned.

Review: Generalized Motor Programs and Parameters

Recall from chapter 5 that the skill of throwing, for example, represents a *class* of movements. For example, in American football, skill in passing is reflected by the capability to produce many different throwing distances, with arched or flat trajectories, and to stationary or moving targets, and also involves many other potential variables (the defense, the weather, and so on). Even with all of these variations, there is something fundamental, consistent, and characteristic about a football pass, such as the particular grip on the ball, the step and the follow-through, the arm action, and the wrist movement that produces a spiral. These features are called invariances (chapter 5). One can determine that an action is a member of a particular class of actions because it has the same invariant features as the other members of the class. Also, these features differ between classes, as there is no way to change a putting stroke into a football pass, for example. Members of a class have these characteristics:

- Common movement sequencing exists among the elements.
- Common temporal, or rhythmical, organization exists.
- The same action can often be carried out with different effectors (e.g., limbs).
- The same action can differ in surface features (e.g., speed) on two different occasions, which is specified by different movement parameters.

Return now to the conceptual model of human performance developed earlier for the example in figure 8.1. Discrete movement patterns are governed by generalized motor programs (GMPs), each with an almost invariant temporal organization. Once learned, a GMP for football passing can be applied to many specific throwing situations by specifying parameters in the movement programming stage, which define how the movement is produced for any one instance. The learner evaluates the environment, decides what kind of pass is required in this particular case, and then specifies the proper parameters to the program (those that are likely to achieve the movement goals as assessed). The parts of the conceptual model involved in this process are shown in figure 8.1. The questions are: How are the proper parameters selected? How does the performer learn to *generalize* to all of the throwing distances in the class?

Schema Theory

One conceptualization to answer these questions is provided by **schema theory** (Schmidt, 1975), in which the learner acquires a set of rules, called schemas, that relate the surface features of throwing (e.g., distances, speeds, forces) to the parameter values necessary to produce those actions. Figure 10.7 illustrates how this could work for the distance dimension in the football pass as an example. On the horizontal axis are all the possible distances the football has been thrown in the past, with a maximum of 40 m for this learner. Whenever a ball is thrown, the learner briefly stores in memory the distance the ball went as well as the parameter that was applied to the GMP for that throw. Over time and many such throws, the learner then abstracts (or generalizes) the relationship between the past throwing distances and the task parameters that were used for the GMP (Schmidt, 1975). Figure 10.7 illustrates how the abstraction process might occur. To avoid a storage problem the learner remembers these values just long enough to update the schema after each throw, and then the details are discarded or forgotten. According to schema theory, this process

Passing a football accurately requires the player to throw with different speeds and trajectories under variable conditions. How can a learner practice to maximize the ability to perform this skill?

is responsible for learning to parameterize the GMPs—a common problem for the player using the same GMP over and over again.

An important question for researchers is how the schema is learned. The learning process, according the schema theory, is also illustrated in figure 10.7. Suppose the learner begins the learning process by generating parameter A (e.g., a moderate level of force), which leads to a throwing distance of 29 m. On subsequent attempts, the learner chooses parameter B (a lesser force), which leads to a throw of approximately 18 m, and then the learner issues parameter C (a larger force), which leads to a throw of about 34 m, and so on. With each throw, the learner reduces the information about the value of the parameter applied to the GMP, along with the resulting distance thrown, to a single data point, as illustrated by the collection of individual (blue) data points in figure 10.7.

Over time, practice results in building a large collection of individual (blue) data points. Figure 10.7 illustrates just six data points (A, B, C, D, E, F), but you can imagine many thousands of such data points being accumulated for a football player. The critical point made by schema theory is this: Learning is a process of abstracting or generalizing a rule (the schema) that relates specific parameters to specific outcomes. In Figure 10.7, that rule is represented by the straight, blue line. In future throws, the decision about what parameter is used to apply to the GMP is based on the relation of the goal outcome to the schema. For example, to throw a distance of X_1 m, the player chooses the distance of X_1 on the horizontal-axis in Figure 10.7, uses the vertical red line to access the schema (blue line), and this results in selecting a parameter value of Y_1 to apply to the GMP. In the same way, desiring a longer throwing distance of X_2 m would require a parameter value of Y_2.

This process generates a movement with parameter values based on the learner's past experience in using this program. Most important, this process allows the learner to make a movement that has never been made previously. Suppose that this learner has never produced a 45 m pass before (X_2 in figure 10.7). The learner simply provides the best estimate of the required parameter values from the schema, and then runs off the GMP with this parameter value (Y_2 in figure 10.7), thereby producing a novel action that has not been performed before.

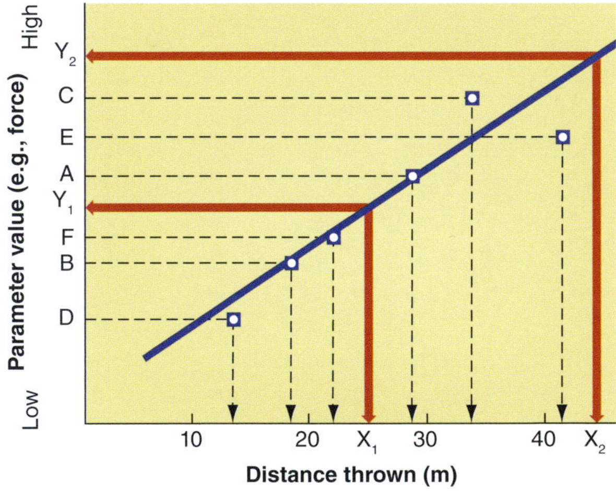

FIGURE 10.7 The schema relates parameter values to outcome distances. To produce a throw of 25 m (X_1) or 45 m (X_2), the learner relies on the schema to generate parameter values equal to Y_1 and Y_2, respectively.

Two important implications about schema learning can be readily understood from figure 10.7. One is that the strength of the schema—the blue line that forms a general relationship between parameters and outcomes—will be enhanced with practice. In figure 10.7, it is inferred that a schema (the straight line) is a representation of better skill when based on many thousands of data points than when based on only a few. The second implication is that schema learning is predicted to be better when the breadth of parameters and outcomes experienced is wide (variable practice) than when narrow (or nonvariable), which is discussed in the next section.

Variable Practice Enhances Schema Learning

Considerable evidence suggests that variable practice is particularly effective in schema learning. A basic research paradigm contrasts two groups of learners: One is a nonvariable or **constant-practice** group, practicing only a single member of a class of tasks; the other is a **variable-practice** group, practicing several members of the class of tasks (for the football passing example, this could mean practicing varying football passing distances). The two groups have the same amount of practice and differ only in the amount of practice variability they receive.

The constant group typically outperforms the variable group during the acquisition phase. Typically a learner can produce instances of a single version of a movement more effectively than multiple versions, particularly if these multiple versions are performed in a random order (or interleaved—more on this issue in the next section).

However, when participants in both groups are switched to a novel version of the task in a transfer test, the group that received variable practice performs at least as well as the constant group, and frequently they do so more skillfully (e.g., Kerr & Booth, 1978; McCracken & Stelmach, 1977). This finding has been interpreted as evidence that learners acquire schemas when they practice and that variable practice enhances schema development, allowing more effective novel-task performance in the future. In other words, variable practice enhances *generalizability*, allowing the performer to apply past learning to actions not specifically experienced before in practice.

An example of this generalization can be seen in figure 10.8 (from Catalano & Kleiner, 1984). Groups practiced a coincident-timing task (coinciding with the arrival of a moving light simulating a moving ball by making a hand response) with target velocities of only one speed (5, 7, 9, *or* 11 mph) under constant-practice conditions. Another group practiced all speeds (5, 7, 9, *and* 11 mph) under variable-practice conditions, with the different target velocities presented in a random order over trials. Transfer tests were then given on task versions that were not experienced previously by either group (at 1, 3, 13, and 15 mph). Figure 10.8 illustrates that in three of the four transfer velocity tests, variable practice led to much smaller errors than did constant practice; hence variable practice produced generalization. Many skills require us to produce variations that have never been produced before, and variable practice is one means of maximizing the capability to move effectively in this way.

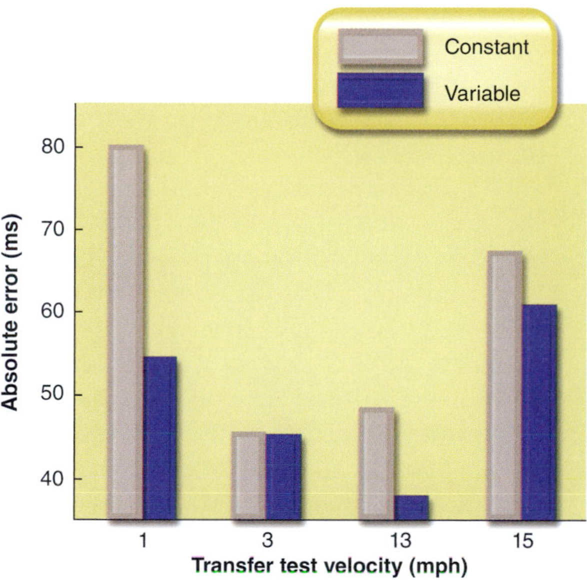

FIGURE 10.8 Mean absolute timing errors in four coincident-timing transfer target speeds following practice in either a constant (gray) or variable (blue) practice condition.

Blocked and Random Practice

In many, if not most, real-world settings, the learner's goal is to acquire more than a single skill or task in a limited practice period, sometimes even in a single practice period. Physicians practice different skills related to surgery (such as suturing and knot-tying skills), musicians practice multiple songs at a time, tennis players practice serving and volleying as well as the more usual ground strokes during a single session, and so on. An important question confronting the learner or instructor is how to sequence the practice of these various tasks during the practice session so as to maximize learning. Two variations have powerful effects on learning: **blocked practice** (sometimes called drilled or repetitive practice) and **random practice** (sometimes called interleaved practice). Their respective effects on learning have been termed the **contextual-interference effect**.

Suppose that your student has three tasks to learn in a practice session (tasks A, B, and C). A commonsense method of scheduling such tasks would be to practice all trials of one task before shifting to the second, then to finish practice on the second before switching to the third. This is called blocked practice, in which all the trials of a given task (for that day) are completed before moving on to the next task. Blocked practice is typical of some drills in which a skill is repeated over and over, with minimal interruption by other activities. This kind of practice seems to make

Focus on
RESEARCH 10.1

Especial Skills: An Exception to Variable Practice?

Schema theory, and indeed just common sense, suggests that if someone is faced with learning to produce a class of actions, that practice ought to be structured to be variable, taking into account the unlimited variations to be experienced in the criterion version of the skill. But how would practice be structured if only one variation of the criterion task would ever be experienced? In other words, are skills that are to be performed in only one way represented differently in memory than a class of skills that can be performed in infinite ways?

The latter question was addressed in a series of experiments involving skilled basketball players (Keetch, Lee, & Schmidt, 2008; Keetch et al., 2005), and more recently in skilled archers and baseball pitchers (Nabavinik et al., 2018; Simons et al., 2009). Two types of shots are commonly used in basketball—jump shots (which, as the name implies, involve the player leaping into the air before releasing the ball), and set shots (in which the player remains in contact with the ground during the shot). Jump shots are taken anywhere on the court and are used in most game situations; set shots are typically taken only at the foul (or free-throw) line.

Keetch and colleagues predicted that if variable (jump shot) practice results in the development of a schema for a class of actions, then performance at one location should be highly related to performance at all other locations, including shots at the free-throw line. In contrast, constant practice of the set shot, practiced only at the free-throw line, might result in a specific advantage for performance at that one particular location. Moreover, this prediction should be particularly strong for highly experienced players, who have taken thousands of set-shot practice shots in the development of their expertise.

Data from college basketball players shooting set shots and jump shots from five locations perpendicular to the basket (including one from 15 ft—the foul line) are presented in figure 10.9. Jump-shot accuracy decreased almost linearly as the player moved farther from the basket, as expected. In contrast, even though the set-shot performance decreased in accuracy as distance increased, performance at the 15 ft mark was much more accurate than would be expected based on the performances at the other shot locations.

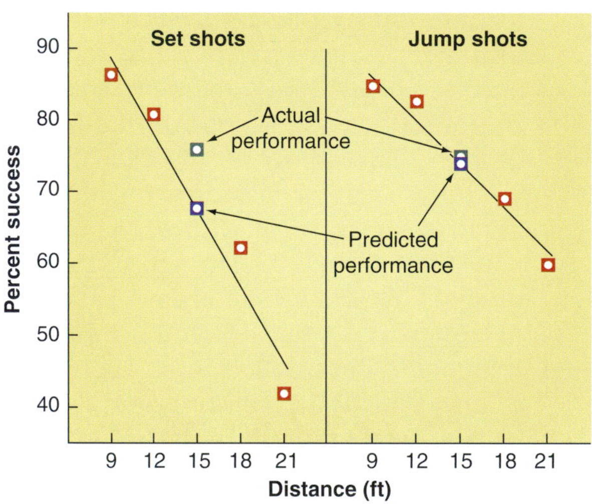

FIGURE 10.9 Performance of set and jump shots from five different locations. The blue data points represent the expected performances for the set and jump shots at the foul line (15 ft) based on linear regression analyses from the four other locations. The green data points represent the actual performance scores. Set-shot performance shows an advantage at the foul line (green data point much higher than predicted), whereas no specific advantage is seen for jump shots at the foul line (green and blue data points overlap).

These findings have some interesting implications for learning, as they seem to suggest that practice be structured according to the criterion demands of the task—how the skills will be performed in the test situation. If flexibility in producing a variation of a class of skills is required, then it makes sense to continue with variable practice. However, if only one version of the task will ever be performed, then concentrating practice from the one location appears to have practical merit (Breslin et al., 2012).

Exploring Further

1. Name another skill usually performed from only one specific location that might show an effect similar to the set shot in basketball.
2. For the task named in question 1, describe an experimental methodology that would assess whether or not performance would show a specific advantage from that location.

---

sense in that it allows the learners to concentrate on one particular task at a time and to refine and correct it, without any interference from practice of the other tasks. Indeed, a blocked schedule has been and continues to be (unfortunately, in our opinion) the dominant practice strategy used in skills training across many disciplines.

Another practice scheduling variation is called random (interleaved) practice, where the order of task presentation is mixed, or interleaved, across the practice period. Learners switch practice attempts among the three tasks so that, in the more extreme cases, they never (or rarely) practice the same task on two consecutive attempts. From a commonsense perspective, the random method, with its high level of trial-to-trial variability and its high level of interference between tasks, might seem to be disruptive to the learning process. At least, that is what many believed until the publication of a landmark experiment.

The Shea and Morgan Experiment

John Shea and Robyn Morgan (1979) conducted a groundbreaking experiment that revolutionized the way researchers think of the processes involved in practice. Following some of the original ideas of William Battig (1966), Shea and Morgan had participants practice three different tasks (A, B, and C) that involved responding to a stimulus light with a series of rapid arm movements, with each task having a different predetermined sequence. One group of participants practiced the tasks in a blocked order, completing all trials of task A before moving to task B trials, which they completed before completing the trials of task C. A second group practiced in a random order; no more than two consecutive trials could occur for any one task. It is important to remember that the two groups had exactly the same amount of practice on tasks A, B, and C and the same amount of total practice—the two groups differed only in the *order* in which the tasks were practiced.

The results are presented in figure 10.10. The goal was to respond to the stimulus and complete the movements as quickly as possible, so lower total times indicate more-skilled performance. Notice that, during acquisition, the blocked condition was far more effective for performance (with shorter times) than the random condition. But recall that differences during acquisition cannot be interpreted as differences in learning; rather, delayed retention (or transfer) tests are needed to evaluate learning (these concepts were presented in chapter 8).

Shea and Morgan tested for learning by conducting retention tests after 10 min and 10 days; these tests were conducted under either random or blocked conditions, which produced four subgroups. The following

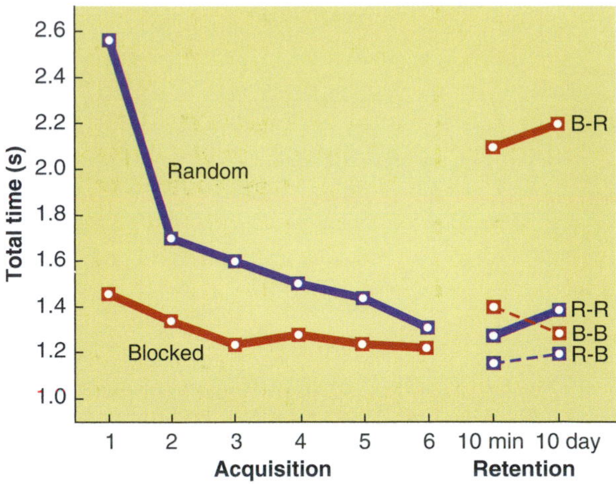

FIGURE 10.10 Performance on speeded movement tasks under random-practice and blocked-practice conditions during acquisition, and in random-ordered and blocked-ordered retention tests.

abbreviations indicate the condition in acquisition and the condition in retention, respectively: R-B, R-R, B-R, and B-B. The first character in the pair indicates the condition during acquisition (random R and blocked B), and the second member of the pair indicates the performance conditions in retention.

When the retention tests were performed under random conditions, the group that had random practice in acquisition (R-R, solid blue line) greatly outperformed the group with blocked conditions in acquisition (B-R, solid red line). When the retention tests were under blocked conditions, again the random condition in acquisition (R-B, dotted blue line) outperformed those who had blocked conditions in acquisition (B-B, dotted red line), but these differences were much smaller than for the random retention tests. Clearly, the random conditions in acquisition were always more effective for retention, but this benefit was clearly dependent on the nature of the retention test.

An issue regarding variable practice was alluded to earlier. A very important factor concerns how variable practice is scheduled; this issue now becomes better understood due to the results of Shea and Morgan (1979). Studies in which variable practice was scheduled in a trial-by-trial random order tended to show larger advantages compared to constant practice (e.g., Catalano & Kleiner, 1984; also Pigott & Shapiro, 1984). The Shea and Morgan findings suggest that scheduling how variable practice is ordered influences its effectiveness.

Visit the web study guide to read "But I Was Great on the Practice Range" and complete the self-directed learning activities.

Why Random Practice Is So Effective

The Shea and Morgan findings surprised many researchers in the field by showing that, even though random conditions result in much less-skilled performance than blocked conditions in acquisition, random-practice conditions produce more learning. The findings were a large surprise because most conventional viewpoints would suggest that learning should be maximized by those conditions that make learners most proficient *during* practice—there was no motor learning theorizing that could explain this opposite result. As a result, some interesting new hypotheses were offered to explain the findings.

Shea and Morgan (1979; also Shea & Zimny, 1983) argued that changing the task on every random-practice trial made the tasks more distinct from each other and more meaningful, resulting in more *elaborate* memory representations. As revealed in participant interviews after the experiment, random-practice participants tended to relate the task structure to concepts already in memory (creating meaningfulness), such as discovering that the arm movement pattern for task B had essentially the shape of an upside-down Z. Also, they would make distinctions between tasks, such as "Task A is essentially like task C, except that the first part is reversed" (creating distinctiveness). The blocked-practice participants, on the other hand, tended not to make such statements. Instead they talked of running off the performances more or less automatically and without thinking much about the movements. Blocked practice did not induce the kind of comparative and contrastive efforts in practice that were experienced during random practice. According to this **elaboration hypothesis**, increased meaningfulness and distinctiveness produce more durable memories for the tasks, and thus increased performance capabilities in tests of retention and transfer.

An alternative hypothesis explains the beneficial effects of random practice somewhat differently. Lee and Magill (1983) suggested that when the learner shifts from task A to task B, the solution that was generated and stored in short-term memory (see chapter 2) for performing task B causes the solution previously generated for task A to be forgotten. When task A is encountered again a few trials later, the learner must generate the solution again; therefore, performance in practice is relatively poor. Yet this solution-generating process is assumed to be beneficial for learning (see also Cuddy & Jacoby, 1982). In blocked practice, on the other hand, the performer remembers the solution generated on a given trial and simply applies it to the next trial, which minimizes the number of times the learner must generate new solutions. Therefore, performance during practice in a blocked schedule is very effective because the solution, once generated, is remembered for a series of trials. Yet learning is poor because the learner is not required to generate a new solution to the task on every trial. In this way, the key focus of the forgetting hypothesis is the fact that new solutions are required frequently in random practice but not in blocked practice; thus, the development of the solution for the task is the key feature that facilitates learning. Interestingly, the **forgetting hypothesis** suggests the somewhat ironic and counterintuitive idea that forgetting benefits learning (Cuddy & Jacoby, 1982).

A number of investigations have evaluated and provided support for each of the hypotheses. For example, in a study by Wright (1991), members of a blocked-practice group were encouraged to make explicit comparisons of the task just practiced with one of the other tasks to be learned—essentially inducing this group to mentally practice the tasks with meaningful and distinctive processing. This special blocked-practice group outperformed the other practice groups that had a similar intervention but without the benefits of the explicit comparative and contrastive processing. The results supported the elaboration hypothesis predictions because of the insertion of these specific mental processing activities.

A key prediction of the forgetting hypothesis was that random practice forces more extensive planning operations on each trial compared to blocked practice. A study by Lee and colleagues (1997) attempted to reduce the need for these planning operations by presenting a powerful model just before each practice trial. This model was designed so that it would inform participants how to perform the next trial, and because it provided extremely strong memory guidance for the upcoming trial, the model was hypothesized to prevent the construction process (because the model provided the solution for the next trial). In the experiment, the presence of the model was combined with random practice. The model, eliminating as it did the participant's requirement to reconstruct the solution for the next trial, would interfere with performance in acquisition more or less as blocked practice does. As figure 10.11 shows, the model obliterated the usual benefits of random practice.

In the experiment, the random and blocked conditions are contrasted with this special "random + model" condition. Clearly, the model was beneficial for performance during acquisition (when the model was present), as seen on the left side of figure 10.11 where the random + model group was far more skilled than the group that had only random practice. However, in the retention tests, where the model was withdrawn, the random + model group regressed considerably, to the point that this condition led to the most error in the delayed retention test. Providing the powerful model before each practice trial, while it was beneficial for performance when it was present, was disastrous for learning. The model obliterated the beneficial advantages

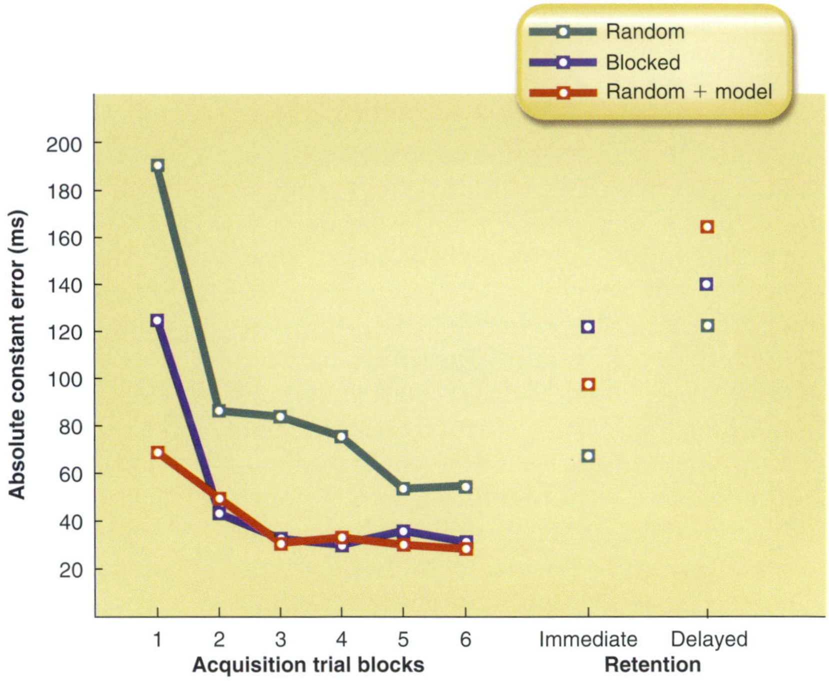

FIGURE 10.11 Providing a powerful guiding model reduced planning operations in a random+model practice group obliterated the usual random-practice benefit for learning (from Lee et al., 1997).

of random practice. These findings support strongly the forgetting hypothesis for the random-practice versus blocked-practice effect, and they also show that random practice is not necessarily the magic bullet for effective motor learning.

A number of studies have provided evidence supporting the elaboration hypothesis, and a number have supported the forgetting hypothesis. As a result, it is perhaps best to consider these hypotheses as complementary rather than competing explanations of contextual interference effects. Other explanations have been provided as well (e.g., Broadbent et al., 2017; Wright et al., 2016), and as more research emerges these important theoretical debates should become clearer.

Research Since Shea and Morgan

Shea and Morgan's findings have been very influential. Hundreds of studies have been conducted on random and blocked practice effects since their research was published, and many discussion articles have been written about how to conduct practice in everyday activities (e.g., Lee & Schmidt, 2014). The next sections summarize some of the research that has emerged in the years since the publication of this landmark study.

Contextual-Interference Effects in Non-laboratory Tasks

As might be expected, the Shea and Morgan (1979) study motivated a large number of researchers to examine random- and blocked-practice schedules in non-laboratory tasks. Goode and Magill (1986) found similar effects in participants who were learning three different types of badminton serves. Hall, Domingues, and Cavazos (1994) produced an analogous effect using a group of college baseball players who engaged in extra batting practice, hitting different types of pitches thrown in random or blocked orders. Ste-Marie and colleagues (2004) found similar beneficial effects for random practice in schoolchildren who were learning handwriting skills. Carter and Grahn (2016) reported similar benefits for random practice by experienced clarinetists who learned new musical pieces. Many other studies involving the learning of sport, music, and everyday skills have been published as well—the Shea and Morgan laboratory findings extend to the acquisition of real-world tasks too.

This walking garden allows rehabilitation patients to practice walking with crutches over many surfaces, allowing for variable and random practice.

Random-Practice Limitations

The beneficial effects of random practice are not universal, however, and some studies have resulted in no learning differences. Lee (unpublished data, Louisiana State University, 1981), using the pursuit-rotor task, failed to produce the expected random-practice benefits. The pursuit rotor, however, a continuous, tracking task, does not require much advance preparation between trials. Perhaps this can be taken as evidence that the random-practice benefits might only occur in tasks for which considerable pretrial preparation is needed.

Guadagnoli and Lee (2004) reviewed the varieties of evidence and suggested that random practice is likely to be least effective when the task demands are so high to begin with that performers have a difficult time producing even a single trial of the behavior. This could occur when individuals are practicing a very difficult task, or when the learners themselves are in some way not appropriate for the task to be learned. A good example might be attempting to teach very young learners an adult task that demands too much. In such cases, random practice would make the practice environment too challenging and perhaps counterproductive to effective learning.

Alternatives to Blocked and Random Practice

Blocked and random practice represent extreme ends of the practice-schedule continuum—random practice involves very little (or no) repetition of the same task from one practice trial to the next, and blocked practice involves almost no interleaving of practice on other tasks. These scheduling extremes might be responsible for the rather dramatic shifts seen in performance and retention, with blocked practice facilitating performance in practice, but having a detrimental effect on retention (and vice versa for random practice). Thus, one need for seeking an alternative to choosing random or blocked practice concerns the fact that neither optimizes both performance *and* learning. One solution, involving so-called hybrid schedules, is presented in the next section.

There is another reason for seeking alternatives to blocked and random practice—the learners' perception of the progress of their own learning. Simon and Bjork (2001) asked their participants to make predictions about their performance just before a retention test. The results, presented in figure 10.12, revealed that participants had an illusion about their learning. When asked to predict how they would do in a retention test, blocked practice fooled the participants into thinking that they had learned much more than they really had, whereas random practice led the participants to believe that they had learned less than they had. Thus, giving learners a more accurate sense of how learning is proceeding might be another reason to seek alternatives to blocked and random practice.

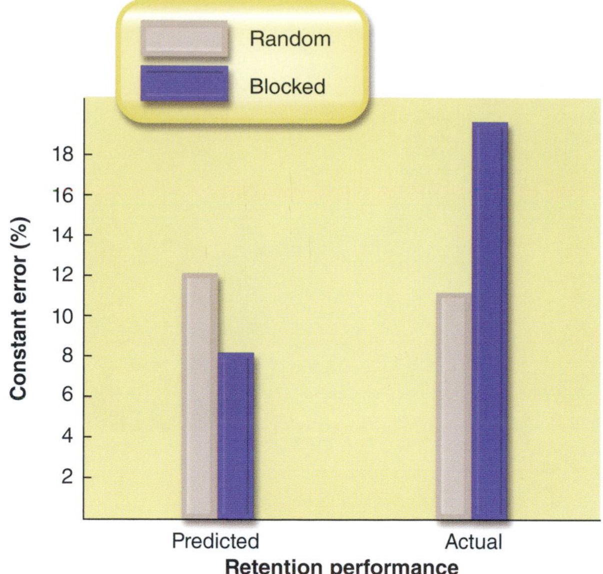

FIGURE 10.12 Before performance in a retention test, individuals who had practiced in a blocked order (blue) predicted that they would be more skilled than those who practiced in a random order (gray, the predicted bars). In reality, the retention performance of the blocked group was less skillful than that of the random group (the actual bars).

Hybrid Schedules Some researchers have found that moderate levels of random practice, with the practice schedule including interleaved short strings of blocked practice, for example, are beneficial for performance and learning. For example, Landin and Hebert (1997) had novices practice a basketball shooting task from different locations on the court according to either a blocked order, a serial order (a quasi-random condition, but more structured than purely random practice), or a moderate order in which practice rotated from task to task after mini-blocks of three attempts from the same distance were performed. This moderate practice format was successful in reducing the performance deficit normally seen during purely random practice *and* facilitated learning as measured in both a blocked- and a random-retention test (see also Pigott & Shapiro, 1984, and Porter & Magill, 2010).

Practice Contingencies Although the hybrid approach to practice would appear to represent the best of both worlds, it is not sensitive to individual differences. For example, although three blocked trials might be optimal for one person, five blocked trials might be better for another person, or no task repetitions at all for someone else.

A type of schedule that is more sensitive to individual differences is a contingency schedule, whereby the difficulty of the task (Choi et al., 2008) and the decision to repeat the same task or switch to an easier or more difficult task depend on the performance success of the individual (Simon et al., 2008). For example, if someone is having considerable difficulty with performance on a task, an instructor might consider some repetition until the difficulties are overcome. The obvious problem with this approach, however, is that performance change (or lack of change) does not necessarily reflect learning (as discussed in chapter 8). Approaches to better understand these contingencies and their effects on performance versus learning represent an intriguing theoretical challenge for researchers but an exciting new practical approach to the topic of practice scheduling for skill learners.

Summary

Physical practice is just one way to rehearse a task. Several methods not involving physical rehearsals have also been shown to enhance learning. Observation of a human model provides objective information that learners can use to organize their thinking about the task. Mental practice and imagery reflect important methods to undertake this organization of thoughts.

Rest periods during physical practice (relative to no-rest conditions) produce gains in learning, especially so for continuous tasks. However, long rest periods have the disadvantage of making practice less time efficient. Research suggests that these rest periods can be used more efficiently if combined with periods of observation, mental practice, or both.

Variable practice involves intentional breadth of experiences with a given task. Compared to constant practice, in which only a single variant is practiced, varied practice facilitates retention and generalizability to a novel situation whose specific variant has not received prior practice. Variable practice is thought to operate by generating stronger schemas, which define the relationship between parameters for a GMP and the movement's outcome.

Large learning gains can be made through effective practice organization and scheduling. An important concept is random (or interleaved) practice, in which the practice order of trials of several tasks is interleaved during acquisition. Relative to blocked practice, in which trials of a single given task are presented repeatedly, random practice produces far more skilled performance at retention (i.e., more learning). Random practice operates by preventing the learner from repeating the same movement plan on successive trials and by interleaving experience gained from performing different activities on adjacent trials.

WEB STUDY GUIDE ACTIVITIES

The student web study guide offers these activities to help you build and apply your knowledge of the concepts in this chapter.

Interactive Learning

Activity 10.1: Better conceptualize the possible ways of organizing practice by identifying the pattern represented by each of five graphical representations and the type of practice illustrated.

Activity 10.2: Explore the ways that random practice leads to better learning than blocked practice by matching descriptions to either the elaboration hypothesis or the forgetting hypothesis.

Activity 10.3: Answer a series of questions on how instructors can influence learners' levels of motivation.

Principles-to-Application Exercise

Activity 10.4: The principles-to-application exercise for this chapter prompts you to choose an activity that involves several motor skills, then identify a specific learner and design a practice session that would include blocked practice and random practice and why these types of practices are used for each skill.

Motor Control in Everyday Actions Narratives

Bend It like Becker

But I Was Great on the Practice Range

Check Your Understanding

1. Explain how rest and cognitive activities between periods of practice influence motor learning.
2. Explain why including variable and random practice when teaching a person to play volleyball can be beneficial to learning. Are there any volleyball skills for which this type of practice would not be beneficial? Why or why not?
3. Discuss the differences between internal focus and external focus instructions. Give an example of each for someone learning to play the piano. Which of your examples would be more beneficial to learning for an intermediate student?

Apply Your Knowledge

1. Discuss three motivational tools or techniques that a physical therapist could use to help ensure a client is motivated during a recovery program. What factors would you consider in order to integrate observational learning or mental practice into the client's schedule?
2. You have volunteered to coach your nephew's soccer team for the summer. Two of the skills that you would like to work on with your team this season are penalty kicks and dribbling the ball down the field. How might you organize work and rest periods during practice for each of these skills? How might you include an amount of task variability appropriate to each skill? Are there any characteristics of your players that you would need to take into consideration when organizing practice? Why?

Suggestions for Further Reading

The review by Ste-Marie and colleagues (2012) provides a solid framework for considering various factors related to observational learning. A meta-analysis (statistical review) of the mental practice literature is provided by Feltz and Landers (1983). A distribution-of-practice meta-analysis and review was published by Lee and Genovese (1988). A different analysis of the distribution-of-practice literature was presented by Verhoeven and Newell (2018). For more on variable practice and schema development, see Schmidt (1975) and Schmidt et al. (2019, ch. 13). The variability-of-practice literature is reviewed in Shapiro and Schmidt (1982). And numerous reviews of the contextual-interference literature exist, including those by Magill and Hall (1990), Merbah and Meulemans (2011), and Lee (2012). See the reference list for these additional resources.

11

Augmented Feedback

How Supplemental Feedback Influences Learning

KEY TERMS

absolute frequency of feedback
augmented feedback
average feedback
bandwidth feedback
concurrent feedback
error amplification
faded feedback
feedback
feedback delay interval
guidance
guidance hypothesis
inherent feedback
instantaneous feedback
knowledge of performance (KP)
knowledge of results (KR)
postfeedback delay
precision of feedback
relative frequency of feedback
summary feedback
trials-delay of feedback

CHAPTER OUTLINE

CHAPTER OBJECTIVES

Chapter 11 describes the influence of augmented feedback on motor performance and learning. This chapter will help you to understand

- the types of augmented feedback,
- how augmented feedback functions to influence performance and learning,
- the various properties of augmented feedback, and
- the influence of the various ways in which augmented feedback can be delivered.

One of the most important learning processes concerns the use of feedback about movements attempted in practice. As discussed in chapter 4, feedback may be a natural consequence of the movement, such as seeing a hammered nail become flush with a block of wood or hearing the sound of a typed key on a keyboard. Feedback can also be supplemented in various artificial forms that are not so obvious to the learner, such as the performer's score in a rifle range test or a comment about a swimmer's leg kick when performing the breaststroke. Often, this feedback is under the instructor's direct control; thus, it makes up a large part of practice.

This chapter can be considered an extension of chapters 9 and 10 because it also concerns practice and learning. In this chapter the focus is on how learners receive supplemental **feedback**—information about performance or errors that the learner can use for making future corrections. Here we discuss some principles of how supplemental feedback influences learning, examining questions about its frequency, timing, and the most effective kinds for learning.

Feedback Classifications

The term *feedback* originally emerged from the analysis of closed-loop control systems, referring to information about the difference between performance and some desired goal-state (see chapter 4). In closed-loop system terminology, feedback is considered to be information about error. In human performance systems, however, the term takes on a more general meaning: information about the movement and movement outcomes, not just errors.

It is helpful to form a clear feedback classification system because the terms and what they refer to can be confusing. One classification appears in figure 11.1, where the global category of all sensory information available to the learner is divided into several subclasses. First, of course, there is a great deal of sensory information in our environment, most of which is not related to the movements we make. But of the information that is related to movement, it is useful to categorize the information as either naturally available in our environment, which is termed *inherent* feedback (sometimes called intrinsic

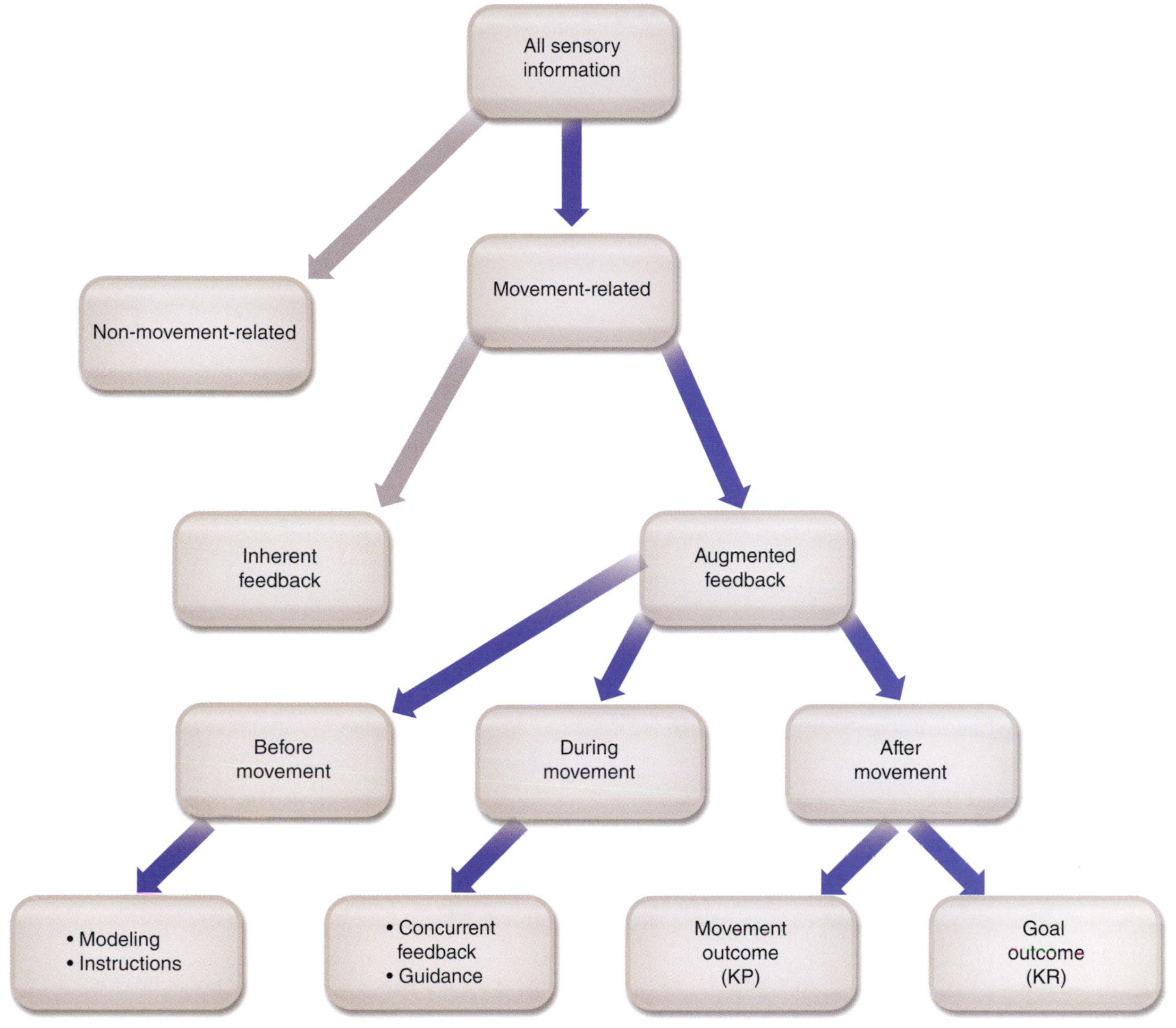

FIGURE 11.1 A feedback classification scheme.

feedback; discussed in detail in chapter 4), or information that is supplemented to the learning environment, called **augmented feedback** (sometimes called extrinsic feedback). It is also useful to distinguish between three types of augmented information in terms of when it has been supplemented to the learner: before, during, or after the movement. (Strictly speaking, only information provided during or after the movement fits the definition as feedback, because it is information arising from moving or having moved that is being "fed back" to the learner. But we will consider supplemental information provided before movement in this discussion as well.)

Inherent Feedback

Discussed previously in chapter 4, **inherent feedback** is information provided as a natural consequence of making an action. When you take a swing at a tennis ball, you feel your hips, shoulders, and arms moving; you see the racket travel; you see, hear, and feel the ball's contact; and you see where the ball travels. All these types of information are inherent to the task, and most performers can perceive them more or less directly, without special methods or devices. Other kinds of inherent information might be the sounds or smells made by a race car engine, or seeing and hearing the progress of a saw blade as a carpenter cuts through a piece of wood or as a surgeon operates on a bone. This general class of feedback has been discussed throughout the text during the development of the conceptual model of human performance.

Augmented Feedback

Augmented feedback is information supplied to the learner that is in addition to the information contained in inherent feedback. As the name suggests, augmented feedback serves to supplement the naturally available (inherent) information. Most importantly, this feedback is information about which the instructor has control; thus, it can be given or not given, given in different forms, and given at different times to influence learning.

Before Movement

Information provided by an instructor or coach to the learner before a movement begins was discussed in chapter 10 under the terms *modeling* and *instructions*. This type of information is supplemental to the learner's practice experience and is provided to augment the way the learner thinks about or conceptualizes how to approach the task. This type of information is not feedback in the strict sense because it is not usually information about what the learner has done but, instead, what could be done.

During Movement

Information provided during movement often occurs when the learner is performing a continuous task, such as walking, in which the augmented feedback can be used to alter an ongoing movement. This type of information has been termed *concurrent feedback* because it is augmented information provided to the learner concurrently with ongoing movement. Visual, auditory, and haptic feedback about gait in stroke rehabilitation are forms of concurrent feedback. Guidance devices, which provide feedback in the form of physical restriction during movement execution, also provide concurrent augmented feedback because they are usually intended to help contain movement within prescribed limits of motion. Newer cars provide examples both of these types of augmented feedback while driving: for example, the car's lane departure feature can provide visual, auditory, or haptic concurrent feedback when a lane is unexpectedly crossed, and can also nudge the steering wheel in the opposite direction of the departure, a type of physical guidance.

After Movement

The most common use of augmented feedback occurs when provided after a movement. Postmovement feedback can be provided about the results of the movement or the movement itself, used for learning both discrete as well as continuous skills. It has been the research focus for many years and, due to its significance in motor learning, has been added as an integral part of our conceptual model, completing the bottom line feedback loop in figure 11.2.

Knowledge of results (KR) represents one category of postmovement augmented feedback. KR is usually verbal (or at least verbalizable) information about the success of an action with respect to the environmental goal. In many daily activities, KR is redundant with the inherent feedback. Telling someone he missed the nail with the hammer or telling a basketball player she missed the free throw are examples of KR (the verbal information) that duplicates the information the performer received anyway. However, KR is not always redundant with inherent feedback. Surgical residents, springboard divers, and dancers must wait for the assessment scores to know the success of their performance. In riflery and archery it is not always possible to see where the projectile hit the target area, so augmented KR information must be received from a coach or a scoring device. In these cases, KR is critically important for performance and learning because, in tasks in which the inherent feedback is absent or incomplete, learners cannot know about the outcomes of their actions without some form of KR.

KR is frequently used in research, where specific aspects regarding how information is given to learners can be controlled.

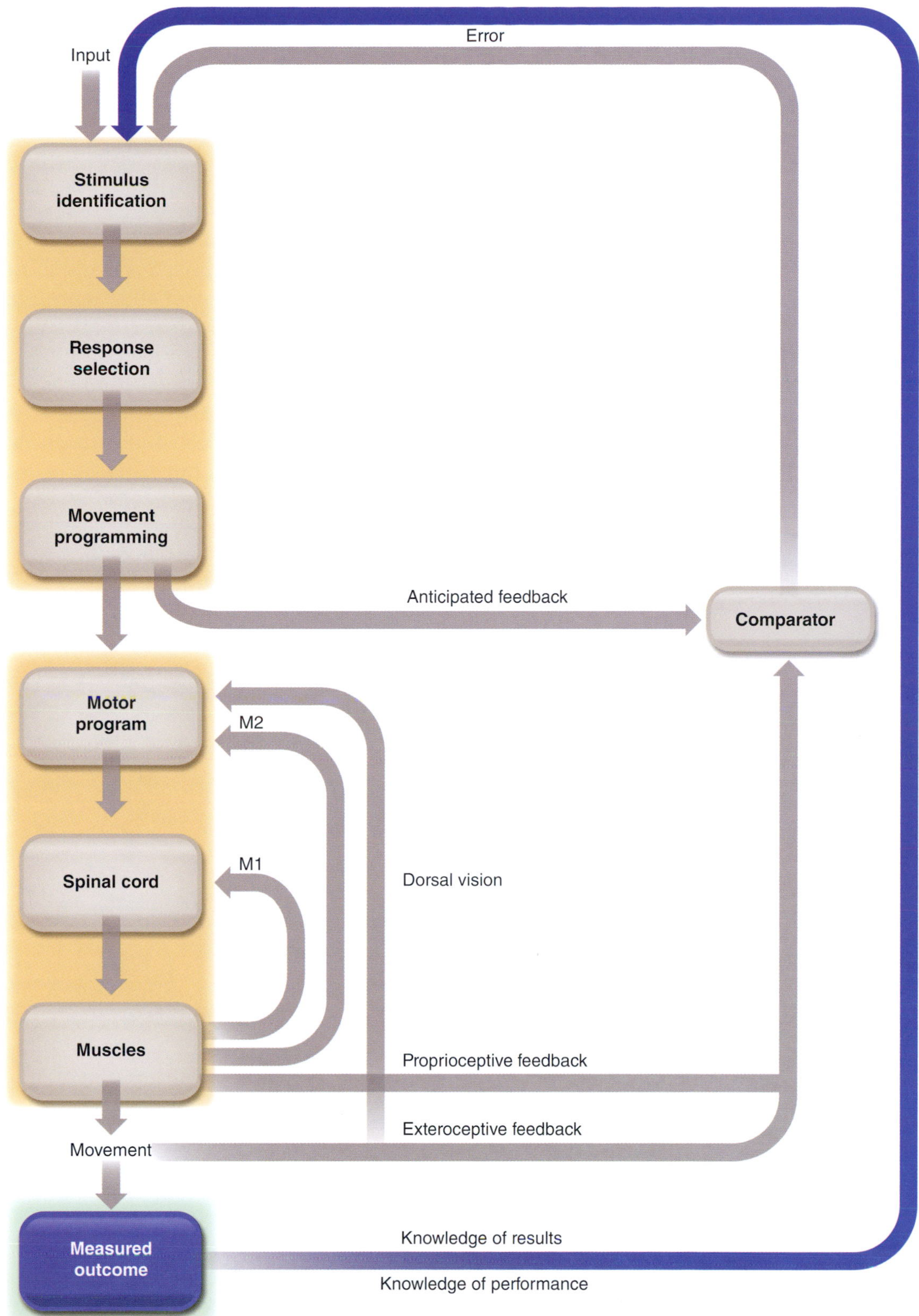

FIGURE 11.2 Conceptual model with the addition of augmented feedback.

Researchers use this general method to examine how feedback processes influence learning. Older research was often conducted with very simple tasks, such as blindfolded limb-positioning tasks, where the learners could not use the most important inherent feedback (vision). These experiments generally showed that, without any KR, there was no learning at all (e.g., Thorndike, 1927; Trowbridge & Cason, 1932). On the other hand, providing KR about errors facilitated improvements across practice that remained in retention tests even when KR was withdrawn. These results suggest that when learners cannot detect their own performance errors through inherent feedback, no learning occurs at all unless *some* form of augmented feedback is provided. This is one of the reasons that feedback is considered the single most important variable for learning except for practice itself (Bilodeau, 1966). Thus, the principle is as follows: Some information relative to goal achievement must be received, either through inherent sources or augmented sources, for learning to occur.

Knowledge of performance (KP), sometimes referred to as kinematic feedback, is augmented information about the movement the learner has just made. It is frequently used by instructors in real-world settings. For example, you often hear coaches say things like "Your tuck was not tight enough" in a springboard dive or "Your backswing was too short" in golf. These forms of KP tell the learner something about kinematics of the movement or movement pattern. Note that KP information, unlike KR, does not necessarily inform the learner about success in terms of meeting the environmental goal. Rather, kinematic feedback provides information about the nature of the movement pattern that the learner actually produced.

For a diver, augmented feedback could be provided as either KR or KP. Identify two examples of diver augmented feedback each for KR and KP.

Functions of Augmented Feedback

After a movement attempt, a music instructor says to the learner, "The rhythm was pretty good, but try to slow everything down a little next time." Think of all the meanings that such a simple statement could have to the learner. First, the feedback could have a motivating or discouraging function: It could make the learner more enthusiastic about the activity and encourage her to try harder, or it might be construed in a negative way and have a detrimental impact. Second, feedback helps to direct the learner's attention either toward the production of the movement (an internal focus of attention) or toward the effect of the movement in the environment (an external focus). Third, the feedback provides information about the rhythm and absolute timing of the movements, which can be combined with other information (e.g., how the movement felt) to generate new knowledge and take corrective actions. Finally, feedback can also produce a kind of dependency in the learner, such that performance is enhanced when feedback is present because of its influence on the next attempt but causes performance to deteriorate when it is later withdrawn.

Generally in real-world settings, augmented feedback operates in four interdependent ways simultaneously and is very difficult to separate. To summarize, augmented feedback can do these four things:

- Motivates or discourages the learner
- Directs the learner's focus of attention
- Provides information about errors to be corrected
- Creates a dependency, potentially leading to problems later

Motivational Properties

The music instructor tells the struggling piano student, "Keep it up, you're doing fine." This casual comment motivates the student to keep going a little longer in practice. Certainly, one important function of feedback is to motivate the learner, for example, in helping a tired learner to bring more effort to bear on the task. In addition, early research revealed that if performance was deteriorating (in so-called vigilance tasks), performers showed an immediate increase in proficiency, as if the feedback was acting as a kind of stimulant to energize them again (Arps, 1920). Learners who are given feedback say they like the task more, they try harder at it, and they are willing to practice longer. In short, unless it is overdone, learners seem to benefit from feedback. Even when an instructor has another primary reason for giving feedback (e.g., to correct an error), it usually has an extra motivational effect that benefits learning.

The effects of feedback as a motivating tool just discussed are primarily *indirect* in their influence. That is, KR encourages the learner to keep practicing, and the results of this additional practice are what influences learning. However, feedback can also have a *direct* motivational effect on learning. Consider the study by Chiviacowsky and Wulf (2007), for example. Learners in this study practiced a beanbag-tossing task in which vision of the end-result accuracy was obstructed, making feedback from the experimenter (KR) critical for improving performance. Participants in one group were provided with feedback about performance on their three best performances out of the previous six trials, over repeated blocks of practice. Participants in another group received information about their three worst performances over these same practice periods. When assessed later in a retention test, the group that had received KR on their best performances showed superior learning compared to the other group, suggesting that this feedback was having a positive motivational effect on learning.

The implications of positive motivational effects of augmented feedback on learning have also been investigated in other experimental paradigms by Wulf and her colleagues. For example, a study by Chiviacowsky and Wulf (2002) revealed that learners requested feedback more frequently following trials that they perceived as having been performed well, as compared to trials thought to have been

Focus on RESEARCH 11.1

How Feedback Works

Research traditions that were established in the animal-learning literature early in the 20th century strongly influenced the thinking about how feedback must work in motor learning. In one example, a food reward was given if a hungry animal pressed a lever within 5 s of hearing a tone. Over trials, the animal learned to press the lever quite reliably when the sound occurred. Your new puppy quickly learns to sit on command if you give a biscuit or a friendly pat when the puppy performs the action. In this case, the food reward is serving as feedback for correctly responding to the stimulus (to sit on command).

Scientists realized that the nature and timing of the feedback had a marked influence on learning the desired behavior. These findings were summarized by Thorndike's (1927) Law of Effect, in which feedback played a prominent role—associations (or bonds) between the stimulus and the correct behavior were presumably strengthened when reinforced by feedback. Learning was enhanced by the immediacy or frequency of such feedback presentations, presumably by strengthening these bonds. Conversely, if feedback was withheld, there could be no increment of bond strengthening for that trial, rendering that practice trial essentially useless for enhancing learning. These basic notions gave rise to the general idea that any variation of feedback during practice that makes the information more immediate, more precise, more frequent, more informationally rich, or generally more useful would be beneficial for learning, including motor learning. Such a view made good common sense—it just seems logical that giving more information to the learner should benefit learning—and this view became widely adopted as a result. The principle has strong implications for the structure of practice, encouraging just about anything that would provide more information to the learner.

As you will see throughout this chapter, however, the above generalization is probably wrong in several ways. One of the major difficulties with this principle emerged from research on the relative frequency of feedback—a key variable that defines how frequently feedback is scheduled in a learning session. Other variables, such as feedback delay, feedback summaries, and bandwidth feedback, failed to operate in ways predicted by Thorndike's views.

In the end, these early theoretical beginnings were important because they led to more research, new ideas, and a better understanding of feedback processes in motor learning. These more modern interpretations of the research constitute most of the theorizing presented in this chapter. An important review of the feedback literature by Salmoni, Schmidt, and Walter (1984) provides much more on the historical context of this work.

Exploring Further

1. Why does the typical experiment in animal conditioning provide an "extinction" period?
2. In what ways does augmented feedback in motor learning work similarly to the provision of feedback in animal conditioning studies? In what ways do the principles differ?

performed poorly. Moreover, simply having the option or control over when, how, or what feedback will be provided appears to have a beneficial effect on motor learning (e.g., Janelle et al., 1997; see review by Sanli et al., 2013). These and other findings (see chapter 10) have been summarized in a theoretical model by Wulf and Lewthwaite (2016) that further develops the motivational roles of feedback (see also chapters 11 and 12 in Schmidt et al., 2019).

Attentional-Focusing Properties

Important discussions earlier in the book addressed the role of attentional focus on performance (chapter 3) and learning (chapter 10). In most situations, it is likely that performance and learning are enhanced when the learner's attention is directed to the end-product of movement (or the effect of the movement on the environment)—typically referred to as an external focus of attention. In contrast, an attentional focus that is directed toward the movement itself (an internal focus) usually leads to poor performance and learning.

Now consider the effects of KR and KP on attentional focus. By its very nature, KR provides information about success of performance relative to the movement goal. Put differently, KR directs the learner to think about externally directed information. The informational content of KP, on the other hand, is about the nature of the movement that was produced, such as the spatial or temporal form of the action. Thus, the information content of KP directs the learner to think about movement-related information—an internally focused process.

The attentional-focusing properties of KR and KP set up the learner for a potential conflict in practice goals. Since KP is often considered to be the preferred form of augmented feedback for making changes in the kinematics and kinetics of the action itself (e.g., Newell & Walter, 1981), how can it be used without the detrimental impact of directing the learner to an internally focused attention? One solution has been to reduce the frequency of providing feedback that induces an internal focus of attention (e.g., Wulf et al., 2002). These and other issues regarding scheduling and provision of feedback are discussed in the sections that follow.

Informational Properties

Consider now the example mentioned earlier, in which the music instructor tells the student that the rhythm was fine but the speed could be slower overall. This information defines the basis for making corrections on the next attempt, bringing the performance closer to the values that characterize more-skilled performance. There is no doubt that giving information guides the learner toward the movement goal. Feedback helps the learner problem-solve the process of detecting and correcting errors while learning a more-skilled movement pattern.

Recognizing that augmented feedback has a critical informational role raises many important questions for the instructor. For example, in what form is the information best provided (e.g., verbally, in video replays, graphically), how often should it be provided (on every trial, only some trials), and when is it best provided (immediately after an action, delayed somewhat)? These questions are addressed in detail later in this chapter.

Dependency-Producing Properties

When feedback that contains information for error correction is given frequently, it tends to guide behavior toward the goal movement. In a sense, this process operates in very much the same way guidance procedures do, as we discuss later in this chapter. Physical **guidance** acts very powerfully to reduce errors, sometimes preventing them almost completely. This is fine as long as the guidance is present, but the learner can also become dependent on the guidance, allowing performance to deteriorate markedly when the guidance is removed and the learner attempts to perform without it (Salmoni, Schmidt, & Walter, 1984).

Just as with physical guidance, augmented feedback can have a powerful role in allowing the learner to correct errors quickly and thereby maintain the movement's form or outcome. The problem led to the **guidance hypothesis** (Salmoni, Schmidt, & Walter, 1984), which holds that the learner can become dependent on the augmented source of information instead of internally generated processes to keep the movement on target. If the instructor's feedback is then removed in a retention test, the performance could suffer markedly if the learner has not developed the capability to produce the movement independently. Various ways have been developed to structure feedback to minimize dependency-producing effects, as discussed in the sections that follow.

Visit the web study guide to read "The Coach as a Dictionary" and complete the self-directed learning activities.

What Feedback to Give

An instructor could give feedback about countless features of the action after every performance attempt. Thus, overloading the learner with too much information is a potential problem. Information-processing and memory capabilities are limited, so it is doubtful that the learner can take in and retain very much information during an onslaught of feedback presentations. It is also doubtful that the learner can be very effective in correcting the next action in more than one way, particularly with feedback about motor patterning. As well, providing too much feedback could lead to an abundance of thought processes during action, many leading to an internal focus of attention, as depicted in the illustration in figure 11.3. A good rule of thumb is to decide what error is most fundamental and provide feedback on that.

Precision of Feedback

Feedback about movement errors can be expressed in terms of either the direction of the error, the magnitude of the error, or both, and with varying levels of precision. The following are some of the principles involved.

Qualitative information about the direction of the learner's error (early versus late, high versus low, left versus right, and so on) is critical to bring the movement into line with the goal. In addition, it is generally helpful to report some quantitative magnitude of the errors as part of the feedback. **Precision of feedback** refers to the level of accuracy with which the feedback describes the movement or outcome. You can imagine feedback that

FIGURE 11.3 Providing more feedback than can be processed effectively can lead to an abundance of internal focus of attention thoughts during movement.

Technology has made providing video feedback to athletes easier than ever, but it is more effective when accompanied by cues to help the learner focus on the relevant details. Name two important cues that might be important to the dancer receiving feedback.

only roughly approximates the movement feature, as in learning to do partial weight bearing on crutches. Feedback such as "You put a little too much weight through your left leg that time" would be considered less precise than "You put 4.3 pounds too much weight through your left leg that time."

The level of feedback precision to provide seems to depend on the learner's skill. Early in practice, the learner's errors are so large that precise information about the exact size of the errors does not matter, simply because the learner does not have the movement-control precision to match the precision of correction specified by the feedback. By the same argument, movement control will be much more precise at higher levels of skill, so more precise feedback can be used effectively as a consequence.

Video Feedback

Knowledge of performance (KP) has a long history in motor skills research. Early pioneers in feedback methods recorded force–time tracings in sprint starts on strip-chart paper (Howell, 1956). The recordings were then displayed to the learner as KP feedback together with the correct tracing superimposed over the learner's tracing (see Tiffin & Rogers, 1943, for a very early study using similar methods with industrial tasks).

Films were also popular, particularly among professional sport teams; these were used as feedback so that a player could analyze mistakes and determine more effective actions to use next time. As learning tools, though, films were limited because the time required for developing film was usually quite long, troublesome, and costly. Videotape solved many of the problems with film: Feedback about whole performances could be viewed after only a few seconds of tape rewind, and these replays would capture the details of the movement very well. And, of course, digital imagery has taken this kind of feedback to a whole new level. Crisp, clear, high-definition videos can be recorded with a cell phone and instantly distributed to others around the world. Providing live feedback to the user has never been easier, cheaper, or more informative.

But an important question remains for all of these video forms: Is replaying a video of the performance an effective method of providing augmented feedback? Early on, Rothstein and Arnold (1976) reviewed the evidence on videotape replays and, surprisingly, found that this feedback was not always useful for learning. One explanation is that videotape replays provide *too much* information, so the learner becomes confused about what is important and what is not. This led to the suggestion that cuing, in which the instructor directs the learner to examine some particular feature of the movement as feedback, should be combined with video to enhance its effectiveness.

Kernodle and Carlton (1992) provided evidence to support Rothstein and Arnold's suggestions. Participants in each of four groups practiced a throwing task (using a lightweight foam ball, arranged so that the learner could not assess accuracy from inherent feedback) with their nondominant limb and were given retention tests for learning immediately before each of five practice sessions. One group received only KR about the distance of the throw. The other three groups all received videotape replays of their performances—one group with no additional feedback, another group with cues to direct attention to certain parts of the video, and a

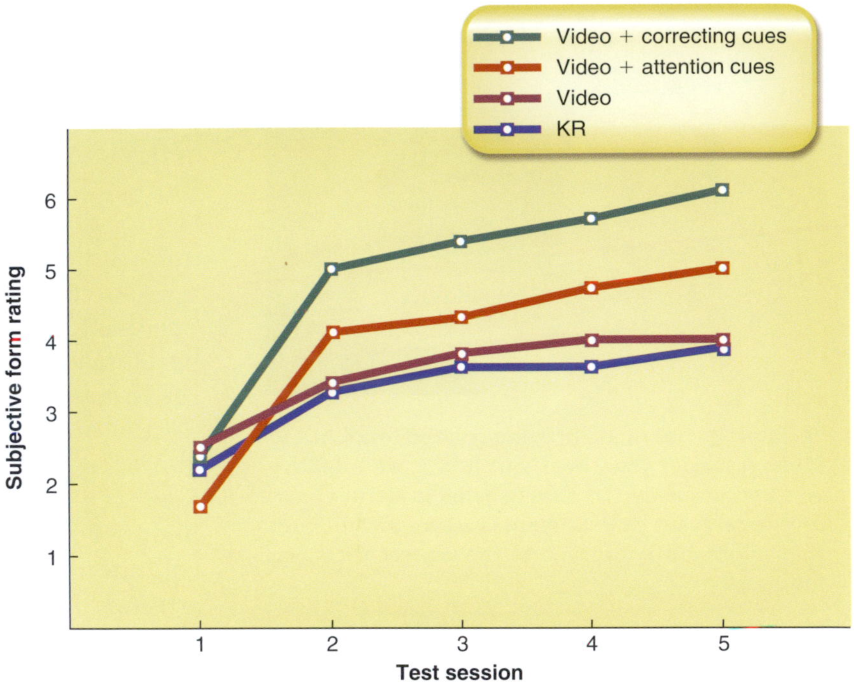

FIGURE 11.4 Providing real-time augmented feedback facilitates learning only if supplemented with additional cuing, as indicated by five retention tests conducted before practice over several days.

third group with supplemental cues indicating what changes to make on the next attempt. The results, illustrated in figure 11.4, were quite clear. Providing video feedback KP without additional information was no more effective than just providing KR. However, video feedback given with the addition of attention-directing cues, or even better, with cues about what errors to correct, was most effective for learning.

KP Versus KR?

On the surface, the question of whether to provide KP to a learner or to provide KR seems easy to answer. Since KP provides more precise information about how to change a movement pattern, it would seem to be a natural preference. However, as we have seen in previous sections, the answer is not so simple or obvious. KP can lead to an internal focus of attention, which can be a detriment to learning. And because KP is so informative, there often needs to be an expert who provides cuing in order to focus the learner to specific information in the feedback.

Some additional evidence suggests that since KP is so directed in content, it removes some of the problem-solving efforts that would otherwise be engaged by KR (Swinnen et al., 1993). For example, in learning to use a limb prosthesis in a virtual ball-throwing task, participants transferred more effectively to novel force-production tasks following KR-feedback training than after KP-feedback training (Bouwsema et al., 2014). Perhaps the information content provided by the KR in this task was sufficient to engage problem-solving analyses during practice that enabled later transfer performance. Using feedback to *assist* the learning process, without *guiding* the process, is often not revealed until learning is examined in retention or transfer tests.

How Much Feedback to Give

One of the challenges faced in education and skills instructions is the student–teacher ratio. Small student–teacher ratios (e.g., one-on-one instruction) have often been viewed as ideal because the student gains from the teacher's full attention and maximizes the amount of augmented feedback that can be delivered to the student. But, do the effects of frequent feedback last beyond the lesson into tests of learning? For very practical reasons, assessing the influence of feedback frequency should be an important consideration in designing skills-learning instruction.

Absolute and Relative Frequency of Feedback

The feedback literature has defined two general descriptors for feedback frequency. **Absolute frequency of feedback** refers to the total number of feedback presentations given to a learner across a set of trials in practice. If there are 400 trials and the instructor gives feedback on 100 of them, then the absolute frequency is 100—simply, the total number of feedback presentations. **Relative frequency of feedback**, on the other hand, refers to the percentage of trials receiving feedback. In this example, the relative frequency of feedback is 25% (100 feedback trials out of a total of 400 trials).

Consider this situation: A learner practices a task such as rifle shooting at a distant target, where errors cannot be detected without augmented feedback. Because the instructor is busy giving feedback to other students, information about the performances can be given only occasionally. We have discussed the learning benefits of the trials that actually receive feedback, but what about the trials in between that are not provided feedback? Are they useful for learning? Do these so-called blank (no-feedback) trials have any function for learning at all, or are they simply a waste of time?

Such questions about blank trials can be answered by examining the effect of relative frequency of feedback for learning. Perhaps of some surprise, research has shown that blank trials can be beneficial for learning, even though participants receive no feedback on them (Winstein & Schmidt, 1990). This can be seen in figure 11.5. Using a limb patterning task, the 100% group received feedback after every trial (100% relative frequency), and the 50% group received feedback after only half of the trials (50% relative frequency), with the same total number of trials. The groups improved at about the same rate in acquisition. However, in the tests of learning performed without any feedback, there was a strong effect for the 50% group to have learned more than the 100% group, even

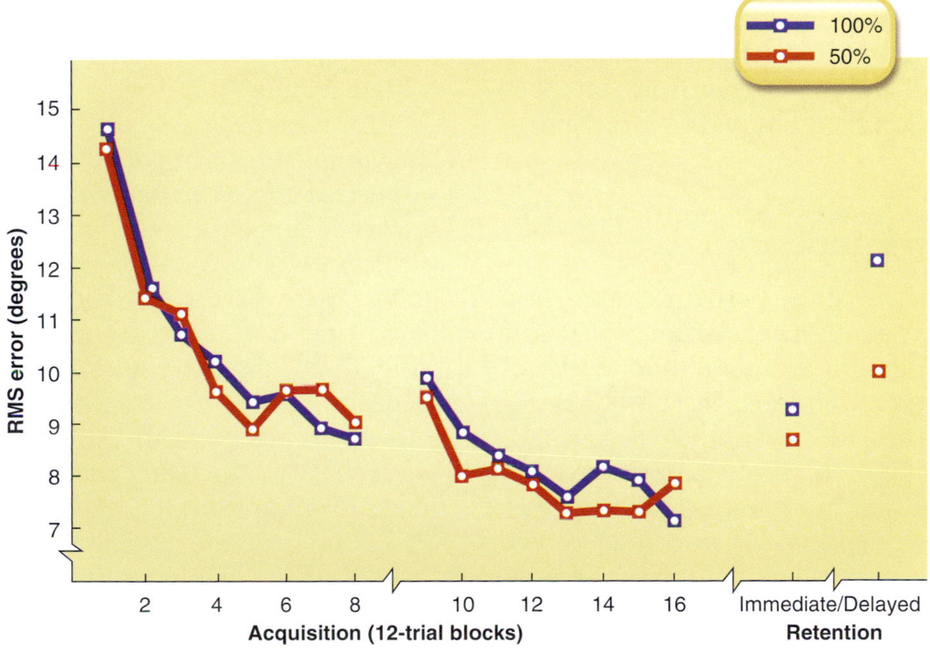

FIGURE 11.5 Reducing relative frequency of feedback from 100% to 50% during acquisition has beneficial effects on learning. RMSE = root-mean-squared error.

though half of the 50% group's trials involved no feedback.

A key feature in the Winstein and Schmidt (1990) study was that reduced feedback frequency was achieved using a **faded feedback** method. Here, the learner is given feedback at high relative frequencies (essentially 100%) in early practice, which has the effect of guiding the learner toward the movement goal. The experimenter then gradually reduces the relative frequency as skill develops such that presentation of feedback is infrequent when higher skill levels have been achieved. With advanced skill, the performance does not deteriorate much when feedback is totally withdrawn for a few trials. If performance does begin to drop off, the instructor can give feedback again for a trial or two to bring behavior back to the target, then withdraw the feedback again. The instructor can adjust feedback scheduling to the proficiency level and improvement rate of each learner separately, thus tailoring feedback to individual differences in capabilities. The ultimate goal is to generate the capability for the learner to produce the action on her own, without a dependency on feedback. Even though feedback is critical for developing the movement into a skilled pattern, it appears that it must be eventually removed to accomplish permanent skill learning. Thus the faded feedback idea is both a practical and theoretically sound method to prevent the learner from developing a feedback dependency (see also Krause et al., 2018).

Bandwidth Feedback

A method that produces both qualitative and quantitative types of information, discussed earlier, as well as the faded method of reducing the relative frequency of feedback, is known as **bandwidth feedback** (Sherwood, 1988). In this method, the decision to provide a learner with feedback is based on a preset degree of acceptability of performance. For example, if a resident is suturing a wound after a surgery, the instructing physician might say, "Good job" if the stitches were performed satisfactorily or if the time to perform the surgery was acceptable. If either the accuracy or time was not acceptable, however, the physician might provide precise feedback about the nature of the errors made and what aspects of the performance needed to be improved.

There are two general rules in using the bandwidth method (Sherwood, 1988). First, precise feedback indicating the amount and direction of the error is given only when performance falls outside a range of acceptability. Second, if performance lies within the bandwidth of acceptability, then no feedback is given—the learner being told ahead of time to interpret the absence of feedback as meaning that performance was essentially correct.

A key issue in using the bandwidth method is deciding what level of error tolerance is appropriate for a learner. A simple illustration of this concept is presented in figure 11.6. The darker orange band in the figure illustrates a narrow bandwidth (–1 to +1 mm). In this case, the learner would receive no feedback on trials 5, 8, 9, and 10 (because performance levels were inside the dark orange area). Given prior instructions, the learner would interpret the absence of feedback as meaning that those movements were essentially correct, and given precise feedback on the other trials. The lighter orange band (–2 to +2 mm) illustrates a larger bandwidth that could be used instead. Here, the learner would not be given feedback on trials 2, 3, 4, 5, 8, 9, and 10 and given precise error feedback only on trials 1, 6, and 7.

Although the size of the bandwidth seems very simplistic, its impact produces some very important effects on learning. Obviously, the tolerance levels set will have a determining influence on how frequently the learner is given precise error feedback versus indications that performance was correct. And indeed, the bandwidth size itself has an important effect on learning. For example, Sherwood (1988) found that a larger bandwidth (10% of the target goal) produced more learning than smaller bandwidths (5% or 1%). Moreover, the feedback provided by the bandwidth method (combining both error and correct types of feedback) has a larger impact on learning than comparable amounts of only error feedback frequency (Agethen & Krause, 2016; Lee & Carnahan, 1990).

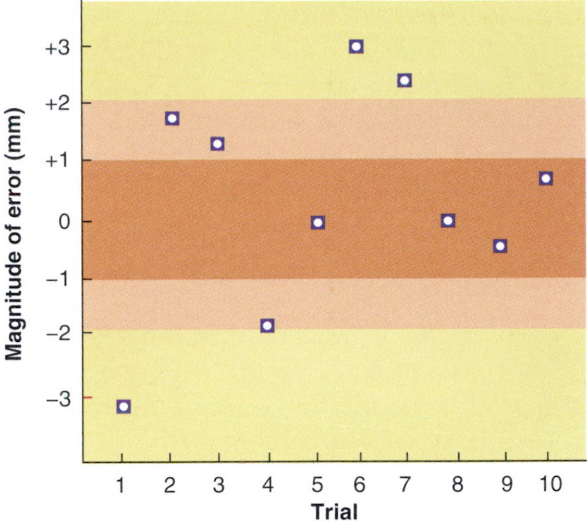

FIGURE 11.6 An illustration of the bandwidth-feedback method. Establishing a preset level of tolerance determines what type of feedback is given to the learner. Two potential bands of correctness are shown here—a narrow band (the darker orange) and a wider band (which includes both the lighter and darker orange regions). If performance falls outside of the tolerance band chosen, then and only then is error feedback given. Performance that falls within the band chosen results in no feedback, which the learner has been told beforehand to mean that performance was correct.

The effects of the bandwidth method are consistent with a number of well-established principles for learning. First, the method produces a natural way of fading the frequency of feedback (see previous section). When the learner is just beginning, the movements often tend to be outside the tolerance level, leading to frequent feedback from the instructor. As skill improves, more performances fall within the band, leading to less frequent error feedback. Therefore, the bandwidth creates a natural fading of error feedback because it is sensitive to the performance levels and progression of the individual over practice. Second, with improvements in performance (resulting in more performances inside the bandwidth), there is a decreased frequency of error feedback and an increased frequency of motivating feedback, indicating to the learner that performance had been accurate. And as we have discussed twice previously, providing learners with motivating feedback has a strong learning function. Finally, withholding information on a set of trials that fall within the bandwidth fosters more stable, consistent actions. Eliminating these small trial-to-trial corrections has a stabilizing influence on performance, because the learner is not encouraged to change the action on every trial. This seems especially important when the movement had been essentially correct on the previous attempt.

Summary Feedback

Another way to avoid the detrimental effects of too-frequent feedback is to give feedback summaries. In this method, feedback is withheld for a series of trials—say, following a series of 5 to 20 performance attempts—after which feedback for the entire series is summarized for the learner, perhaps by providing a graph of all of the previous performance attempts in that block of trials. On the surface, summary feedback would seem to be particularly ineffective for learning. The informational content of the feedback would be seriously degraded because the learner wouldn't be able to associate the feedback with any particular practice attempt, and thus would have no basis for making trial-to-trial corrections to improve performance.

But research has shown that **summary feedback** can be particularly effective for learning (e.g., Lavery, 1962; Schmidt et al., 1989). Even though summary feedback is less effective than every-trial feedback for performance during practice, when feedback was withdrawn in retention tests, participants who had received summary feedback performed more skillfully than participants who had received every-trial feedback.

How Many Trials to Summarize?

How many trials should you include in summary feedback? Can there be too many summarized trials? Evidence suggests that there may be an optimal number of trials to include in summary-feedback reports, with either too few or too many trials decreasing learning. Why? With every-trial feedback (a one-trial summary), the learner is guided strongly to the goal, but this also maximizes the dependency-producing effects. If the feedback summarizes too many trials (say 100), however, the dependency-producing effects are greatly reduced, but the learner also loses some of the error-correction benefits of directive feedback. This rationale suggests the existence of an optimal number of summary-feedback trials in which the benefits from being directed to the goal are balanced just right with costs of the dependency-producing properties.

This prediction was confirmed in experiments by Schmidt, Lange, and Young (1990) and Guadagnoli, Dornier, and Tandy (1996). These findings are important because they revealed that the optimal summary depended on a combination of learner experience and task complexity. For example, the Guadagnoli et al. retention results, illustrated in figure 11.7, revealed that larger (15-trial) summaries produced more learning than small (1-trial) summaries for experienced learners, regardless of the task complexity. However, for novice learners, large summaries produced more learning for simple tasks, but small summaries enhanced learning for complex tasks. The finding makes sense: experienced performers can gather and benefit from larger summaries regardless of the task; however, novices require smaller feedback summaries, especially for more complex tasks.

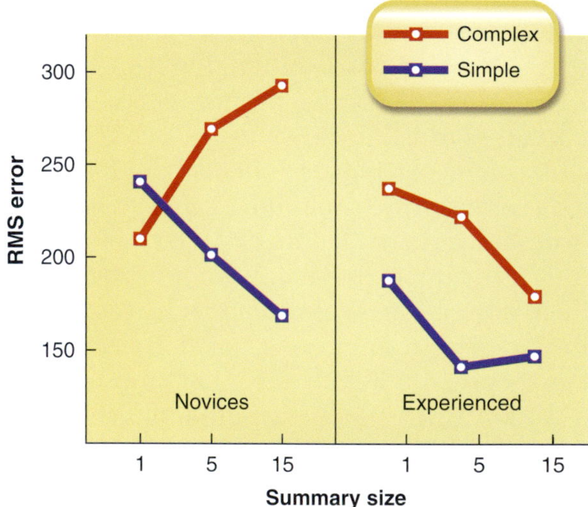

FIGURE 11.7 The optimal summary size in a study by Guadagnoli et al. (1996) was a function of learner experience and task complexity. For both simple and complex tasks, experienced learners benefited from larger summaries. However, novices only benefited from larger summaries for the simple task—the complex task was learned better when given smaller summaries.

How Does Summary Feedback Work?

What are the processes behind the benefits of summary feedback? The following are three ways summary feedback could function to aid learning:

1. Summary feedback might prevent the dependency-producing effects of frequent feedback because it causes the learner to perform independently for several trials before finally receiving feedback. Then the learner can make corrections to the general movement pattern produced in the earlier trials.
2. Summary feedback might produce more stable movements because feedback is withdrawn for several trials, giving the learner no basis for a change in the movement from trial to trial. Frequent feedback, on the other hand, more or less encourages the learner to change the movement on every trial, which prevents the movement from achieving the stability needed for subsequent performance.
3. Summary feedback appears to encourage learners to analyze their inherent movement-produced feedback (kinesthetic, visual, and so on) to learn to detect their own errors (this concept was discussed in chapter 9). Frequent feedback tells learners about errors, eliminating the need to process inherent feedback, so the learners do not need to process information about their errors, as augmented feedback provides this for them.

Average Feedback

In a variant of summary feedback called **average feedback**, the learners wait for a series of trials before receiving feedback information about their scores (as with summary feedback), but now receive only the *average* score on those trials instead of a trial-by-trial (e.g., graphical) summary. For example, the golf instructor might watch the learner make 10 swings before commenting, "Your backswing was about 6 inches too short on those last 10 shots." Results from studies by Young and Schmidt (1992) and Yao, Fischman, and Wang (1994) showed that average feedback and feedback summaries were far more effective for learning (i.e., retention) than every-trial feedback. The Yao et al. retention results, shown in figure 11.8, revealed an optimal summary size of 5 trials, with average feedback conditions (green bars) slightly more effective for learning than summary feedback conditions (red bars).

Average feedback and summary feedback might operate in the same general way—by blocking the detrimental, dependency-producing effects of every-trial feedback. Average feedback also allows the instructor to formulate a more complete idea of what the learner's error tendency happens to be. On any one attempt, many things can occur by chance alone (because performances vary greatly from trial to trial). However, by watching the learner do a number of performances, the instructor can filter out the variability (i.e., by averaging) to detect the error that a learner typically (i.e., on average) tends to make. Thus, average feedback gives the learner more reliable information about what to change, and how much to change, on the next few practice attempts.

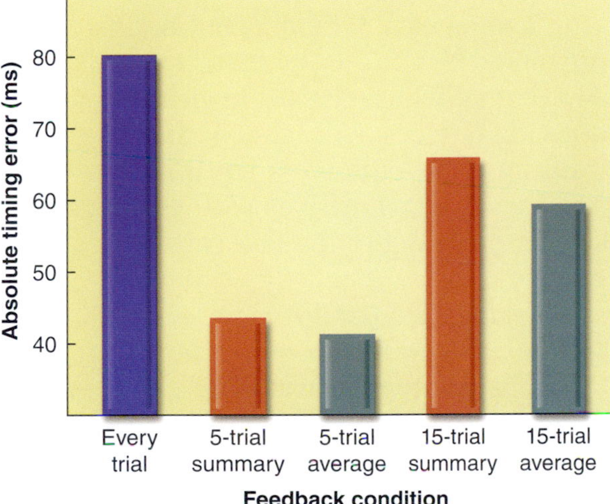

FIGURE 11.8 Retention performance (over two retention intervals) for various feedback conditions. In this study (Yao et al., 1994), average feedback conditions produced slightly better retention than summary feedback conditions, and 5-trial summary or average conditions were optimal.

Feedback Timing

Assuming that it is desirable to provide feedback about a particular performance, an important question that remains is *when* should it be given? A common myth is that immediate feedback is desirable, leading to the idea that an instructor should strive to give feedback as quickly as possible after a performance to maximize learning. As we will present in the next sections, however, that advice is undesirable for a number of reasons.

Feedback timing can be described in terms of three intervals, shown in figure 11.9. When delivered during the ongoing movement, it is typically called **concurrent feedback**. Note that *physical guidance* falls within this definition since it consists of augmented information that serves to signal errors and is provided during an ongoing movement. (As mentioned earlier, concurrent feedback is often reserved for tasks in which there is sufficient time to use the augmented feedback to correct an ongoing performance.) The interval of time after the completion of movement until feedback is presented is called the **feedback delay interval**. And the interval after the provision of feedback until the next movement starts is the **postfeedback delay** interval.

Feedback During the Movement

One of the most powerful ways to deliver feedback is to provide it while the movement is ongoing. The information can be used to regulate ongoing actions by giving a basis for correcting errors and pushing the movement closer to the action goals. Two methods

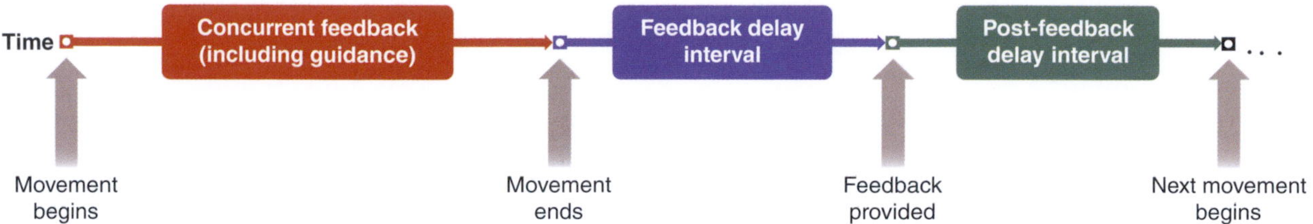

FIGURE 11.9 Terms used to describe the various times when feedback can be delivered.

are typically used to provide ongoing information: (1) concurrent feedback, in which augmented information about the movement error (or the correct movement) is provided by verbal, visual, or auditory means, and (2) physical guidance, in which haptic or kinesthetic information is signaled to the learner by means of a physically restrictive guidance device or a person (e.g., therapist) who physically restricts the movement. Despite their apparent differences, the two methods influence similar processes that govern motor learning.

Concurrent Feedback

A classic experiment, providing considerable insight into some of the processes involved in concurrent feedback, was conducted by Annett (1959). He asked participants to learn to produce a given amount of pressure against a hand-operated lever. During the movement, one group of participants received concurrent visual feedback on a display showing the amount of pressure they exerted in relation to the goal pressure. Another group received feedback after the movement. As expected, the concurrent feedback facilitated performance greatly during practice. However, in a retention test with the feedback removed, this group performed very poorly, with some participants pressing so hard that they damaged the apparatus! Participants who had learned the task with this concurrent feedback were unable to perform without it. Similar results, showing enhanced performance but poor retention, were shown in Schmidt and Wulf (1997), and as part of an important, larger study by Armstrong (1970), described in more detail below.

Physically Restrictive Guidance

Concurrent feedback, such as that provided in the studies just cited, provides information that helps the learner avoid making errors, correct errors quickly, or both. Guidance techniques often work in a more direct way—to *prevent* the learner from making errors by physical means (e.g., see Focus on Application 11.1).

Physical guidance techniques represent a large class of methods in which the learner is forced to produce the correct movement. Guidance devices have several goals; the main one is to reduce or eliminate errors and ensure that the learner performs the ideal or proper movement pattern. Another goal of guidance devices is to provide a measure of safety when the movement is dangerous, as in gymnastics, where harmful falls can be prevented by various spotting methods, or in swimming, where fearful beginners can use flotation devices. Guidance is also useful for training with expensive equipment, where mistakes can be costly as well as dangerous, as with learning to drive a car or fly an airplane.

Guidance methods vary widely across settings. Some forms of guidance are very loose, giving the learner only slight aids to performance. An example is the instructor who provides very slight hand pressure to guide the learner or talks the learner through the action. Other forms of guidance are far more powerful and invasive. An instructor can constrain the learner's movements physically, as when the physical therapist forces the patient's movements into the proper path, preventing a serious fall. Physically restrictive guidance devices are particularly

Focus on APPLICATION 11.1

Physical Guidance in Stroke Rehabilitation

The effects of acute stroke are often devastating, and many individuals who experience a stroke never fully regain the motor capability that was lost due to the brain damage. But many individuals do indeed recover. Some of this recovery is spontaneous, as the brain heals itself following the trauma. And some of the recovery can also be attributed to intense therapeutic interventions involving movement.

Physical guidance is a frequently used technique in rehabilitation and is typically based on two basic fundamental assumptions: (1) that learning is a process of repetition and (2) that repeating an optimal or correct movement pattern results in more learning than repeating a movement that is suboptimal, incorrect, or errorful. Physical guidance techniques are designed with both of these assumptions in mind. Both of these assumptions have questionable validity, though, that we'll cover in a later section.

Patients who have had a stroke often tire easily because of extreme weakness. One advantage of upper limb guidance techniques, for example, is that they can be used to move the limb for the patient (passive movement) or to support the weight of the limb at least partially so that active movement can be done with minimized effort. An advantage, therefore, is that much less fatigue occurs during a therapy session with a guidance device, and more repetitions can be performed as a result, satisfying the first principle. By this view, then, more practice should lead to more complete rehabilitation outcomes (see Barnett et al., 1973).

The second principle is more contentious. The view of optimizing learning as a process of repeating a correct or desirable movement pattern is basically an extension of Thorndike's Law of Effect (see Focus on Research 11.1). This view characterizes learning as a process of strengthening the association between a goal (e.g., to move in a certain way, correctly) and a response (e.g., actually moving correctly). For Thorndike, augmented feedback, in the form of reward, was the agent that served to increase the repetition of this association. So, in theory, physically restricting the response so that *only* the correct movement can be performed should optimize the Law of Effect.

As we discuss in this chapter, however, the evidence from studies with healthy adults suggests that physical guidance is an ineffective method of practice, for several important reasons. Moreover, the use of physical guidance as a therapy intervention in stroke rehabilitation has come under increasing criticism (Mehrholz et al., 2008; Timmermans et al., 2009). The result is that new techniques are now being devised, with the aim of maximizing the positive benefits conferred by guidance devices that provide assistance only when needed—allowing the patient to make and experience some errors in movement, but not ones that would lead to further injury (Banala et al., 2009).

---

popular in sports such as golf, where the aids constrain the movement pattern physically in several ways, with the hope that participants will memorize the ideal movement pattern.

Each method provides the learner with some kind of temporary aid during practice. The desire, of course, is that learning, as measured by performance in the future without the aid, will be enhanced. But the research suggests that while learning might be facilitated by small amounts of guidance, perhaps in the very early stages of practice, the negative impact on learning accumulates quickly (Hodges & Campagnaro, 2012).

A study by Armstrong (1970) provides an important statement about the effects of guidance and an empirical comparison of concurrent feedback and terminal feedback as well. Over three days of practice, participants learned to move a lever with elbow extension and flexion movements in order to produce a specific, timed kinematic pattern (illustrated by the blue line in figure 5.5). Performance on the three days of practice and in retention tests (with no augmented feedback) for the three experimental groups is illustrated in figure 11.10. Most of the movement error was prevented in a guidance group in which a physical restriction essentially forced the participants to produce the correct movement pattern. Movement error was not prevented entirely but was eliminated quickly in a concurrent-feedback group, whose participants were able to see the ongoing movement's kinematic trace on a computer screen, overlaid on the target template. And error was eliminated gradually over practice in a group that received terminal KP feedback after the completion of a trial. Figure 11.10 shows that, even after three days of practice, participants in the terminal-feedback group never did achieve the level of performance of the other groups. Clearly, the guidance procedure did its job, ensuring that the learners remained on target.

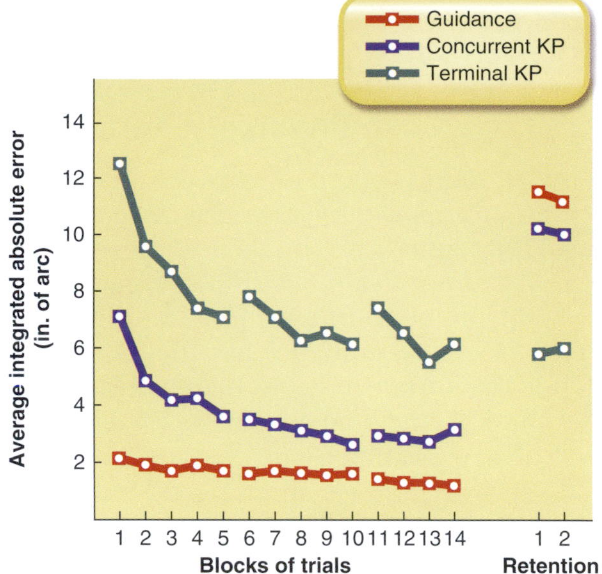

FIGURE 11.10 Effects of guidance (red), concurrent feedback (blue), and terminal feedback (green) on performance and in a no-feedback retention test.

But now consider the respective performances of these groups in a retention test, in which all groups were transferred to a test condition without the benefit of any augmented guidance or augmented feedback (far right side of figure 11.10). Several things are of interest to note here. First, the terminal-feedback group, which had been the most errorful of the three groups during practice, clearly showed the most learning as measured in these retention trials. Second, in the absence of augmented feedback, the terminal feedback group maintained the level of performance that had been achieved at the end of the practice trials. And finally, the performance of the physical-guidance group was most errorful of all in retention, showing that guidance during practice was particularly horrible for learning. Note also that both the guidance group and the concurrent-feedback group deteriorated remarkably following the removal of their respective augmented feedback. In fact, the performance of both of these groups deteriorated almost to the level of performance displayed by the terminal-feedback group on their very first block of practice, suggesting that guidance and concurrent feedback were almost completely ineffective for learning.

Visit the web study guide to read "The Golfer's Little Helper" and complete the self-directed learning activities.

If the findings on the negative effects of physical guidance were not surprising enough for some, then more recent research on the effects of **error amplification** might be. In this research, computers use restrictive-guidance devices to pull movements *away from* the intended movement goal, rather than toward it. The idea here is simple: Rather than restricting the error that can be made in performing a movement, error amplification methods serve to increase the magnitude of the error with the purpose of generating explicit, error-correction techniques by the learner. These methods are providing some provocative results that show benefits to learning that outweigh many traditional methods, and certainly, much better than error-restriction methods (reviewed in Heuer & Lüttgen, 2016), despite their unpopularity with participants (Marchal-Crespo et al., 2017). Future research in this area will be interesting to follow.

Common Processes in Concurrent Feedback and Physical Guidance

The evidence discussed in the previous sections points to an important principle. Guidance and concurrent feedback, almost by definition, are effective for performance when present during practice. After all, these augmented supplements are designed to help the performer make the correct action, to prevent errors, to aid in confidence, and so on, so there is little surprise that performance benefits from guidance. But the real test of guidance effectiveness is how well participants do when the intervention is removed, and here is where these procedures often fail. When the ongoing information source is removed for retention tests, performance usually falls to the level of, or sometimes below, that of learners who had no guidance at all. That is, guidance is not a very effective variable for learning if it is not used wisely.

How can these principles of guidance be understood? Probably the best interpretation is that, during practice where guidance is present, the learner relies too strongly on its powerful performance-enhancing properties, which actually changes the task in several ways. Physical guidance can modify the feel of the task. Decision-making processes change when the instructor or the guidance device tells the learner what to do. Also, the learner does not have the opportunity to experience errors, or to correct errors, during the guided movement or on the next movement. The learner will have failed to acquire the capability necessary to perform in a retention test or in a competition when the guidance is not present.

Notice that this interpretation is really a statement of the specificity view discussed in chapter 9. If guided practice changes the task requirements markedly (as it does), the task is not really the same task it was under the unguided conditions. If these modifications are large (as in very strong physical guidance procedures), then practice on the guided version can be thought of as involving practice on a different task rather than practice on the unguided version. Perhaps this was seen most clearly in the Armstrong (1970) study in which the guided and concurrent feedback groups' retention performance reverted to the level of the terminal KP group's first block of trials—essentially, these two groups had not practiced the task that was tested in retention.

Feedback After the Movement

The information-processing perspective about feedback holds that the learner uses feedback to correct errors. If the feedback presentation is separated in time (feedback delay) from the action and the learner forgets various aspects of the movement by the time feedback arrives, wouldn't the feedback be less useful in making corrections? In animal conditioning experiments, laboratory rats learning to press a bar after a presented tone suffer a decrement to learning from feedback delays; and, if the delay is long enough, there is no learning at all. Some researchers believed that the same would apply to humans and motor learning. But what does the evidence say?

Empty Feedback Delays

First, consider simply lengthening the time interval between a movement and its feedback, with the interval free of other attention-demanding activities (conversations, other trials, and so on). The information-processing view would expect longer intervals to interfere with learning (see the section "Short-Term Memory" in chapter 2 and figure 2.12). Yet when empty feedback delays, ranging from several seconds to several minutes, have been examined in human research, scientists have almost never found systematic effects on learning (Salmoni, Schmidt, & Walter, 1984). The lack of any degraded learning when the feedback delays are lengthened has been surprising. In any case, the evidence seems to suggest that, without other activities in the interval between a movement and its feedback, the instructor doesn't need to worry about the delay in giving feedback.

Focus on

APPLICATION 11.2

Physical Guidance in Learning to Swim

As mentioned previously, not all physical guidance is detrimental to learning. Guidance certainly plays an important role in dangerous or frightening situations; here it would be undesirable to continue practice in the absence of guidance. And guidance may also serve a useful function in the beginning stages of learning a skill. Here is an example from personal experience. When one of us (RAS) was a graduate student he was assigned to teach a course in beginning swimming. This course should have been called "Teaching the Persistent Nonswimmer to Swim," as many of these students could not swim a stroke, and many were truly terrified of the water.

After a week or so of learning to become familiar with water (e.g., in the shallow end of the pool, blowing bubbles, and so on), the next task was for the students to learn the elementary backstroke as a lifesaving stroke in case they were to fall into the water somewhere. This process involved the usual techniques (in the shallow end of the pool): learning to float on the back, gliding on the back after a push-off from the side of the pool, then adding a frog kick and eventually adding an arm stroke.

Then came the terrifying part: swimming with the elementary backstroke in the deep end of the pool. Naturally, most of the students were quite apprehensive about this task, so we developed various methods to alleviate their fear. One of these involved the use of long wooden poles. On the first attempt the instructor would walk along the poolside adjacent to the swimmer in the water just touching the pole against the swimmer's far-side hip. This did two things: First, it provided a measure of assurance for the swimmer, since all he had to do in an emergency was to grasp the pole, and the instructor could pull him to the pool edge. Second, the pole did not interfere with the swimmer's own strokes, allowing him to gain confidence and to learn the stroke unimpeded by the guide.

This method was enormously successful. By the end of the course most of the students had been weaned from the assistance of the wooden pole, and were quite capable of swimming relatively long distances (albeit very slowly). Over the course of about 10 years in which this course was taught, the average percentage of students who completed the 1 mi swim was over 70%! The look of pride on these students' faces was impossible to describe.

These were the two major keys to the success of this procedure:

- Alleviating nearly completely the learner's fear so that the student could learn the stroke
- Doing so in a very noninvasive way so that the guidance did not interfere with the actions the student was trying to produce

Instantaneous Feedback

There is one exception to this generalization about feedback delay, however—situations in which feedback is presented very soon after the completion of a movement. Under the belief that feedback given quickly will be beneficial for learning, many instructors have tried to minimize feedback delays, essentially giving feedback that is almost simultaneous with the completion of movement. Instantaneous feedback is common in many simulators, for example, such as medical mannequins, in which feedback about pressure is displayed immediately after a chest compression is performed.

Note that **instantaneous feedback** is not, technically, the same as concurrent feedback, because feedback is being delivered after the movement has finished (and often because the movement is completed too quickly for concurrent feedback to be useful). But the effects on performance and learning are remarkably similar to those for concurrent feedback. Research shows that giving feedback instantaneously, as opposed to delaying it even by a few seconds, is actually *detrimental* to learning (Swinnen et al., 1990). This can be seen in figure 11.11: Participants in the instantaneous-feedback condition (blue) performed a simulated batting task more poorly than the delayed group (red) on the second day of practice and on several retention tests given up to four months later. One interpretation is that feedback given instantaneously blocks the participant from processing inherent feedback (i.e., how the movement felt, sounded, looked), thereby restricting the learning of error-detection capabilities, as discussed in chapter 9.

Filled Feedback-Delay Intervals

When the delays are long in many real-world settings, other attention-demanding activities can occur between the completion of a given movement and the augmented feedback. These intervening activities may include conversing with a friend, practicing some other task, or even attempting other trials of the given movement as with the summary- and average-feedback methods discussed earlier in this chapter. The research findings fall into two classes, depending on the nature of the intervening task.

Intervening Activities of a Different Task

Imagine that the activity occurring between a given movement and its feedback is a different task that interferes in some way. This activity could be a trial of a different motor task or even a task involving mental operations, such as recording one's scores or giving feedback to a friend. Performing these events during the feedback-delay interval generally degrades learning as measured on retention tests (Marteniuk, 1986; Swinnen, 1990).

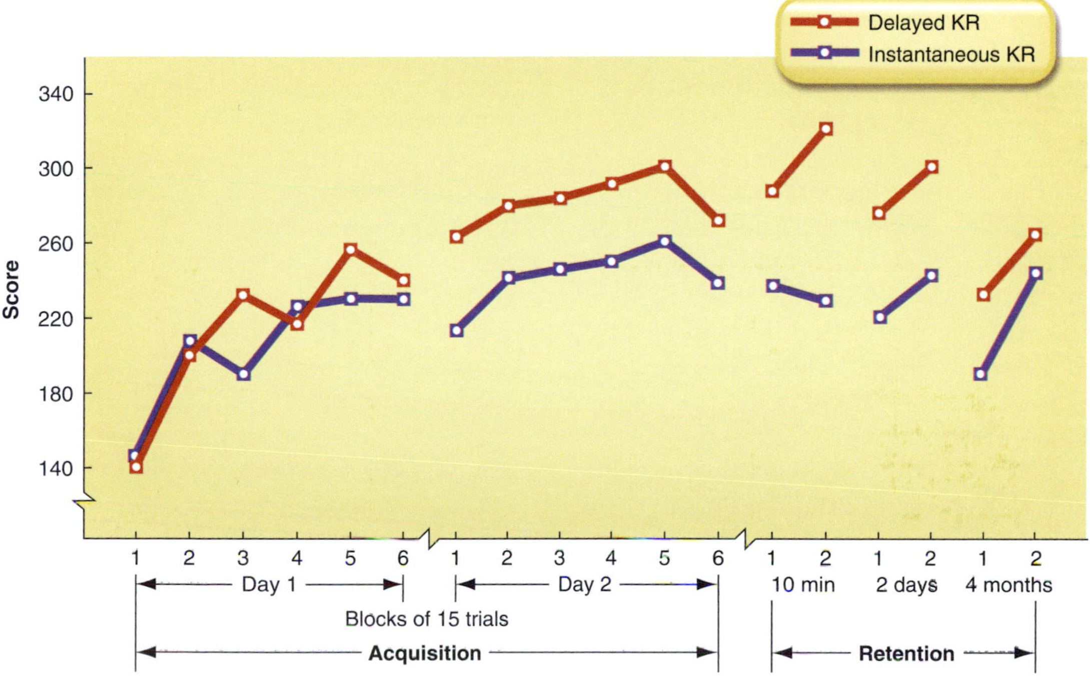

FIGURE 11.11 Instantaneous feedback degraded learning compared to delayed feedback.

Trials-Delay Technique But what if the intervening activity is just another trial of the same motor task? For example, the instructor might give the learner several minutes to practice a skill, then give feedback about the first movement after the learner has completed several more attempts in the interim. For instance, feedback from a therapist to a patient when practicing to stand from a seated position might include statements such as "On your first attempt you started to stand before your feet were properly positioned under your knees," but this is provided after several more attempts at the sit-to-stand have already been completed. This has been called **trials-delay of feedback**, with other trials of a given action intervening between the movement and its feedback.

Although the trials-delay procedure would seem to prevent the learner from associating the movement and the corresponding feedback, the evidence says that it is not detrimental at all, and it may be more effective for learning than presenting feedback after each trial (Lavery & Suddon, 1962). In fact, researchers have suggested that the performance of intervening trials before the delivery of feedback has the effect of raising awareness of the inherent feedback available after performing the task, perhaps making it more important or valuable when it is then presented to the learner (Anderson et al., 2005).

Intervening Subjective Estimations The conclusions of Anderson and colleagues (2005) just discussed support a view that learning is enhanced when processing of the inherent feedback occurs before augmented feedback is provided. This idea has been examined more directly in studies that promoted subjective estimation of task performance during the KR-delay period. For example, learners who practiced a throwing task with their nondominant limb performed more skillfully in retention tests if they made subjective estimates of their throwing technique during practice (Liu & Wrisberg, 1997). A study by Guadagnoli and Kohl (2001) further revealed the impact of making subjective estimations. They found that the

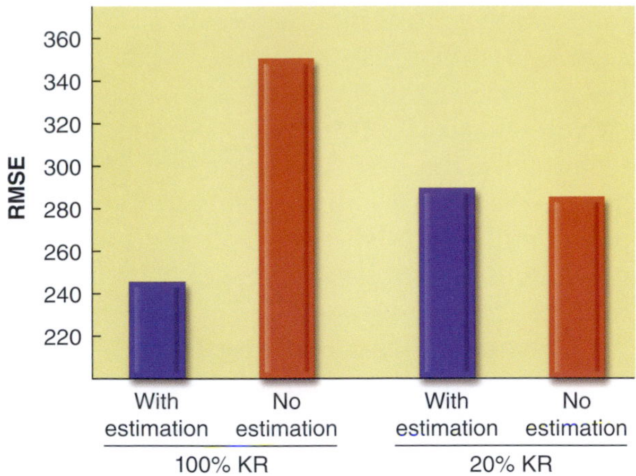

FIGURE 11.12 The negative effects of presenting feedback on every trial (100% KR) were reversed in retention when participants performed an error-estimation procedure. There were no effects on groups that received only 20% relative feedback. RMSE = root-mean-square-error (see chapter 1).

negative effects of 100% KR frequency (see earlier discussion) were eliminated in retention if learners had made subjective estimates of error before the delivery of the feedback on each trial (see figure 11.12). In contrast, the benefit of reduced relative frequency of feedback was not further enhanced from error estimation, perhaps because this 20% group was estimating spontaneously on the no-feedback trials.

Together with the results of the trials-delay studies, these subject-estimation findings support a strong role for processing inherent feedback information that leads, of course, to a score estimation. It is important to remember that retention tests in all of these studies were performed without augmented feedback. Thus, the only information that a learner could use to check on performance accuracy in retention was the inherent sources of feedback that were always available. Conditions of practice that encourage a more thorough appreciation and use of the information provided by inherent feedback promote learning. These conditions are suited to performance in both (1) these no-augmented-feedback tests and (2) most real-world applications of these ideas.

Postfeedback Delay Intervals

After receiving feedback for one movement, in the postfeedback delay (see figure 11.9) the learner attempts to create another movement that is at least somewhat different from the previous one—a movement that will eliminate the errors signaled by feedback. How much time is required for processing this information, and how soon can the next movement begin? The research on these questions shows that if this interval is too short (less than 5 s), performance on the next trial will suffer, probably because of insufficient time for evaluation and planning. Overall, though, the postfeedback interval is not particularly powerful in determining learning, and you can focus on more important aspects of the learning environment.

Summary

A learner can receive various kinds of sensory information, but augmented feedback about errors from the instructor is one of the most critical aspects of the learning environment. This kind of information can have several simultaneous roles: It can serve as a motivator; it can influence where the focus of attention is directed; it can provide information about errors and how to correct them; and it can produce a learner dependency, in which case performance suffers when the information is withdrawn. Feedback can take on many forms, such as videos and verbal descriptions. Verbal feedback is best when it is simple and refers to only one movement feature at a time, a movement feature that the learner can control.

Augmented feedback can be provided at various time periods relative to the performance—before, during, and after a movement. A number of feedback-related factors have strong influences on learning, such as feedback frequency (including bandwidth and summary procedures) as well as guidance and concurrent feedback effects. An early principle that anything making feedback more frequent, accurate, and useful will enhance learning has been found to be false and has been replaced by newer viewpoints that focus on the feedback's nature, scheduling, and motivational properties.

WEB STUDY GUIDE ACTIVITIES

The student web study guide offers these activities to help you build and apply your knowledge of the concepts in this chapter.

Interactive Learning

Activity 11.1: Review the types of feedback by matching each with its definition.

Activity 11.2: Given examples of feedback, determine whether each represents knowledge of results or knowledge of performance.

Activity 11.3: Answer a series of questions that will help you understand the effects of concurrent feedback and physical guidance.

Activity 11.4: Tie together concepts discussed throughout the textbook by selecting labels to complete a conceptual model of motor performance.

Principles-to-Application Exercise

Activity 11.5: The principles-to-application exercise for this chapter prompts you to choose an activity and a learner along with an aspect of the learner's current performance. You will then create a strategy for providing feedback to that learner in the most beneficial way possible.

Motor Control in Everyday Actions Narratives

The Coach as a Dictionary

The Golfer's Little Helper

Check Your Understanding

1. Define inherent and augmented feedback, highlighting the differences between them. Define knowledge of results and knowledge of performance, highlighting the differences between them. Provide an example of each of these types of feedback that a beginner watercolor artist might experience.
2. Briefly explain how each of the following can affect learning:
   - Frequency of feedback
   - Precision of feedback
   - Feedback schedules
   - Timing of feedback presentation
3. List and briefly discuss four properties of augmented feedback.

Apply Your Knowledge

1. A university wrestling coach is teaching his team some new ways to finish a takedown. One wrestler has been competing for 10 years and is the current national champion, while another is in her first year of university and has much less experience. Discuss some factors that the coach might consider when providing feedback to each of the wrestlers. Explain how the coach might provide feedback in order to benefit learning of the new skills and transfer to a wrestling match.
2. A physical education teacher is beginning a new unit, teaching the game of goalball to her high school class. (In the game of goalball each player is blindfolded, and the ball used for play emits an auditory signal.) Discuss three types of augmented feedback the teacher can use to provide feedback to the students during the class. Would the amount, precision, and frequency of feedback change from her earlier unit teaching handball? If so, how would it change?

Suggestions for Further Reading

A thorough review of the published research on feedback and motor learning by Salmoni, Schmidt, and Walter (1984) offers fuller details of the principles discussed here. The OPTIMAL theory of motor learning by Wulf and Lewthwaite (2016) provides an outstanding review of the motivational impact of augmented feedback on learning. An excellent review of the guidance research was written by Hodges and Campagnaro (2012). An important early review on videotape replays for motor learning was presented by Rothstein and Arnold (1976) and remains relevant today. And chapter 12 of Schmidt and Lee (2011) provides more detail on each of the sections presented in this chapter. See the reference list for these additional resources.

Glossary

ability—A stable, enduring, mainly genetically-defined trait that underlies skilled performance, is largely inherited, and is not modifiable by practice.

absolute constant error (|CE|)—The absolute value of CE for a participant; a measure of amount of bias without respect to its direction.

absolute error (AE)—The average absolute deviation of each of a set of scores from a target value; a measure of overall error.

absolute frequency of feedback—The actual number of feedback presentations given in a series of practice trials.

Adams (closed-loop) theory—A theory of motor learning proposed by Adams (1971), focusing heavily on the learning of slow positioning movements.

amplitude—The distance between the two target centers in aiming tasks ("A" in Fitts' Law).

anti-phase—A coordination timing pattern in which two movement components oscillate in opposition (180° relative phase).

arousal—An internal state of alertness or excitement.

attention—A limited capacity or set of capacities to process information.

augmented feedback—Information from the measured performance outcome that is fed back to the learner by some artificial means; sometimes called extrinsic feedback.

automatic processing—A mode of information processing that is fast, is done in parallel, is not attention demanding, and is often involuntary.

autonomous stage—The third of three stages of learning proposed by Fitts, in which the attention demands of performing a task have been greatly reduced.

average feedback—A type of augmented feedback that presents a statistical average of two or more trials, rather than results on any one of them.

bandwidth feedback—A procedure for delivering feedback in which errors are signaled only if they fall outside some range of correctness.

blindsight—A medical condition in which the patient can respond to certain visual stimuli while being judged legally blind by other criteria.

blocked practice—A schedule in which many trials on a single task are practiced consecutively; sometimes called drilled or repetitive practice, or low contextual interference.

capability—The internal representation of skill, acquired during practice, that supports performance on some task.

central pattern generator (CPG)—A centrally located control mechanism that produces mainly genetically defined actions such as walking.

choice reaction time—A variation in RT procedure in which the performer, when a particular stimulus is given, must choose one response (the "correct" response) from a number of possible predetermined responses; the temporal interval between the presentation of a given stimulus and the start of its associated response.

choking—Scenario in which a performer changes a normal routine or fails to adapt to a changing situation, resulting in a failed performance.

closed-loop control system—A type of system control involving feedback, error detection, and error correction that is applicable to maintaining a system goal.

closed skill—A skill for which the environment is stable and predictable, allowing advance organization of movement.

cocktail-party effect—A phenomenon of attention in which humans can attend to a single conversation at a noisy gathering, neglecting most (but not all) other inputs.

cognitive stage of learning—The first of three stages of learning proposed by Fitts, in which the learners' performances are heavily based on cognitive or verbal processes.

comparator—A component of closed-loop control that compares anticipated feedback with actual feedback, finally outputting an error signal.

concurrent feedback—Augmented (usually continuous) feedback that is presented simultaneously with an ongoing action.

constant error (CE)—The signed difference of a score on a given trial from a target value; a measure of bias for that trial.

constant practice—A practice sequence in which only a single variation of a given class of tasks is experienced.

constrained action hypothesis—An explanation of focus of attention effects that attributes an internal focus to conscious movement control and external focus to automated movement control.

constraints—Features that contain or act as boundaries to performance.

constraints-led approach—A view of motor learning as a problem-solving process involving the interaction of organismic, task, and environmental constraints.

contextual interference—The interference in performance and learning that arises from performing one task in the context of other tasks; blocked practice has low contextual interference, and random or (interleaved) practice has high contextual interference.

contextual-interference effect—The finding that groups of participants who practice under high contextual interference (random practice) do not perform well relative to low contextual interference participants (blocked practice) during acquisition, but outperform blocked-practice participants when evaluated in retention and transfer tests.

continuous skill—A task in which the action is performed without any recognizable beginning or end.

control parameter—A variable that when altered can lead to a change in coordination patterns.

controlled processing—A mode of information processing that is relatively slow, serial, attention demanding, and voluntary.

coordination—How individual degrees of freedom interact to produce movement.

coordination dynamics—The study of movement systems as they interact with the environment over time.

correlation coefficient *(r)*—A statistical method that evaluates the strength of a relationship between two variables; it does not imply causality.

criterion task—The ultimate version, condition, or situation in which the skill learned in practice is to be applied; the ultimate goal of practice.

cutaneous receptor—A receptor located in the skin that provides inherent information about touch (haptic sensations).

deafferentation—A surgical procedure that involves cutting one or more of an animal's dorsal roots, preventing nerve impulses from the periphery from traveling to the spinal cord.

degrees of freedom—The collection of separate movements of a system that need to be controlled.

degrees of freedom problem—The problem of explaining how a movement with many degrees of freedom is controlled or coordinated.

deliberate practice—The type of practice that is effortful and conducted specifically for the purpose of improving skilled performance.

demonstration—Performance of a skill by an instructor (or a model) to facilitate observational learning.

differential method—A method of understanding behavior by focusing on individual differences and abilities.

discrete skill—A task that has a recognizable beginning and end; usually brief in duration.

distributed practice—A practice schedule in which the duration of rest between practice trials is "relatively long"; the time in practice is often less than the time at rest.

dorsal stream—Visual information, used specifically for the control of movement within the visual environment, that is sent from the eye to the posterior parietal cortex.

double stimulation paradigm—A method for studying information processing in which a given stimulus (leading to one response) is followed closely by a second stimulus (leading to another response).

effective target width (W_e)—The amount of spread, or variability, of movement end points about a target in an aiming task; represents the performer's "effective" target size; the within-participant standard deviation of the movement distances for a set of trials.

elaboration hypothesis—The idea that frequent switching among tasks (e.g., in random practice) renders the tasks more distinct from each other and more meaningful, resulting in stronger memory representations; one explanation of the contextual-interference effect.

error amplification—A technique in which a guidance device amplifies the error made during movement production.

error-detection capability—The learned capability to detect one's own errors through analyzing inherent feedback.

especial skills—A specific representation for one skill (e.g., free throw in basketball) within a broader class of skills (e.g., set shots in basketball).

experimental method—A method of understanding behavior emphasizing common principles among people and through the use of experiments.

external focus of attention—Attention directed outside the body to an object or environmental goal.

exteroception—Sensory information arising primarily from outside the body.

extrinsic feedback—See *augmented feedback*.

faded feedback—The practice in delivering feedback whereby the frequency of feedback is decreased systematically across trials.

faded frequency—A feedback schedule in which the relative frequency is high in early practice and reduced in later practice.

false-negative normative feedback—An experimental procedure in which learners are (mis)informed that their performance is less skilled than that of others.

false-positive normative feedback—An experimental procedure in which learners are (mis) informed that their performance on some task is more skilled than that of others.

far transfer—Transfer of learning from one task to another, very different task or setting.

feedback—Information provided to the learner about the action just made; often synonymous with augmented feedback.

feedback delay interval—The interval of time from the end of the movement until the feedback is presented.

feedforward—Anticipated sensory consequences of movement that should occur if the movement is correct.

Fitts' Law—The principle that movement time in aiming tasks is linearly related to the $\text{Log}_2(2A/W)$, where $A = \text{amplitude}$ and $W = \text{target width}$.

fixation (associative) stage—The second of three stages of learning proposed by Fitts, in which learners establish motor patterns.

foreperiod—In a reaction time task, the interval of time between a warning signal and a stimulus to respond.

forgetting—The loss of an acquired capability for responding; loss of memory.

forgetting hypothesis—The hypothesis that frequent task switching in random practice causes forgetting of the planning done on the previous trials, therefore leading to more next-trial planning and resulting in stronger memory representations; a hypothesis to explain the contextual-interference effect.

gearshift analogy—A model regarding the learning of motor programs using the analogy of learning to shift gears in a standard-transmission automobile.

generalized motor program (GMP)—A motor program whose output can vary along certain dimensions to produce novelty and generalizability in movement.

general motor ability—An older, incorrect view in which a single, general ability was thought to underlie individual differences in motor behavior; sometimes called motor educability.

goal setting—A motivational procedure in which the learner is encouraged to set personal performance goals during practice.

Golgi tendon organs—Small stretch receptors located in the tendons that provide precise information about muscle tension.

guidance—A procedure used in practice in which the learner is physically or verbally directed through the performance in order to minimize errors during performance.

guidance hypothesis—A view emphasizing the guidance properties of augmented feedback, which promotes effective performance when it is present but has dependency-producing (guidance-like) effects on retention tests of learning.

Hick's Law—The mathematical descriptor showing a linear relationship between choice reaction time and the logarithm (to the base 2) of the number of stimulus–response alternatives.

hypervigilance—A heightened state of arousal that leads to ineffective decision making and poor performance; panic.

inattentional blindness—A failure to perceive objects in the visual environment when attention is directed to other objects or events.

index of difficulty (ID)—The theoretical "difficulty" of a movement in the Fitts tapping task, or $\text{ID} = \text{Log}_2(2A/W)$, where A is target amplitude and W is target width.

individual differences—Stable, enduring differences among people in terms of some measurable characteristic or performance of some task (e.g., reaction time).

information-processing approach—Approaches to the study of behavior that treat the human as a processor of information, focusing on storage, coding, retrieval, and transformation of information.

inherent feedback—Information provided as a natural consequence of making an action; sometimes called intrinsic feedback.

in-phase—A coordination timing pattern in which two movement components oscillate in synchrony (0° relative phase).

instantaneous feedback—Augmented feedback delivered immediately after completion of movement (with no delay).

internal focus of attention—Attention directed to locations inside the body, or to motor or sensory information.

invariant feature—A feature of a class of movements that remains constant, or invariant, while surface features change (e.g., relative timing).

inverted-U principle—The principle that increased arousal improves performance only to a point, with degraded performance as arousal is increased further.

ironic effects—The tendency to do exactly what you consciously intend *not* to do.

joint receptors—Sensory receptors located in the joint capsule that provide information about joint position.

knowledge of performance (KP)—Augmented information about the movement pattern the learner has just made; sometimes referred to as kinematic feedback.

knowledge of results (KR)—Augmented verbal (or at least verbalizable) information fed back to the learner about the success of an action with respect to the environmental goal.

lead-up activities—Special tasks designed to be learned before the practice of a more complicated or dangerous criterion task.

learner-determined feedback—A schedule in which the provision of feedback is determined by the learner.

learning curves—A label sometimes applied to a performance curve (a plot of average performance against trials), in the mistaken belief that the changes in performance mirror changes in learning.

long-term memory (LTM)—A virtually limitless memory store for information, facts, concepts, and relationships; presumably storage for movement programs.

"looked-but-failed-to-see" accidents—Traffic accidents in which the driver looked at, but failed to notice (to see) the presence of a cyclist or pedestrian; believed to be related to inattention blindness.

M1 response—The monosynaptic stretch reflex, with a latency of 30 to 50 ms.

M2 response—The polysynaptic, or functional, stretch reflex, with a latency of 50 to 80 ms.

M3 response—The voluntary reaction-time response to a stimulus, with a latency of 120 to 180 ms.

massed practice—A practice schedule in which the amount of rest between practice trials is relatively short (often less than the time for a trial).

mental practice—A practice procedure in which the learner imagines successful action without overt physical practice.

modeling—A practice procedure in which another person demonstrates the skills to be learned.

motor learning—A set of internal processes associated with practice or experience leading to relatively permanent gains in the capability for skilled performance.

motor program—A prestructured set of movement commands that defines the essential details of skilled action, with minimal (or no) involvement of sensory feedback.

movement programming—The third stage of information processing in which the motor system is readied for the planned action.

movement time (MT)—The interval from the initiation of a movement until its termination.

muscle spindle—Structure located in parallel with muscle fibers that provides information about muscle length.

near transfer—Transfer of learning from one task or setting to another that is very similar.

novelty problem—The concern that simple theories cannot account for the production of novel, unpracticed movements.

observational learning—The process by which the learner acquires the capability for action by observing model demonstrations.

open-loop control—A type of system control in which instructions for the effector system are determined in advance and run off without feedback.

open skill—A skill for which the environment is unpredictable or unstable, preventing advance organization of movement.

optical array—The collection of rays of light that are reflected from objects in the visual environment.

optical flow—The change in patterns of light rays from the environment as they "flow" over the retina during continuous movement of the eye through the environment, allowing perception of motion, position, and timing.

parameterized—The process whereby parameters are supplied to the generalized motor program to define its surface features.

parameters—Values applied to a generalized motor program that determine a movement's surface features, such as speed, amplitude, or limb used.

part practice—A procedure in which a complex skill is broken down into parts that are practiced separately.

perceptual narrowing—The tendency for the perceptual field to "shrink"; sometimes called tunnel vision, or "weapon focus" in police work.

performance curve—Graphs of average performance for an individual or a group plotted against practice trials; sometimes incorrectly called a learning curve.

physical fidelity—The degree to which the surface features of a simulation and the criterion task are identical.

population stereotypes—Habitual stimulus–response relationships that dominate behavior due to specific cultural learning.

postfeedback delay—The interval of time between the presentation of augmented feedback and the start of the next movement.

precision of feedback—The level of precision with which augmented feedback describes the movement or outcome produced.

prediction—The process of using people's abilities to estimate their probable success in various situations.

probe-task technique—A method that uses an RT task as a secondary task during the performance of a primary, criterion task to assess the attention demands of the criterion task.

proprioception—Sensory information arising from within the body, resulting in the sense of position and movement; sometimes called kinesthesis.

psychological fidelity—The degree to which the behaviors produced in a simulator are identical to the behaviors required by the criterion task.

psychological refractory period (PRP)—The delay in responding to the second of two closely spaced stimuli.

quiet-eye effect—The period of time when a performer fixates the eyes on a target just before movement onset.

random (or interleaved) practice—A schedule in which practice trials on several different tasks are mixed, or interleaved, across the practice period; also called high contextual interference.

reaction time (RT)—The interval from presentation of an unanticipated stimulus until the beginning of the response.

reflex-reversal phenomenon—The phenomenon by which a given stimulus can produce two different reflexive responses depending on the function of the limb in a movement.

relative-age effect—Phenomenon in which members of an age-normative group who are born early in a given year are "relatively older" than participants born late in the year.

relative frequency of feedback—The proportion of trials during practice on which feedback is given; absolute frequency divided by the number of trials.

relative phase—A measure of coordination that describes the motor behavior of two oscillating limbs or objects.

relative timing—The temporal structure or rhythm of action; the durations of various segments of an action divided by the total movement time.

repetition—A type of ineffective practice in which a movement is repeated again and again.

response selection—The second stage of information processing in which the system selects a response from a number of alternatives.

response time—The sum of reaction time plus movement time; sometimes called total time.

retention test—A performance test on a given task provided after a retention interval without practice; sometimes called a transfer test.

root-mean-square error (RMSE)—The square root of the average squared deviations of a set of values from a target value; typically used as a measure of overall tracking proficiency.

schema—A learned rule relating the outcomes of members of a class of actions to the parameters that were used to produce those outcomes.

schema theory—A theory of motor control and learning based on generalized motor programs and schemata.

Schmidt's Law—The principle that effective target width (W_e) in rapid aiming tasks is linearly related to movement velocity (A/MT), where A = amplitude and MT = movement time.

self-organization—A view that describes motor control as emerging from the interaction of the components of the movement system and the environment.

self-regulation—Technique used in motor learning studies in which the learners determine how to schedule practice or feedback or some other aspect of scheduling.

sensory neuropathy—A medical condition in patients who are unable to process and respond to most of their own sensory feedback.

serial skill—A task composed of several discrete actions strung together, often with the order of actions being critical for success.

set—A collection of psychological activities or adjustments that underlie performance but that can be "lost" after a rest.

short-term memory (STM)—A memory store with a capacity of about seven elements, capable of holding information briefly (perhaps up to 30 s); sometimes called "working memory."

short-term sensory store (STSS)—A functionally limitless memory store for holding literal, sensory information from the various senses very briefly (for only about 1 s).

simple RT—A reaction-time situation in which there is only one possible stimulus and one response.

simulator—A training device that mimics various features of some real-world task.

skill—The capability to bring about an end result with maximum certainty, minimum energy, or minimum time; task proficiency that can be modified by practice.

spatial anticipation—The anticipation of which of several possible stimuli will occur; sometimes called event anticipation.

specificity hypothesis—The hypothesis that individual differences are based on many independent abilities.

specificity of learning—A view that what you practice is what you learn.

speed–accuracy trade-off—The tendency for accuracy to decrease as the movement speed or velocity of a movement increases and vice versa.

startle RT—A rapid (<100 ms latency) reaction to an unexpected, often very strong, stimulus; used to study the involuntary release of motor programs.

stimulus identification—The first stage of information processing in which a stimulus is recognized and identified.

stimulus-onset asynchrony (SOA)—The interval between the onsets of the two stimuli in a double-stimulation paradigm; sometimes called the interstimulus interval (ISI).

stimulus–response (S-R) compatibility—The degree of "naturalness" (or directness) between the stimulus and the response assigned to it.

storage problem—The concern that simple program theories would require an almost limitless storage capacity for nearly countless different movements.

summary feedback—Information about the effectiveness of performance on a series of trials that is presented only after the series has been completed.

surface feature—An easily changeable aspect of a movement, such as movement time or amplitude, that does not affect the "deep structure" (the invariant features).

sustained attention—Maintenance of attention over long periods of work, such as monitoring a radar-based aircraft detection device; sometimes called vigilance.

Tau (τ)—A variable providing optical information about time-to-contact; the size of the retinal image divided by the rate of change of the image.

temporal anticipation—The anticipation of when a given stimulus will arrive or when a movement is to be made.

tracking—A class of tasks in which a moving track must be followed, typically by movements of a manual control.

transfer of learning—The gain or the loss in proficiency on one task as a result of practice or experience on another task.

transfer test—A performance test in which the task or task conditions have changed; often provided after a retention interval without practice.

trials-delay of feedback—A procedure in which the presentation of feedback for a movement is delayed; during the delay the learner practices one or more other trials of the same task.

triggered reactions—Coordinated, learned reactions to perturbations that are manifest in large segments of the body; the triggered reaction has a latency shorter than RT yet longer than the long-loop reflex (50 to 80 ms).

unintended acceleration—Sudden, uncommanded, violent acceleration of a vehicle accompanied by the perception of a loss of braking effectiveness.

variable error (VE)—The standard deviation of a set of scores about the participant's own average (CE) score; a measure of movement (in)consistency.

variable practice—A schedule of practice in which many variations of a class of actions are practiced.

ventral stream—Information useful for the identification of an object that is sent to the inferotemporal cortex.

vestibular apparatus—Receptors in the inner ear that are sensitive to the orientation of the head with respect to gravity, to rotation of the head, and to balance.

warm-up decrement—Temporary worsening of performance that is brought on by the passage of time away from a task and that is eliminated quickly when the performer begins again.

whole practice—A procedure in which a skill is practiced in its entirety, without separation into its parts.

width—The size of a target in aiming tasks ("W" in Fitts' Law).

yoking—A type of control procedure in which a practice schedule is determined by (and matched to) a learner in a different experimental group or condition.

References

Abbs, J.H., Gracco, V.L., & Cole, K.J. (1984). Control of multimovement coordination: Sensorimotor mechanisms in speech motor programming. *Journal of Motor Behavior, 16,* 195–232.

Abernethy, B., Farrow, D., Gorman, A., & Mann, D. (2012). Anticipatory behavior and expert performance. In N.J. Hodges & A.M. Williams (Eds.), *Skill acquisition in sport: Research, theory, and practice* (2nd ed.) (pp. 287–305). London, UK: Routledge.

Abernethy, B., & Wood, J.M. (2001). Do generalized visual training programmes for sport really work? An experimental investigation. *Journal of Sports Sciences, 19,* 203–222.

Adams, J.A. (1953). *The prediction of performance at advanced stages of training on a complex psychomotor task.* Res. Bull. 5349. Lackland Air Force Base, TX: Human Resources Research Center.

Adams, J.A. (1956). *An evaluation of test items measuring motor abilities.* Research Rep. AFP-TRCTN5655. Lackland Air Force Base, TX: Human Resources Research Center.

Adams, J.A. (1961). The second facet of forgetting: A review of warmup decrement. *Psychological Bulletin, 58,* 257–273.

Adams, J.A. (1971). A closed-loop theory of motor learning. *Journal of Motor Behavior, 3,* 111–150.

Adams, J.A. (1976). *Learning and memory: An introduction.* Homewood, IL: Dorsey.

Adams, J.A. (1987). Historical review and appraisal of research on the learning, retention, and transfer of human motor skills. *Psychological Bulletin, 101,* 41–74.

Adams, J.A., & Dijkstra, S. (1966). Short-term memory for motor responses. *Journal of Experimental Psychology, 71,* 314–318.

Agethen, M., & Krause, D. (2016). Effects of bandwidth feedback on the automatization of an arm movement sequence. *Human Movement Science, 45,* 71–83.

Ahmad, N., Szymkowiak, A., & Campbell, P.A. (2013). Keystroke dynamics in the pre-touchscreen era. *Frontiers in Human Neuroscience, 7,* 835. doi: 10.3389/fnhum.2013.00835.

Alexander, R.M. (2003). *Principles of animal locomotion.* Princeton, NJ: Princeton University Press.

Allard, F., & Burnett, N. (1985). Skill in sport. *Canadian Journal of Psychology, 39,* 294–312.

Ammons, R.B., Farr, R.G., Block, E., Neumann, E., Dey, M., Marion, R., & Ammons, C.H. (1958). Long-term retention of perceptual motor skills. *Journal of Experimental Psychology, 55,* 318–328.

Ammons, R.B., & Willig, L. (1956). Acquisition of motor skill: IV. Effects of repeated periods of massed practice. *Journal of Experimental Psychology, 51,* 118–126.

Anderson, D.I., Magill, R.A., Sekiya, H., & Ryan, G. (2005). Support for an explanation of the guidance effect in motor skill learning. *Journal of Motor Behavior, 37,* 231–238.

Annett, J. (1959). Learning a pressure under conditions of immediate and delayed knowledge of results. *Quarterly Journal of Experimental Psychology, 11,* 3–15.

Anson, J.G., Elliott, D., & Davids, K. (2005). Information processing and constraints-based views of skill acquisition: Divergent or complementary? *Motor Control, 9,* 217–241.

Armstrong, T.R. (1970). *Training for the production of memorized movement patterns.* Tech. Rep. No. 26. Ann Arbor, MI: University of Michigan, Department of Psychology.

Arps, G.F. (1920). Work with knowledge of results versus work without knowledge of results. *Psychological Monographs, 28,* 1–41.

Asundi, K., & Odell, D. (2011). Effects of keyboard keyswitch design: A review of the current literature. *Work, 39,* 151–159.

Attneave, F. (1959). *Applications of information theory to psychology: A summary of basic concepts, methods, and results.* New York: Holt, Rinehart & Winston.

Ayres, T.J., Schmidt, R.A., Steele, B.D., & Bayan, F.P. (1995). Visibility and judgment in car-truck night accidents. In D.W. Pratt (Ed.), *Safety engineering and risk analysis—1995* (pp. 43–50). New York: American Society of Mechanical Engineers.

Baddeley, A.D., & Longman, D.J.A. (1978). The influence of length and frequency of training session on the rate of learning to type. *Ergonomics, 21,* 627–635.

Bahrick, H.P., Fitts, P.M., & Briggs, G.E. (1957). Learning curves—facts or artifacts? *Psychological Bulletin, 54,* 256–268.

Banala, S.K., Kim, S.H., Agrawal, S.K., & Scholz, J.P. (2009). Robot assisted gait training with active leg exoskeleton (ALEX). *IEEE Transactions on Neural Systems and Rehabilitation Engineering, 17,* 2–8.

Barnett, J.L., Ross, D., Schmidt, R.A., & Todd, B. (1973). Motor skills learning and the specificity of training principle. *Research Quarterly, 44,* 440–447.

Barnsley, R.H., Thompson, A.H., & Legault, P. (1992). Family planning: Football style. The relative age effect in football. *International Review for the Sociology of Sport, 27,* 77–87.

Bartlett, F.C. (1932). *Remembering: A study in experimental and social psychology.* Cambridge: Cambridge University Press.

Battig, W.F. (1966). Facilitation and interference. In E.A. Bilodeau (Ed.), *Acquisition of skill* (pp. 215–244). New York: Academic Press.

Beilock, S.L. (2010). *Choke: What the secrets of the brain reveal about success and failure at work and at play.* New York: Simon & Schuster.

Belen'kii, V.Y., Gurfinkel, V.S., & Pal'tsev, Y.I. (1967). Elements of control of voluntary movements. *Biofizika, 12,* 135–141.

Bender, P.A. (1987). *Extended practice and patterns of bimanual interference.* Unpublished doctoral dissertation, University of Southern California.

Bernstein, N.A. (1967). *The co-ordination and regulation of movements.* Oxford: Pergamon Press.

Bernstein, N.A. (1996). On dexterity and its development. In M.L. Latash & M.T. Turvey (Eds.), *Dexterity and its development.* Mahwah, NJ: Erlbaum.

Bilodeau, I.M. (1966). Information feedback. In E.A. Bilodeau (Ed.), *Acquisition of skill* (pp. 255–296). New York: Academic Press.

Blouin, J., Gauthier, G.M., Vercher, J.L., & Cole, J. (1996). The relative contribution of retinal and extraretinal signals in determining the accuracy of reaching movements in normal subjects and a deafferented patient. *Experimental Brain Research, 109,* 148–153.

Bourne, L.E. Jr., & Archer, E.J. (1956). Time continuously on target as a function of distribution of practice. *Journal of Experimental Psychology, 51,* 25–33.

Boutcher, S.H., & Crews, D.J. (1987). The effect of a preshot attentional routine on a well-learned skill. *International Journal of Sport Psychology, 18,* 30–39.

Bouwsema, H., van der Sluis, C.K., & Bongers, R.M. (2014). Effect of feedback during virtual training of grip force control with a myoelectric prosthesis. *PLoS ONE, 9*: e98301. doi:10.1371/journal.pone.0098301.

Boyce, B.A. (1992). Effects of assigned versus participant-set goals on skill acquisition and retention of a selected shooting task. *Journal of Teaching in Physical Education, 11,* 220–234.

Breslin, G., Hodges, N.J., Steenson, A., & Williams, A.M. (2012). Constant or variable practice: Recreating the especial skill effect. *Acta Psychologica, 140,* 154–157.

Bridgeman, B., Kirch, M., & Sperling, A. (1981). Segregation of cognitive and motor aspects of visual information using induced motion. *Perception & Psychophysics, 29,* 336–342.

Broadbent, D.P., Causer, J., Williams, A.M., & Ford, P.R. (2017). The role of error processing in the contextual interference effect during the training of perceptual-cognitive skills. *Journal of Experimental Psychology: Human Perception and Performance, 43,* 1329–1342.

Brosnan, K.C., Hayes, K., & Harrison, A.J. (2017). Effects of false-start disqualification rules on response-times of elite-standard sprinters. *Journal of Sports Sciences, 35,* 925–935.

Brown, I.D. (2005). *Review of the "looked but failed to see" accident causation factor.* Road Safety Res. Rep. No. 60. Cambridge, England: Ivan Brown Associates.

Brown, I.D., Tickner, A.H., & Simmons, D.C.V. (1969). Interference between concurrent tasks of driver and telephoning. *Journal of Applied Psychology, 53,* 419–424.

Bryan, W.L., & Harter, N. (1897). Studies in the physiology and psychology of the telegraphic language. *Psychological Review, 4,* 27–53.

Bryan, W.L., & Harter, N. (1899). Studies on the telegraphic language: The acquisition of a hierarchy of habits. *Psychological Review, 6,* 345–375.

Cahill, L., McGaugh, J.L., & Weinberger, N.M. (2001). The neurobiology of learning and memory: Some reminders to remember. *Trends in Neurosciences, 24,* 578–581.

Caird, J.K., Simmons, S.M., Wiley, K., & Johnston, K.A. (2018). Does talking on a cell phone, with a passenger, or dialing affect driving performance? An updated systematic review and meta-analysis of experimental studies. *Human Factors, 60,* 101–133.

Cañal-Bruland, R., Müller, F., Lach, B., & Spence, C. (2018). Auditory contributions to visual anticipations in tennis. *Psychology of Sport & Exercise, 36,* 100–103.

Card, S.K., English, W.K., & Burr, B.J. (1978). Evaluation of mouse, rate-controlled isometric joystick, step keys, and text keys for text selection on a CRT. *Ergonomics, 21,* 601–613.

Carlsen, A.N., Maslovat, D., Lam, M.Y., Chua, R., & Franks, I.M. (2011). Considerations for the use of a startling acoustic stimulus in studies of motor preparation in humans. *Neuroscience and Biobehavioral Reviews, 35,* 366–376.

Carron, A.V. (1967). *Performance and learning in a discrete motor task under massed versus distributed conditions.* Unpublished doctoral dissertation, University of California, Berkeley.

Carron, A.V., Loughhead, T.M., & Bray, S.R. (2005). The home advantage in sport competitions: Courneya and Carron's (1992) conceptual framework a decade later. *Journal of Sports Sciences, 23,* 395–407.

Carter, C.E., & Grahn, J.A. (2016). Optimizing music learning: Exploring how blocked and interleaved practice schedules affect advanced performance. *Frontiers in Psychology, 7,* 1251. doi: 10.3389/fpsyg.2016.01251.

Catalano, J.F., & Kleiner, B.M. (1984). Distant transfer in coincident timing as a function of practice variability. *Perceptual and Motor Skills, 58,* 851–856.

Cattell, J.M. (1893). Aufmerksamkeit und reaction. *Philosophische Studien, 8,* 403–406. English translation in R.S. Woodworth (1947). *Psychological research* (vol. 1, pp. 252–255). Lancaster, PA: Science Press.

Cha, Y.J., Yoo, E.Y., Jung, M.Y, Park, S.H., & Park, J.H. (2012). Effects of functional task training with mental practice in stroke: A meta analysis. *NeuroRehabilitation, 30,* 239–246.

Chabris, C.F., & Simons, D.J. (2010). *The invisible gorilla: And other ways our intuitions deceive us.* New York: Crown.

Chase, W.G., & Simon, H.A. (1973). Perception in chess. *Cognitive Psychology, 4,* 55–81.

Chauvel, G., Wulf, G., & Maquestiaux, F. (2015). Visual illusions can facilitate sport skill learning. *Psychonomic Bulletin & Review, 22,* 717–721.

Cherry, E.C. (1953). Some experiments on the recognition of speech, with one and two ears. *Journal of the Acoustical Society of America, 25,* 975–979.

Chiviacowsky, S., & Wulf, G. (2002). Self-controlled feedback: Does it enhance learning because performers get feedback when they need it? *Research Quarterly for Exercise and Sport, 73,* 408–415.

Chiviacowsky, S., & Wulf, G. (2007). Feedback after good trials enhances learning. *Research Quarterly for Exercise and Sport, 78,* 40–47.

Choi, Y., Qi, F., Gordon, J., & Schweighofer, N. (2008). Performance-based adaptive schedules enhance motor learning. *Journal of Motor Behavior, 40,* 273–280.

Christina, R.W. (1992). The 1991 C.H. McCloy research lecture: Unraveling the mystery of the response complexity effect in skilled movements. *Research Quarterly for Exercise and Sport, 63,* 218–230.

Chubb, C., Dosher, B.A., Lu, Z-L., & Shiffrin, R.M. (2013). *Human information processing: Vision, memory, and attention.* Washington: American Psychological Association.

Chun, M.M., Golomb, J.D., & Turk-Browne, N.B. (2011). A taxonomy of external and internal attention. *Annual Review of Psychology, 62,* 73–101.

Cignetti, F., Schena, F., Zanone, P.G., & Rouard, A. (2009). Dynamics of coordination in cross-country skiing. *Human Movement Science, 28,* 204–217.

Cobley, S., Baker, J., Wattie, N., & McKenna, J. (2009). Annual age-grouping and athlete development: A meta-analytical review of relative age effects in sport. *Sports Medicine, 39,* 235–256.

Cooper, J.M., & Strayer, D.L. (2008). Effects of simulator practiced and real-world experience on cellphone related driver distraction. *Human Factors, 50,* 893–902.

Cormier, S.M., & Hagman, J.D. (Eds.) (1987). *Transfer of learning: Contemporary research applications.* New York: Academic Press.

Coughlan, E.K., Williams, A.M., McRobert, A.P., & Ford, P.R. (2014). How experts practice: A novel test of deliberate practice theory. *Journal of Experimental Psychology: Learning, Memory, and Cognition, 40,* 449–458.

Crossman, E.R.F.W. (1959). A theory of the acquisition of speed skill. *Ergonomics, 2,* 153–166.

Cuddy, L.J., & Jacoby, L.L. (1982). When forgetting helps memory. An analysis of repetition effects. *Journal of Verbal Learning and Verbal Behavior, 21,* 451–467.

Currin, A. (2018). *U Drive. U Text. U Pay.* www.nhtsa.gov/risky-driving/distracted-driving.

Davids, K., Button, C., & Bennett, S. (2008). *Dynamics of skill acquisition: A constraints-led approach.* Champaign, IL: Human Kinetics.

Davies, D.R., & Parasuraman, R. (1982). *The psychology of vigilance.* New York: Academic Press.

Davis, R. (1988). The role of "attention" in the psychological refractory period. *Quarterly Journal of Experimental Psychology, 11,* 211–220.

Deci, E.L., & Ryan, R.M. (2000). The "what" and "why" of goal pursuits: Human needs and the self-determination of behavior. *Psychological Inquiry, 11,* 227–268.

de Gelder, B., Tamietto, M., van Boxtel, G., Goebal, R., Sahraie, A., van den Stock, J., Stienen, B.M.C., Weiskranz, L., & Pegna, A. (2008). Intact navigation skills after bilateral loss of striate cortex. *Current Biology, 18,* R1128-R1129.

deGroot, A.D. (1946/1978). *Thought and choice in chess.* The Hague: Mouton. (Original work published in 1946).

Dickstein, R., & Deutsch, J.E. (2007). Motor imagery in physical therapist practice. *Physical Therapy, 87,* 942–953.

Diedrich, F.J., & Warren, W.H. Jr. (1995). Why change gaits? Dynamics of the walk-run transition. *Journal of Experimental Psychology: Human Perception and Performance, 21,* 183–202.

Donders, F.C. (1969). On the speed of mental processes. In W.G. Koster (Ed. & Trans.), *Attention and performance II.* Amsterdam: North-Holland. (Original work published in 1868).

Drowatzky, J.N., & Zuccato, F.C. (1967). Interrelationships between selected measures of static and dynamic balance. *Research Quarterly, 38,* 509–510.

Easterbrook, J.A. (1959). The effect of emotion on cue utilization and the organization of behavior. *Psychological Review, 66,* 183–201.

Eliasz, K.L. (2016). The effects of social-comparative feedback during motor skill acquisition in highly-motivated learners: Applications to medical education. PhD thesis, McMaster University. hdl.handle.net/11375/20515.

Elliott, D., Lyons, J., Hayes, S.J., Burkitt, J.J., Roberts, J.W., Grierson, L.E.M., Hansen, S., & Bennett, S.J. (2017). The multiple process model of goal-directed reaching revisited. *Neuroscience & Biobehavioral Reviews, 72,* 95–110.

Elliott, D., Helsen, W.F., & Chua, R. (2001). A century later: Woodworth's (1899) two-component model of goal-directed aiming. *Psychological Bulletin, 127,* 342–357.

Elliott, D., Hansen, S., & Grierson, L.E.M. (2010). The legacy of R.S. Woodworth: The two-component model revisited. In D. Elliott & M. Khan (Eds.), *Vision and goal-directed movement: Neurobehavioral perspectives* (pp. 5–19). Champaign, IL: Human Kinetics.

Elliott, D., & Khan, M. (Eds.) (2010). *Vision and goal-directed movement: Neurobehavioral perspectives.* Champaign, IL: Human Kinetics.

Elliott, D., & Lee, T.D. (1995). The role of target information on manual aiming bias. *Psychological Research, 58,* 2–9.

Ericsson, K.A., & Pool, R. (2016). *Peak: Secrets from the new science of expertise.* Boston: Houghton, Mifflin, Harcourt.

Eysenck, M.W., Derakshan, N., Santos, R., & Calvo, M.G. (2007). Anxiety and cognitive performance: Attentional control theory. *Emotion, 7,* 336–353.

Farrell, J.E. (1975). The classification of physical education skills. *Quest, 24,* 63–68.

Feltz, D.L., & Landers, D.M. (1983). The effects of mental practice on motor skill learning and performance: A meta-analysis. *Journal of Sport Psychology, 5,* 25–57.

Fischman, M.G., Christina, R.W., & Anson, J.G. (2008). Memory drum theory's C movement: Revelations from Franklin Henry. *Research Quarterly for Exercise and Sport, 79,* 312–318.

Fitts, P.M. (1954). The information capacity of the human motor system in controlling the amplitude of movement. *Journal of Experimental Psychology, 47,* 381–391.

Fitts, P.M. (1964). Perceptual-motor skills learning. In A.W. Melton (Ed.), *Categories of human learning* (pp. 243–285). New York: Academic Press.

Fitts, P.M., Bahrick, H.P., Noble, M.E., & Briggs, G.E. (1959). *Skilled performance.* Contract No. AF 41 [657]-70. Columbus, OH: Ohio State University, Wright Air Development Center.

Fitts, P.M., & Peterson, J.R. (1964). Information capacity of discrete motor responses. *Journal of Experimental Psychology, 67,* 103–112.

Fitts, P.M., & Posner, M.I. (1967). *Human performance.* Belmont, CA: Brooks/Cole.

Fleishman, E.A. (1956). Psychomotor selection tests: Research and application in the United States Air Force. *Personnel Psychology, 9,* 449–467.

Fleishman, E.A., & Parker, J.F. (1962). Factors in the retention and relearning of perceptual motor skill. *Journal of Experimental Psychology, 64,* 215–226.

Forssberg, H., Grillner, S., & Rossignol, S. (1975). Phase dependent reflex reversal during walking in chronic spinal cats. *Brain Research, 85,* 103–107.

Fritsch, G., & Hitzig, E. (1870). Über die elektrische Erregbarkeit des Grosshirns. *Archiv Anatomie Physiologie, 37,* 300–332.

Fujii, S., Kudo, K., Ohtsuki, T., & Oda, S. (2010). Intrinsic constraint of asymmetry acting as a control parameter on rapid, rhythmic bimanual coordination: A study of professional drummers and nondrummers. *Journal of Neurophysiology, 104,* 2178–2186.

Fullerton, G.S., & Cattell, J. (1892). On the perception of small differences. *University of Pennsylvania Philosophical Series,* No. 2.

Furley, P., Memmert, D., & Heller, C. (2010). The dark side of visual awareness in sport: Inattentional blindness in a real-world basketball task. *Attention, Perception & Psychophysics, 72,* 1327–1337.

Garrison, K.A., Winstein, C.J., & Aziz-Zadeh, L. (2010). The mirror neuron system: A neural substrate for methods in stroke rehabilitation. *Neurorehabilitation and Neural Repair, 24,* 404–412.

Gentile, A.M. (1972). A working model of skill acquisition with application to teaching. *Quest, 17,* 3–23.

Gentile, A.M. (2000). Skill acquisition: Action, movement, and neuromotor processes. In J.H. Carr & R.H. Shepherd (Eds.), *Movement science: Foundation for physical therapy in rehabilitation* (2nd ed.) (pp. 111–180). Gaithersburg, MD: Aspen.

Gentili, R., Han, C.E., Schweighofer, N., & Papaxanthis, C. (2010). Motor learning without doing: Trial-by-trial improvement in motor performance during mental training. *Journal of Neurophysiology, 104,* 774–783.

Gentner, D.R. (1987). Timing of skilled motor performance: Tests of the proportional duration model. *Psychological Review, 94,* 255–276.

Ghez, C., & Krakauer, J. (2000). The organization of movement. In E.R. Kandel, J.H. Schwartz, & T.M. Jessell (Eds.), *Principles of neural science* (pp. 653–673). New York: McGraw-Hill.

Giboin, L.-S., Gruber, M., Kramer, A. (2018). Three months of slackline training elicit only task specific improvements in balance performance. *PLoS ONE, 13*: e0207542. doi:10.1371/journal.pone.0207542.

Gibson, J.J. (1966). *The senses considered as perceptual systems.* Boston: Houghton Mifflin.

Gladwell, M. (2008). *Outliers: The story of success.* New York: Little, Brown.

Goode, S., & Magill, R.A. (1986). Contextual interference effects in learning three badminton serves. *Research Quarterly for Exercise and Sport, 57,* 308–314.

Gray, R. (2008). Multisensory information in the control of complex motor actions. *Current Directions in Psychological Science, 17,* 244–248.

Gray, R. (2009). How do batters use visual, auditory, and tactile information about the success of a baseball swing? *Research Quarterly for Exercise and Sport, 80,* 491–501.

Gray, R. (2018). Comparing cueing and constraints interventions for increasing launch angle in baseball batting. *Sport, Exercise and Performance Psychology, 7,* 318–332.

Greenlee, E.T., DeLucia, P.R., & Newton, D.C. (2018). Driver vigilance in automated vehicles: Hazard detection failures are a matter of time. *Human Factors, 60,* 465–476.

Griffith, C.R. (1931). An experiment on learning to drive a golf ball. *Athletic Journal, 11,* 11–13.

Grillner, S. (1975). Locomotion in vertebrates: Central mechanisms and reflex interaction. *Physiological Reviews, 55,* 247–304.

Guadagnoli, M.A., Dornier, L.A., & Tandy, R.D. (1996). Optimal length for summary knowledge of results: The influence of task-related experience and complexity. *Research Quarterly for Exercise and Sport, 67,* 239–248.

Guadagnoli, M.A., & Kohl, R.M. (2001). Knowledge of results for motor learning: Relationship between error estimation and knowledge of results frequency. *Journal of Motor Behavior, 33,* 217–224.

Guadagnoli, M.A., & Lee, T.D. (2004). Challenge point: A framework for conceptualizing the effects of various practice conditions in motor learning. *Journal of Motor Behavior, 36,* 212–224.

Guthrie, E.R. (1952). *The psychology of learning.* New York: Harper & Row.

Haken, H., Kelso, J.A.S., & Bunz, H. (1985). A theoretical model of phase transitions in human hand movements. *Biological Cybernetics, 51,* 347–356.

Hall, K.G., Domingues, D.A., & Cavazos, R. (1994). Contextual interference effects with skilled baseball players. *Perceptual and Motor Skills, 78,* 835–841.

Hancock, P.A. (2017). On the nature of vigilance. *Human Factors, 59,* 35–43.

Helmuth, L.L., & Ivry, R.B. (1996). When two hands are better than one: Reduced timing variability during bimanual movement. *Journal of Experimental Psychology: Human Perception and Performance, 22,* 278–293.

Henry, F.M. (1968). Specificity vs. generality in learning motor skill. In R.C. Brown & G.S. Kenyon (Eds.), *Classical studies on physical activity* (pp. 331–340). Englewood Cliffs, NJ: Prentice Hall. (Original work published in 1958).

Henry, F.M., & Rogers, D.E. (1960). Increased response latency for complicated movements and a "memory drum" theory of neuromotor reaction. *Research Quarterly, 31,* 448–458.

Heuer, H. (1985). Wiewirktmentale Übung? [How does mental practice operate?] *Psychologische Rundschau, 36,* 191–200.

Heuer, H. (1988). Testing the invariance of relative timing: Comment on Gentner (1987). *Psychological Review, 95,* 552–557.

Heuer, H., Schmidt, R.A., & Ghodsian, D. (1995). Generalized motor programs for rapid bimanual tasks: A two-level multiplicative-rate model. *Biological Cybernetics, 73,* 343–356.

Heuer, H., & Lüttgen, L. (2016). Robot assistance of motor learning: A neuro-cognitive perspective. *Neuroscience and Biobehavioral Reviews, 56,* 222–240.

Hick, W.E. (1952). On the rate of gain of information. *Quarterly Journal of Experimental Psychology, 4,* 11–26.

Higgins, J.R. (1977). *Human movement: An integrated approach.* St. Louis: Mosby.

Hird, J.S., Landers, D.M., Thomas, J.R., & Horan, J.J. (1991). Physical practice is superior to mental practice in enhancing cognitive and motor task performance. *Journal of Sport and Exercise Psychology, 13,* 281–293.

Hodges, N.J., & Campagnaro, P. (2012). Physical guidance research: Assisting principles and supporting evidence. In N.J. Hodges & A.M. Williams (Eds.), *Skill acquisition in sport: Research, theory and practice* (2nd ed.) (pp. 150–169). London, UK: Routledge.

Hollerbach, J.M. (1978). *A study of human motor control through analysis and synthesis of handwriting.* Unpublished doctoral dissertation, Massachusetts Institute of Technology, Cambridge.

Howell, M.L. (1953). Influence of emotional tension on speed of reaction and movement. *Research Quarterly, 24,* 22–32.

Howell, M.L. (1956). Use of force-time graphs for performance analysis in facilitating motor learning. *Research Quarterly, 27,* 12–22.

Hoyt, D.F., & Taylor, C.R. (1981). Gait and the energetics of locomotion in horses. *Nature, 292,* 239–240.

Hubbard, A.W., & Seng, C.N. (1954). Visual movements of batters. *Research Quarterly, 25,* 42–57.

Humphrey, N. (1974). Vision in a monkey without striate cortex: A case study. *Perception, 3,* 241–255.

Hyman, I.E. Jr., Boss, S.M., Wise, B.M., McKenzie, K.E., & Caggiano, J.M. (2010). Did you see the unicycling clown? Inattentional blindness while walking and talking on a cell phone. *Applied Cognitive Psychology, 24,* 597–607.

Hyman, R. (1953). Stimulus information as a determinant of reaction time. *Journal of Experimental Psychology, 45,* 188–196.

Ille, A., Selin, I., Do, M.-C., & Thon, B. (2013). Attentional focus effects on sprint start performance as a function of skill level. *Journal of Sports Sciences, 31,* 1705–1712.

Irion, A.L. (1966). A brief history of research on the acquisition of skill. In E.A. Bilodeau (Ed.), *Acquisition of skill* (pp. 1–46). New York: Academic Press.

Ishigami, Y., & Klein, R.M. (2009). Is a hands-free phone safer than a handheld phone? *Journal of Safety Research, 40,* 157–164.

Jagacinski, R.J., & Flach, J.M. (2003). *Control theory for humans: Quantitative approaches to modeling performance.* Mahwah, NJ: Erlbaum.

James, W. (1890). *The principles of psychology* (Vol. 1). New York: Holt.

James, W. (1891). *The principles of psychology* (Vol. 2). New York: Holt.

Janelle, C.M. (1999). Ironic mental processes in sport: Implications for sport psychologists. *The Sport Psychologist, 13,* 201–220.

Janelle, C.M., Barba, D.A., Frehlich, S.G., Tennant, L.K., & Cauraugh, J.H. (1997). Maximizing performance feedback effectiveness through videotape replay and a self-controlled learning environment. *Research Quarterly for Exercise and Sport, 68,* 269–279.

Janssen, L., Crajé, C., Weigelt, M., & Steenbergen, B. (2010). Motor planning in bimanual object manipulation: Two plans for two hands? *Motor Control, 14,* 240–254.

Kahneman, D. (2011). *Thinking, fast and slow.* New York: Farrar, Straus, and Giroux.

Kantak, S.S., & Winstein, C.J. (2012). Learning–performance distinction and memory processes for motor skills: A focused review and perspective. *Behavioural Brain Research, 228,* 219–231.

Keele, S.W. (1968). Movement control in skilled motor performance. *Psychological Bulletin, 70,* 387–403.

Keele, S.W., & Posner, M.I. (1968). Processing of visual feedback in rapid movements. *Journal of Experimental Psychology, 77,* 155–158.

Keetch, K.M., Lee, T.D., & Schmidt, R.A. (2008). Especial skills: Specificity embedded within generality. *Journal of Sport and Exercise Psychology, 30,* 723–736.

Keetch, K.M., Schmidt, R.A., Lee, T.D., & Young, D.E. (2005). Especial skills: Their emergence with massive amounts of practice. *Journal of Experimental Psychology: Human Perception and Performance, 31,* 970–978.

Kelso, J.A.S. (1984). Phase transitions and critical behavior in human bimanual coordination. *American Journal of Physiology: Regulatory, Integrative and Comparative Physiology, 246,* R1000-R1004.

Kelso, J.A.S. (1995). *Dynamic patterns: The self-organization of brain and behavior.* Cambridge, MA: MIT Press.

Kelso, J.A.S. (2009). Coordination dynamics. In R.A. Meyers (Ed.), *Encyclopedia of complexity and systems sciences* (pp. 1537–1564). Berlin: Springer-Verlag.

Kelso, J.A.S., & Engstrøm, D.A. (2005). *The complementary nature.* Cambridge, MA: MIT Press.

Kelso, J.A.S., Tuller, B., Vatikiotis-Bateson, E., & Fowler, C.A. (1984). Functionally specific articulatory cooperation following jaw perturbations during speech: Evidence for coordinative structures. *Journal of Experimental Psychology: Human Perception and Performance, 10,* 812–832.

Kelso, J.A.S., Putnam, C.A., & Goodman, D. (1983). On the space-time structure of human interlimb co-ordination. *Quarterly Journal of Experimental Psychology, 35A,* 347–375.

Kelso, J.A.S., Southard, D.L., & Goodman, D. (1979). On the coordination of two-handed movements. *Journal of Experimental Psychology: Human Perception and Performance, 5,* 229–238.

Kelso, J.A.S., Scholz, J.P., & Schöner, G. (1986). Nonequilibrium phase transitions in coordinated biological motion: Critical fluctuations. *Physics Letters A, 118,* 279–284.

Kelso, J.A.S., Scholz, J.P., & Schöner, G. (1988). Dynamics governs switching among patterns of coordination in biological movement. *Physics Letters A, 134,* 8–12.

Kernodle, M.W., & Carlton, L.G. (1992). Information feedback and the learning of multiple-degree-of-freedom activities. *Journal of Motor Behavior, 24,* 187–196.

Kerr, R., & Booth, B. (1978). Specific and varied practice of motor skill. *Perceptual and Motor Skills, 46,* 395–401.

Klapp, S.T. (1996). Reaction time analysis of central motor control. In H.N. Zelaznik (Ed.), *Advances in motor learning and control* (pp. 13–35). Champaign, IL: Human Kinetics.

Klapp, S.T. (2010). Comments on the classic Henry and Rogers (1960) paper on its 50th anniversary. *Research Quarterly for Exercise and Sport, 81,* 108–112.

Klapp, S.T., Maslovat, D., & Jagacinski, R.J. (2019). The bottleneck of the psychological refractory period involves timing of response initiation rather than response selection. *Psychonomic Bulletin & Review, 26,* 29–47.

Konczak, J., vander Velden, H., & Jaeger, L. (2009). Learning to play the violin: Motor control by freezing, not freeing degrees of freedom. *Journal of Motor Behavior, 41,* 243–252.

Kozlowski, S.W.J., & DeShon, R.P. (2004). A psychological fidelity approach to simulation-based training: Theory, research, and principles. In E. Salas, L.R. Elliott, S.G. Schflett, & M.D. Coovert (Eds.), *Scaled worlds: Development, validation, and applications* (pp. 75–99). Burlington, VT: Ashgate.

Krause, D., Agethen, M., & & Zobe, C. (2018). Error feedback frequency affects automaticity but not accuracy and consistency after extensive motor skill practice. *Journal of Motor Behavior, 50,* 144–154.

Kunde, W., Skirde, S., & Weigelt, M. (2011). Trust my face: Cognitive factors of head fakes in sports. *Journal of Experimental Psychology: Applied, 17,* 110–127.

Kunde, W., & Weigelt, M. (2005). Goal congruency in bimanual object manipulation. *Journal of Experimental Psychology: Human Perception and Performance, 31,* 145–156.

LaDelfa, N.J., Garcia, D.B.L., Cappelletto, J.A.M., McDonald, A.C., Lyons, J.L., & Lee, T.D. (2013). The gunslinger effect: Why are movements made faster when responding to vs. initiating an action? *Journal of Motor Behavior, 45,* 85–90.

Landin, D., & Hebert, E.P. (1997). A comparison of three practice schedules along the contextual interference continuum. *Research Quarterly for Exercise and Sport, 68,* 357–361.

Langham, M., Hole, G., Edwards, J., & O'Neil, C. (2002). An analysis of "looked but failed to see" accidents involving parked police vehicles. *Ergonomics, 45,* 167–185.

Lashley, K.S. (1917). The accuracy of movement in the absence of excitation from the moving organ. *American Journal of Physiology, 43,* 169–194.

Lashley, K.S. (1942). The problem of cerebral organization in vision. In J. Cattell (Ed.), *Biological symposia. Vol. VII. Visual mechanisms* (pp. 301–322). Lancaster, PA: Jaques Cattell Press.

Lavery, J.J. (1962). Retention of simple motor skills as a function of type of knowledge of results. *Canadian Journal of Psychology, 16,* 300–311.

Lavery, J.J., & Suddon, F.H. (1962). Retention of simple motor skills as a function of the number of trials by which KR is delayed. *Perceptual and Motor Skills, 15,* 231–237.

Lawrence, M., & Barclay, D.M. (1998). Stuttering: A brief review. *American Family Physician, 57,* 2175–2178.

Leavitt, J.L. (1979). Cognitive demands of skating and stickhandling in ice hockey. *Canadian Journal of Applied Sports Science, 4,* 46–55.

Lee, D.N. (1980). Visuo-motor coordination in space-time. In G.E. Stelmach & J. Requin (Eds.), *Tutorials in motor behavior* (pp. 281–295). Amsterdam: North-Holland.

Lee, D.N., & Aronson, E. (1974). Visual proprioceptive control of standing in human infants. *Perception & Psychophysics, 15,* 529–532.

Lee, D.N., & Young, D.S. (1985). Visual timing of interceptive action. In D. Ingle, M. Jeannerod, & D.N. Lee (Eds.), *Brain mechanisms and spatial vision* (pp. 1–30). Dordrecht: Martinus Nijhoff.

Lee, T.D. (2012). Contextual interference: Generalizability and limitations. In N.J. Hodges & A.M. Williams (Eds.), *Skill acquisition in sport: Research, theory, and practice* (2nd ed.) (pp. 79–93). London, UK: Routledge.

Lee, T.D., & Carnahan, H. (1990). Bandwidth knowledge of results and motor learning: More than just a relative frequency effect. *Quarterly Journal of Experimental Psychology, 42A,* 777–789.

Lee, T.D., Wishart, L.R., Cunningham, S., & Carnahan, H. (1997). Modeled timing information during random practice eliminates the contextual interference effect. *Research Quarterly for Exercise and Sport, 68,* 100–105.

Lee, T.D., & Genovese, E.D. (1988). Distribution of practice in motor skill acquisition: Learning and performance effects reconsidered. *Research Quarterly for Exercise and Sport, 59,* 277–287.

Lee, T.D., & Genovese, E.D. (1989). Distribution of practice in motor skill acquisition: Different effects for discrete and continuous tasks. *Research Quarterly for Exercise and Sport, 60,* 59–65.

Lee, T.D., Ishikura, T., Kegel, S., Gonzalez, D., & Passmore, S. (2008). Do expert golfers really keep their heads still while putting? *Annual Review of Golf Coaching, 2,* 135–143.

Lee, T.D., & Magill, R.A. (1983). The locus of contextual interference in motor-skill acquisition. *Journal of Experimental Psychology: Learning, Memory, and Cognition, 9,* 730–746.

Lee, T.D., Magill, R.A., & Weeks, D.J. (1985). Influence of practice schedule on testing schema theory predictions in adults. *Journal of Motor Behavior, 17,* 283–299.

Lee, T.D., & Schmidt, R.A. (2014). PaR (Plan-act-Review) golf: Motor learning research and improving golf skills. *International Journal of Golf Science,3,* 2–25.

Lee, T.D., & Swinnen, S.P. (1993). Three legacies of Bryan and Harter: Automaticity, variability and change in skilled performance. In J.L. Starkes & F. Allard (Eds.), *Cognitive issues in motor expertise* (pp. 295–315). Amsterdam: Elsevier.

Lee, W.A. (1980). Anticipatory control of postural and task muscles during rapid arm flexion. *Journal of Motor Behavior, 12,* 185–196.

Lersten, K.C. (1968). Transfer of movement components in a motor learning task. *Research Quarterly, 39,* 575–581.

Levac, D., Pierrynowski, M.R., Canestraro, M., Gurr, L., Leonard, L., and Neeley, C. (2010). Exploring children's movement characteristics during virtual reality video game play. *Human Movement Science, 29,* 1023–1038.

Levac, D., Rivard, L., & Missiuna, C. (2012). Defining the active ingredients of interactive computer play interventions for children with neuromotor impairments: A scoping review. *Research in Developmental Disabilities, 33,* 214–223.

Lewthwaite, R., & Wulf, G. (2010). Social-comparative feedback affects motor skill learning. *Quarterly Journal of Experimental Psychology, 63,* 738–749.

Lewthwaite, R., & Wulf, G. (2012). Motor learning through a motivational lens. In N.J. Hodges & A.M. Williams (Eds.), *Skill acquisition in sport: Research, theory and practice* (2nd ed.) (pp. 173–191). London, UK: Routledge.

Lindeburg, F.A. (1949). A study of the degree of transfer between quickening exercises and other coordinated movements. *Research Quarterly, 20,* 180–195.

Liu, J., & Wrisberg, C.A. (1997). The effects of knowledge of results delay and the subjective estimation of movement form on the acquisition and retention of a motor skill. *Research Quarterly for Exercise and Sport, 68,* 145–151.

Locke, E.A., & Latham, G.P. (1985). The application of goal setting to sports. *Sport Psychology Today, 7,* 205–222.

Lohse, K.R., Wulf, G., & Lewthwaite, R. (2012). Attentional focus affects movement efficiency. In N.J. Hodges & A.M. Williams (Eds.), *Skill acquisition in sport: Research, theory and practice* (2nd ed.) (pp. 40–58). London, UK: Routledge.

Mackworth, N.H. (1948). The breakdown of vigilance during prolonged visual search. *Quarterly Journal of Experimental Psychology, 1,* 6–21.

MacLeod, C.M. (1991). Half a century of research on the Stroop effect: An integrative review. *Psychological Bulletin, 109,* 163–203.

MacLeod, C.M. (2015). Attention: Beyond Stroop's (1935) colour-word interference phenomenon. In M.W. Eysenck & D. Groome (Eds.), *Cognitive psychology: Revisiting the classic studies* (pp. 60–70). London: Sage.

Magill, R.A., & Anderson, D. (2017). *Motor learning and control: Concepts and applications* (11th ed.). Columbus, OH: McGraw-Hill.

Magill, R.A., & Hall, K.G. (1990). A review of the contextual interference effect in motor skill acquisition. *Human Movement Science, 9,* 241–289.

Marchal-Crespo, L., Rappo, N., & Riener, R. (2017). The effectiveness of robotic training depends on motor task characteristics. *Experimental Brain Research, 235,* 3799–3816.

Marteniuk, R.G. (1974). Individual differences in motor performance and learning. *Exercise and Sport Sciences Reviews, 2,* 103–130.

Marteniuk, R.G. (1976). *Information processing in motor skills.* New York: Holt, Reinhart & Winston.

Marteniuk, R.G. (1986). Information processes in movement learning: Capacity and structural interference effects. *Journal of Motor Behavior, 18,* 55–75.

Martinez De Quel, O. & Bennett, S.J. (2014). Kinematics of self-initiated and reactive karate punches. *Research Quarterly for Exercise and Sport, 85,* 117–123.

McCracken, H.D., & Stelmach, G.E. (1977). A test of the schema theory of discrete motor learning. *Journal of Motor Behavior, 9,* 193–201.

McLeod, P. (1980). What can probe RT tell us about the attentional demands of movement? In G.E. Stelmach & J. Requin (Eds.), *Tutorials in motor behavior* (pp. 579–589). Amsterdam: Elsevier.

Mehrholz, J., Platz, T., Kugler, J., & Pohl, M. (2008). Electromechanical and robot-assisted arm training for improving arm function and activities of daily living after stroke. *Cochrane Database of Systematic Reviews, 4.* CD006876. doi:10.1002/14651858.CD006876.pub2.

Merbah, S., & Meulemans, T. (2011). Learning a motor skill: Effects of blocked versus random practice. A review. *Psychologica Belgica, 51,* 15–48.

Merkel, J. (1885). Die zeitlichen Verhaltnisse der Willensthaütigkeit. *Philosophische Studien, 2,* 73–127. (Cited in Woodworth, R.S. [1938]. *Experimental psychology.* New York: Holt.)

Merton, P.A. (1972). How we control the contraction of our muscles. *Scientific American, 226,* 30–37.

Meyer, D.E., Abrams, R.A., Kornblum, S., Wright, C.E., & Smith, J.E.K. (1988). Optimality in human motor performance: Ideal control of rapid aimed movements. *Psychological Review, 95,* 340–370.

Meyer, D.E., Smith, J.E.K., Kornblum, S., Abrams, R.A., & Wright, C.E. (1990). Speed-accuracy tradeoffs in aimed movements: Toward a theory of rapid voluntary action. In M. Jeannerod (Ed.), *Attention and performance XIII* (pp. 173–226). Hillsdale, NJ: Erlbaum.

Miller, J., & Ulrich, R. (2008). Bimanual response grouping in dual-task paradigms. *Quarterly Journal of Experimental Psychology, 61,* 999–1019.

Nabavinik, M., Abaszadeh, A., Mehranmanesh, M., & Rosenbaum, D.A. (2018). Especial skills in experienced archers. *Journal of Motor Behavior, 50,* 249–253.

Nacson, J., & Schmidt, R.A. (1971). The activity-set hypothesis for warm-up decrement. *Journal of Motor Behavior, 3,* 1–15.

Nashner, L., & Berthoz, A. (1978). Visual contribution to rapid motor responses during postural control. *Brain Research, 150,* 403–407.

National Hockey League Official Rules (2018–2019). National Hockey League, New York.

Néda, Z., Ravasz, E., Brechet, Y., Vicsek, T., & Barabasi, A.L. (2000). The sound of many hands clapping: Tumultuous applause can transform itself into waves of synchronized clapping. *Nature, 403,* 849–850.

Neisser, U., & Becklen, R. (1975). Selective looking, attending to visually specified events. *Cognitive Psychology, 7,* 480–494.

Neumann, E., & Ammons, R.B. (1957). Acquisition and long-term retention of a simple serial perceptual-motor skill. *Journal of Experimental Psychology, 53,* 159–161.

Newell, K.M. (1986). Constraints on the development of coordination. In M.G. Wade & H.T.A. Whiting (Eds.), *Motor development in children: Aspects of coordination and control* (pp. 341–360). Boston: Nijhoff.

Newell, K.M., Liu, Y.-T., & Mayer-Kress, G. (2001). Time scales in motor learning and development. *Psychological Review, 108,* 57–82.

Newell, K.M., Liu, Y.-T., & Mayer-Kress, G. (2009). Time scales, difficulty/skill duality, and the dynamics of motor learning. In D. Sternad (Ed.), *Progress in motor control* (pp. 457–476). Berlin: Springer.

Newell, K.M., & Vaillancourt, D.E. (2001). Dimensional change in motor learning. *Human Movement Science, 20,* 695–715.

Newell, K.M., & Walter, C.B. (1981). Kinematic and kinetic parameters as information feedback in motor skill acquisition. *Journal of Human Movement Studies, 7,* 235–254.

Nilsen, D.M., Gillen, G., & Gordon, A.M. (2010). Use of mental practice to improve upper-limb recovery after stroke: A systematic review. *American Journal of Occupational Therapy, 64,* 695–708.

Norman, J. (2002). Two visual systems and two theories of perception: An attempt to reconcile the constructivist and ecological approaches. *Behavioral and Brain Sciences, 25,* 73–144.

Ong, N.T., & Hodges, N.J. (2012). Mixing it up a little: How to schedule observational practice. In N.J. Hodges & A.M. Williams (Eds.), *Skill acquisition in sport: Research, theory and practice* (2nd ed.) (pp. 22–39). London, UK: Routledge.

Oullier, O., & Kelso, J.A.S. (2009). Social coordination from the perspective of coordination dynamics. In R.A. Meyers (Ed.), *Encyclopedia of complexity and systems sciences* (pp. 8198–8212). Berlin: Springer-Verlag.

Pearson, K., & Gordon, J. (2012). Spinal reflexes. In E.R. Kandel, J.H. Schwartz, T.M. Jessell, S.A. Siegelbaum, & A.J Hudspeth (Eds.), *Principles of neural science* (pp. 790–811). New York: McGraw-Hill.

Peterson, L.R., & Peterson, M.J. (1959). Short-term retention of individual verbal items. *Journal of Experimental Psychology, 58,* 193–198.

Pew, R.W. (1994). Paul Morris Fitts (1912–1965). In H.L. Taylor (ed.), *Division 21 members who made distinguished contributions to engineering psychology* (pp. 23–44). Washington: American Psychological Association.

Pfordresher, P.Q., & Dalla Bella, S. (2011). Delayed auditory feedback and movement. *Journal of Experimental Psychology: Human Perception and Performance, 37,* 566–579.

Pigott, R.E., & Shapiro, D.C. (1984). Motor schema: The structure of the variability session. *Research Quarterly for Exercise and Sport, 55,* 41–45.

Plamondon, R., & Alimi, A.M. (1997). Speed/accuracy tradeoffs in target-directed movements. *Behavioral and Brain Sciences, 20,* 279–349.

Platz, T., Roschka, S., Christel, M.I., Duecker, F., Rothwell, J.C., & Sack, A.T. (2012a). Early stages of motor skill learning and the specific relevance of the cortical motor system—a combined behavioural training and theta burst TMS study. *Restorative Neurology and Neuroscience, 30,* 199–211.

Platz, T., Roschka, S., Doppl, K., Roth, C., Lotze, M., Sack, A.T., & Rothwell, J.C. (2012b). Prolonged motor skill learning—a combined behavioural training and theta burst TMS study. *Restorative Neurology and Neuroscience, 30,* 213–224.

Porter, J.M., & Magill, R.A. (2010). Systematically increasing contextual interference is beneficial for learning sport skills. *Journal of Sports Sciences, 28,* 1277–1285.

Posner, M.I., & Keele, S.W. (1969). Attentional demands of movement. *Proceedings of the 16th Congress of Applied Psychology.* Amsterdam: Swets and Zeitlinger.

Poulton, E.C. (1957). On prediction in skilled movements. *Psychological Bulletin, 54,* 467–478.

Poulton, E.C. (1974). *Tracking skill and manual control.* New York: Academic Press.

Proctor, R.W., & Vu, K-P.L. (2006). *Stimulus-response compatibility principles: Data, theory, and application.* Boca Raton, FL: Taylor & Francis.

Proteau, L. (1992). On the specificity of learning and the role of visual information for movement control. In L. Proteau & D. Elliott (Eds.), *Vision and motor control* (pp. 67–103). Amsterdam: Elsevier.

Raibert, M.H. (1977). *Motor control and learning by the state space model.* Tech. Rep. No. AI-TR-439. Cambridge: Massachusetts Institute of Technology, Artificial Intelligence Laboratory.

Rasmussen, J. (1986). *Information processing and human-machine interaction: An approach to cognitive engineering.* New York: North-Holland.

Rawlings, E.I., Rawlings, I.L., Chen, S.S., & Yilk, M.D. (1972). The facilitating effects of mental rehearsal in the acquisition of rotary pursuit tracking. *Psychonomic Science, 26,* 71–73.

Redelmeier, D.A., & Tibshirani, R.J. (1997). Association between cellular-telephone calls and motor vehicle collisions. *New England Journal of Medicine, 336,* 453–458.

Robinson, G.H., & Kavinsky, R.C. (1976). On Fitts' law with two-handed movement. *IEEE Transactions on Systems, Man, and Cybernetics, 6,* 504–505.

Roediger, H.L., III (Ed.) (2008). *Learning and memory: A comprehensive reference.* Oxford: Elsevier.

Rosenbaum, D.A. (2010). *Human motor control* (2nd ed.). Burlington, MA: Elsevier.

Rosenbaum, D.A., Chapman, K.M., Coelho, C.J., Gong, L., and Studenka, B.E. (2013). Choosing actions. *Frontiers in Psychology, 4,* 273. doi:10.3389/fpsyg.2013.00273.

Rothstein, A.L., & Arnold, R.K. (1976). Bridging the gap: Application of research on videotape feedback and bowling. *Motor Skills: Theory Into Practice, 1,* 35–62.

Salmoni, A.W., Schmidt, R.A., & Walter, C.B. (1984). Knowledge of results and motor learning: A review and critical reappraisal. *Psychological Bulletin, 95,* 355–386.

Sanli, E.A., Patterson, J.T., Bray, S.R., & Lee, T.D. (2013). Understanding self-controlled motor learning protocols through the self-determination theory. *Frontiers in Movement Science and Sport Psychology, 3,* 611. doi:10.3389/fpsyg.2012.00611.

Schmidt, R.A. (1969). Movement time as a determiner of timing accuracy. *Journal of Experimental Psychology, 79,* 43–47.

Schmidt, R.A. (1975). A schema theory of discrete motor skill learning. *Psychological Review, 82,* 225–260.

Schmidt, R.A. (1982). *Motor control and learning: A behavioral emphasis.* Champaign, IL: Human Kinetics.

Schmidt, R.A. (1985). The search for invariance in skilled movement behavior. *Research Quarterly for Exercise and Sport, 56,* 188–200.

Schmidt, R.A. (1989). Unintended acceleration: A review of human factors contributions. *Human Factors, 31,* 345–364.

Schmidt, R.A., Zelaznik, H.N., and Frank, J.S. (1978). Sources of inaccuracy in rapid movement. *Information Processing in Motor Control and Learning.* New York: Academic Press, 197.

Schmidt, R.A., Zelaznik, H.N., Hawkins, B., Frank, J.S., & Quinn, J.T. Jr. (1979). Motor-output variability: A theory for the accuracy of rapid motor acts. *Psychological Review, 86,* 415–451.

Schmidt, R.A., Heuer, H., Ghodsian, D., & Young, D.E. (1998). Generalized motor programs and units of action in bimanual coordination. In M. Latash (Ed.), *Progress in motor control, Vol. 1: Bernstein's traditions in movement studies* (pp. 329–360). Champaign, IL: Human Kinetics.

Schmidt, R.A., Wood, C.T., Young, D.E., & Kelkar, R. (1996). *Evaluation of the BIC J26 child guard lighter.* Tech. Rep. Los Angeles: Failure Analysis Associates, Inc.

Schmidt, R.A., Lange, C., & Young, D.E. (1990). Optimizing summary knowledge of results for skill learning. *Human Movement Science, 9,* 325–348.

Schmidt, R.A., & Lee, T.D. (2011). *Motor control and learning: A behavioral emphasis* (5th ed.). Champaign, IL: Human Kinetics.

Schmidt, R.A., Lee, T.D., Winstein, C.J., Wulf, G., & Zelaznik, H.N. (2019). *Motor control and learning: A behavioral emphasis* (6th ed.). Champaign, IL: Human Kinetics.

Schmidt, R.A., Young, D.E., Swinnen, S., & Shapiro, D.C. (1989). Summary knowledge of results for skill acquisition: Support for the guidance hypothesis. *Journal of Experimental Psychology: Learning, Memory, and Cognition, 15,* 352–359.

Schmidt, R.A., & Sherwood, D.E. (1982). An inverted-U relation between spatial error and force requirements in rapid limb movements: Further evidence for the impulse-variability model. *Journal of Experimental Psychology: Human Perception and Performance, 8,* 158–170.

Schmidt, R.A., & Wulf, G. (1997). Continuous concurrent feedback degrades skill learning: Implications for training and simulation. *Human Factors, 39,* 509–525.

Schmidt, R.A., & Young, D.E. (1987). Transfer of movement control in motor learning. In S.M. Cormier & J.D. Hagman (Eds.), *Transfer of learning* (pp. 47–79). Orlando, FL: Academic Press.

Schmidt, R.C., Carello, C., & Turvey, M.T. (1990). Phase transitions and critical fluctuations in the visual coordination of rhythmic movements between people. *Journal of Experimental Psychology: Human Perception and Performance, 16,* 227–247.

Schneider, D.M., & Schmidt, R.A. (1995). Units of action in motor control: Role of response complexity and target speed. *Human Performance, 8,* 27–49.

Schneider, W., & Shiffrin, R.M. (1977). Controlled and automatic human information processing: I. Detection, search, and attention. *Psychological Review, 84,* 1–66.

Schutz, R.W., & Roy, E.A. (1973). Absolute error: The devil in disguise. *Journal of Motor Behavior, 5,* 141–153.

Scripture, C.W. (1905). *The new psychology.* New York: Scott.

Seifert, L., Komar, J., Barbosa, T., Toussaint, H., Millet, G., & Davids, K. (2014). Coordination pattern variability provides functional adaptations to constraints in swimming performance. *Sports Medicine, 44,* 1333–1345.

Selverston, A.I. (2010). Invertebrate central pattern generator circuits. *Philosophical Transactions of the Royal Society B, 365,* 2329–2345.

Shapiro, D.C., Zernicke, R.F., Gregor, R.J., & Diestel, J.D. (1981). Evidence for generalized motor programs using gait pattern analysis. *Journal of Motor Behavior, 13,* 33–47.

Shapiro, D.C., & Schmidt, R.A. (1982). The schema theory: Recent evidence and developmental implications. In J.A.S. Kelso & J.E. Clark (Eds.), *The development of movement control and co-ordination* (pp. 113–150). New York: Wiley.

Shea, J.B., & Morgan, R.L. (1979). Contextual interference effects on the acquisition, retention, and transfer of a motor skill. *Journal of Experimental Psychology: Human Learning and Memory, 5,* 179–187.

Shea, J.B., & Zimny, S.T. (1983). Context effects in memory and learning movement information.

In R.A. Magill (Ed.), *Memory and control of action* (pp. 345–366). Amsterdam: Elsevier.

Shergill, S.S., Bays, P.M., Frith, C.D., & Wolpert, D.M. (2003). Two eyes for an eye: The neuroscience of force escalation. *Science, 301,* 187.

Sherrington, C.S. (1906). *The integrative action of the nervous system.* New Haven, CT: Yale University Press.

Sherwood, D.E. (1988). Effect of bandwidth knowledge of results on movement consistency. *Perceptual and Motor Skills, 66,* 535–542.

Sherwood, D.E., Lohse, K.R., & Healy, A.F. (2014). Judging joint angles and movement outcome: Shifting the focus of attention in dart-throwing. *Journal of Experimental Psychology: Human Perception and Performance, 40,* 1903–1914.

Sherwood, D.E., Schmidt, R.A., & Walter, C.B. (1988). The force/force-variability relationship under controlled temporal conditions. *Journal of Motor Behavior, 20,* 106–116.

Simmons, S.M., Hicks, A., & Caird, J.K. (2016). Safety-critical event risk associated with cell phone tasks as measured in naturalistic driving studies: A systematic review and meta-analysis. *Accident Analysis and Prevention, 87,* 161–169.

Simon, D.A., & Bjork, R.A. (2001). Metacognition in motor learning. *Journal of Experimental Psychology: Learning, Memory, and Cognition, 27,* 907–912.

Simon, D.A., Lee, T.D., & Cullen, J.D. (2008). Win-shift, lose-stay: Contingent switching and contextual interference in motor learning. *Perceptual and Motor Skills, 107,* 407–418.

Simons, D.J., & Chabris, C.F. (1999). Gorillas in our midst: Sustained inattentional blindness for dynamic events. *Perception, 28,* 1059–1074.

Simons, D.J., & Levin, D.T. (1998). Failure to detect changes to people in a real-world interaction. *Psychonomic Bulletin & Review, 5,* 644–649.

Simons, J.P., Wilson, J. M., Wilson, G. J., & Theall, S. (2009). Challenges to cognitive bases for an especial motor skill at the regulation baseball pitching distance. *Research Quarterly for Exercise and Sport, 80,* 469–479.

Sinnett, S., & Kingstone, A. (2010). A preliminary investigation regarding the effect of tennis grunting: Does white noise during a tennis shot have a negative impact on shot perception? *PLoS One, 5*: e13148. doi:10.1371/journal.pone.0013148.

Slater-Hammel, A.T. (1960). Reliability, accuracy and refractoriness of a transit reaction. *Research Quarterly, 31,* 217–228.

Smith, K.L., Weir, P.L., Till, K., Romann, M., & Cobley, S. (2018). Relative age effects across and within female sport contexts: A systematic review and meta-analysis. *Sports Medicine, 48,* 1451–1478.

Snoddy, G.S. (1926). Learning and stability: A psychophysical analysis of a case of motor learning with clinical applications. *Journal of Applied Psychology, 10,* 1–36.

Snyder, C., & Abernethy, B. (Eds.) (1992). *The creative side of experimentation: Personal perspectives from leading researchers in motor control, motor development, and sport psychology.* Champaign, IL: Human Kinetics.

Soderstrom, N.C., & Bjork, R.A. (2015). Learning versus performance: An integrated review. *Perspectives on Psychological Science, 10,* 176–199.

Sperling, G. (1960). The information available in brief visual presentations. *Psychological Monographs, 74* (11, Whole No. 498).

Starkes, J.L., & Ericsson, K.A. (2003). *Expert performance in sports.* Champaign, IL: Human Kinetics.

Ste-Marie, D.M., Clark, S.E., Findlay, L.C., & Latimer, A.E. (2004). High levels of contextual interference enhance handwriting skill acquisition. *Journal of Motor Behavior, 36,* 115–126.

Ste-Marie, D.M., Law, B., Rymal, A.M., O, J., Hall, C., & McCullagh, P. (2012). Observation interventions for motor skill learning and performance: An applied model for the use of observation. *International Review of Sport and Exercise Psychology, 5,* 145–176.

Stephen, L., Macknik, S.L., King, M., Randi, J., Robbins, A., Teller, J.T., & Martinez-Conde, S. (2008). Attention and awareness in stage magic: Turning tricks into research. *Nature Reviews: Neuroscience, 9,* 871–879.

Sternberg, R.J. (Ed.) (1989). *Advances in the psychology of human intelligence* (Vol. 5). Hillsdale, NJ: Erlbaum.

Sternberg, S. (1969). The discovery of processing stages: Extensions of Donders' method. In W.G. Koster (Ed.), *Attention and performance II* (pp. 276–315). Amsterdam: North-Holland.

Stratton, S.M., Liu, Y.T., Hong, S.L., Mayer-Kress, G., & Newell, K.M. (2007). Snoddy (1926) revisited: Time scales of motor learning. *Journal of Motor Behavior, 39,* 503–515.

Strayer, D.L., & Johnston, W.A. (2001). Driven to distraction: Dual-task studies of simulated driving and conversing on a cellular telephone. *Psychological Science, 12,* 462–466.

Stroop, J.R. (1935). Studies of interference in serial verbal reactions. *Journal of Experimental Psychology, 18,* 643–662.

Swinnen, S.P. (1990). Interpolated activities during the knowledge-of-results delay and post-knowledge-of-results interval: Effects on performance and learning. *Journal of Experimental Psychology: Learning, Memory, and Cognition, 16,* 692–705.

Swinnen, S.P., Walter, C.B., Lee, T.D., & Serrien, D.J. (1993). Acquiring bimanual skills: Contrasting forms of information feedback for interlimb decoupling. *Journal of Experimental Psychology: Learning, Memory, and Cognition, 19,* 1328–1344.

Swinnen, S.P., Schmidt, R.A., Nicholson, D.E., & Shapiro, D.C. (1990). Information feedback for skill acquisition: Instantaneous knowledge of results degrades learning. *Journal of Experimental Psychology: Learning, Memory, and Cognition, 16,* 706–716.

Swinnen, S.P., & Wenderoth, N. (2004). Two hands, one brain: Cognitive neuroscience of bimanual skill. *Trends in Cognitive Sciences, 8,* 18–25.

Taub, E. (1976). Movement in nonhuman primates deprived of somatosensory feedback. *Exercise and Sport Sciences Reviews, 4,* 335–374.

Taub, E., & Berman, A.J. (1968). Movement and learning in the absence of sensory feedback. In S.J. Freedman (Ed.), *The neuropsychology of spatially oriented behavior* (pp. 173–192). Homewood, IL: Dorsey.

Taylor, J.E.T., Witt, J.K., & Sugovic, M. (2011). When walls are no longer barriers: Perception of wall height in parkour. *Perception, 40,* 757–760.

Thompson, L.L., Rivara, F.P., Ayyagari, R.C., & Ebel, B.E. (2013). Impact of social and technological distraction on pedestrian crossing behaviour: An observational study. *Injury Prevention, 19,* 232–237.

Thorndike, E.L. (1927). The law of effect. *American Journal of Psychology, 39,* 212–222.

Thorndike, E.L., & Woodworth, R.S. (1901). The influence of improvement in one mental function upon the efficiency of other functions. *Psychological Review, 8,* 247–261.

Tiffin, J., & Rogers, H.B. (1943). The selection and training of inspectors. *Personnel, 22,* 3–20.

Timmermans, A.A.A., Seelen, H.A.M., Willmann, R.D., & Kingma, H. (2009). Technology-assisted training of arm-hand skills in stroke: Concepts on reacquisition of motor control and therapist guidelines for rehabilitation technology design. *Journal of Neuroengineering and Rehabilitation, 6,* 1. doi:10.1186/1743-0003-6-1.

Tresilian, J. (2012). *Sensorimotor control and learning: An introduction to the behavioral neuroscience of action.* New York: Palgrave Macmillan.

Trowbridge, M.H., & Cason, H. (1932). An experimental study of Thorndike's theory of learning. *Journal of General Psychology, 7,* 245–260.

Turvey, M.T. (1977). Preliminaries to a theory of action with reference to vision. In R. Shaw & J. Bransford (Eds.), *Perceiving, acting, and knowing* (pp. 211–265). Hillsdale, NJ: Erlbaum.

Umiltà, C., Priftis, K., & Zorzi, M. (2009). The spatial representation of numbers: Evidence from neglect and pseudoneglect. *Experimental Brain Research, 192,* 561–569.

Ungerleider, L.G., & Mishkin, M. (1982). Two cortical visual systems. In D.J. Ingle, M.A. Goodale, & R.J.W. Mansfield (Eds.), *Analysis of visual behavior* (pp. 549–586). Cambridge, MA: MIT Press.

Urbin, M.A., Stodden, D., Boros, R., & Shannon, D. (2012). Examining impulse-variability in overarm throwing. *Motor Control, 16,* 19–30.

Urbin, M.A., Stodden, D.F., Fischman, M.G., & Weimar, W.H. (2011). Impulse-variability theory: Implications for ballistic, multijoint motor kill performance. *Journal of Motor Behavior, 43,* 275–283.

Valls-Solé, J., Kumru, H., & Kofler, M. (2008). Interaction between startle and voluntary reactions in humans. *Experimental Brain Research, 187,* 497–507.

van Ulzen, N.R., Lamoth, C.J., Daffertshofer, A., Semin, G.R., & Beek, P.J. (2008). Characteristics of instructed and uninstructed interpersonal coordination while walking side-by-side. *Neuroscience Letters, 432,* 88–93.

Varlet, M., & Richardson, M.J. (2015). What would be Usain Bolt's 100-meter sprint world record without Tyson Gay? Unintentional interpersonal synchronization between the two sprinters. *Journal of Experimental Psychology: Human Perception and Performance, 41,* 36–41.

Verbruggen, F., & Logan, G.D. (2008). Response inhibition in the stop-signal paradigm. *Trends in Cognitive Sciences, 12,* 418–424.

Verhoeven, F.M., & Newell, K.M. (2018). Unifying practice schedules in the timescales of motor learning and performance. *Human Movement Science, 59,* 153–169.

Vickers, J. (2007). *Perception, cognition, and decision training.* Champaign, IL: Human Kinetics.

Vidmar, P. (1984). *Public-domain comments.* New York: American Broadcasting Company.

Wadman, W.J., Denier van der Gon, J.J., Geuze, R.H., & Mol, C.R. (1979). Control of fast goal-directed arm movements. *Journal of Human Movement Studies, 5,* 3–17.

Watson, J.M., & Strayer, D.L. (2010). Supertaskers: Profiles in extraordinary multi-tasking ability. *Psychonomic Bulletin and Review, 17,* 479–485.

Wegner, D.M. (1994). Ironic processes of mental control. *Psychological Review, 101,* 34–52.

Weinberg, R.S., & Gould, D. (2019). *Foundations of sport and exercise psychology* (7th ed.). Champaign, IL: Human Kinetics.

Weinberg, R.S., & Ragan, J. (1978). Motor performance under three levels of trait anxiety and stress. *Journal of Motor Behavior, 10,* 169–176.

Weiskrantz, L. (2007). Blindsight. *Scholarpedia, 2* (4), 3047. www.scholarpedia.org/article/Blindsight.

Weiskrantz, L., Warrington, E.K., Sanders, M.D., and Marshall, J. (1974). Visual capacity in the hemianopic field following a restricted occipital ablation. *Brain, 97,* 709–728.

Welchman, A., Stanley, J., Schomers, M., Miall, R., & Bulthoff, H. (2010). The quick and the dead: When reaction beats intention. *Proceedings of the Royal Society of Biological Sciences, 277,* 1667–1674.

Welford, A.T. (1952). The "psychological refractory period" and the timing of high-speed performance—a review and a theory. *British Journal of Psychology, 43,* 2–19.

Welford, A.T. (1980). *Reaction times.* London: Academic Press.

Weller, L., Kunde, W., & Pfister, R. (2018). Disarming the gunslinger effect: Reaction beats intention for cooperative actions. *Psychonomic Bulletin & Review, 25,* 761–766.

Weltman, G., & Egstrom, G.H. (1966). Perceptual narrowing in novice divers. *Human Factors, 8,* 499–505.

Wickens, C.D., & McCarley, J.S. (2008). *Applied attention theory.* Boca Raton, FL: CRC Press.

Williams, A.M., Ward, P., & Smeeton, N.J. (2004). Perceptual and cognitive expertise in sport: Implications for skill acquisition and performance enhancement. In A.M. Williams & N.J. Hodges (Eds.), *Skill acquisition in sport: Research, theory and practice* (pp. 328–347). London: Routledge.

Wing, A.M. (2002). Voluntary timing and brain function: An information processing approach. *Brain and Cognition, 48,* 7–30.

Wing, A.M., & Kristofferson, A.B. (1973). The timing of interresponse intervals. *Perception & Psychophysics, 13,* 455–460.

Winstein, C.J., & Schmidt, R.A. (1990). Reduced frequency of knowledge of results enhances motor skill learning. *Journal of Experimental Psychology: Learning, Memory and Cognition, 16,* 677–691.

Witt, J.K., Linkenauger, S.A., & Proffitt, D.R. (2012). Get me out of this slump! Visual illusions improve sports performance. *Psychological Science, 23,* 397–399.

Wolfe, J.M., Horowitz, T.S., & Kenner, N.M. (2005). Rare items often missed in visual searches: Errors in spotting key targets soar alarmingly if they appear only infrequently during screening. *Nature, 435,* 439–440.

Wood, G., Vine, S.J., & Wilson, M.R. (2013). The impact of visual illusions on perception, action planning, and motor performance. *Attention, Perception & Psychophysics, 75,* 830–834.

Woodworth, R.S. (1899). The accuracy of voluntary movement. *Psychological Review Monographs, 3* (Whole No. 13).

Woodworth, R.S. (1938). *Experimental psychology.* New York: Holt.

Wright, D.L. (1991). The role of intertask and intratask processing in acquisition and retention of motor skills. *Journal of Motor Behavior, 23,* 139–145.

Wright, D.L., Verwey, W., Buchanan, J., Chen, J., Rhee, J., & Immink, M. (2016). Consolidating behavioural and neurophysiologic findings to explain the influence of contextual interference during motor sequence learning. *Psychonomic Bulletin & Review, 23,* 1–21.

Wulf, G. (2007). *Attention and motor skill learning.* Champaign, IL: Human Kinetics.

Wulf, G. (2013). Attentional focus and motor learning: A review of 15 years. *International Review of Sport and Exercise Psychology, 6,* 77–104.

Wulf, G., McConnel, N., Gärtner, M., & Schwarz, A. (2002). Feedback and attentional focus: Enhancing the learning of sport skills through external-focus feedback. *Journal of Motor Behavior, 34,* 171–182.

Wulf, G., & Lewthwaite, R. (2016). Optimizing performance through intrinsic motivation and attention for learning: The OPTIMAL theory of motor learning. *Psychonomic Bulletin & Review, 23,* 1382–1414.

Wulf, G., Weigelt, M., Poulter, D.R., & McNevin, N.H. (2003). Attentional focus on supra-postural tasks affects balance learning. *Quarterly Journal of Experimental Psychology, 56A,* 1191–1211.

Wulf, G., McNevin, N.H., & Shea, C.H. (2001). The automaticity of complex motor skill learning as a function of attentional focus. *Quarterly Journal of Experimental Psychology, 54A,* 1143–1154.

Wulf, G., & Toole, T. (1999). Physical assistance devices in complex motor skill learning: Benefits of a self-controlled practice schedule. *Research Quarterly for Exercise and Sport, 70,* 265–272.

Yamanishi, J., Kawato, M., & Suzuki, R. (1980). Two coupled oscillators as a model for the coordinated finger tapping by both hands. *Biological Cybernetics, 37,* 219–225.

Yao, W., Fischman, M.G., & Wang, Y.T. (1994). Motor skill acquisition and retention as a function of average feedback, summary feedback, and performance variability. *Journal of Motor Behavior, 26,* 273–282.

Yerkes, R.M., & Dodson, J.D. (1908). The relation of strength of stimulus to rapidity of habit-formation.

Journal of Comparative Neurology and Psychology, 18, 459–482.

Young, D.E., & Schmidt, R.A. (1990). Units of motor behavior: Modifications with practice and feedback. In M. Jeannerod (Ed.), *Attention and performance XIII* (pp. 763–795). Hillsdale, NJ: Erlbaum.

Young, D.E., & Schmidt, R.A. (1992). Augmented kinematic feedback for motor learning. *Journal of Motor Behavior, 24,* 261–273.

Zehr, E.P. (2005). Neural control of rhythmic human movement: The common core hypothesis. *Exercise and Sport Sciences Reviews, 33,* 54–60.

Index

Note: The italicized *f* and *t* following page numbers refer to figures and tables, respectively.

C

D

E

About the Authors

Richard A. Schmidt, PhD (1941–2015) was a professor emeritus in the department of psychology at UCLA. At the time of his death, Schmidt ran his own business, Human Performance Research, conducting research and consulting in the area of human factors and human performance. Widely acknowledged as one of the leaders in research on motor behavior, he had more than 40 years of experience in the area of motor learning and performance.

The originator of both schema theory and impulse-variability theory (aka "Schmidt's Law"), he founded the *Journal of Motor Behavior* in 1969 and was editor for 11 years. He authored the first edition of *Motor Control and Learning* in 1982 and the first edition of this book, *Motor Learning and Performance,* in 1991.

Schmidt was highly recognized for his contribution of a lifetime of research and writing. In recognition of his work, he received honorary doctorates from the Catholic University of Leuven in Belgium (in 1992) and the Université Joseph Fourier in France (in 1998). He was a longtime member of the North American Society for the Psychology of Sport and Physical Activity (NASPSPA), where he served as president in 1982 and received the organization's two highest honors: the Distinguished Scholar Award for lifetime contributions to research in motor control and learning (in 1992) and the President's Award for significant contributions to the development and growth of NASPSPA (in 2013). He was also a member of the Human Factors and Ergonomics Society and the Psychonomic Society and received the C.H. McCloy Research Lectureship from the American Alliance for Health, Physical Education, Recreation and Dance. His leisure-time passions included sailboat and Porsche racing.

Timothy D. Lee, PhD, is a professor emeritus in the department of kinesiology at McMaster University in Hamilton, Ontario. He has published extensively in motor behavior and psychology journals since 1980, served as an editor for the *Journal of Motor Behavior* and *Research Quarterly for Exercise and Sport*, and has been an editorial board member for *Psychological Review*. Until his retirement in 2014, his research was supported primarily by grants from the Natural Sciences and Engineering Research Council of Canada.

Tim has been a member, secretary-treasurer, and president of the Canadian Society for Psychomotor Learning and Sport Psychology (SCAPPS) and a member of the North American Society for the Psychology of Sport and Physical Activity (NASPSPA), the Psychonomic Society, and the Human Factors and Ergonomics Society. In 1980 Tim received the inaugural Young Scientist Award from SCAPPS, and in 2011 he was named a fellow of the society—its highest honor. He was named an international fellow by the National Academy of Kinesiology in 1999 and awarded the Distinguished Scholar Award by NASPSPA in 2017.

Tim is an avid golfer who competes in local, national, and international tournaments. He teamed with a good friend, Frank Morris, to win the Ontario Senior Better Ball Championship in 2017.